TJ Publishers
Advantage Business Centre
132-134 Great Ancoats Street
Manchester
M4 6DE

Tel: 01207 582 344 or 0141 880 6839
Fax: 01912 478 290
e-mail: info@teejaymaths.com
web : teejaymaths.com

Second Edition published by TeeJay Publishers - May 2017

Printed by :-

Elanders Ltd
Merlin Way
New York Business Park
North Tyneside NE27 0QG
Registered in England number 3788582
http://www.elanders.com/uk

Year 5 Textbook

Book 5

Produced by members of the TeeJay Writing Group.

T Strang, J Geddes and J Cairns.

Front and Back Cover designed by *Fraser McKie*.
(http://www.frasermckie.com)

TEXTBOOK
5

National Curriculum TextBook 5

- This book covers every outcome of the Year 5 course, as laid out in the National Curriculum England Framework Document, (September 2013).

- There are no A and B exercises. The book covers the entire Year 5 course without the teacher having to pick and choose which questions to leave out and which exercises are important. They all are !

- The book follows on directly from TeeJay's Year 4 Book and includes revision and consolidation of the work covered in the Year 4 course.

- The Year 5 Book contains an 8 page "Chapter Zero" which primarily revises every topic from the Year 4 course and can be used as a diagnostic tool. This could be followed by TeeJay's diagnostic assessments * of the work covered in our Year 4 book.

- It also contains a Chapter 19 which revises every topic from the Year 5 course, prior to an end of year assessment.

- Non-calculator skills are emphasised and encouraged throughout the book.

- Each chapter has a "Revisit - Review - Revise" exercise as a summary.

- Homework*, mirroring exercise by exercise, the topics in this book, is available as a photocopiable pack.

- TeeJay's Assessment Pack* for Year 5 work, is also available as a photocopiable pack, and can be used topic by topic or combined to form a series of Year 5 Cumulative Tests. It also contains a series of longer assessments covering the Outcomes as laid out in the National Curriculum England framework document (Sept 2013).

We make no apologies for the multiplicity of colours used throughout the book, both for text and in diagrams - we feel it helps brighten up the pages !!

T Strang, J Geddes, J Cairns

(*June 2014*)

* Available for purchase separately.

Contents

Chapter 0

Revision - Year 4

1. Write out the number 8056 fully in words.

2. Write the number seven thousand four hundred and one using digits.

3. Rearrange the numbers given below in order, starting with the smallest :-

   6051 7040 7001 6688 7018 7051.

4. What numbers are represented by P, Q, R and S on the given scales ?

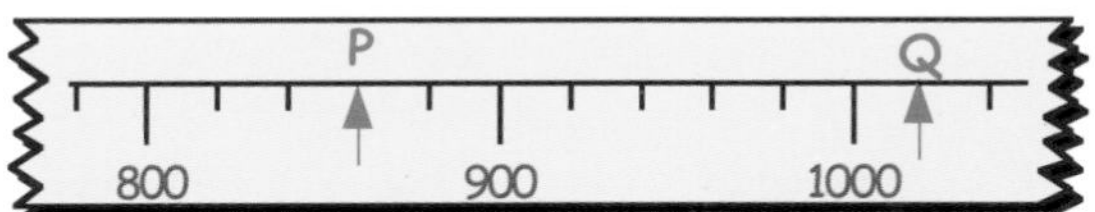

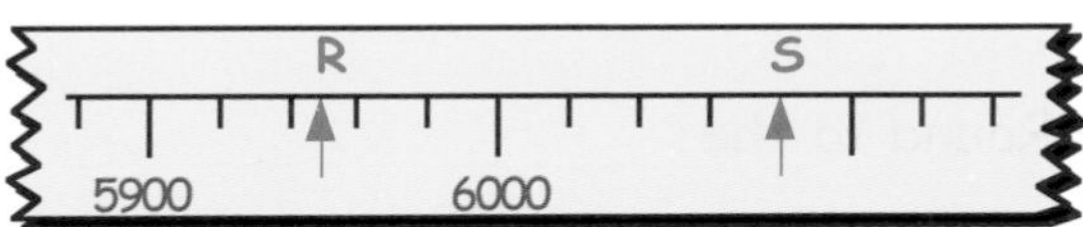

5. What number lies halfway between 3200 and 7200 ?

6. Write down the number that is 3000 less than 8100.

7. Write down the next two numbers each time :-

   a 975, 970, 965, ..., ...
   b 480, 500, 520, ..., ...
   c 7100, 6800, 6500, ..., ...
   d 8000, 6500, 5000, ..., ...

8. a Change to number form :- (i) XXVI (ii) LXIX (iii) XCIV.

   b Change to Roman numerals :- (i) 29 (ii) 57 (iii) 99.

9. How many lines of symmetry do each of these shapes have ?

a
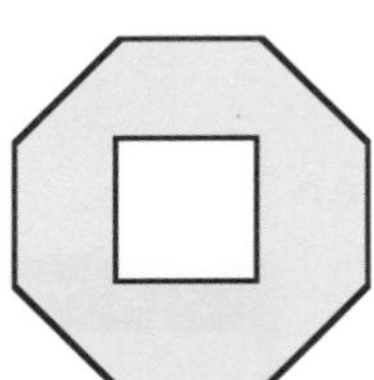
b

c

d

10. Trace or copy this shape and draw the other half so the red dotted line is a line of symmetry.

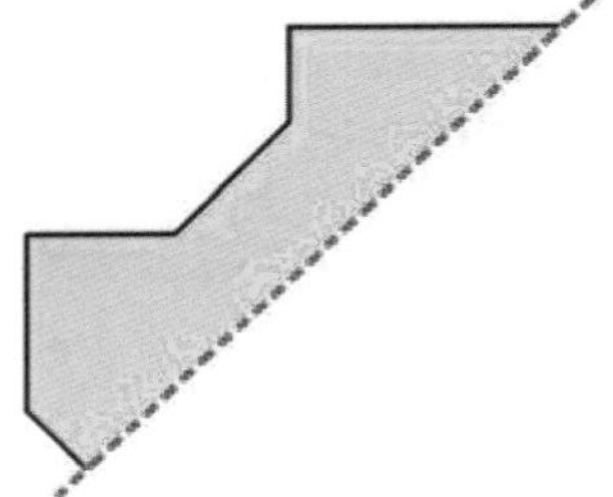

11. Set down and then work out :-

   a $\begin{array}{r} 6486 \\ +\ 2827 \\ \hline \end{array}$
   b 6327 - 1853
   c $\begin{array}{r} 7896 \\ +\ 999 \\ \hline \end{array}$
   d $\begin{array}{r} 10000 \\ -\ 2475 \\ \hline \end{array}$

12. From London to New York is 3458 miles.
From London to Bangkok is 5921 miles.

a How much further is it from London to Bangkok than from London to New York ?

b If Nikki flew from Bangkok to London, then on to New York, how far would she have flown altogether ?

13. Do the following mentally (*no working should be seen*) :-

a 49 + 35 b 349 + 99 c 6300 + 3500 d 81 - 18

e 4800 - 650 f 10 000 - 6400 g 3146 + 2999 h 5000 - 19.

14. Round to the :-

a nearest 10 :- (i) 73 (ii) 297 (iii) 625.

b nearest 100 :- (i) 549 (ii) 2951 (iii) 9805.

c nearest 1000 :- (i) 3847 (ii) 8099 (iii) 6500.

15. Change these times to 24 hour format :-

a 7.40 am b 11.10 at night c 20 to 5 in the afternoon.

16. Write the following in 12 hour format :- (*remember to use am or pm*)

a 0855 b 1350 c 1135 d 2240.

17. How many minutes are there between :-

a 8 pm and 9.30 pm b noon and 1310 c 1555 and 1640 ?

18. a How many days are there in :- (i) April (ii) December ?

b How many months are there in 5 years ?

c How many days are there from the 28th of March to the 9th of April, including both dates ?

19. Copy and complete :-

a 9 x 6 = ... b 5 x 11 = ... c 8 x 8 = ...

d 10 x 12 = ... e 7 x 9 = ... f 2 x 5 x 7 = ...

20. What numbers are missing ?

a 7 x .... = 49 b .... x 6 = 300 c .... x 8 = 72

d .... x 11 = 110 e 9 x .... = 108 f .... x 5 = 500.

21. Copy and complete these multiplications :-

a $\begin{array}{r} 65 \\ \times 9 \\ \hline \end{array}$ b $\begin{array}{r} 207 \\ \times 8 \\ \hline \end{array}$ c $\begin{array}{r} 387 \\ \times 7 \\ \hline \end{array}$

d $\begin{array}{r} 203 \\ \times 10 \\ \hline \end{array}$ e $\begin{array}{r} 178 \\ \times 5 \\ \hline \end{array}$ f $\begin{array}{r} 345 \\ \times 6 \\ \hline \end{array}$

22. Lucy lives in Nottingham, which is 129 km by road from London.

She drove back and forwards 4 times last month.

How far in total did she drive ?

23. State what temperatures are represented on these thermometers :-

a

b

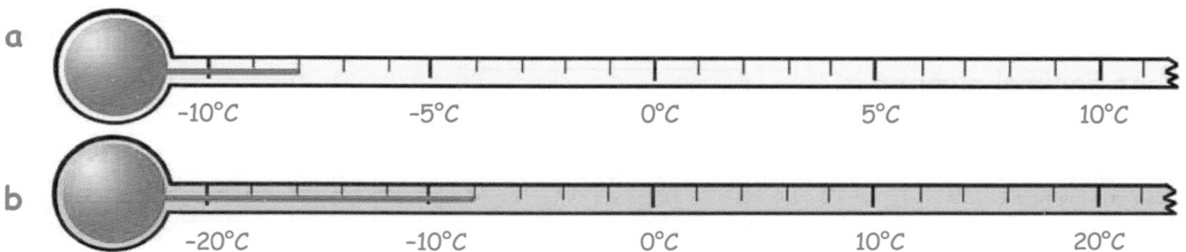

24. What is the temperature :-

a 10°C up from 3°C
b 8°C down from 2°C
c 5°C up from -6°C
d 3°C down from -7°C ?

25. Which integer is halfway between :-

a 20 and 28
b -30 and 30
c -8 and -2 ?

26. Copy and complete :-

a $5\overline{)35}$ b $7\overline{)84}$ c $8\overline{)112}$ d $6\overline{)138}$

e $9\overline{)207}$ f $4\overline{)264}$ g $8\overline{)256}$ h $10\overline{)250}$.

27. Write in the form $6\overline{)72}$ and work out the answer :-

a $91 \div 7$
b $\frac{265}{5}$
c 144 divided by 8
d 6 into 78
e $\frac{196}{4}$
f 135 divided by 9
g 10 into 4700
h $360 \div 8$.

28. Four new tyres cost £188. What is the cost of 1 tyre ?

29. When Bill and his 5 friends shared a pools win, they **each** got £275.

How much did the group win in total ?

30. **Copy** the coordinate grid shown opposite.

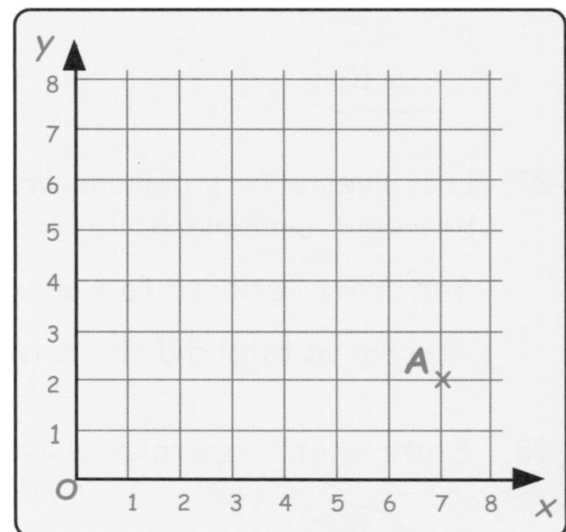

a Write down the coordinates of point **A**.

b Plot the 3 points **P**(0, 2), **Q**(1, 6) and **R**(5, 7).

S is a point to be put on the grid so that figure **PQRS** is a **rhombus**.

c On your diagram plot the point **S** and write down its coordinates.

31. What decimal number is represented by this diagram ?

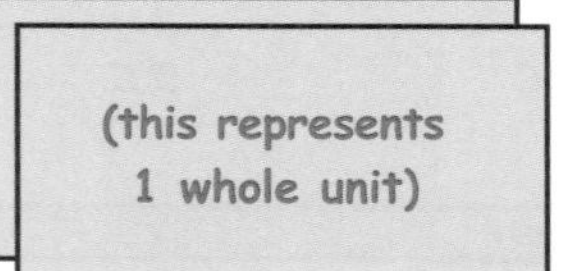

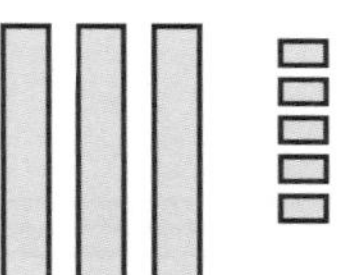

32. Draw diagrams (similar to Question **31**) to represent :- a 3·2 b 1·43.

33. In the decimal number 4·96, what does the :-

a 9 represent b 4 represent c 6 represent ?

34. Write down the number that is :-

a 0·5 up from 7·5 b 0·03 down from 2·42 c $\frac{7}{10}$ up from 5·4.

35. What number is **halfway** between :-

a 0·2 and 0·8 b 6·6 and 7·0 c 0·34 and 0·38 ?

36. a Arrange in order, **smallest** first :- 3·9, 3·28, 3·67, 4, 3·3, 3·23.

b Arrange in order, **largest** first :- 5·77, 5·8, 6·62, 6·18, 7·9, 6·05.

37. To what decimal numbers are the arrows pointing ?

a

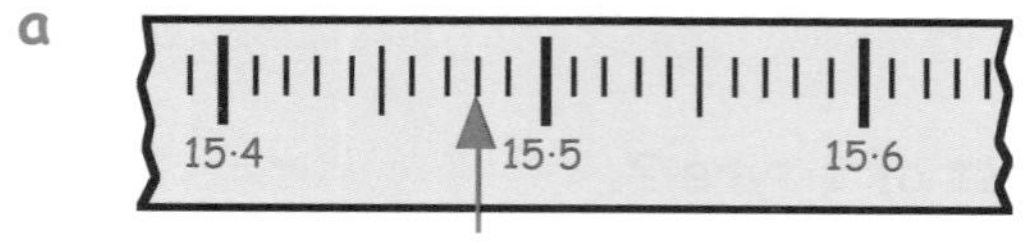

b

38. This triangle can be described as follows :-

Triangle PQR is an obtuse angled isosceles triangle.

Name and describe both of these triangles fully :-

a

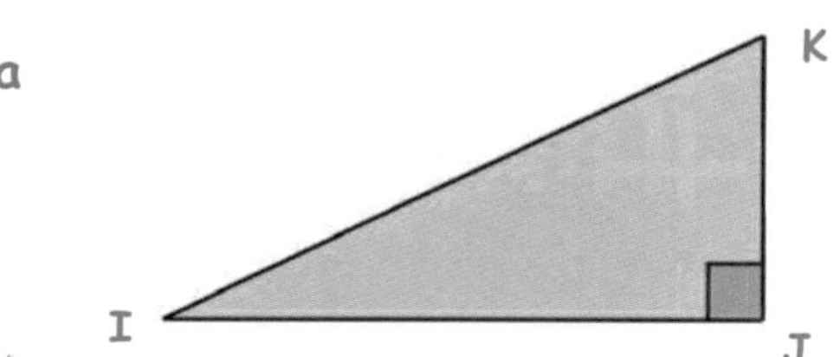

b

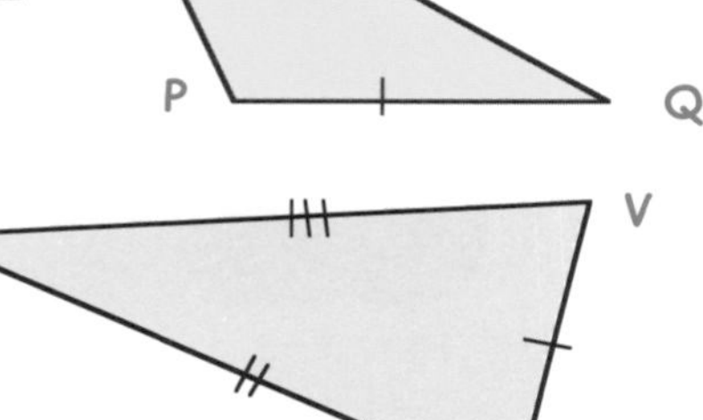

39. Round the following to the nearest whole number :-

a 9·3   b 11·8   c 32·51   d 88·45.

40. Do the following mentally (*no working*) :-

a 3·6 + 8·2   b 11·3 + 6·47   c 9·6 – 3·4   d 0·92 – 0·88.

41. Copy the following and find :-

a 3·82 + 2·49   b 35·54 + 6·72   c 10·8 – 6·3   d 15·65 – 9·87

e £3·87 + £4·95   f £24·48 + £5·32   g £5·63 – £2·87   h 15·05 - 2·95

i 45·42 – 9·73   j 30 – 2·45   k 85·7 – 38·49   l 100 - 13·99.

42. Nadia buys a denim jacket for £27·49 and a pair of jeans for £19·99.

How much change should she receive from a £50 note ?

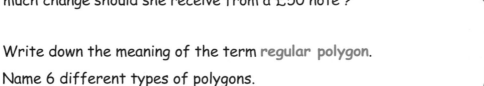

43. a Write down the meaning of the term regular polygon.

b Name 6 different types of polygons.

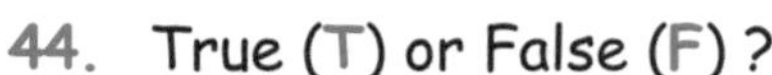

44. True (T) or False (F) ?

a A rectangle is made up of 2 identical isosceles triangles.

b The opposite angles of a rhombus are equal.

c A kite has 2 pairs of equal sides.

d A parallelogram has at least 1 line of symmetry.

e A square can only fit onto itself 4 times, allowing for turning over and rotating.

45. Write down 2 ways in which a rectangle is different from a parallelogram.

46. Name the quadrilateral with 2 lines of symmetry but with no right angles.

47. Write each of these amounts using a decimal point :-

a 

b 

c 

48. Find :-

a £39·56 + £25·48

b £172·69 − £83·45

c £37·43 − £28·69

d £137·46 + £62·54.

49. a Nina spent £7·89 and gave a £20 note. How much change did she receive ?

b Nigel got £6·95 change from a £10 and a £20 note. How much had he spent ?

50. How many :-

a minutes in 5 hours

b seconds in 3 minutes

c weeks in 2 years ?

51. How many days are there in :-

a March

b August

c November ?

52. Change each of these to minutes and seconds :-

a 100 secs

b 360 secs

c 1000 secs.

53. Change each of these to hours and minutes :-

a 70 mins

b 210 mins

c 600 mins.

54. Change each of these from minutes and seconds to seconds :-

a 2 mins 15 secs

b 3 mins 40 secs

c 5 mins 55 secs.

55. Change each of these from hours and minutes to minutes :-

a 2 hrs 50 mins

b 6 hrs 1 min

c 20 hrs 20 mins.

56. Copy and complete :-

a 3 mins 25 secs + 4 mins 30 secs

b 9 mins 55 secs − 6 mins 20 secs

c 4 hrs 10 mins − 2 hrs 50 mins

57. Write down the answer to each of these :-

a	3250 x 10	b	43 x 100	c	7 x 1000	d	820 ÷ 10
e	9000 ÷ 100	f	3000 ÷ 1000	g	8 x 9	h	15 x 10
i	84 ÷ 12	j	110 ÷ 11	k	144 ÷ 9	l	220 ÷ 11.

58. Polythene CD covers come in boxes of 100.

A company bought in 25 boxes.

How many covers was that ?

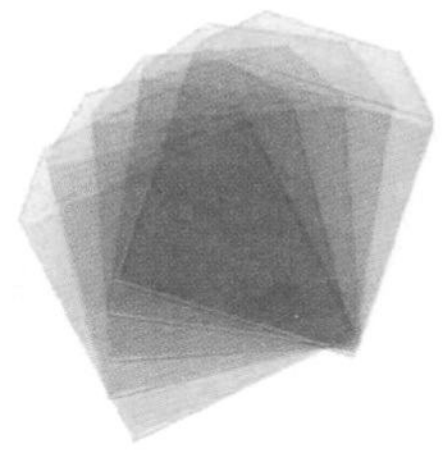

59. 

A football team consists of 11 players.

12 teams entered a football tournament.

How many players is that altogether ? (*Forget subs*).

60. In the "olden" days, there were 12 old pennies to an old shilling.

How many shillings would I have if I had 156 pennies ?

61. Change :-

a	5 cm 6 mm to mm	b	2000 mm to cm	c	125 mm to cm & mm
d	3 m 75 cm to cm	e	560 cm to m & cm	f	2 km 900 m to m
g	8250 m to km & m	h	3 m to mm	i	$2\frac{1}{4}$ km to m.

62. Change :-

a	3 litres 800 ml to ml	b	5200 ml to L & ml	c	$4\frac{1}{2}$ litres to ml.

63. Change :-

a	5 kg 650 g to g	b	9050 g to kg & g	c	$10\frac{1}{4}$ kg to g.

64. Which of these two shapes has the bigger **perimeter** and by how much is it bigger ?

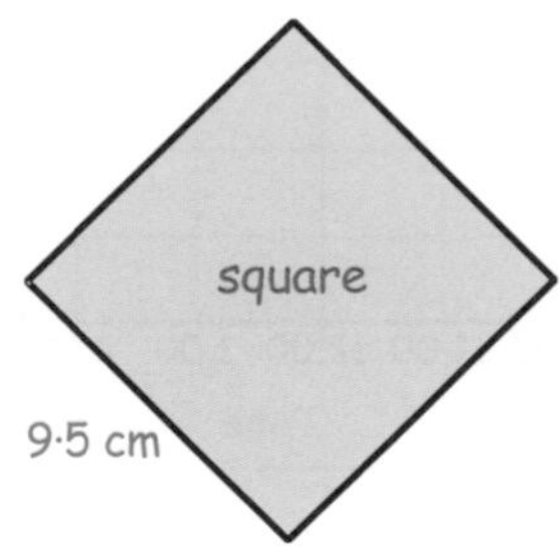

10·3 cm

7·6 cm

rectangle

65. Write down the shaded area of this shape in cm^2. →

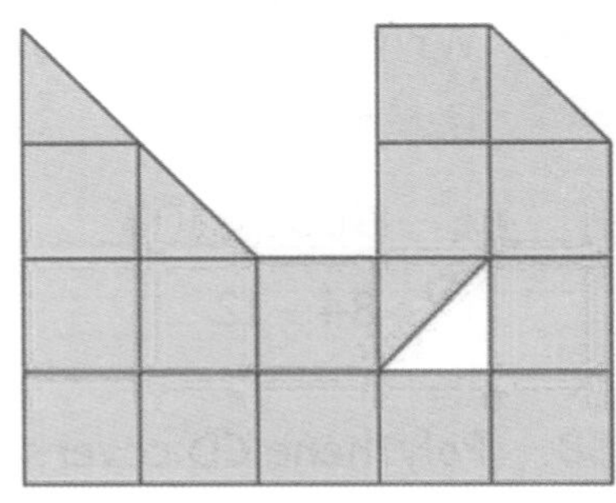

66. Simplify each of these fractions as far as possible :-

a $\frac{10}{15}$ b $\frac{12}{16}$ c $\frac{5}{35}$ d $\frac{28}{35}$.

67. Find :-

a $\frac{1}{6}$ of 42 b $\frac{2}{3}$ of 120 c $\frac{7}{8}$ of 1600 d $\frac{2}{9}$ of 36.

68. Find :-

a $\frac{1}{7} + \frac{3}{7}$ b $\frac{5}{8} - \frac{1}{8}$ c $2\frac{1}{10} + 4\frac{3}{10}$ d $6\frac{3}{4} - 1\frac{1}{4}$.

69. Write as a decimal :- a $\frac{1}{4}$ b $\frac{77}{100}$ c $\frac{9}{10}$.

70. A group of children was asked to list the first thing that came into their heads when asked the question - "What would you take to the beach with you ?"

bucket/spade	ball	costume	bucket/spade	towel	costume
bucket/spade	ball	bucket/spade	ball	bucket/spade	suncream
towel	costume	bucket/spade	towel	ball	costume
bucket/spade	ball	ball	bucket/spade	ball	towel
suncream	costume	bucket/spade	ball	bucket/spade	costume

a Draw a frequency table to represent the above information.

b Now draw a neat labelled bar chart.

71. A lady made a note of the number of butterflies in her garden one day over a 7 hour period from 9 in the morning.

a How many butterflies were there at :-

(i) 10.00 (ii) 11.00 ?

b At what time was there the largest number of butterflies present ?

c Between which two times did the number of butterflies appear to remain unchanged ?

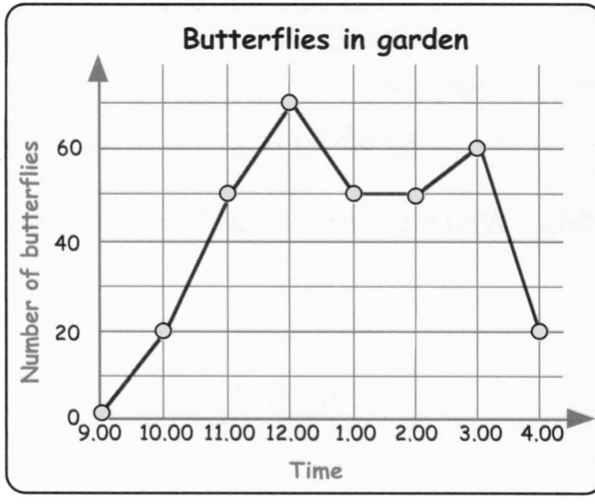

d Why do you think the number began to drop off quickly at 4 o'clock ?

Chapter 1

Whole Numbers

Place Values

Understand place value for numbers up to 1 000 000.
Three hundred and forty six thousand, seven hundred and eighty five. 346 785 ✓

Example :-

In the number 346 785,

100000	10000	1000	100	10	1
3	4	6	7	8	5

the 3 stands for three hundred thousand	300 000
the 4 stands for forty thousand	40 000
the 6 stands for six thousand	6 000
the 7 stands for seven hundred	700
the 8 stands for eight tens	80
the 5 stands for five units	5
	346 785

Exercise 1

1. What do the following digits stand for in the number 487 293 :-

   a 2   b 7   c 8   d 4 ?

2. What does the 7 stand for in each of these numbers :-

   a 58 740   b 35 279   c 647 900   d 740 601 ?

3. Write the following numbers out fully in words :-

   a 4080   b 21 900   c 71 350   d 235 080
   e 703 460   f 870 000   g 493 070   h 750 062.

4. Write the following numbers using digits :-

   a four thousand, two hundred and one
   b seventeen thousand and fifty
   c two hundred and thirty thousand and four
   d four hundred and seven thousand and eighty
   e one hundred thousand and seven
   f five hundred and sixty thousand and forty.

5. Put the following sets of numbers in order, smallest first :-

   a 7068, 6876, 7086, 6786, 7008, 7080, 6867.
   b 100 870, 99 924, 100 086, 98 999, 90 887, 100 076.

6. Write down the number that is :-

a 80 more than 290
b 70 less than 3240
c 900 more than 290
d 500 less than 1200
e 4000 more than 8300
f 6000 less than 12 200
g 50 000 more than 70 000
h 30 000 less than 120 000
i 700 000 more than 250 000
j 600 000 less than 1 000 000.

7. Look at the following scales. To what numbers do the letters A, B, C, ... point ?

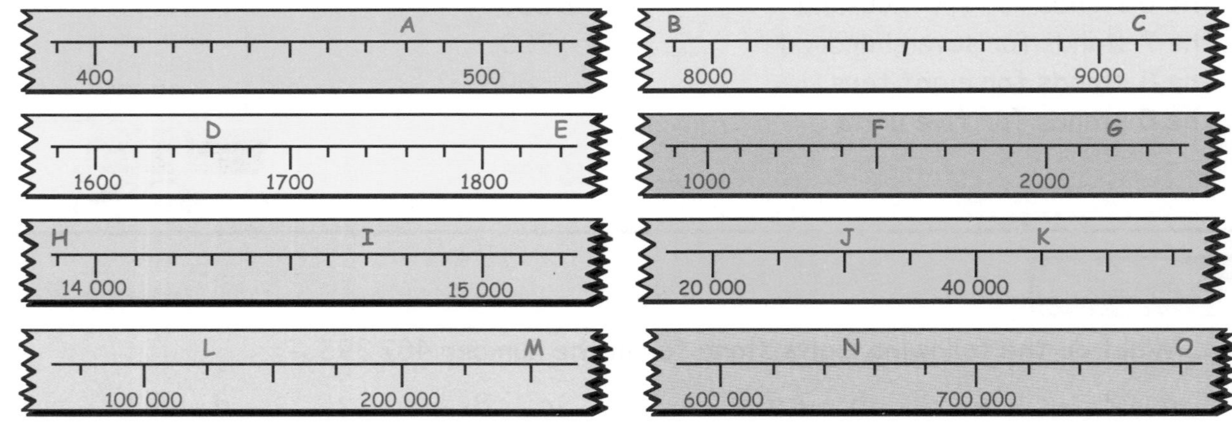

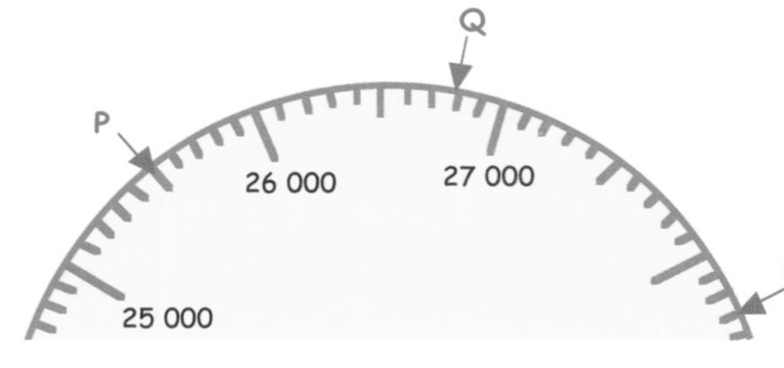

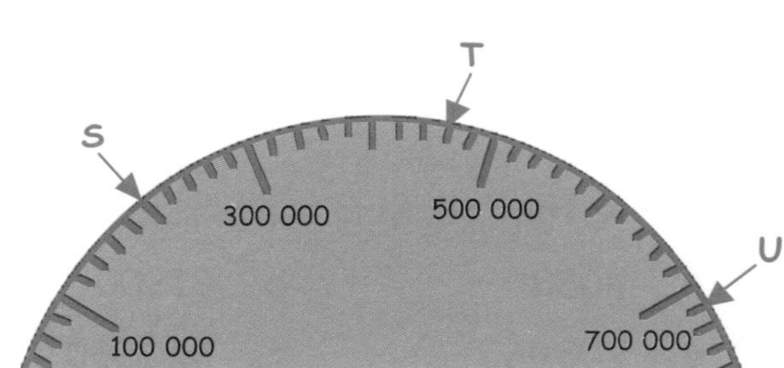

8. What number lies halfway between :-

a 970 and 980
b 3400 and 3500
c 44 000 and 44 500
d 820 000 and 880 000
e 630 500 and 830 500
f 900 000 and 1 000 000 ?

9. Write out in figures :-

a 1 million
b $\frac{1}{2}$ million
c $\frac{1}{4}$ million
d $\frac{3}{4}$ million.

10. The Dukes from St. Annes won $98\frac{1}{2}$ thousand pounds in the Eurolottery. That was the largest amount ever won in the North West.

a Write out this amount of money in full, in figures.
b Now write it out filly, using words.

Going up by 10, 100, 1000, 10 000 & 100 000

Numbers going up by 10, 100, 1000, 10000 & 100000.

Look at these patterns :-

a	50, 60, 70, 80, ...	Numbers go up in 10's.	Next number 90.
b	300, 400, 500, ...	Numbers go up in 100's.	Next number 600.
c	4000, 5000, 6000	Numbers go up in 1000's.	Next number 7000.
d	50000, 60000, 70000	Numbers go up in 10000's.	Next number 80000.
e	100000, 200000, 300000	Numbers go up in 100000's.	Next number 400000.

Exercise 2

1. Write down the next 2 numbers in each of these patterns :-

a 80, 90, 100, 110, ..., ...

b 240, 230, 220, 210, ..., ...

c 600, 700, 800, 900, ..., ...

d 2200, 2100, 2000, ..., ...

e 7000, 8000, 9000, ..., ...

f 23000, 22000, 21000, ..., ...

g 40000, 50000, 60000, ..., ...

h 150000, 140000, 130000, ..., ...

i 600000, 700000, 800000, ..., ...

j 400000, 300000, 200000, ..., ...

2. Find the missing numbers :-

a 45, 55, ..., 75, ...

b 112, 102, ..., 82, 72, ...

c 320, ..., 520, 620, ..., 820

d 930, 920, ..., 900, ..., 880

e ..., 2400, 3400, ..., 5400

f 9100, 8100, ..., 6100, ...

g 37000, ..., 57000, ..., 77000

h 99000, 89000, ..., 69000, ...

i 1240, 1230, ..., 1210, ...

j 5380, 5390, ..., 5410, ...

k 3620, ..., 3420, 3320, ..., 3120

l 7125, 8125, ..., 10125, ...

m 50600, ..., 48600, 47600

n ..., 43910, 44910, 45910

o 641000, ..., 441000, 341000

p 700000, 800000, 900000 ....

Rounding to the nearest 10, 100, 1000, 10 000 & 100 000

Be able to round a number to the nearest 10, 100, 1000, 10 000 and 100 000.

In Year 4, you learned how to round a number to the nearest 10, 100 and 1000.

A few examples are shown to remind you.

Revision of rounding to the nearest 10, 100, 1000.

157 —> 160 (10)

2374 —> 2400 (100)

9488 —> 9000 (1000)

In the same way :-

To round to the nearest 10 000 look at the thousands digit :-

- if it is a 0, 1, 2, 3 or 4 - leave the 10 000's digit as it is.
- if it is a 5, 6, 7, 8 or 9 - round the 10 000's digit up by one.

137 650 —> 140 000

To round to the nearest 100 000 look at the ten thousands digit :-

- if it is a 0, 1, 2, 3 or 4 - leave the 100 000's digit as it is.
- if it is a 5, 6, 7, 8 or 9 - round the 100 000's digit up by one.

642 486 —> 600 000

Exercise 3

1. Round to the nearest 10 :-

   a 69 b 34 c 183 d 375
   e 429 f 2766 g 9804 h 25 678.

2. Round to the nearest 100 :-

   a 784 b 777 c 4656 d 9480
   e 26 284 f 29 850 g 16 050 h 212 450.

3. Round to the nearest 1000 :-

   a 8700 b 48 200 c 37 960 d 91 501
   e 83 960 f 357 600 g 436 492 h 799 984.

4. Round to the nearest 10 000 :-

   a 9000 b 25 000 c 32 719 d 62 090
   e 87 500 f 122 300 g 246 700 h 989 699.

5. Round to the nearest 100 000 :-

   a 230 000 b 490 000 c 601 700 d 872 200
   e 599 500 f 750 000 g 649 999 h 919 888.

Using Rounding to Estimate Answers

Be able to estimate an answer to a question using rounding.
Make sure you know your tables !

It is possible to "MENTALLY" estimate the answer to a question by rounding the numbers to "1 figure" accuracy first.

Examples :-

79 x 42 is approximately 80 x 40 ≈ 3200	7982 ÷ 396 is approximately 8000 ÷ 400 ≈ 20

"≈" approximately equal to.

Exercise 4

1. The answer to 62 x 78 is either {486, 4836 or 48 036}. (no calculator !)

   By rounding 62 x 78 = 60 x ..... = ... , decide which of the 3 answers has to be the correct one.

2. Round your numbers before multiplying. Use this to decide which of the 3 given answers is most likely to be the correct one :-

a	39 x 61	Choice of	{237·9,	2379	or	23 799}
b	178 x 18	Choice of	{3204,	32 440	or	32 004}
c	614 x 57	Choice of	{3498,	34 998	or	349 908}
d	293 x 116	Choice of	{323 618,	3988,	or	33 988}
e	283 648 ÷ 277	Choice of	{10 240,	1024	or	104}.

3. Round each number to 1 figure accuracy, then give an estimate for :-

a	71 x 28	b	37 x 52	c	88 x 81	d	397 x 61
e	304 x 78	f	785 x 182	g	796 ÷ 18	h	4031 ÷ 37
i	5918 ÷ 192	j	62 128 ÷ 302	k	18 096 ÷ 188	l	99 909 ÷ 2347.

4. a A tin of green pea soup weighs 415 grams.

   What is the approximate weight of a carton containing 36 tins ?

b 

A company charges a Council £110 624 for 208 laptops.

Approximately, what was the cost of a laptop ?

c On average, a coach driver travels 38 000 miles per year at work.

If a bus company employs 62 drivers, what will be the approximate total mileage travelled by these drivers ?

Roman Numbers

Be able to write numbers to 1000 (and beyond) using Roman Numerals.

In Year 4, you learned how to write all the numbers from 1 to 100 using the Roman Numerals I, V, X, L and C.

Centurion

1	I	21	XXI	41	XLI	61	LXI	81	.....
2	II	22	XXII	42	....	62	LXII	82	LXXXII
3	III	23	.....	43	XLIII	63	LXIII	83	LXXXIII
4	..	24	XXIV	44	XLIV	64	....	84	LXXXIV
5	V	25	XXV	45	...	65	LXV	85	.....
6	..	26	....	46	XLVI	66	LXVI	86	LXXXVI
7	VII	27	XXVII	47	XLVII	67	LXVII	87	LXXXVII
8	....	28	XXVIII	48	XLVIII	68	LXVIII	88	LXXXVIII
9	IX	29	....	49	....	69	....	89	LXXXIX
10	X	30	XXX	50	.	70	LXX	90	..
11	..	31	XXXI	51	LI	71	LXXI	91	XCI
12	XII	32	XXXII	52	LII	72	LXXII	92	XCII
13	....	33	XXXIII	53	....	73	......	93	XCIII
14	XIV	34	.....	54	LIV	74	LXXIV	94	.....
15	XV	35	XXXV	55	LV	75	LXXV	95	...
16	....	36	XXXVI	56	...	76	LXXVI	96	XCVI
17	XVII	37	......	57	LVII	77	LXXVII	97	XCVII
18	.....	38	XXXVIII	58	LVIII	78	LXXVIII	98	XCVIII
19	XIX	39	.....	59	LIX	79	.....	99	....
20	XX	40	..	60	..	80	LXXX	100	C

I'm playing X-pin bowling

As a class, try to work out the Roman symbols used to represent the missing numbers from the above table.

Rules :-

Here are some of the basic rules used when writing Roman symbols :-

1. A symbol can only appear 3 times at most - XXXX not allowed.
2. Only one smaller symbol can appear in front of a bigger one - IIX not allowed.
3. Only I, X and C can appear in front of a larger symbol - LC and VL not allowed.
4. Only subtract 1 type of smaller symbol at a time - IXL not allowed.
5. When a smaller symbol is in front of a larger one, the larger symbol cannot be more than 10 times bigger than the smaller one - VC and IL not allowed.

Exercise 5

1. a Use Rule 1 to decide what to use instead of XXXX for the number 40.

   b Use Rule 2 to decide what to use instead of IIX for the number 8.

   c Use Rule 3 to decide what to use instead of LC and VL for 50 and 45.

1. d Use Rule 4 to decide what to use instead of IIXL for the number 38.

   e Use Rule 5 to decide what to use instead of VC and IL for 95 and 49.

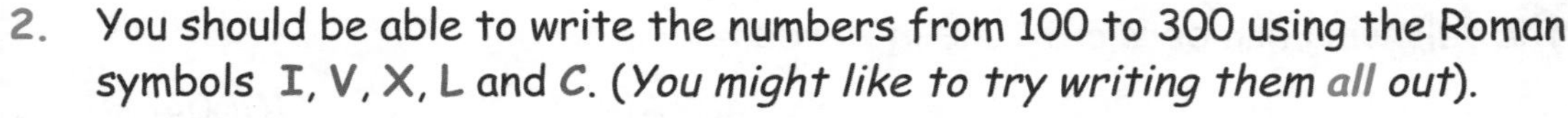

2. You should be able to write the numbers from 100 to 300 using the Roman symbols I, V, X, L and C. (*You might like to try writing them all out*).

   What are the Roman Numerals used to write the number :-

   a 101 b 110 c 125 d 150 e 155 f 188 g 190 h 200

   i 205 j 230 k 239 l 249 m 250 n 275 o 290 p 299 ?

3. What numbers do these Roman symbols represent :-

   a CIII b CIX c CXV d CXXVI e CXXXIX f CLXVI

   g CLXXX h CCXX i CCXLV j CCLIX k CCLXXVI l CCXCV ?

We now introduce the two new Roman Symbols - D = 500 and M = 1000.

Using the symbols I, V, X, L, C, D and M, it is possible to write any number up to 5000.

Here are a few examples of numbers up to 1000 :-

a	400 = CD	b	465 = CDLXV	c	490 = CDXC	d	524 = DXXIV
e	549 = DXLIX	f	600 = DC	g	622 = DCXXII	h	659 = DCLIX
i	780 = DCCLXXX	j	799 = DCCXCIX	k	945 = CMXLV	l	999 = CMXCIX

As a class, study how the above Roman Numbers were formed and try the following :-

4. You should be able to write the numbers from 300 to 1000 using the Roman symbols I, V, X, L, C, D and M. (*You might like to try writing them all out !!!!!*).

   What Roman Numerals are used to write the number :-

   a 360 b 401 c 430 d 450 e 480 f 520 g 570 h 635

   i 684 j 699 k 760 l 845 m 869 n 937 o 966 p 995 ?

5. What numbers do these Roman symbols represent :-

   a CCCLXXX b CDXLV c CDXCI d DXXVI e DL f DCX

   g DCCCL h DCCCXC i CMX j CMLVI k CMLXXI l CMXCI ?

6. 888 is the number under 1000 that needs most symbols - What is it in Roman form ?

7. Obviously, MM stands for 2000, MMMD stands for 3500. Investigate the Roman Numerals up to 4000 and find out the symbols for 5000, 10000, 50000 and 100000.

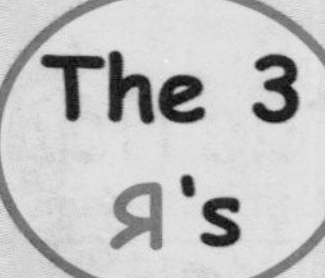

Revisit - Review - Revise

1. Write the following numbers out fully in words :-

   a 7030 b 93 700 c 402 619 d 370 004.

2. Write the following numbers using digits :-

   a Nineteen thousand, one hundred and two

   b Six hundred and three thousand seven hundred and twelve.

3. Write down the number that is :-

   a 8000 more than 12 200 b 240 000 less than 600 000.

4. Find the missing numbers :-

   a 730, 720, ..., 700, ..., 680 b 28 000, ..., ..., 31 000

   c 21 800, ..., 19 800, ... d 1 000 000, ..., 800 000 ...,

5. a Round to the nearest 1000 :- (i) 5548 (ii) 29 672 (iii) 328 299.

   b Round to the nearest 10 000 :- (i) 38 420 (ii) 146 800.

   c Round to the nearest 100 000 :- (i) 481 000 (ii) 929 999.

6. a Round both numbers to the nearest 10, then estimate :- 369 + 395.

   b Round both numbers to the nearest 100, then estimate :- 7682 – 1718.

   c Round both numbers to the nearest 1000, then estimate :- 17 840 + 6399.

7. Cheryl bought two vintage cars - a classic at £43 560 and a convertible costing £38 420.

   Round both these prices to the nearest £10 000 and find an approximate answer for the total amount she paid for the cars.

8. The population of Cardiff in the spring of 2014 was 359 731.

   Round this number to the nearest hundred thousand.

9. What Roman Numerals are used to write the number :-

   a 105 b 210 c 325 d 450 e 655 f 988 ?

10. What numbers do these Roman symbols represent :-

   a CCLXX b CDXLVI c DCXCIV d DCCCXX e CMXXV f CMLIV ?

Chapter 2 — Addition & Subtraction

Add/Subtract Numbers with up to 6 Digits

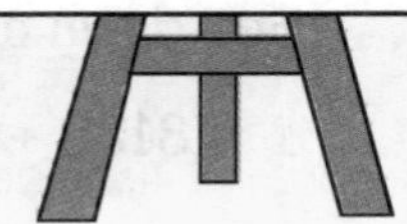

Example 1 :- Add 264 329 + 397 815.

Your teacher will explain.

Set down and work out as before :-

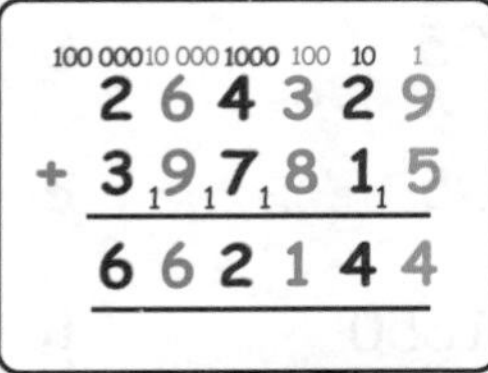

264 329 + 397 815 = 662 144

* Remember to line up the numbers

* Remember to add the numbers you have carried

Example 2 :- Work out 73 246 - 28 739.

Your teacher will explain.

73 246 - 28 739 = 44 507

* note :- The answer can be checked by adding.
=> 44 507 + 28 739 = 73 246. ✓

Exercise 1

*Check your subtraction answers by adding as in the *note above.*

1. Copy each example and work out the answer :-

a 486 + 394

b 825 - 279

c 1646 + 7398

d 8043 - 4825

e 16 252 + 17 438

f 57 089 - 23 462

g 72 435 - 38 279

h 327 425 + 209 782

i 857 733 - 229 492

1.

j	74 289 + 39 364	k	85 326 - 75 608	l	385 237 + 226 748
m	422 684 - 86 705	n	700 499 + 200 687	o	500 000 - 345 432

2. Set down and work out :-

a	8128 + 4795	b	15 254 + 8296	c	9200 - 6850
d	3800 - 1995	e	7400 - 2500	f	10 819 + 15 673
g	13 800 - 11 850	h	27 400 - 19 399	i	54 728 + 45 982
j	200 254 + 179 647	k	892 315 + 107 685	l	1 000 000 - 475 000.

3. There are 49 271 small parakeets and 729 large parakeets in an area of the rain forest.

How many is that altogether ?

4. A technician at a medical laboratory is studying blood samples. Two samples contained a total of 18 225 blood cells. The first sample had 9775 blood cells.

How many blood cells were in the second sample ?

5. 

A fish farm stocked its ponds with 28 500 trout and 17 950 baby salmon.

How many fish altogether ?

6. Rovers paid out £575 400 for a striker and £135 600 for a goalie.

   a How much did they pay out in total ?

   b How much dearer was the striker ?

7. 

Mr Henry paid £368 525 for his bungalow.

Mr Jones paid £540 800 for his bungalow.

How much cheaper was Mr Henry's house ?

8. The local newspaper prints 435 000 copies per week.

The paper sold 397 678 copies last week.

How many copies were not sold ?

Add/Subtract Whole Numbers Mentally

Be able to add & subtract numbers mentally with up to 6 digits.

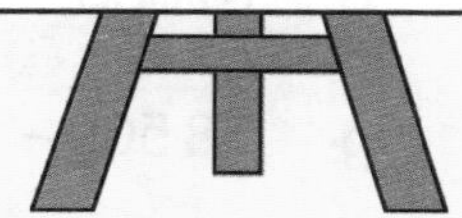

Here are some more quick ways of adding and subtracting numbers.

Example 1 :- To add 19 000 and 27 000,

you could add :-	you could add :-	you could add :-
20 000 + 27 000 = 47 000,	19 000 + 20 000 = 39 000,	19 + 27 = 46,
then subtract 1000	then add 7000	then put on 3 zeros.
= 46 000	= 46 000	= 46 000

Example 2 :- What is 560 000 - 290 000 ?

you could subtract :-	you could subtract :-	you could subtract :-
560 000 - 300 000 = 260 000,	560 000 - 200 000 = 360 000,	56 - 29 = 27,
then add 10 000	then subtract 90 000	then put on 4 zeros.
= 270 000	= 270 000	= 270 000

Example 3 :- Try 12 460 - 2300.

Can you see by easy subtraction in this one, the answer is 10 160 ?

Discuss these and other methods.

Exercise 2 Try to do this exercise mentally.

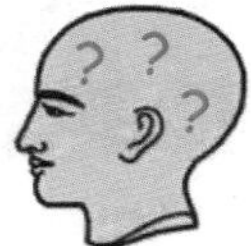

1. *Revision*

Write down the answers to :-

a	67 + 39	b	72 - 48	c	88 + 92
d	91 - 23	e	122 + 78	f	100 - 73
g	340 + 290	h	560 - 180	i	710 + 190
j	790 - 640	k	470 + 750	l	880 - 110
m	971 + 299	n	864 - 398	o	652 + 501
p	1600 - 490	q	7900 + 1200	r	5500 - 4100
s	8900 + 999	t	10 000 - 4100	u	3250 + 6750.

2. Write down the answers to :-

a	19 000 + 9000	b	22 000 - 8000	c	69 200 + 12 000
d	61 000 - 13 000	e	52 000 + 19 000	f	73 000 - 58 000
g	38 500 - 19 000	h	70 200 + 25 800	i	74 000 - 23 800.

3. Write down the answers to :-

a	230 000 - 190 000	b	290 000 + 90 000	c	350 000 - 110 000
d	290 000 + 520 000	e	930 000 - 780 000	f	625 000 + 210 000
g	740 000 - 299 000	h	590 000 + 309 000	i	1 000 000 - 999 000.

4. Work out :-

a	263 410 + 132 562	b	647 289 - 106 173	c	174 293 + 521 604
d	530 284 - 430 172	e	142 215 + 615 384	f	1 000 000 - 999 991.

5. The attendance for the match between Leeds and Doncaster was 25 200.

This was 17 800 fewer than Leeds v Newcastle.

How many people were at that match ?

6. In April 2014, the population of Sheffield was 551 800.

In the same month, the population of Swansea was 240 200.

How many more people lived in Sheffield than Swansea ?

7. The area of Norway is 390 000 square kilometres.

Sweden's area is 450 500 square kilometres.

What is the total area of both countries ?

8. 

A vineyard in France turned 920 000 grapes into wine.

A German vineyard used 790 000 grapes for wine.

How many more grapes did the French vineyard use ?

9. Ternock's made £359 000 from the sales of caramel wafers.

The firm also made £299 000 from tea cake sales.

How much money did they make from both ?

Using Rounding to Estimate Answers

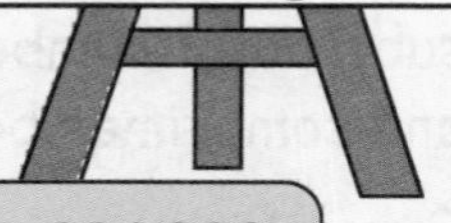

Be able to estimate an answer to a question using rounding.

It is possible to "MENTALLY" estimate the answer to a question by rounding the numbers to "1 figure" or "2 figure" accuracy first.

Examples :-

24 987 + 16 020 is approximately 25 000 + 16 000 ≈ 41 000

499 000 − 296 000 is approximately 500 000 − 300 000 ≈ 200 000

"≈" approximately equal to.

Exercise 3

1. Round each number to 1 figure accuracy, then give an estimate for :-

   a 8920 + 6100 b 54 100 − 19 800 c 61 988 + 18 290

   d 390 000 − 195 000 e 28 990 + 50 777 f 999 000 − 489 899.

2. Round each number to 2 figure accuracy, then give an estimate for :-

   a 25 010 − 12 999 b 72 828 + 13 691 c 748 000 − 219 000

   d 362 500 + 411 600 e 887 000 − 369 000 f 249 320 + 254 320.

3. Last week, 395 000 people watched a new TV show.
   This week, the show's viewing figures dropped by 59 000.
   Using 1 figure accuracy, estimate how many people watched the show in week 2.

4. 

   In winter, a delivery company delivered 28 980 parcels.
   In summer, the company delivered 61 025 more.
   Estimate how many parcels in total, using 2 figure accuracy.

5. Printo's have 297 500 black ink cartridges in stock.
   They also have 104 995 colour ink cartridges.
   Using 1 figure accuracy, estimate how many cartridges they have in stock.

6.  

   A ship full of grain crashed onto a coral reef.
   69 900 tons of the 90 350 tons of grain it was carrying were saved.
   Using 2 figure accuracy, estimate how many tons of grain were lost at sea.

Multi-step Problems Involving Addition & Subtraction

Be able to add and subtract in problems which require more than one operation.

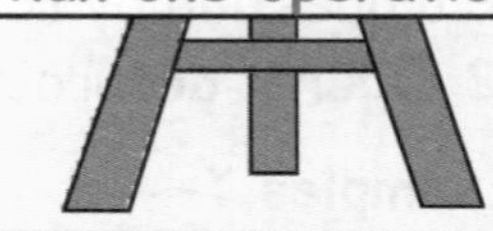

It is not always the case that you will be asked to add or subtract 2 numbers. Often, more than 2 numbers are involved and sometimes both operations (+ and −) appear in the one question.

Example :-

Mrs Doyle bought a vacuum cleaner for £187, a microwave for £96 and a washing machine for £388.

She was given a £45 discount for buying all three items.

What was her **total** bill ?

add → then → subtract

$$\begin{array}{r} 187 \\ 96 \\ +\ 388 \\ \hline £\,671 \end{array} \qquad \begin{array}{r} 671 \\ -\ 45 \\ \hline £\,626 \end{array}$$

Total Bill = £626

Exercise 4

1. Joseph is trying to expand his games collection.

   He got 8 games from his family for Christmas, bought 5 more at a car boot sale and 3 more online. 4 of the games didn't work.

   How many working games did he end up with ?

2. 

   Sandi is making fruit cocktails for her party.

   She adds 350 ml of pineapple juice to 230 ml of orange juice and then adds 45 ml of crushed raspberries.

   How many ml of fruit cocktail has she made ?

3. M&T Bakers make 200 chicken sandwiches and 150 salad sandwiches for sale each day.

   One day last week, 28 chicken and 35 salad sandwiches reached their sell by date and had to be thrown out.

   They managed to sell the rest. How many in total was that ?

4. 

   Asdo Supermarket bought in 2400 Halloween masks and 1700 witchs hats.

   After Halloween, they were left with 180 masks and 620 hats.

   How many masks and hats altogether had Asdo sold ?

5. United bought two players - one for £375000, the other for £448000.

   At the end of the season, they sold both for a total of £950000.

   How much money had United made in these deals ?

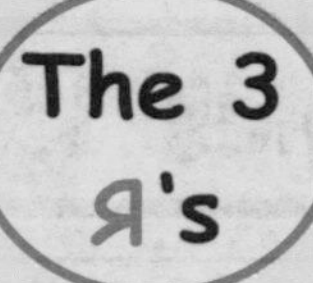

Revisit - Review - Revise

1. Try these mentally. Write down the answers to :-

a 540 + 360 b 8000 - 4900 c 72 000 + 18 000

d 42 500 - 12 500 e 263 124 + 412 805 f 1 000 000 - 997 999.

2. There were 24 200 trees in a forest.

During a harsh winter, 1900 wilted and died.

Write down how many trees were left in the forest.

3. Copy each example and work out the answer :-

a 58 926 − 17 364

b 427 635 + 86 498

c 352 829 − 163 085

4. Set down as in Question 3 and find :-

a 7643 - 2846 b 67 389 + 67 388 c 565 000 - 365 300.

5. A chain of doughnut stores reckons that it sold 628 000 doughnuts last year.

287 500 of these were covered in chocolate icing.

How many doughnuts were sold without that icing ?

6. 

A monument is made up of 86 550 sandstone blocks and 33 080 limestone blocks.

Using **2 figure accuracy**, <u>estimate</u> how many blocks make up the monument.

7. A restaurant has a stock of 117 forks.

It has 25 more knives than forks and twice as many spoons as knives.

How many pieces of cutlery does the restaurant have altogether ?

8. 

A vineyard produced enough grapes to make 327 290 bottles of wine - white, rosé and red.

125 800 were bottles of white wine and 87 450 were of rosé.

How many bottles of red wine ?

Angles 1

Types of Angles

Recognise all types of angles and know their names.

Example :-

An angle is simply a measure of how one line is rotated onto another line.

Angles are not measured in centimetres. They are measured in degrees.

There are various names used to describe angles - based on their sizes.

You should remember these :-

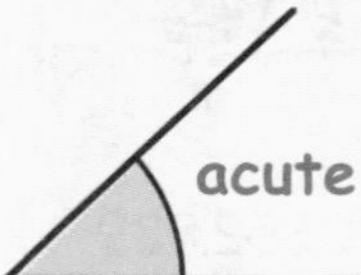

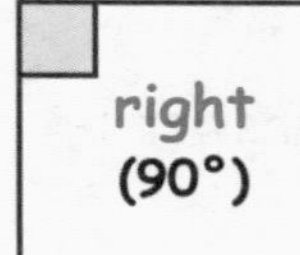

Other angles include :-

Exercise 1

1. Use a word from the above list to describe each of the marked angles :-

a

b

c

d

e

f

g

h

i

2. What type of angle is marked in these triangles :-

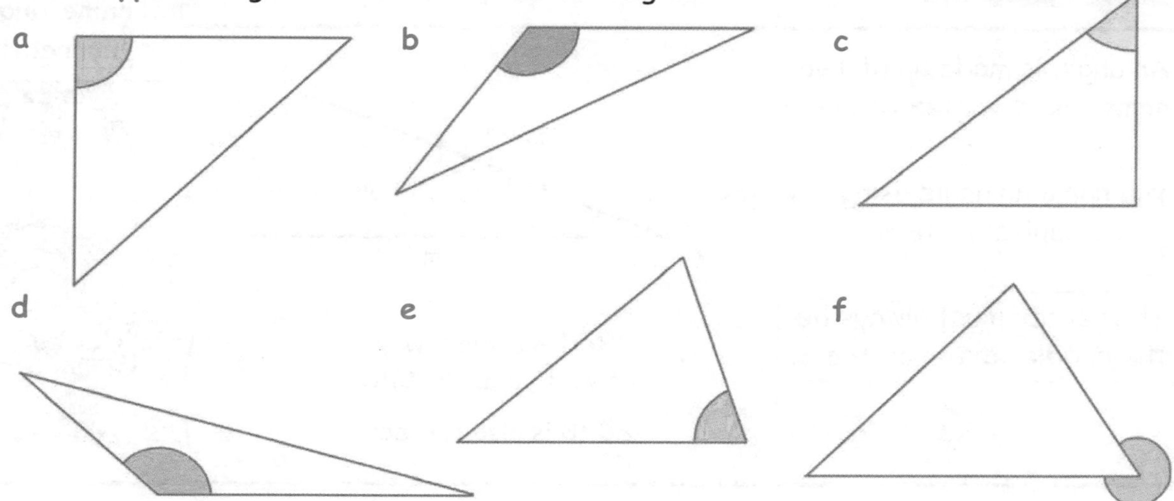

3. What type of angle is marked in these shapes :-

a

b

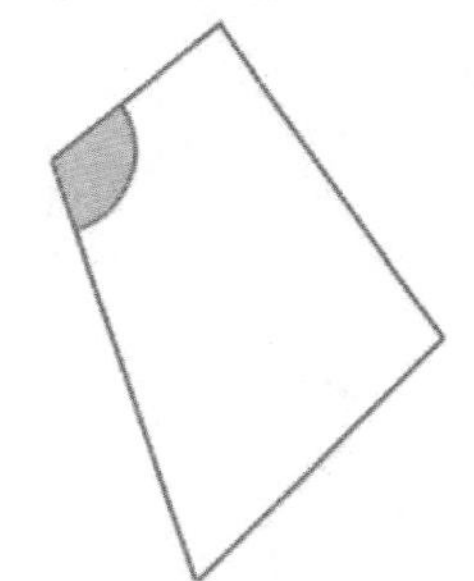

c

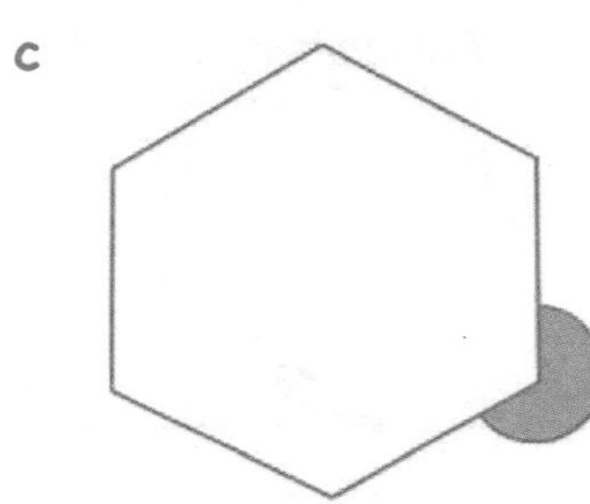

4. Copy the diagrams below and match the type of angle with the given sizes :-

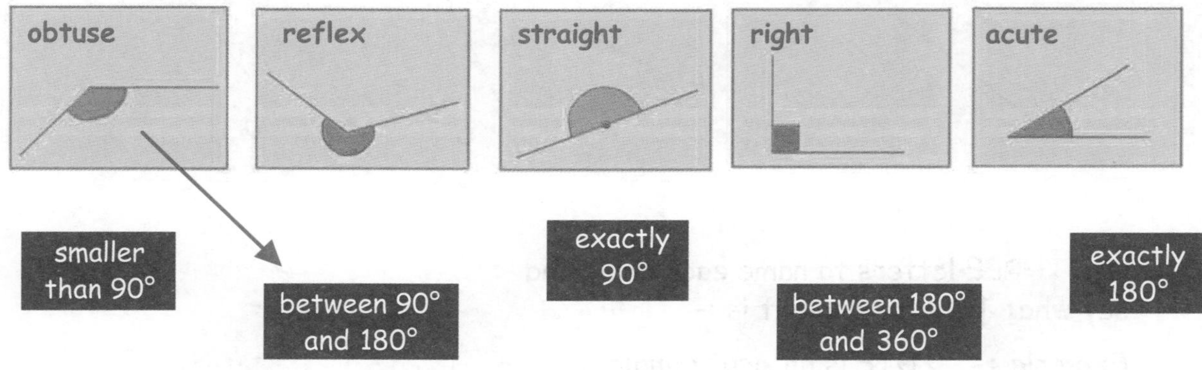

5. Look at the angle sizes listed below :-

210°, 88°, 110°, 17°, 60°, 180°, 176°, 91°, 90°, 335°, 31°, 169°.

Which of the above angles are :-

a acute b obtuse c straight d right e reflex ?

Naming Angles

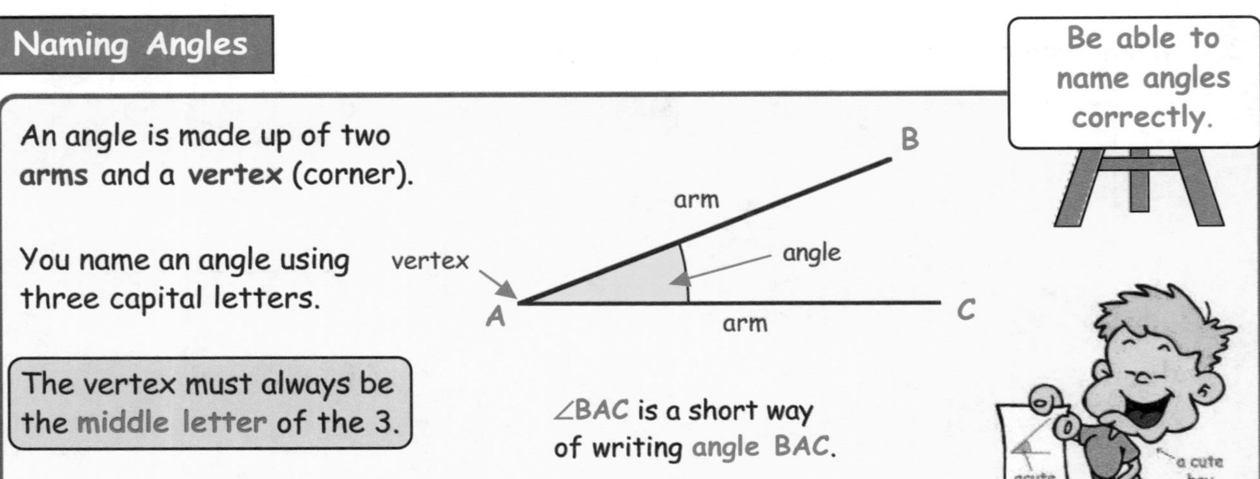

Be able to name angles correctly.
An angle is made up of two **arms** and a **vertex** (corner).
You name an angle using three capital letters.
The vertex must always be the middle letter of the 3.

a cute boy

Exercise 2

1. Use 3 LETTERS each time to name the shaded angle :-
(*Remember to use the "∠" sign*).

a b c

d e f

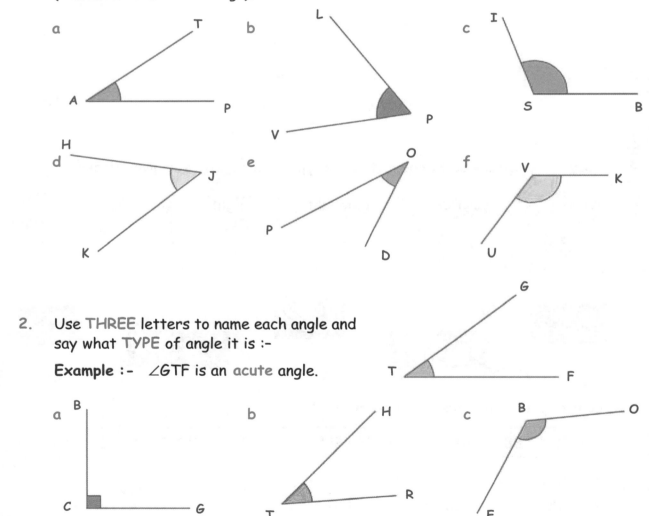

2. Use THREE letters to name each angle and say what TYPE of angle it is :-

Example :- ∠GTF is an acute angle.

arm
vertex

arm
∠BAC is a short way of writing angle BAC.
∠CAB is also correct.

a b c

2. d

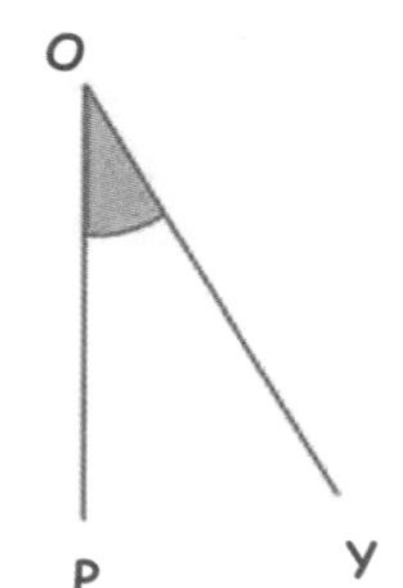

e

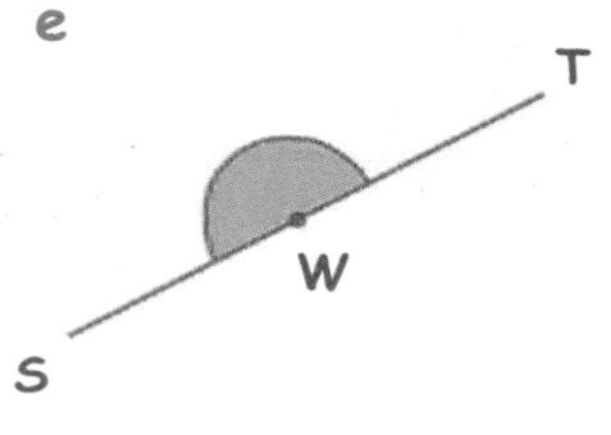

f

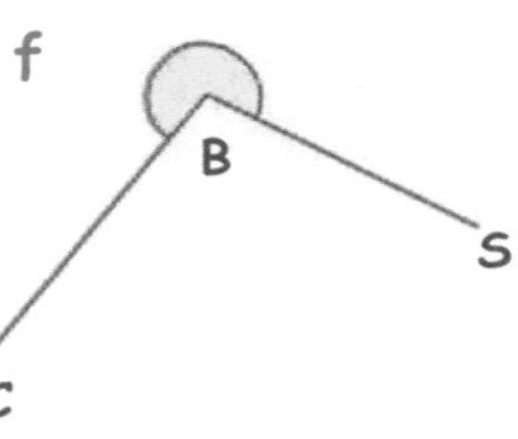

g

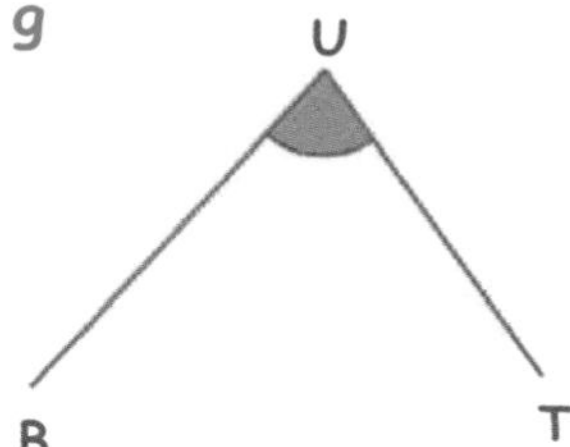

h

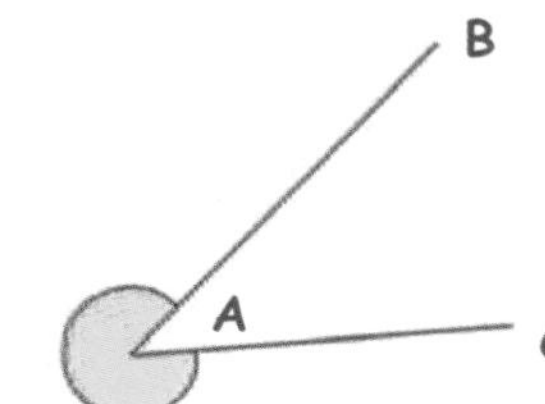

i

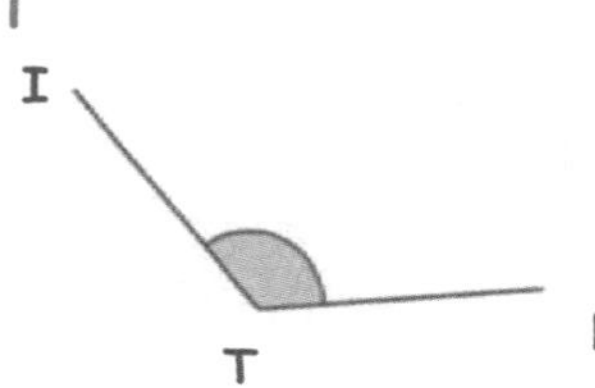

3. Look at triangle TSV :-

Now look at the triangles below :-

∠TSV is **green**.

∠STV is red.

∠TVS is **blue**.

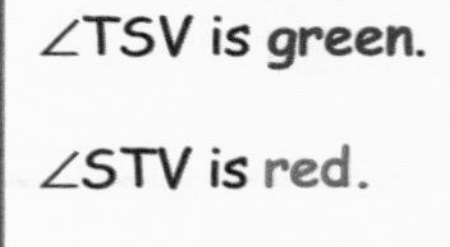

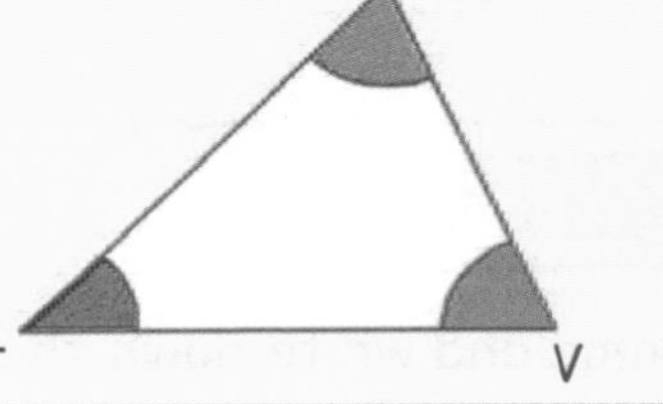

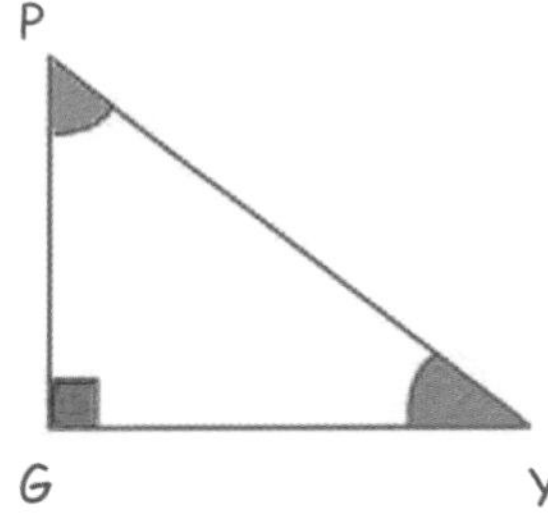

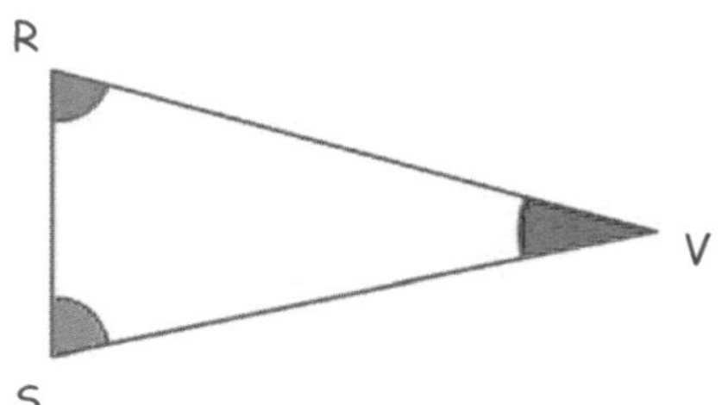

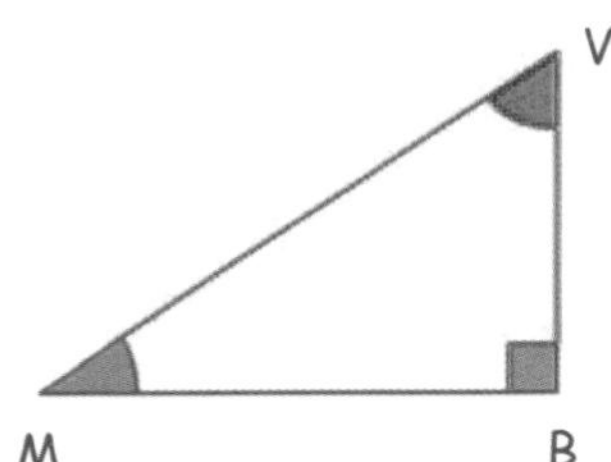

From the triangles above, name each :-

a red angle

b **green** angle

c **blue** angle.

4. Copy the diagram shown.

∠ACD is marked orange.

Colour or mark :-

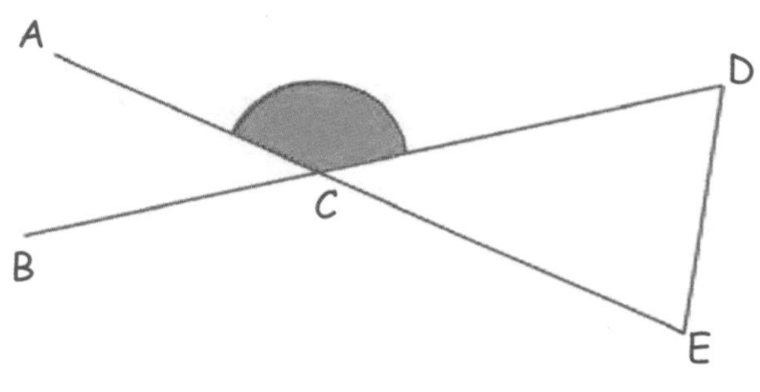

a ∠EDC red

b ∠CED **green**

c ∠ACB and ∠DCE blue

d ∠BCE orange. (*Why do you think ∠ACD and ∠BCE are both coloured orange ?*)

Measuring Angles

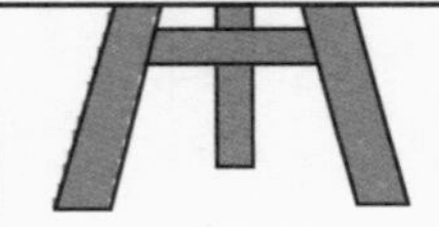

To **measure** an angle with a protractor :-

Step 1 : place the centre of the protractor on the vertex Q.

Step 2 : turn the protractor until the zero line lies along the arm PQ.

Step 3 : count round from the zero (*inside or out*), and read the value where the arm RQ cuts the scale.

You should always estimate the size of an angle, (in degrees), before you measure it.

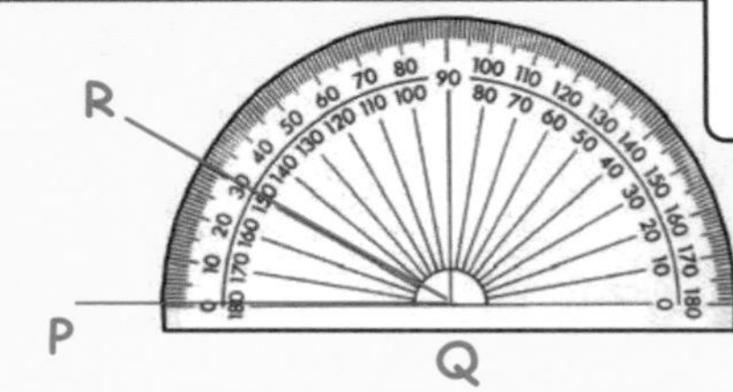

Use outside scale ∠ PQR = 30° .

Example :-

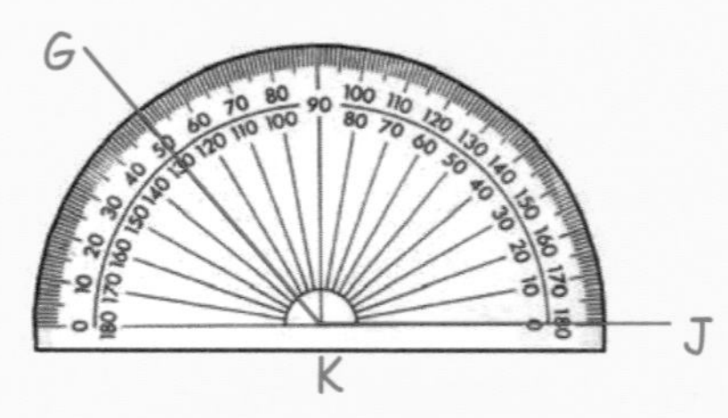

Use inside scale ∠ GKJ = 130°.

Exercise 3

1. Name and write down the size of each angle below. (**Example :-** *∠PQR = 30°*) :-

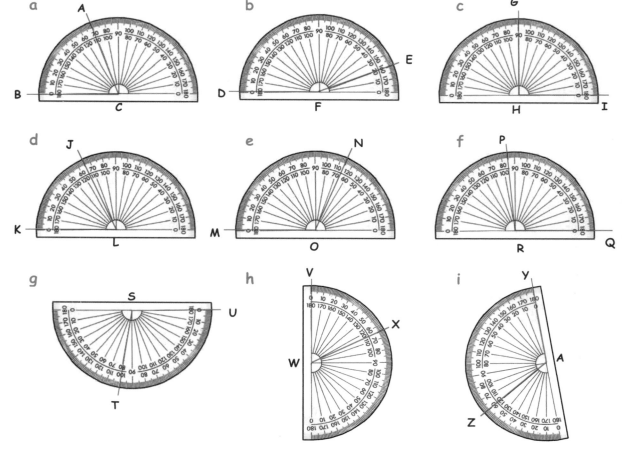

a B, A, C

b D, E, F

c G, H, I

d J, K, L

e M, N, O

f P, R, Q

g S, U, T

h V, X, W

i Y, A, Z

2. Do not use a protractor in this question.

Choose the estimate closest to what you think the angle is :-

a 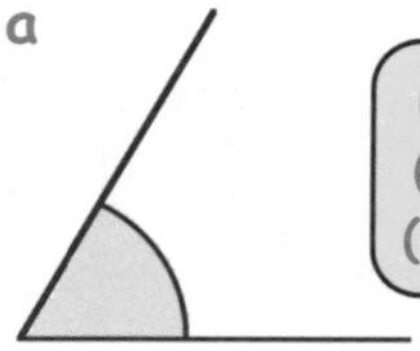
(i) 40°
(ii) 60°
(iii) 88°

b 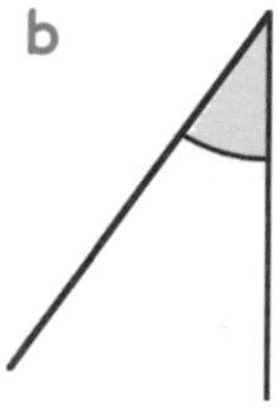
(i) 10°
(ii) 30°
(iii) 70°

c 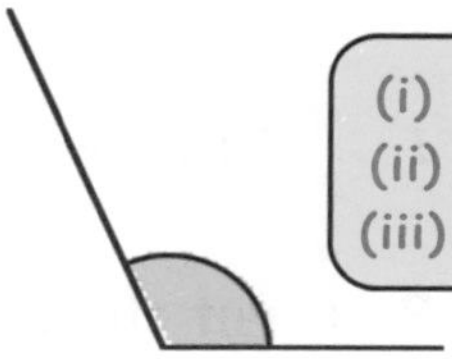
(i) 60°
(ii) 85°
(iii) 110°

d 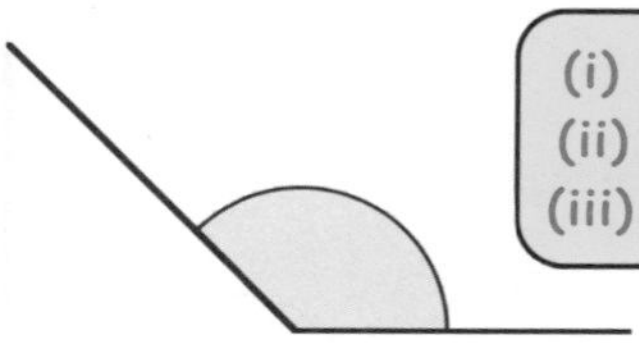
(i) 100°
(ii) 140°
(iii) 170°

e 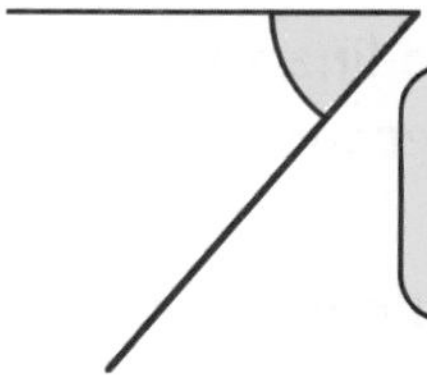
(i) 15°
(ii) 50°
(iii) 75°

f 
(i) 100°
(ii) 150°
(iii) 170°

3. For each coloured angle :- (i) estimate its size

(ii) use a protractor to measure each angle.

a b 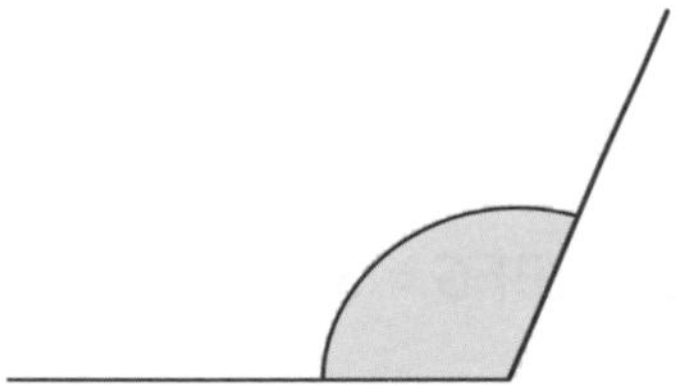 c

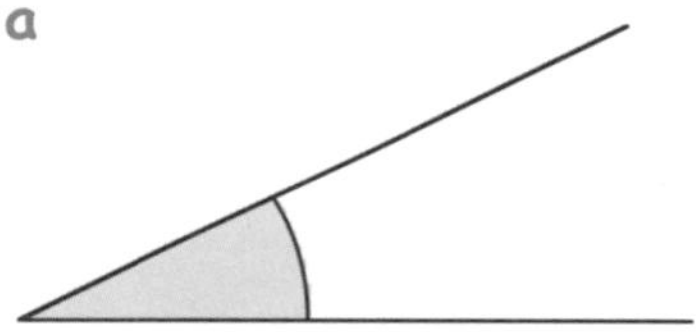

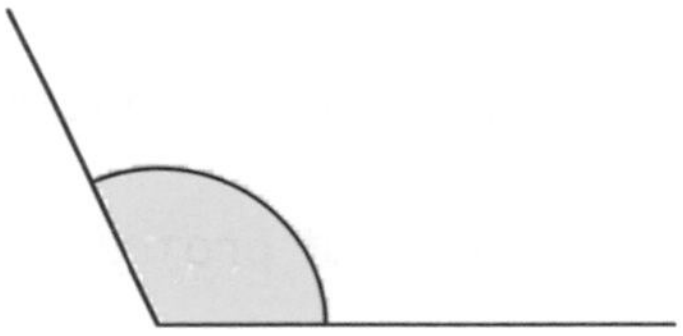

d 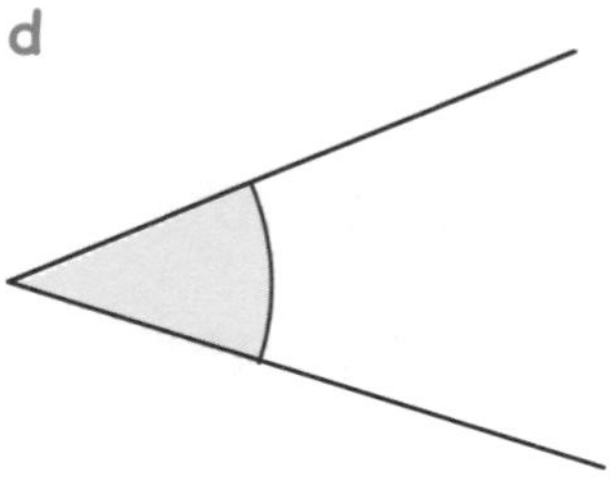 e 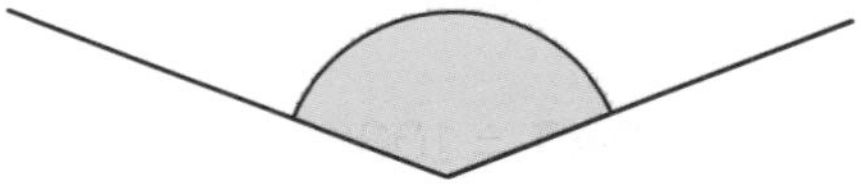 f

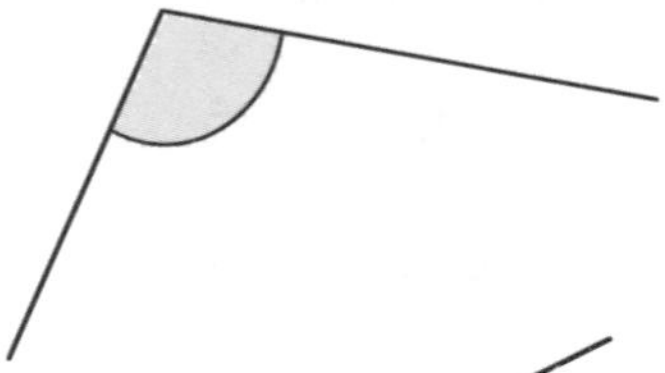

g 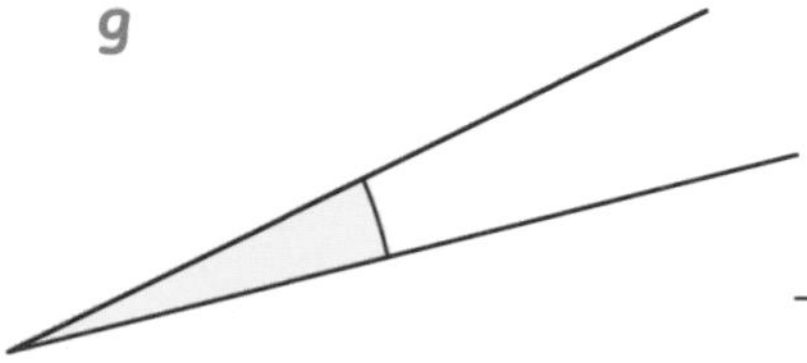 h  i

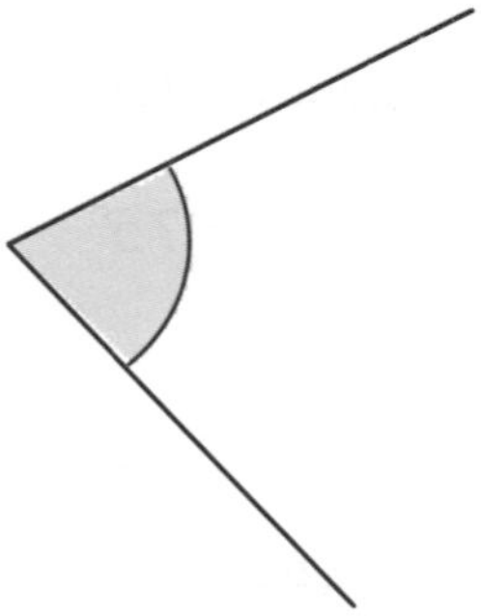

j 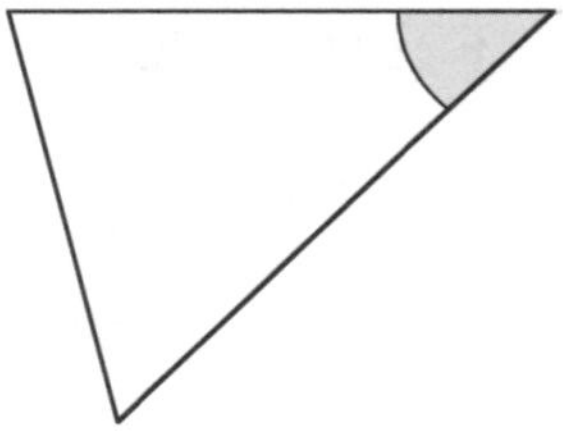 k 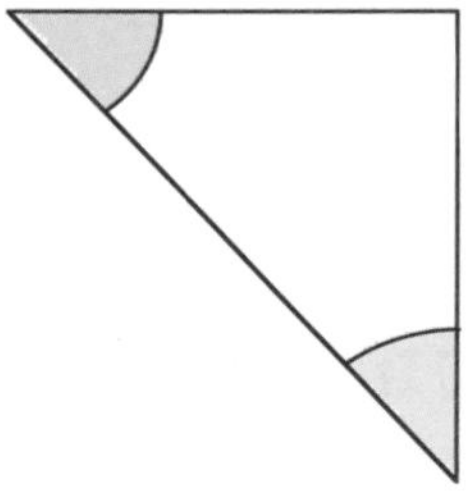 l

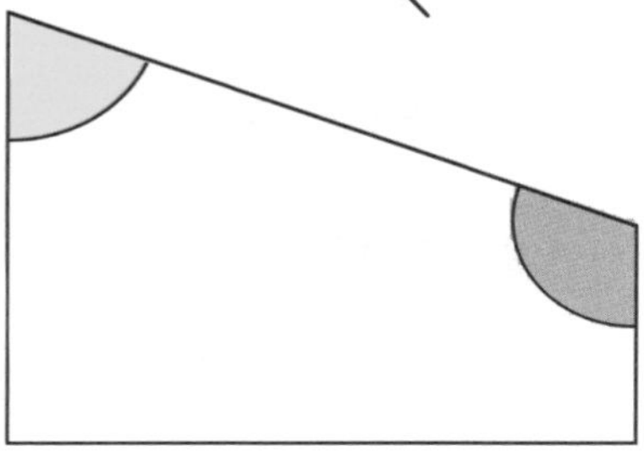

Drawing Angles

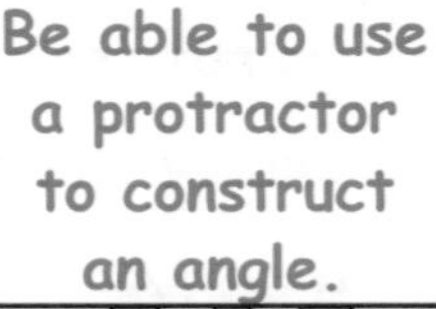

Be able to use
a protractor
to construct
an angle.

Example :- Draw ∠TPQ = 40°.

Step 1 : Start with a line with a dot at one end.

Step 2 : Put the centre of the protractor on the dot and line up with the line.

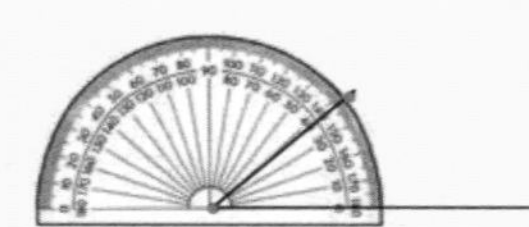

Step 3 : Count round from the zero line to the 40° division and mark with a second dot.

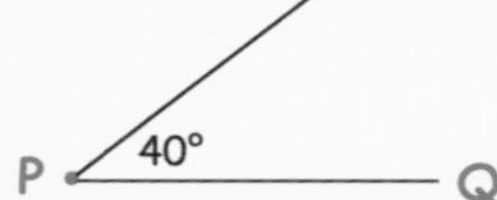

Step 4 : Join the dots and put in the letters, (*middle letter P*).

T
P 40° Q

Exercise 4

1. Draw a 6 centimetre line FG and put a dot on the end (*left side*).

   Use your protractor to show ∠BFG = 30°.

   F ——— G
   6 cm

2. Use the same method to draw and label these angles :-

a ∠ABC = 50°	b ∠PTY = 90°	c ∠LMK = 10°
d ∠RWT = 20°	e ∠RAT = 100°	f ∠WXY = 110°
g ∠ACT = 150°	h ∠QET = 130°	i ∠YUM = 45°
j ∠HJK = 75°	k ∠SWA = 15°	l ∠BRM = 135°.

3. (*Harder*) Draw and label these angles :-

a ∠ABH = 38°	b ∠XTC = 22°	c ∠KLM = 49°
d ∠STV = 76°	e ∠PIJ = 96°	f ∠TRG = 108°
g ∠DAZ = 173°	h ∠YUK = 123°	i ∠FST = 8°
j ∠REW = 111°	k ∠JIL = 144°	l ∠BAD = 190°.

Compass Points   Extension

Know the 8 compass points and the sizes of the angles between them.

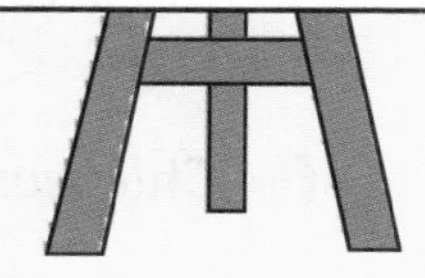

The four points of the compass North, South, East and West can be extended into an eight point compass rose as shown.

NE stands for North-East.

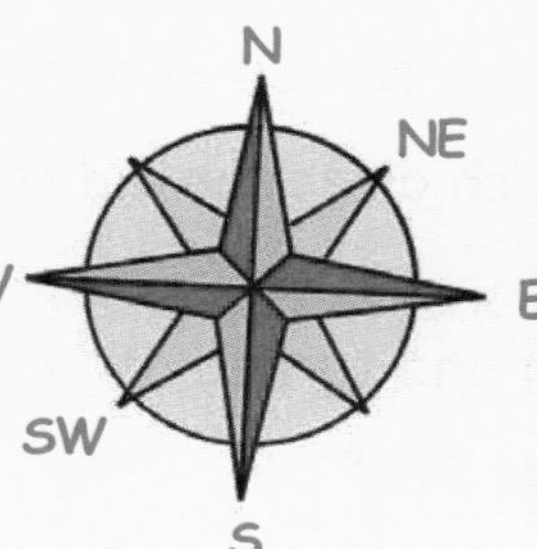

Remember :

360° = 1 full turn

180° = $\frac{1}{2}$ turn

90° = $\frac{1}{4}$ turn

Exercise 5

1. **Copy** this diagram and fill in all 8 points of the compass on it in the correct order.

N

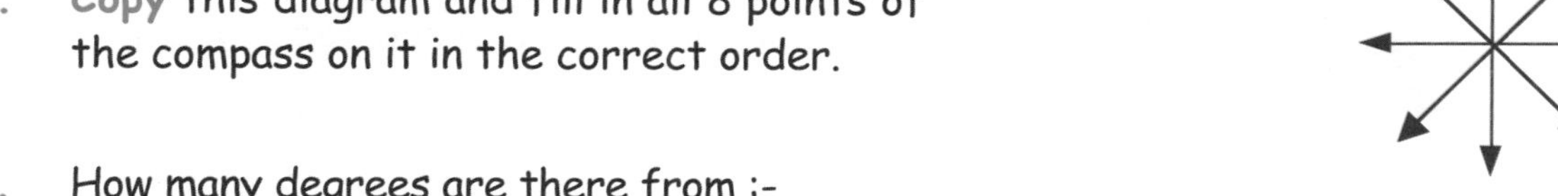

2. How many degrees are there from :-

a	North to East (*clockwise*)	b	East to South (*clockwise*)
c	North to West (*anti-clockwise*)	d	North to West (*clockwise*)
e	North to North East (*clockwise*)	f	West to East (*anti-clockwise*)
g	North to South West (*anti-clockwise*)	h	SW to North (*clockwise*)
i	North to South	j	NW to NE (*anti-clockwise*) ?

3. a

Angela is facing **West**.

She makes a $\frac{1}{4}$ turn clockwise.

In which direction is Angela now facing ?

b Sid was driving **South East** when he came to a roundabout.

He then turned his car through 45° anti-clockwise.

In which direction was Sid then driving ?

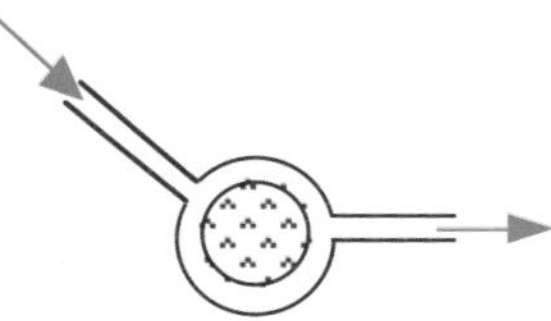

c

A one-seater plane was flying **North East**.

The pilot turned through 90° anti-clockwise.

In which direction was the plane then flying ?

d A tall ship is sailing **SE**, away from a lighthouse.

How many degrees would the ship have to turn to face :-

(i) West (*clockwise*)   (ii) East (*anti-clockwise*)

(iii) NW (*clockwise*)   (iv) South (*anti-clockwise*) ?

3. e 

A witch was travelling North East, but had lost her way.

She turned 90° anticlockwise and moved on a bit.

Then she turned 225° clockwise.

In which direction did she end up facing ?

f Chic was walking North West and turned 45° clockwise.

He then turned anti-clockwise 270°.

In which direction was Chic then facing.

g 

A helicopter is flying North East.

It makes an anti-clockwise turn and now faces West.

How many degrees has the helicopter turned through ?

4. A tourist is given the location of several points of interest.

a In which direction does the tourist need to travel to get to :-

(i) the diving pool

(ii) St Peter's Tower

(iii) the Old High School

(iv) the Horse Statue ?

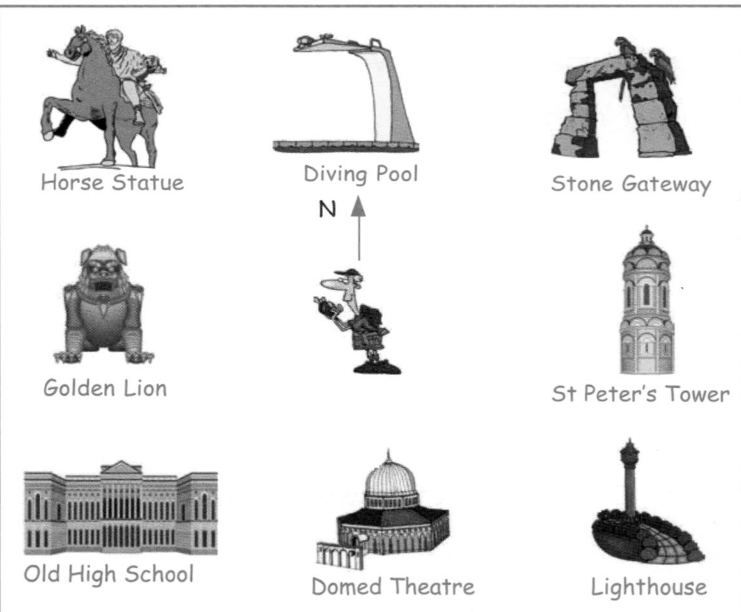

b He is now standing at the top of St Peter's Tower.

From there, in which direction is :-

(i) the Golden Lion

(ii) the Stone Gateway

(iii) the Lighthouse

(iv) the Domed Theatre ?

c The tourist travels from St Peter's Tower to the diving pool.

He then moves on to the Golden Lion and finally ends up at the Old High School.

Describe his movements using compass point directions.

d Facing North from the Old High School he turns 450° (clockwise) !

Where is the first place that this would take him to ?

The 3 Я's

Revisit - Review - Revise

1. Use a word from " acute, right, obtuse, straight **or** reflex" to describe each type of coloured angle below :-

a

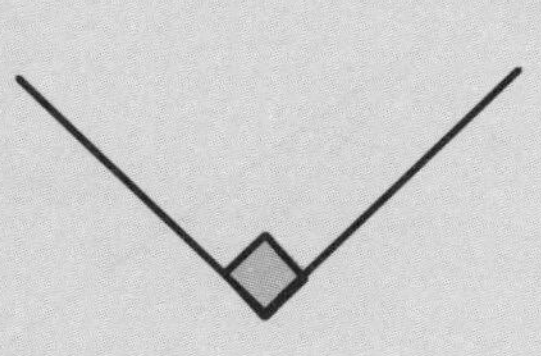

b

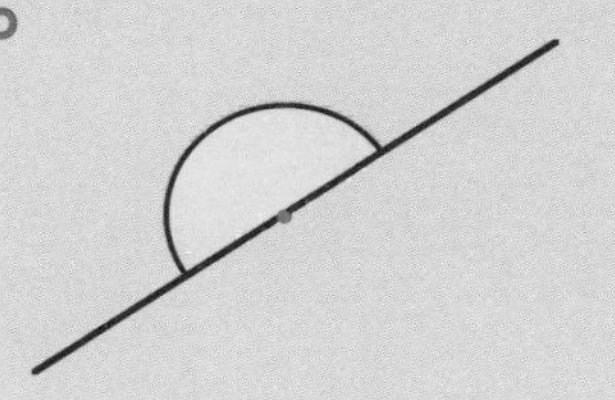

c

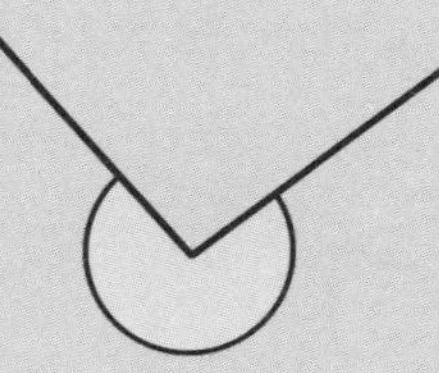

d

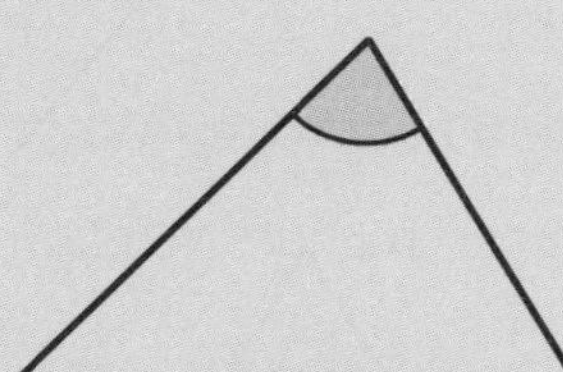

e

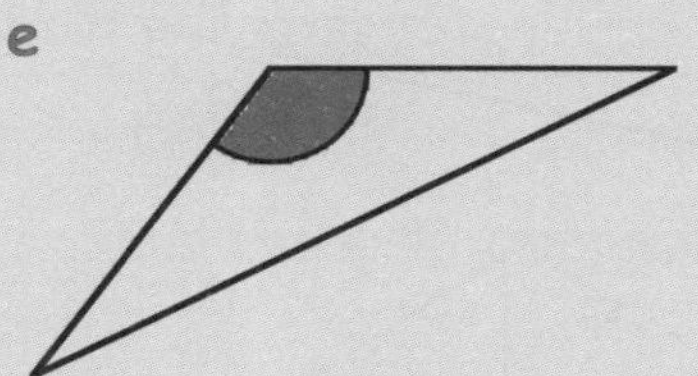

f

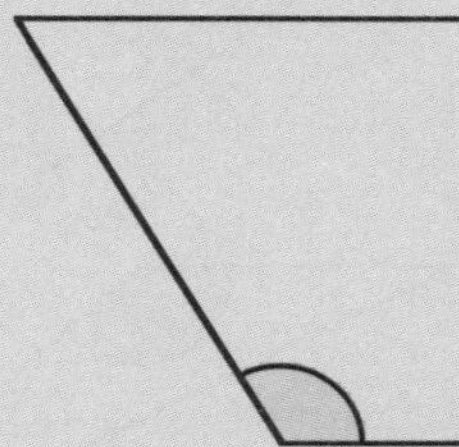

2. Look at the angle sizes listed below :-

54°, 122°, 90°, 189°, 200°, 4°, 179°, 99°, 40°, 67°, 111°, 180°.

Make lists of angles which are :-

a acute b obtuse c right d straight e reflex.

3. Use 3 letters to name each coloured angle :-

a

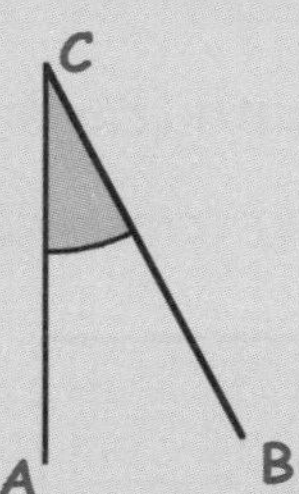

b

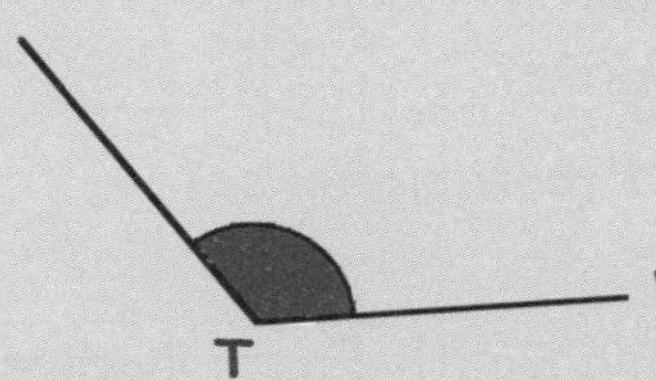

c

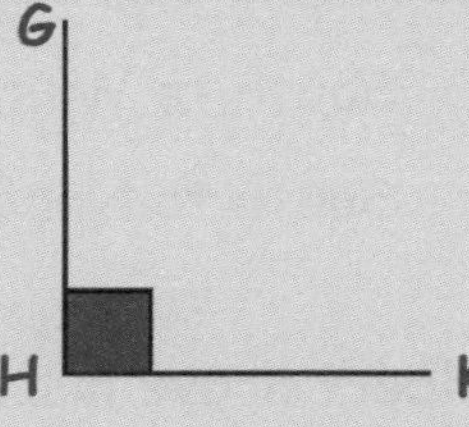

d

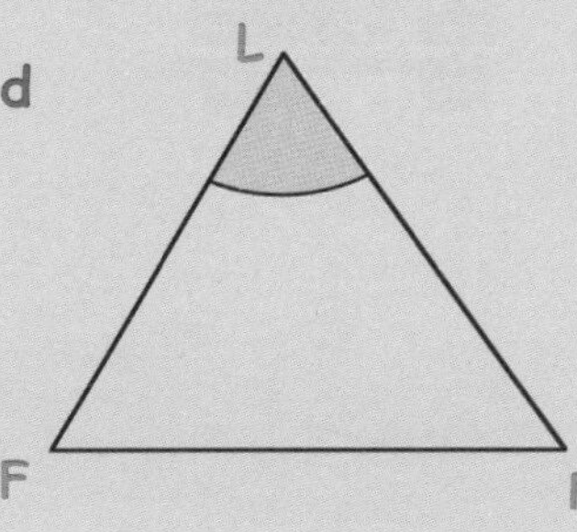

e

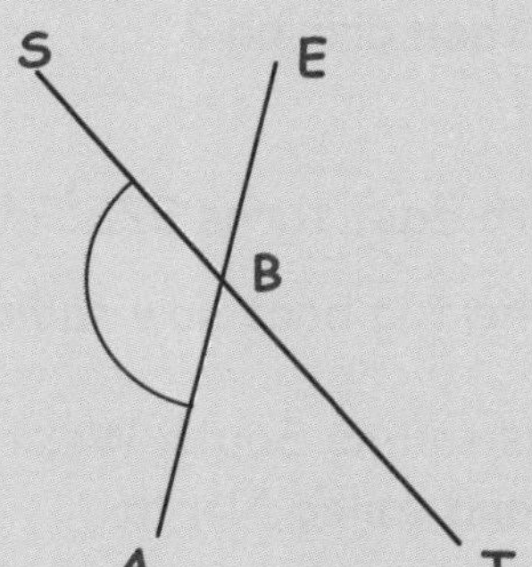

f

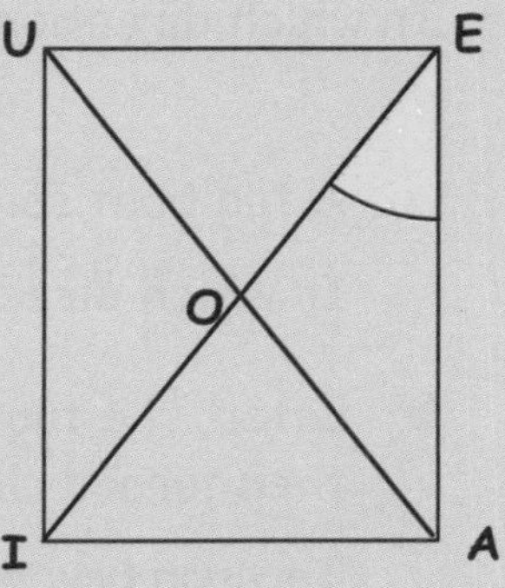

4. For each coloured angle, (i) estimate its size.

(ii) use a protractor to measure the size of the angle.

a

b

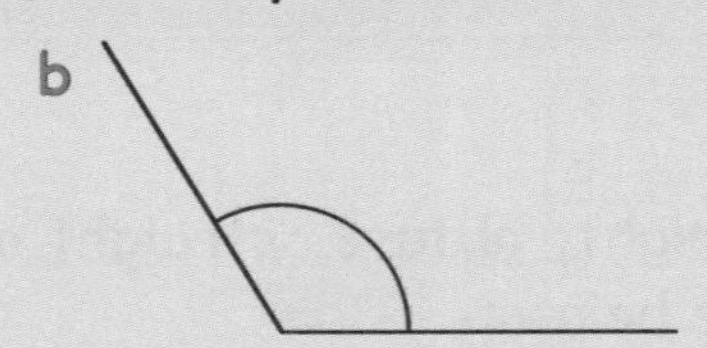

c

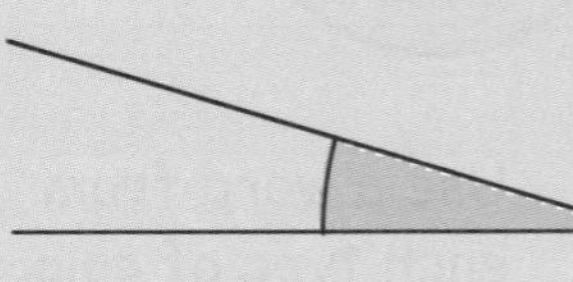

d

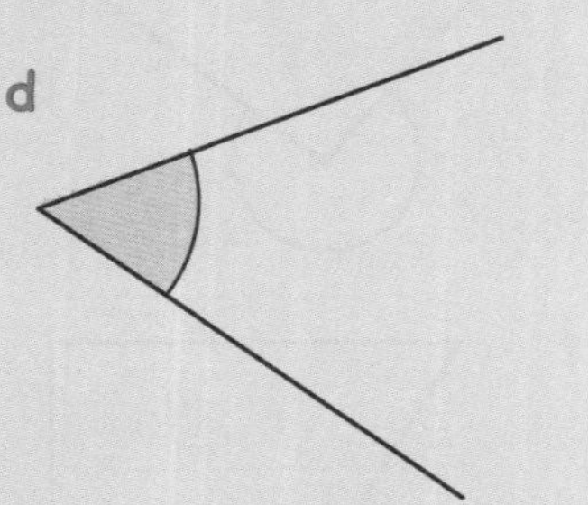

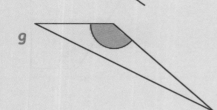

e

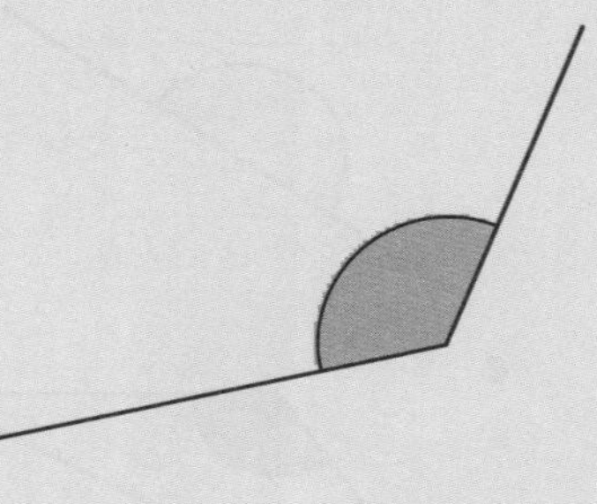

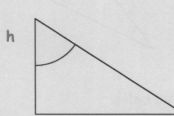

f

g

h

i

5. Carefully draw each of the following angles and label them with their letters :-

a ∠DEF = 20°   b ∠HNJ = 60°   c ∠QWR = 110°

d ∠ASD = 170°   e ∠LHD = 75°   f ∠UTE = 142°.

6. How many degrees are there from :-

a South to West (*clockwise*)   b West to South (*clockwise*)

c South to North West (*anti-clockwise*)   d N to NE (*anti-clockwise*) ?

7. Albert drove his truck in a South-Easterly direction.

He then made a quarter turn anti-clockwise.

In which direction was he then driving ?

8. a A tug boat sailing North East turns 225° clockwise.

In which direction is the tug boat now sailing ?

b Later, the tug boat was sailing South West then turned clockwise and sailed North.

Through how many degrees had the tug boat turned ?

Multiplication & Division

Multiplication by a Single Digit

Be able to multiply a number with up to 4 digits by a single digit.

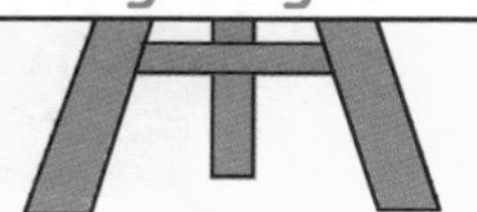

Example 1 :- 78 x 6 **Example 2 :-** 569 x 7

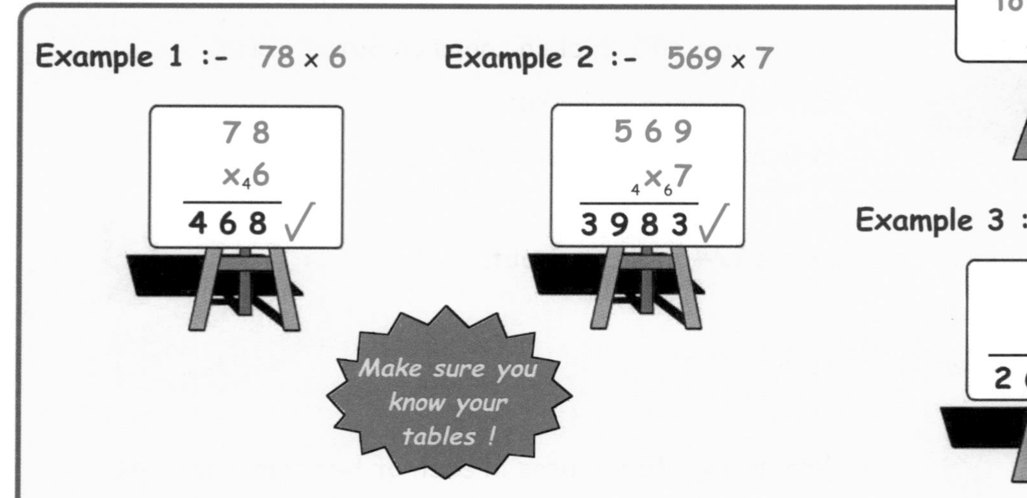

7 8
x₄6
4 6 8
5 6 9
₄x₆7
3 9 8 3
Make sure you know your tables !

Example 3 :- 3276 x 8

Exercise 1

1. Copy the following and complete the calculation :-

a	b	c	d
35 x 6	87 x 4	96 x 7	87 x 9

e	f	g	h
748 x 3	296 x 5	407 x 9	649 x 4

i	j	k	l
5217 x 8	3026 x 7	9070 x 6	9876 x 9

2. Write each of these in the form of Question 1 and work them out :-

a	59 x 8	b	73 x 5	c	87 x 7	d	96 x 9
e	7 x 318	f	5 x 605	g	809 x 9	h	3 x 976
i	1237 x 4	j	8172 x 7	k	6528 x 5	l	1804 x 6
m	7 x 6254	n	5 x 2037	o	1276 x 9	p	3 x 9987.

3. Check your answers to Question 2 by dividing. ....
   e.g. to check if 59 x 8 = 472, divide 472 by 8 to see if you get back to 59.

4. There are 238 steps to the top of a tower.

How many steps will I take if I walk up and down the tower 3 times ?

5. 

There are 345 chicken coops on Bates' Farm.

Each coop has 9 chickens.

How many chickens does Mr Bates have ?

6. At an awards dinner, there were 174 tables set out.

Each table had 8 diners.

How many people were at the dinner ?

7. 

Bronte has 499 photos in each of her family albums.

She has 5 albums altogether.

How many family photos does she have ?

8. Rob and Jane between them earn £2185 per month.

How much will they earn over 6 months ?

9. 

An hour consists of 3600 seconds.

How many seconds are there in 7 hours ?

10. A palette holds 2096 tins of soup.

How many tins in a lorry with 9 palettes ?

11. 

There are 4 schools in Laptown.

Each school was built to take a maximum of 1350 children.

When each school is full, how many children will be attending altogether ?

12. A satellite travels at 7642 kilometres per hour.

How far will it fly in 9 hours ?

Multiplication by Two Digits (Long Multiplication)

Be able to multiply a number with up to 4 digits by a 2 digit number.

Up until now you have only been asked to use one set of "times tables" at a time when you are multiplying.

Now, you may have to use 2 different sets of tables.

Example :- 356 x 47

Step 1 :- multiply the 356 by the 7 (= 2492).

Step 2 :- now multiply by 40, *not 4*. (= 14240)
(it's easier to put a 0 (zero) below the 2, and then multiply by the 4).

Step 3 :- finally ... simply add your 2 answers.

```
   356
  x 47
  ----
  2492
 14240
 -----
 16732 ✓
```

* Your teacher will explain this to you.

Exercise 2

1. Copy this long multiplication and complete it :-

```
   247
  x 36
  ----
  1482
 ......0
 ----------
 ..........
```

2. Set down and work out :-

a 53 x 16 ... 0
b 36 x 48 ... 0
c 804 x 92
d 556 x 55
e 264 x 78
f 2598 x 63
g 4107 x 85
h 1612 x 47

3. Set down the following as in Question 2, then find :-

a	21 x 15	b	35 x 46	c	67 x 58	d	84 x 39
e	236 x 17	f	805 x 25	g	37 x 549	h	52 x 1023
i	8204 x 29	j	7777 x 64	k	4706 x 83	l	67 x 1217.

Multiplication by 10, 100 and 1000

Be able to multiply a number quickly by 10, 100 or 1000.

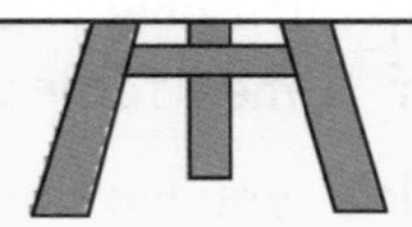

Look at these **examples** :-

32 × 10 = 320	601 × 10 = 6010	274 × 100 = 27 400	98 × 1000 = 98 000	540 × 1000 = 540 000

When you multiply the number 603 by 10 => the figures move 1 place left ..... 6030.

When you multiply 5238 by 100 => the figures move 2 places left ..... 523 800.

When you multiply 40 216 by 1000 => the figures move 3 places left ..... 40 216 000.

Examples :-

46 × 10 = 460	10 × 258 = 2580	6506 × 100 = 650 600
100 × 57 = 5700	260 × 1000 = 260 000	1000 × 3050 = 3 050 000

Exercise 3

1. Write down the answers to the following :-

   a 15 × 10 b 11 × 10 c 56 × 10 d 10 × 98
   e 10 × 125 f 302 × 10 g 10 × 457 h 10 × 1920
   i 3080 × 10 j 8236 × 10 k 10 × 6543 l 46 180 × 10.

2. Write down the answers to the following :-

   a 54 × 100 b 77 × 100 c 100 × 155 d 100 × 700
   e 7020 × 100 f 100 × 2004 g 100 × 8600 h 9050 × 100.

3. Write down the answers to these :-

   a 16 × 1000 b 72 × 1000 c 750 × 1000 d 1000 × 870
   e 1000 × 900 f 246 × 1000 g 1000 × 534 h 1000 × 480.

4. A jar contains 100 jelly beans. How many jelly beans are there in :-

   a 15 jars b 28 jars c 250 jars ?

5. There are 1000 milligrams in 1 gram. How many milligrams are there in :-

   a 6 grams b 37 grams c 620 grams d 701 grams ?

Division by 10, 100 and 1000

Be able to divide a number quickly by 10, 100 or 1000.

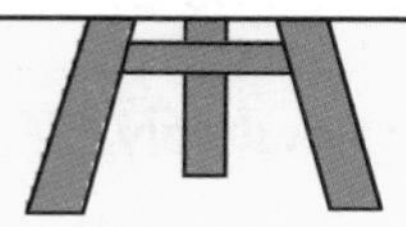

Look at these **examples** :-

10 ⟌ 340 → 34	10 ⟌ 5070 → 507	10 ⟌ 36100 → 3610
100 ⟌ 8500 → 85	100 ⟌ 429000 → 4290	1000 ⟌ 506000 → 506

not needed

When you divide 50 230 by 10 => the figures move 1 place right => 5023(·0)

When you divide 25 700 by 100 => the figures move 2 places right => 257(·00)

When you divide 630 000 by 1000 => the figures move 3 places right => 630(·000).

Examples :-

380 ÷ 10 = 38	25 300 ÷ 10 = 2530	80 200 ÷ 100 = 802
837 000 ÷ 100 = 8370	750 000 ÷ 1000 = 750	2 586 000 ÷ 1000 = 2586

Exercise 4

1. Write down the answers to the following :-

   a 250 ÷ 10   b 370 ÷ 10   c 590 ÷ 10   d 3450 ÷ 10

   e 8900 ÷ 10   f 90 100 ÷ 10   g 54 200 ÷ 10   h 48 000 ÷ 10

   i 40 000 ÷ 10   j 186 000 ÷ 10   k 700 000 ÷ 10   l 330 300 ÷ 10.

2. Write down the answers to the following :-

   a 600 ÷ 100   b 1200 ÷ 100   c 4600 ÷ 100   d 21 000 ÷ 100

   e 9000 ÷ 100   f 308 000 ÷ 100   g 50 000 ÷ 100   h 490 000 ÷ 100.

3. Write down the answers to the following :-

   a 9000 ÷ 1000   b 36 000 ÷ 1000   c 84 000 ÷ 1000   d 50 000 ÷ 1000

   e 415 000 ÷ 1000   f 390 000 ÷ 1000   g 400 000 ÷ 1000   h 625 000 ÷ 1000.

4. A tray holds 100 plants. How many trays are needed to hold :-

   a 1700 plants   b 45 000 plants   c 260 000 plants ?

5. There are 1000 grams in 1 kilogram. How many kilograms are there in :-

   a 23 000 grams   b 49 000 grams   c 160 000 grams   d 2 000 000 grams ?

Multiplying & Dividing Mentally

Finding easier ways to multiply and divide mentally.

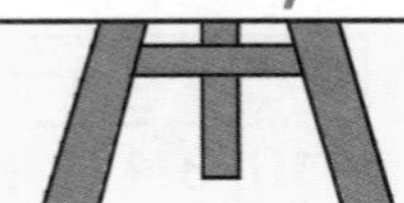

We can do 27 x 200 mentally by using a 2-step approach.

- multiply 27 by 2 first => 27 x 2 = 54
- then multiply your answer by 100 => 54 x 100 = 5400.

This exercise looks at finding easier ways to multiply and divide, so that we are able to carry out many tasks using mental methods.

Some ideas for you to discuss :-

To multiply by 40 .... x 4, then x 10.
To multiply by 700 .... x 7, then x 100.
To multiply by 25 .... x 5, then x 5 again.

To divide by 90 .... ÷ 10, then ÷ 9.
To divide by 5000 .... ÷ 1000, then ÷ 5.
To divide by 24 ... ÷ 6, then ÷ 4, or .. ??

Examples :-

30 x 12 => 3 x 12 x 10 = 36 x 10 = 360

8 x 7000 => 8 x 7 x 1000 = 56 x 1000 = 56 000

2800 ÷ 40 => 2800 ÷ 10 ÷ 4 = 280 ÷ 4 = 70

60 x 25 => 60 x 5 x 5 = 300 x 5 = 1500.

You may even find easier ways yourself ! - Discuss with the class.

Exercise 5

To be attempted mentally - no working to be shown.

Think of an easy way to do each of these, then write down the answer :-

1.	18 x 20	2.	42 x 30	3.	14 x 50	4.	90 x 12
5.	21 x 60	6.	33 x 30	7.	75 x 20	8.	31 x 80
9.	360 ÷ 40	10.	810 ÷ 90	11.	1500 ÷ 30	12.	4500 ÷ 50
13.	8400 ÷ 20	14.	9900 ÷ 30	15.	2400 ÷ 60	16.	5600 ÷ 80
17.	20 x 300	18.	25 x 400	19.	60 x 500	20.	41 x 700
21.	2000 x 20	22.	4000 x 30	23.	5000 x 12	24.	15 000 x 3
25.	60 000 ÷ 20	26.	90 000 ÷ 30	27.	25 000 ÷ 50	28.	42 000 ÷ 60
29.	1600 ÷ 400	30.	12 000 ÷ 200	31.	21 000 ÷ 300	32.	63 000 ÷ 900
33.	12 x 25	34.	25 x 18	35.	22 x 25	36.	140 x 25
37.	150 ÷ 25	38.	200 ÷ 25	39.	2500 ÷ 25	40.	7500 ÷ 25
41.	99 x 7	42.	201 x 12	43.	5 x 399	44.	402 x 11.

Division by a Single Digit (No Remainder)

Be able to divide a number with up to 4 digits by a single digit (no remainder).
Again you must know your tables !

Example 1 :- Divide 175 by 7.

2 5 ✓
7 | 1 7³5

Example 2 :- Divide 5856 by 8.

7 3 2 ✓
8 | 5 8²5¹6

* Note $\frac{175}{5}$ means 175 ÷ 5.

Exercise 6

1. Copy the following and complete each calculation :-

a	7⟌63	b	5⟌895	c	6⟌762	d	8⟌544
e	6⟌6498	f	4⟌9424	g	7⟌81361	h	9⟌88866 .

2. Set the following down in the same way as above and complete each calculation :-

a	96 ÷ 6	b	594 ÷ 2	c	477 ÷ 3	d	783 ÷ 9
e	756 ÷ 7	f	5745 ÷ 5	g	8952 ÷ 4	h	6741 ÷ 3
i	1152 ÷ 9	j	$\frac{7985}{5}$	k	$\frac{2127}{3}$	l	4188 ÷ 6
m	$\frac{9984}{8}$	n	2303 ÷ 7	o	$\frac{30753}{9}$	p	$\frac{95543}{7}$.

3. Show **all** your working in solving the following :-

   a A bar of chocolate has 9 squares.
   How many bars are there if there are 621 squares ?

   b A jar contains 8 lollies.
   How many jars are needed for 2856 lollies ?

   c Seven people are to share **equally** a prize of £2653.
   How much will each receive ?

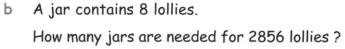

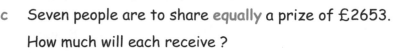

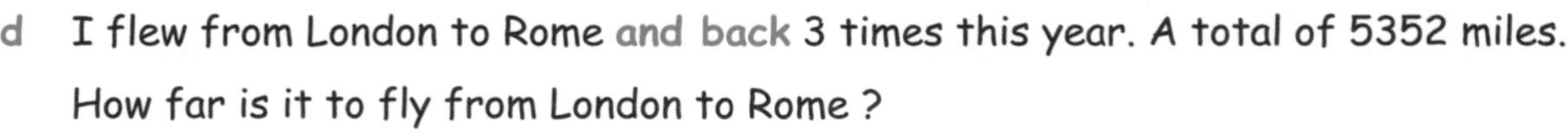

   d I flew from London to Rome **and back** 3 times this year. A total of 5352 miles.
   How far is it to fly from London to Rome ?

4. Try these :- a 96 624 ÷ 4 ÷ 9 b 8 x 495 ÷ 5.

Division by a Single Digit (With a Remainder)

Be able to divide a number with up to 4 digits by a single digit (with a remainder).

NOT all divisions work out exactly.

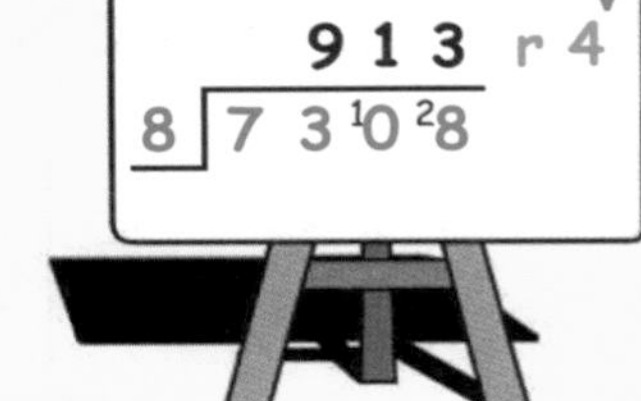

Example 1 :- Divide 7308 by 8.

4 is called the remainder.

Different Forms of Remainders

Example 2 :- A Remainder as a Fraction

$4\overline{)26}$ = 6 r 2

Put the remainder (2) over the divisor (4) to obtain a fraction $\frac{2}{4}$.

Answer :- $6\frac{2}{4}$ or better still $6\frac{1}{2}$.

Example 3 :- A Remainder as a Decimal

$8\overline{)36 \cdot {}^{4}0}$ = 4·5

This time, when you see that there is going to be a remainder - put a decimal point on to the end, followed by a zero (or a few zeros, if needed) and continue to divide until an exact answer is found.

Example 4 :- Using a Remainder to Round to the Nearest Whole Number.

$5\overline{)44}$ = 8 r 4 $= 8\frac{4}{5}$ or $5\overline{)44 \cdot {}^{4}0}$ = 8·8 $= 8 \cdot 8$

Here, 44 ÷ 5 can be done to give an answer with a fraction OR a decimal.

In either case, both answers round to give 9.

Discuss in class when you might use the various ways of presenting remainders.

Exercise 7

1. Carry out the division and write the remainder in the normal " r 5" form.

a	$5\overline{)36}$	b	$4\overline{)47}$	c	$6\overline{)97}$	d	$8\overline{)103}$
e	518 ÷ 3	f	2715 ÷ 6	g	671 ÷ 9	h	6314 ÷ 10
i	$\frac{4444}{6}$	j	$\frac{1827}{8}$	k	$\frac{3143}{5}$	l	$\frac{6172}{3}$.

2. Do these division sums, writing the remainders as fractions :-

a	$3\overline{)7}$	b	$4\overline{)22}$	c	$7\overline{)30}$	d	$8\overline{)47}$
e	$2\overline{)39}$	f	$5\overline{)74}$	g	$6\overline{)94}$	h	$9\overline{)104}$
i	$3\overline{)415}$	j	$6\overline{)725}$	k	$4\overline{)814}$	l	$7\overline{)916}$
m	$5\overline{)3837}$	n	$2\overline{)9131}$	o	$9\overline{)7342}$	p	$8\overline{)8970}$.

3. Do the following divisions, writing the remainders in decimal form :-

a	$5\overline{)8{\cdot}0}$	b	$8\overline{)60}$	c	$2\overline{)35}$	d	$6\overline{)69}$
e	$4\overline{)19}$	f	$5\overline{)103}$	g	$2\overline{)153}$	h	$8\overline{)100}$
i	$6\overline{)117}$	j	$4\overline{)193}$	k	$5\overline{)122}$	l	$8\overline{)468}$
m	$5\overline{)2282}$	n	$2\overline{)9131}$	o	$4\overline{)1706}$	p	$8\overline{)1986}$.

4. Give your answer correct to the nearest whole number :-

a	$13 \div 3$	b	$27 \div 4$	c	$89 \div 5$	d	$104 \div 6$
e	$242 \div 7$	f	$347 \div 8$	g	$674 \div 9$	h	$1045 \div 2$
i	$\frac{1370}{7}$	j	$\frac{4371}{5}$	k	$\frac{7289}{4}$	l	$\frac{1183}{8}$.

5. a Samuel travelled 258 kilometres over 4 days.
He covered the same amount of kilometres each day.
How far did he travel each day ? (*Answer with a fraction remainder*).

b Five gardeners shared 257 ml of liquid lawn feed .
How many ml did they get each ? (*As a decimal number*).

c Jem Paving Company used 824 tonnes of cement to pave 5 miles of road.
How much cement, to the nearest tonne, did the company use per mile ?

The 3 Я's

Revisit - Review - Revise

1. Copy the following and work out the answers :-

a $\begin{array}{r} 84 \\ \times 6 \\ \hline \end{array}$ b $\begin{array}{r} 465 \\ \times 7 \\ \hline \end{array}$ c $\begin{array}{r} 3086 \\ \times 8 \\ \hline \end{array}$ d $\begin{array}{r} 7569 \\ \times 9 \\ \hline \end{array}$

2. Write each of these in the form of Question 1 and work them out :-

a 5 x 97 b 698 x 4 c 7 x 7839 d 1975 x 8.

3. Set down and work out :-

a $\begin{array}{r} 64 \\ \times 52 \\ \hline \end{array}$ b $\begin{array}{r} 378 \\ \times 63 \\ \hline \end{array}$ c $\begin{array}{r} 2609 \\ \times 45 \\ \hline \end{array}$

4. Write down the answer to each of these :-

a 10 x 7835 b 8432 x 100 c 39 247 x 10 d 10 000 x 360.

5. Write down the answers to :-

a 78 000 ÷ 10 b 690 000 ÷ 100 c 427 000 ÷ 1000 d 20 900 ÷ 100.

6. Think of an easy way to do each of the following, then simply write the answer :-

a 32 000 ÷ 40 b 91 x 70 c 25 x 14 d 273 ÷ 21.

7. Set down the following, show your working and complete each calculation :-

a 4060 ÷ 5 b 23 023 ÷ 7 c $\frac{1482}{6}$ d $\frac{53\,800}{8}$.

8. Do these division sums, writing the remainders as fractions :-

a 513 ÷ 2 b 589 ÷ 4 c 4839 ÷ 5 d 7346 ÷ 9.

9. Do these division sums, writing the remainders in decimal form :-

a 42 ÷ 8 b 4002 ÷ 5 c 153 ÷ 6 d 2004 ÷ 8.

10. Give each answer correct to the nearest whole number :-

a 93 ÷ 4 b 743 ÷ 7 c 1347 ÷ 9 d 5988 ÷ 10.

Chapter 5 — Negative Numbers

Integers Revision

Understand and be able to work with integers.

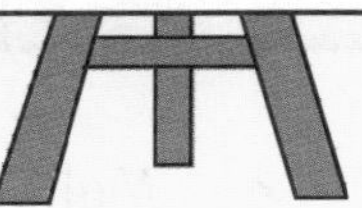

Remember

An integer is a negative whole number, a positive whole number or zero.

Examples :-

-3, -39, 18, 0, 213, -1058, 500 etc. are all integers.

4·6, $5\frac{1}{4}$, -7·3, -1·825, $-35\frac{7}{10}$ etc. are NOT integers.

Exercise 1

1. What temperatures are shown on these thermometers ?

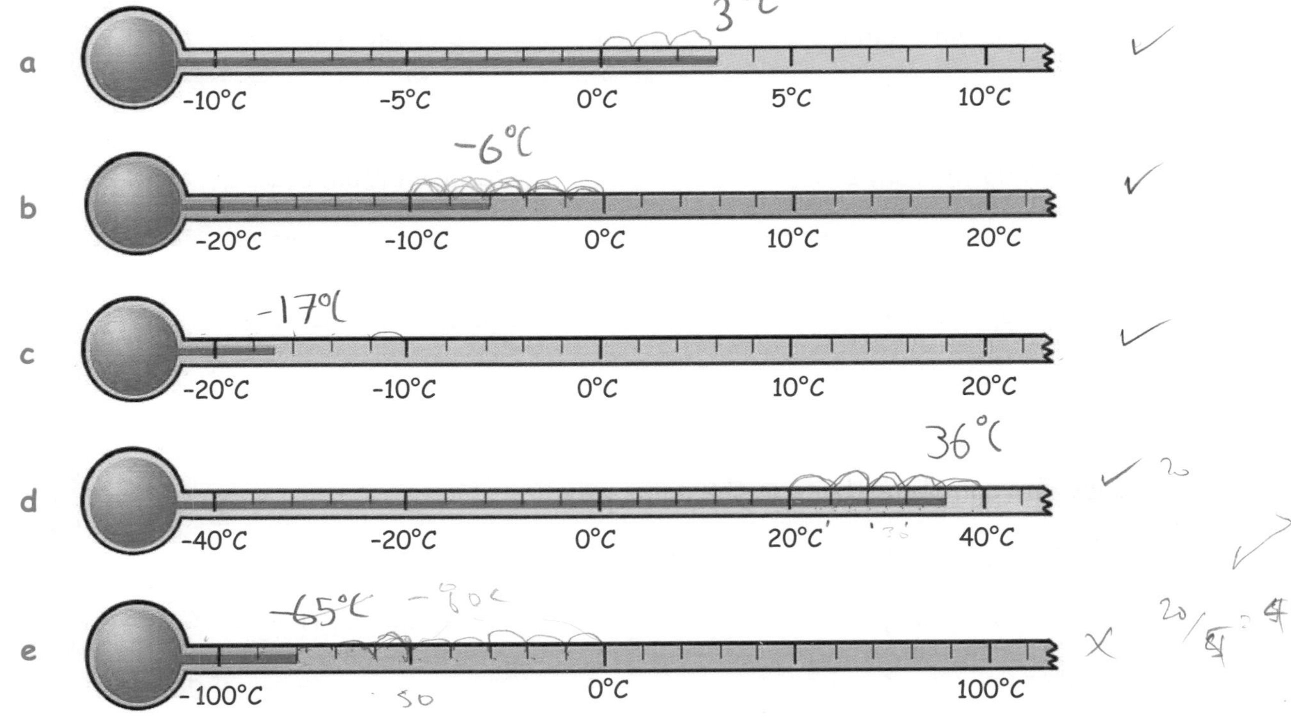

2. Write down the missing numbers :-

a 1, 0, ..., -2, ..., -4 .....

b -5, -4, ... , -2, ... , ..., 1

c -13, -14, ..., -16, ... , -18

d -10, -8, ... , -4, ... , ...

e -90, ..., -50, -30, ... , ...

f -113, -107, ..., ... , ... , -83.

Negative Numbers & the Thermometer

The thermometer drawn down the side of the page can be a great help when studying negative numbers.

Be able to use a thermometer to help with negative numbers.

Exercise 2

1. a Make a neat copy of this thermometer in your exercise book.

   b Write down the temperature shown.

2. Look at your thermometer.

   What is the temperature that is :-

   a 2°C up from 17°C
   b 12°C up from 0°C
   c 18°C up from 3°C
   d 7°C down from 13°C
   e 12°C down from 22°C
   f 3°C up from -1°C
   g 7°C down from -3°C
   h 11°C up from -6°C
   i 9°C down from 2°C
   j 18°C down from 0°C
   k 12°C down from -7°C
   l 16°C down from -5°C
   m 8°C up from -11°C
   n 28°C up from -29°C ?

3. 8°C is *13°C up from* -5°C.

   Copy and complete these in the same way :-

   (state whether it's .. up from or .. down from each time)

   a 7°C is .....°C up from 1°C
   b 12°C is .... from 17°C
   c 0°C is .... from 15°C
   d 8°C is .... from -1°C
   e -9°C is .... from 0°C
   f 4°C is .... from -11°C
   g -21°C is .... from -14°C
   h -3°C is .... from 10°C
   i 40°C is ...... from -40°C
   j -62°C is .... from -50°C
   k 12°C is ..... from -16°C
   l 37°C is ...... from -121°C.

4. 

One winter's day in Leeds, the temperature was -8°C.

In Carlisle it was 8°C colder.

What was the temperature in Carlisle ?

5. On the summit of a mountain in Austria, the temperature was -23°C.

At the foot of the mountain, the temperature was 21°C.

What was the difference between the temperature at the summit and the temperature at the foot ?

6. 

The lowest temperature recorded in the Arizona desert was -25°C

The highest temperature there was 42°C.

Calculate the difference in these temperatures ?

7. Chris made a large batch of chilli con carne and put it in the freezer.

Its temperature fell by a steady amount each hour.

It started at 9°C and fell to 5°C in one hour.

What would the temperature be after :-

a 2 hours	b 3 hours

c 4 hours	d 10 hours ?

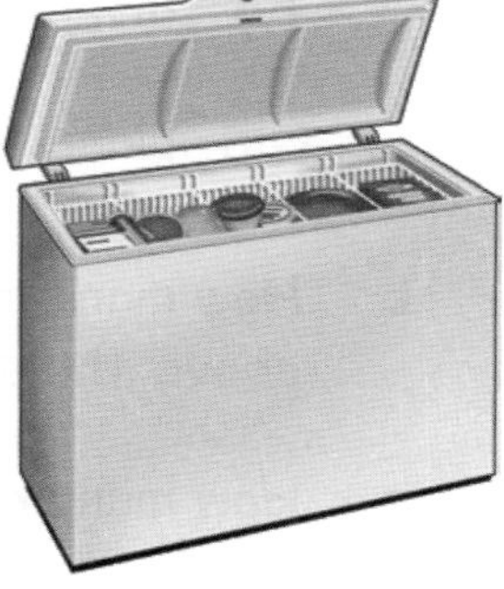

8. Write each set of temperatures in order, coldest first :-

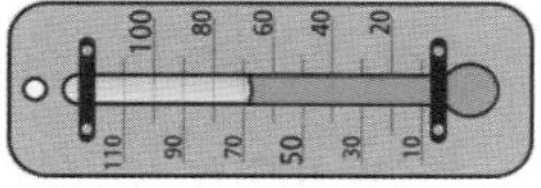

a 18°C, -2°C, -21°C, 0°C, 1°C, -1°C.

b -36°C, -9°C, -17°C, -58°C, 2°C, -2°C.

9. A large warehouse stores goods on 7 levels, 4 above ground and three below.

Each level stores goods as shown in the diagram.

a On which level are these items stored :-

(i) fruit	(ii) tins of soup

(iii) lawnmowers	(iv) frozen peas

(v) trousers	(vi) cabbages ?

Level	Goods
3	Clothes and Shoes
2	Electrical Goods
1	Gardening Equipment
0	Liquid (Juice, water , etc)
-1	Fruit & Veg
-2	Tinned foods
-3	Frozen food

9. b How many levels apart are :-

(i) tins and clothes (ii) water and frozen chicken

(iii) microwaves and garden spades (iv) shoes and bags of ice ?

> **Integer** numbers can also be used to describe heights **above** or **below** sea level.
>
> => Heights **above** sea level are **positive (+)**. ⟶
>
> => Depths **below** sea level are **negative (-)**. ⟶
>
> 

10. Look at the picture of the cliff.

a Write down the heights of each of the following in metres using + or – :-

(i) seagull (ii) pelican

(iii) shark (iv) cliff-top

(v) diver (vi) sea bed

(vii) plane (viii) submarine.

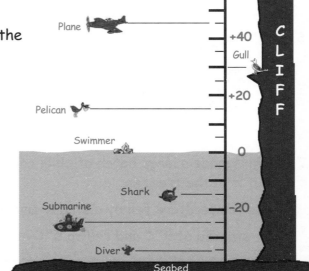

b How many metres is the pelican **above** the shark ?

c How many metres is the plane **above** the diver ?

11. A car park has 5 levels above and 3 levels below the ground floor.

Bob parks his car on level -2. May parks her car on level 3.

How many levels is May's car above Bob's ?

12. Which integer is **halfway** between :-

a 8 and 12 b 25 and 45 c -2 and 4

d -5 and 9 e -2 and -10 f -3 and -11

g -6 and -18 h -17 and -37 i -135 and -235 ?

13. Negative numbers are also used with bank statements. **Investigate** this.

(*You may want to do a poster or project on negative numbers*).

The 3 Я's

Revisit - Review - Revise

1. State what temperatures are represented on these thermometers :-

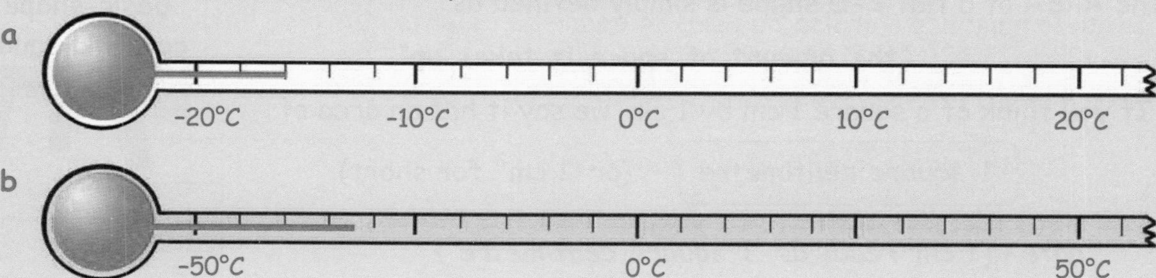

2. Write down the missing numbers :-

a 5, 4, ..., 2, 1, ... , -1, ... , -3

b -7, -5, ... , ... , 1, 3, ... , ...

c 20, 15, 10, ... , ... , -5, ... , ...

d 4, ..., -2, ..., ..., -11, -14, ...

e ... , -11, ... , -17, -20, -23, ...

f ..., ..., ..., -11, ..., ..., 1, 5.

3. What is :-

a 8°C down from 3°C

b 9°C up from -6°C

c 11° up from -6°C

d 14°C down from -88°C ?

4. Put these in order, coldest first :- -7°C, 1°C, -15°C, -2°C, 0°C, -4°C.

5. The temperature at midday on a beach in Florida was 29°C.
By midnight it had fallen to -7°C.
By how many degrees had the temperature fallen ?

6. 

The coldest temperature ever recorded in Wales was -23°C at Rhyader (Powys) on 21 January 1940.

The warmest recorded was 31°C, (Rhyl) on 17th June 2014.

Calculate the difference in temperature.

7. A chemical freezer has a temperature of 8°C when it is switched on at 1 pm.
The temperature in the freezer then drops by 6°C every half hour.
What will the freezer temperature be at 4 pm ?

Measure 1

Area Revision

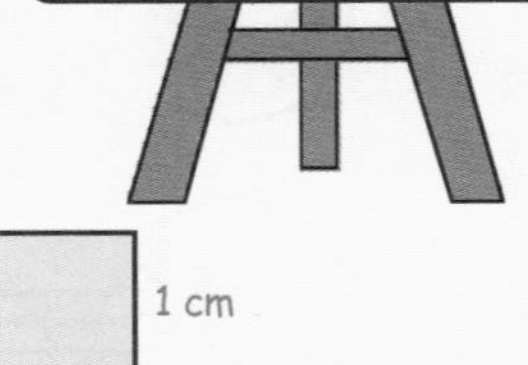

Be able to find the area of a basic shape by counting squares.

The AREA of a flat 2-D shape is simply defined as

"the amount of space it takes up".

If you think of a square 1 cm by 1 cm, we say it has an area of

1 square centimetre (or 1 cm^2 for short).

note - (1 cm^2 reads as "1 square centimetre").

1 cm

1 cm

Exercise 1 *Each box in this exercise represents 1 cm^2.*

1. a How many boxes (*1 cm by 1 cm*) are shown here ?

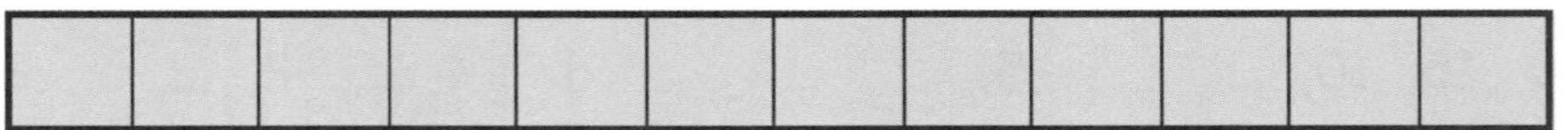

b Write down the area of the shape in square centimetres :- Area = ... cm^2.

2. Write down the areas (use cm^2) of each of the following shapes :-

a

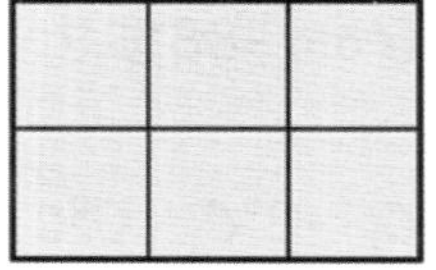

b

c

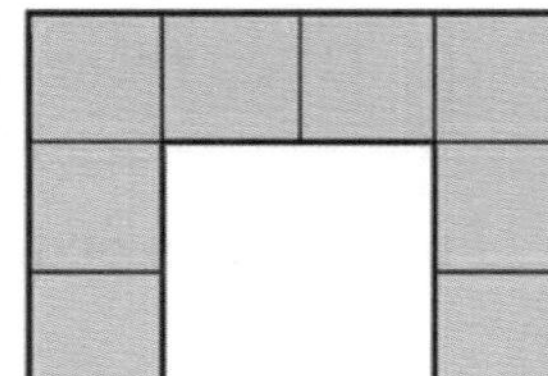

d

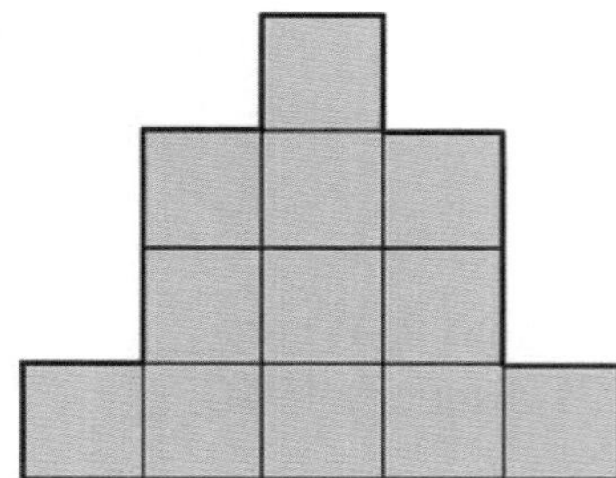

e

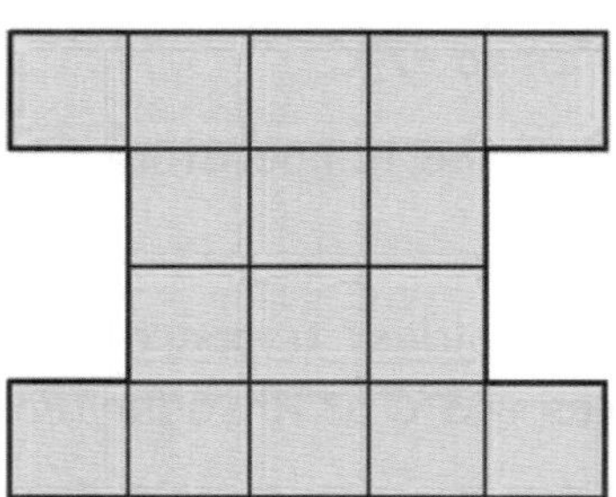

f

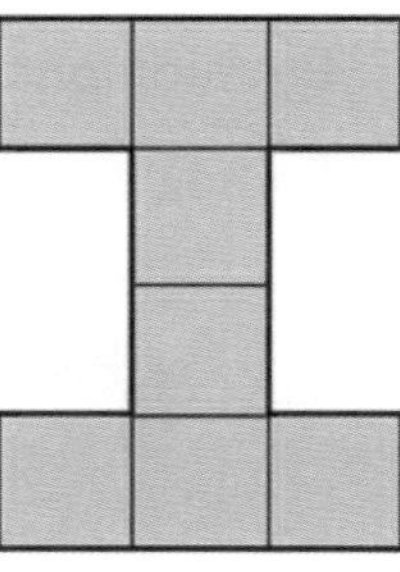

g

$= \frac{1}{2}$ cm^2

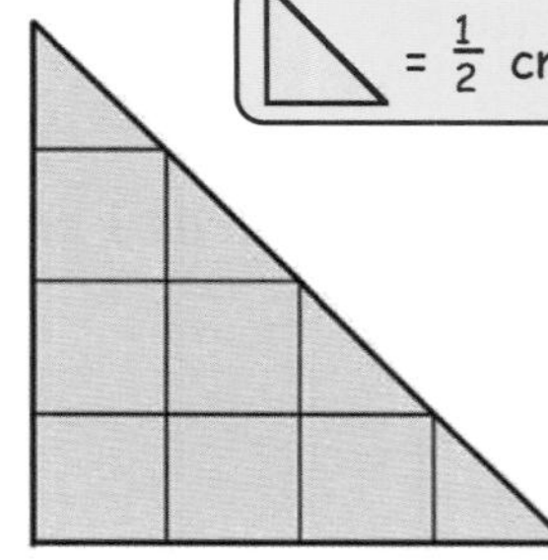

h

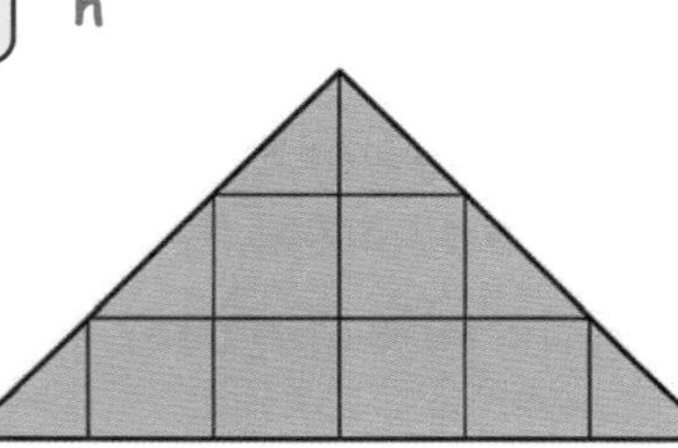

i

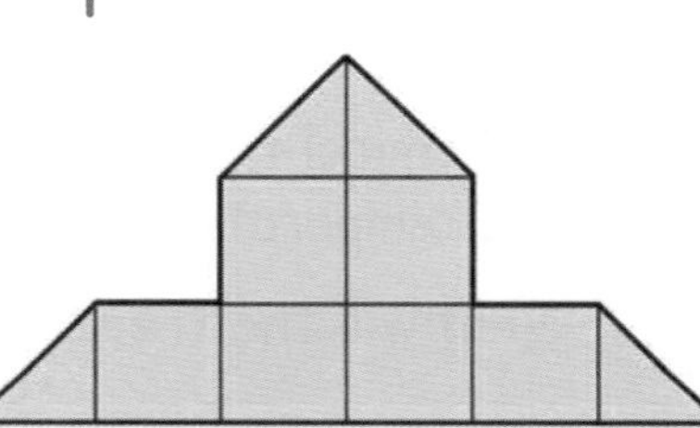

2. j

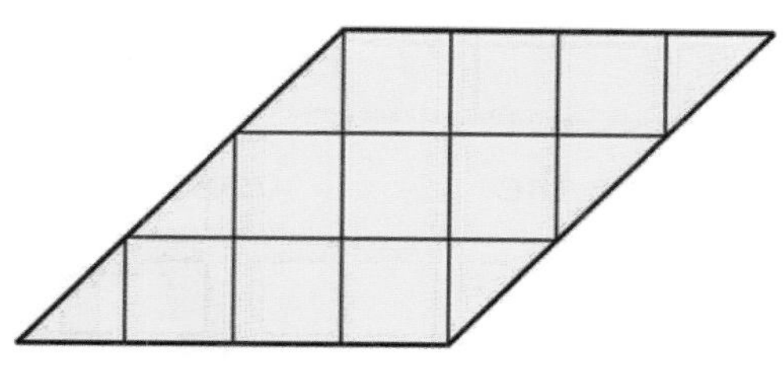

k

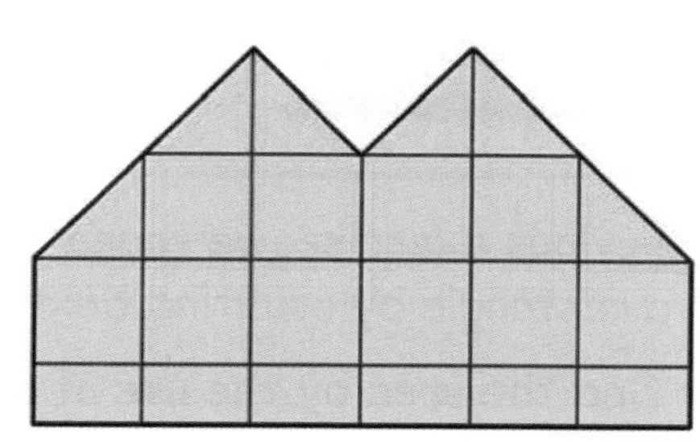

l

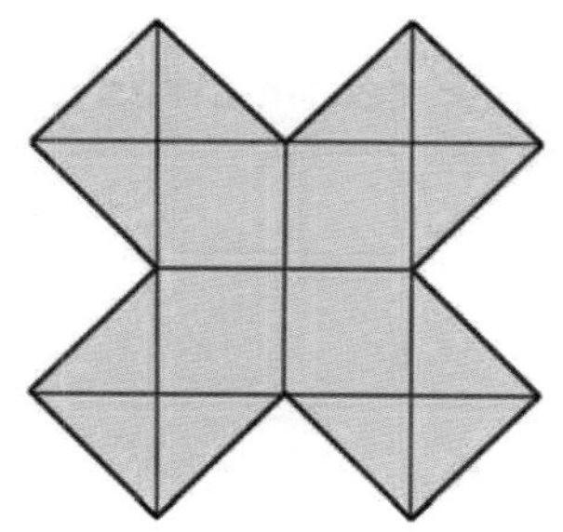

m *careful !*

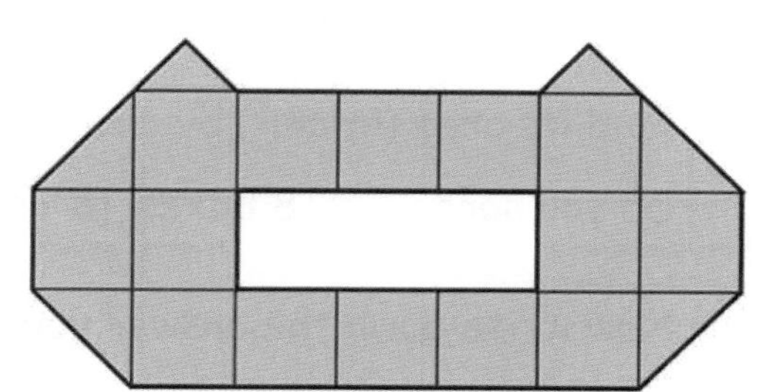

3. Estimate the areas of these shapes as follows :-

If more than $\frac{1}{2}$ a box is covered —> count it as 1 cm^2.

If less than $\frac{1}{2}$ a box is covered —> do not count it at all.

a

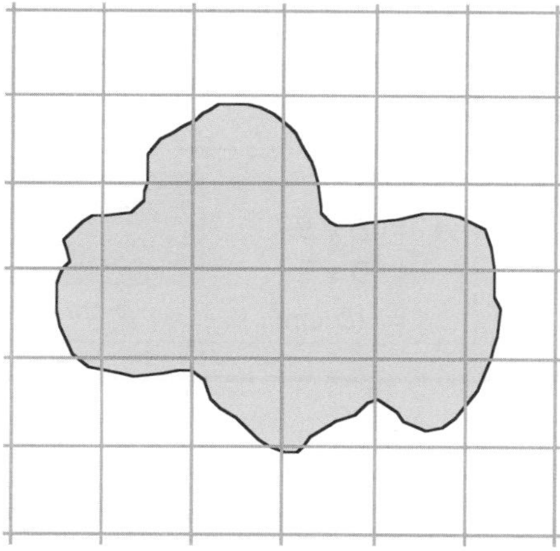

b

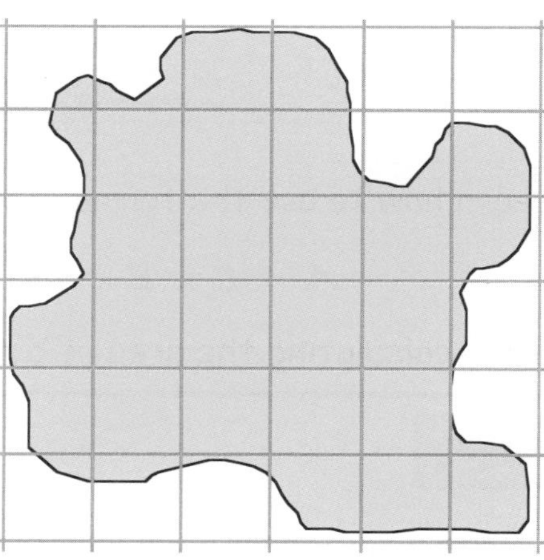

c

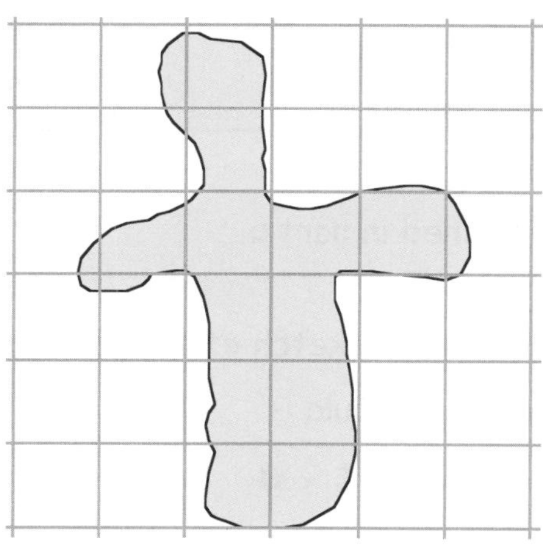

d

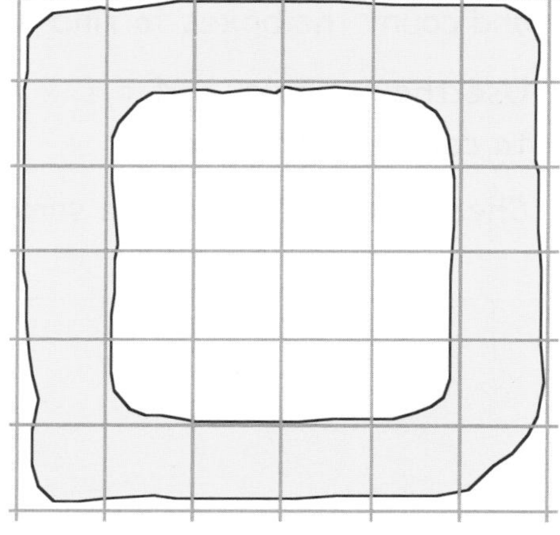

Area of a Rectangle *(A Formula)*

Be able to
calculate the area
of a rectangle
using a formula.

In the previous exercise, we found out how to calculate the area of a rectangle by counting boxes.

We can find the area by the use of a FORMULA, or RULE.

Example :-

The yellow rectangle opposite measures 4 centimetres by 2 centimetres.

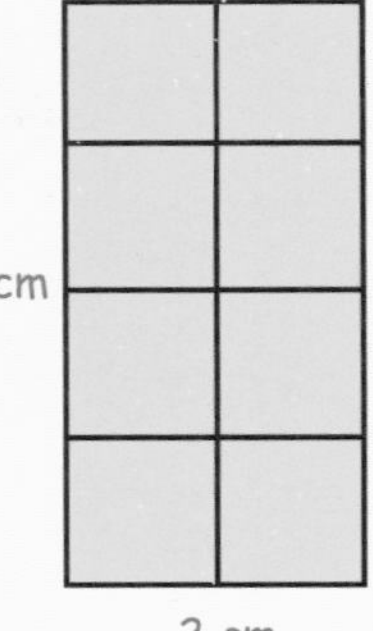

a Find its area (in cm^2) by counting all the boxes.

Do you agree......... 8 boxes, (8 cm^2) ?

b Now write down the answer you get when you multiply its length by its breadth :-

=> 4 cm x 2 cm - (Do you get the same answer ?)

Another way to calculate the AREA of a RECTANGLE is as follows :-

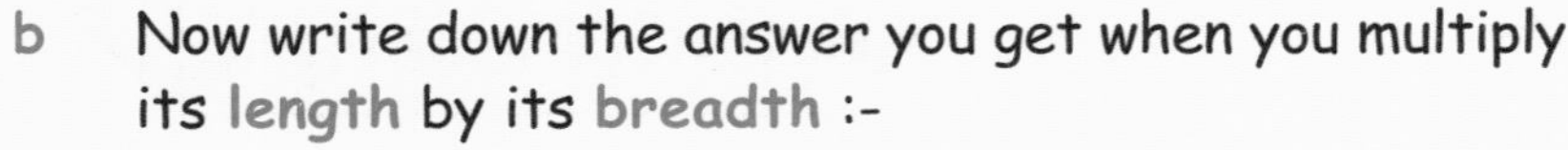

Area = Length × Breadth

or $A = L \times B$

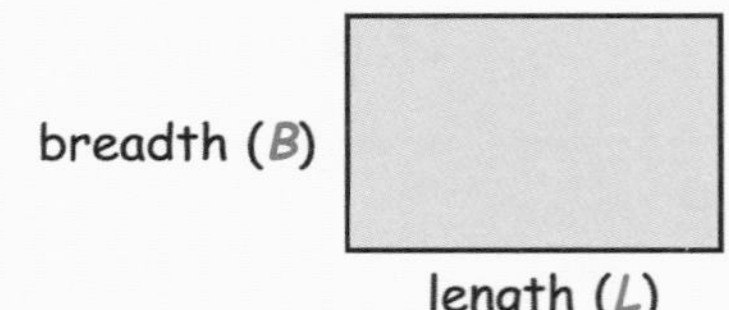

Learn how to use the formula,

$$A = L \times B$$

when calculating the area of a rectangle.

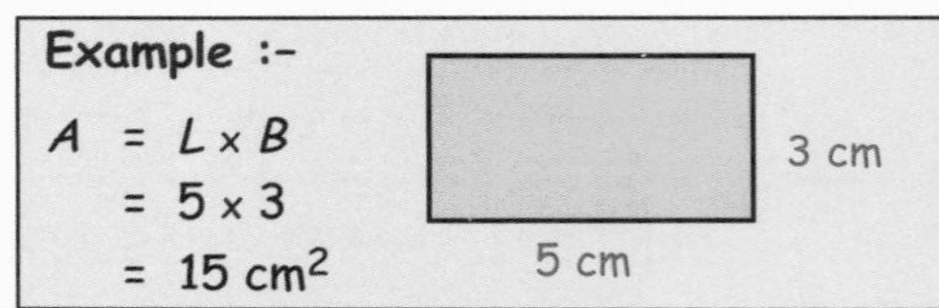

Exercise 2

1. a Draw a rectangle 6 cm long by 3 cm wide.

   b Divide the rectangle neatly into 1 cm square boxes and count the boxes to find the area of the rectangle.

   c Use the formula :- $A = L \times B$, (with $L = 6$, $B = 3$), to calculate the area.

   d Check your answer is the same as that obtained in part b.

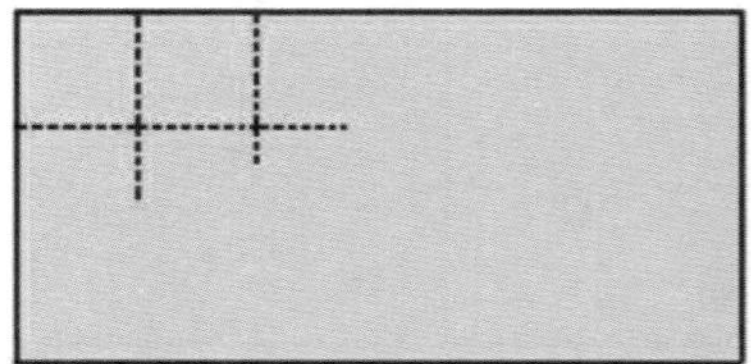

2. 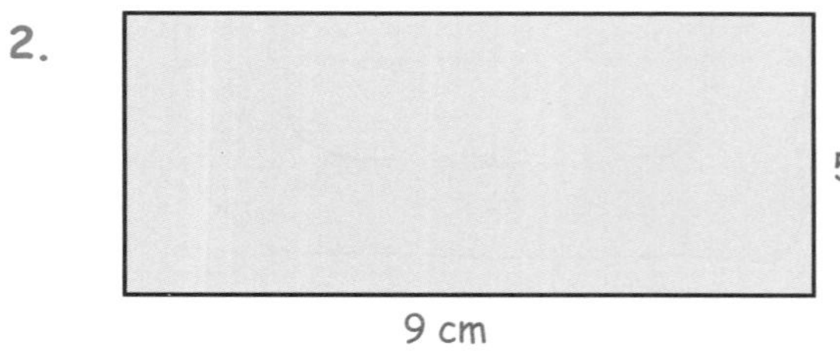

Make a neat sketch of this rectangle.

Use the formula :-

$$A = L \times B$$

to calculate its area (in cm^2).

3. Calculate the area of each of the following rectangles.
In each case, make a small "sketch" of the rectangle first.

Write down and use the rule "$A = L \times B$" to calculate the area in cm^2.

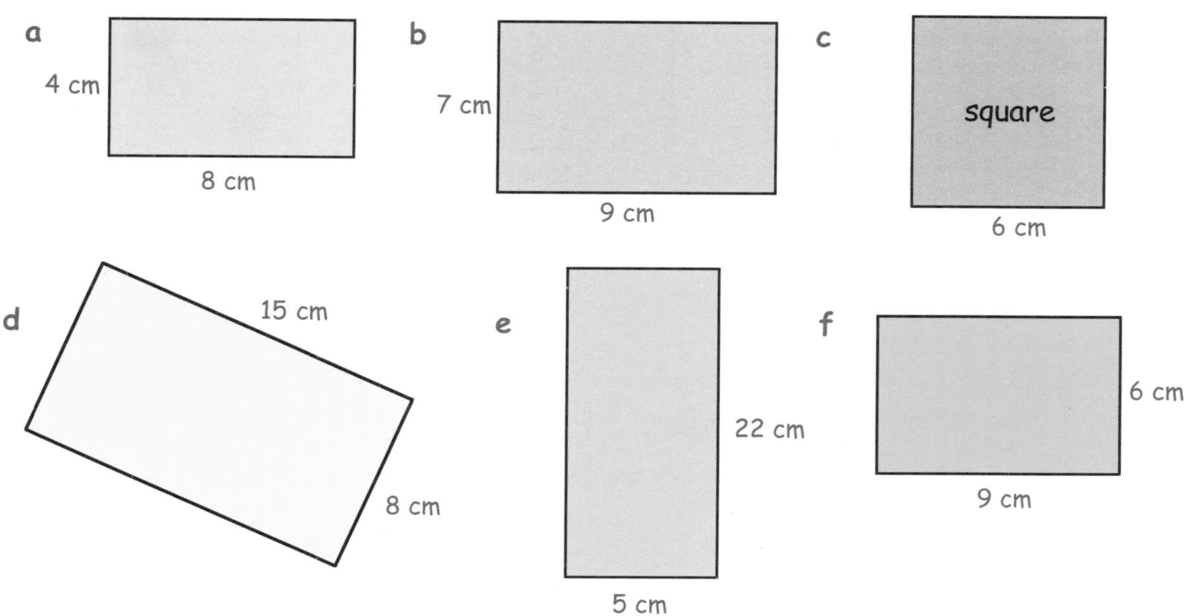

If the length and breadth of the shape are given in metres, then the area will be in **square metres**.

=> The **area** of a box 1 metre by 1 metre would be **1 m^2**.

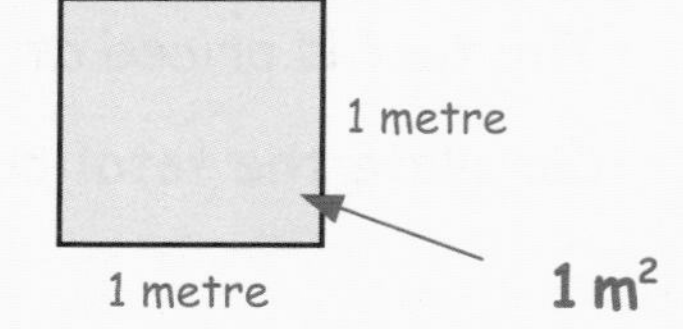

4. A carpet fitter has to lay carpets in 5 rooms in a hotel.

Use $A = L \times B$ to help him calculate the **area** of each of the rooms (in m^2).

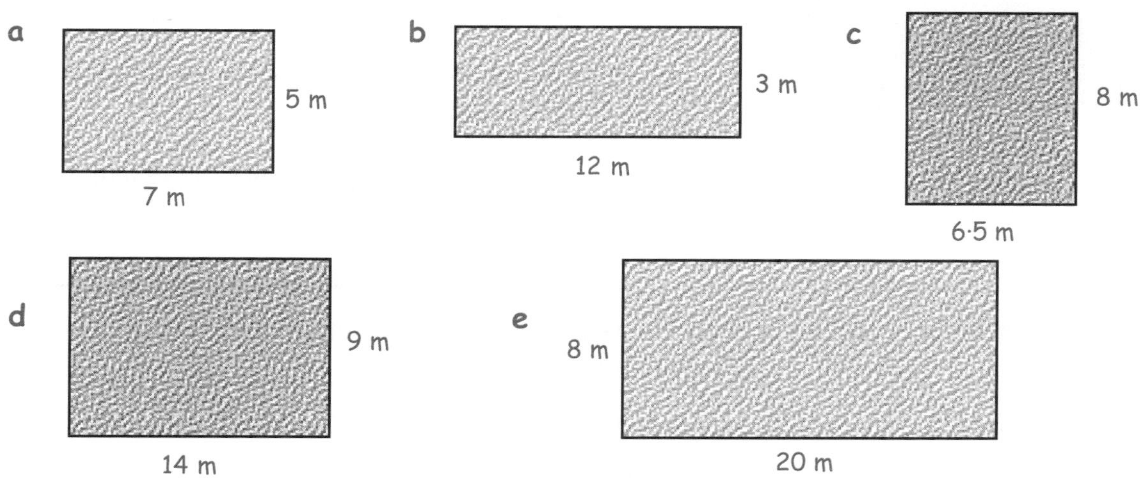

5. He charges £10 per m^2 for the carpet, including fitting.
How much must the hotel owner pay him **altogether** for his work ?

6. A farmer has to spread manure on his fields. He must work out the area of each field. Calculate the **area** of each rectangular field, in m^2 :- (*Use long multiplication here*).

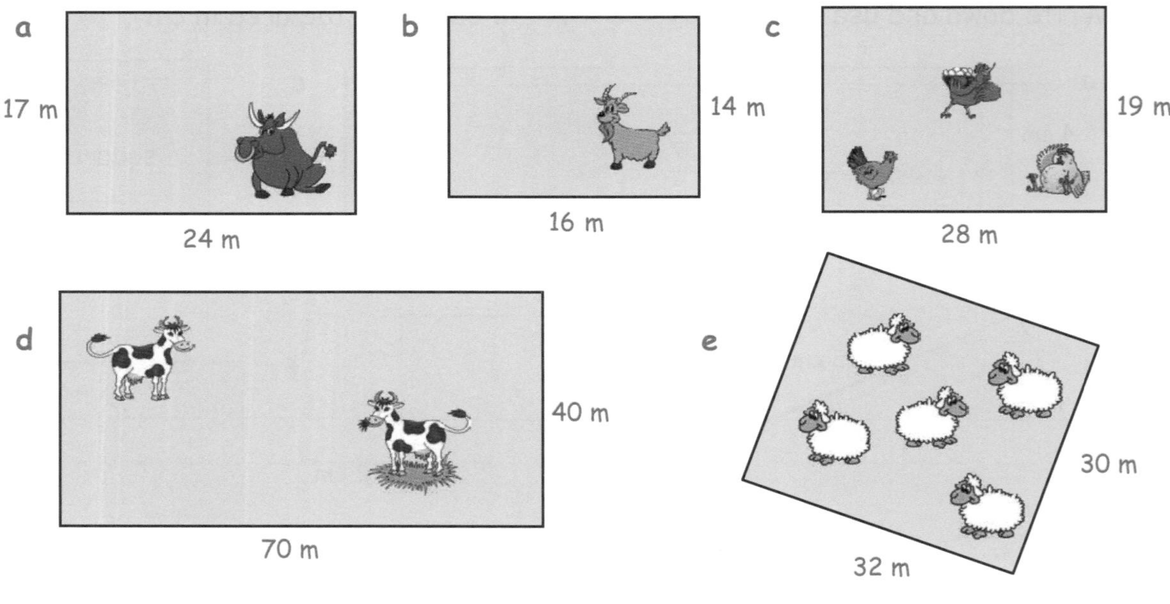

7. Lucy has a rectangular plot of land for which she wishes to buy turf to create a new lawn.

The turf is priced at £3·50 per m^2.

Calculate the **total cost** of turf required.

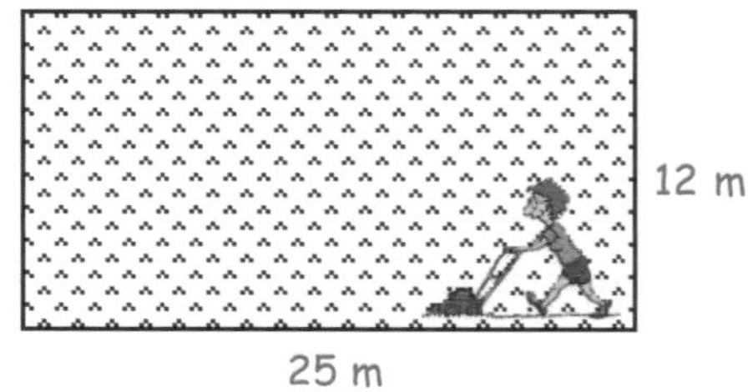

8. 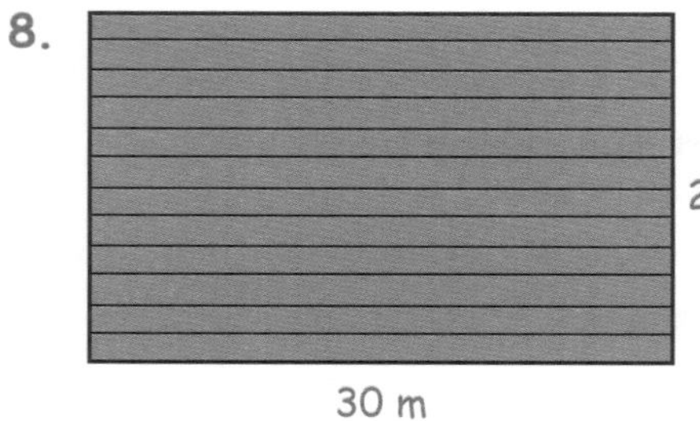

Davie decides to varnish the Scout Hall floor.

a Calculate the **area** of the floor.

b A 5 litre tin of varnish covers 60 m^2.

How many 5 litre tins will be needed for one coat of varnish ?

c If each tin costs £8·50, what will it cost to cover the floor with **two** coats of varnish ?

9.
a Numerically, which is bigger - the **AREA** of a rectangle measuring 3 cm by 5 cm, or its **PERIMETER** ?

b What about a rectangle measuring 6 cm by 2 cm ?

c Is this true for any size of rectangle ?

Investigate by studying various sizes of rectangles.

d What about squares ? - Investigate.

Areas and Perimeters of Simple Composite Shapes

Be able to calculate the area and the perimeter of a shape made up of rectangles.

To calculate the area of this shape, use a two step approach as follows :-

Step 1 - Calculate the area of each rectangle

=> Area (P) = 5 x 3 = 15 cm^2

=> Area (Q) = 4 x 12 = 48 cm^2

Step 2 - Now simply add the 2 answers together

=> Area = 15 cm^2 + 48 cm^2 = 63 cm^2

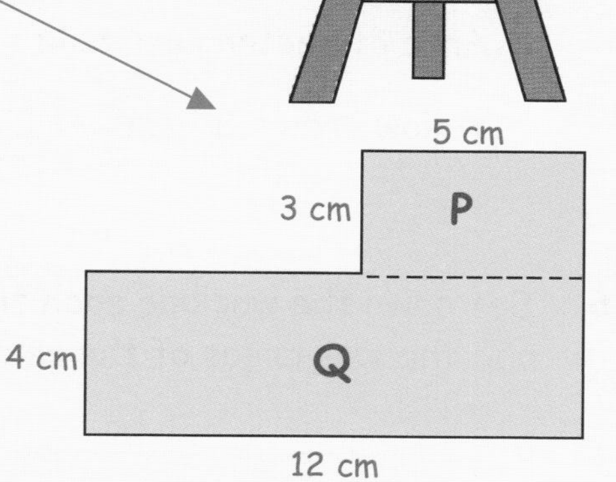

Exercise 3

1. a Calculate the area of rectangle A.
   b Calculate the area of rectangle B.
   c Calculate the area of the whole shape.
   d Now calculate the perimeter of the shape.

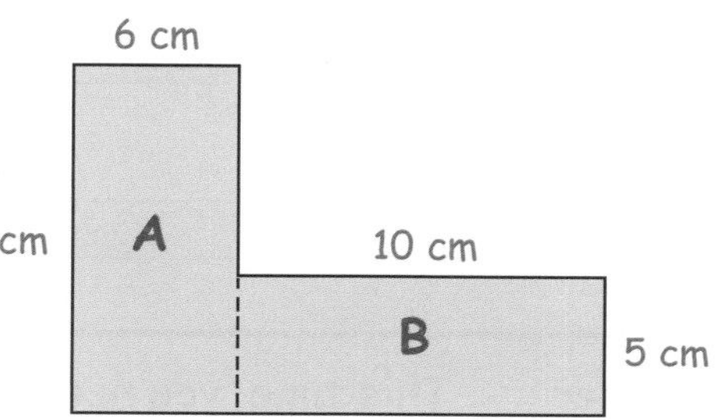

2.

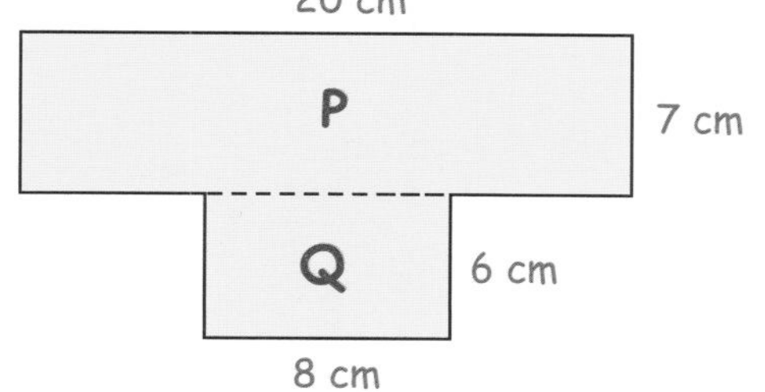

   a Calculate the area of rectangle P.
   b Calculate the area of rectangle Q.
   c Calculate the area of the whole shape.
   d Calculate the perimeter of the shape.

3. a Calculate the area of rectangle R.
   b Calculate the area of square S.
   c Now calculate the area of the whole shape.
   d Calculate the shape's perimeter.

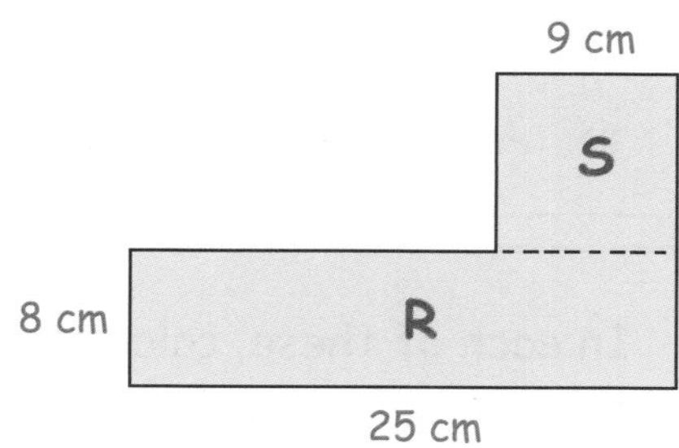

4. Calculate the total area of each of the 2 shapes below, showing 3 lines of working :-

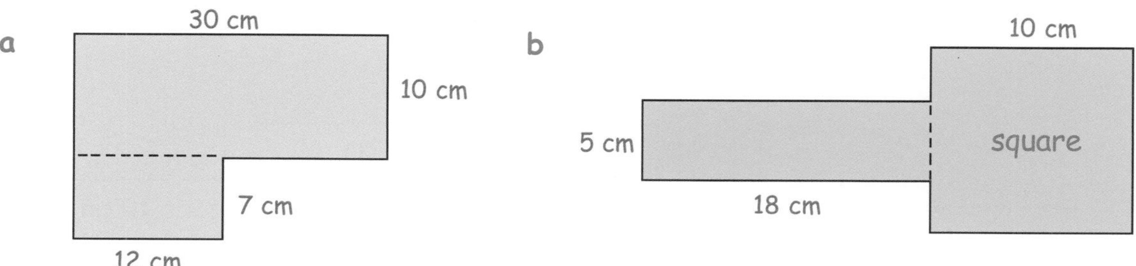

5. This time, the rectangle has a **hole** in it.

Set down the working and complete :-

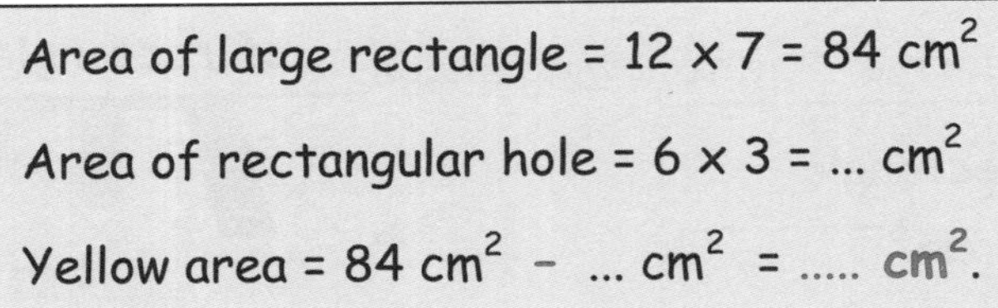

Area of large rectangle = $12 \times 7 = 84$ cm^2

Area of rectangular hole = $6 \times 3 = \ldots$ cm^2

Yellow area = 84 cm^2 $-$ ... cm^2 = ... cm^2.

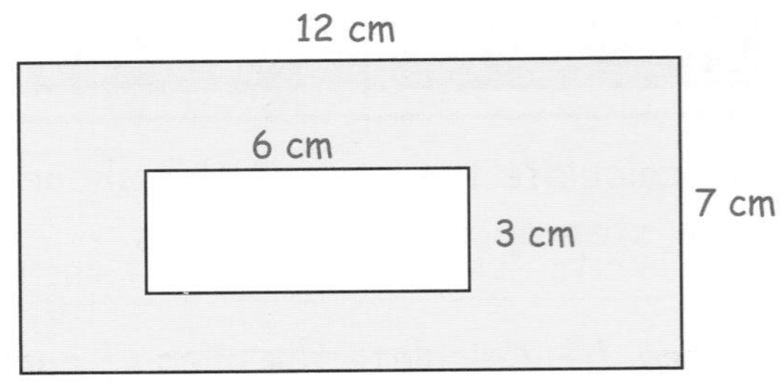

Can you see why it is a "take away" this time ?

6. Set down the working each time here in a similar way and calculate the **green** and the pink areas of the rectangular shapes below :-

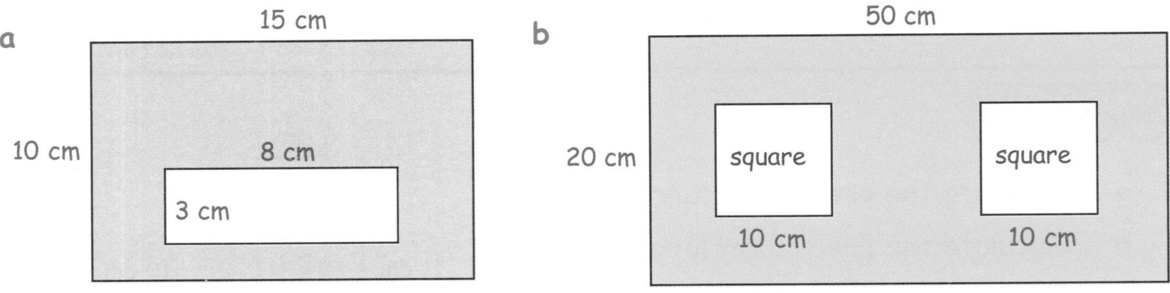

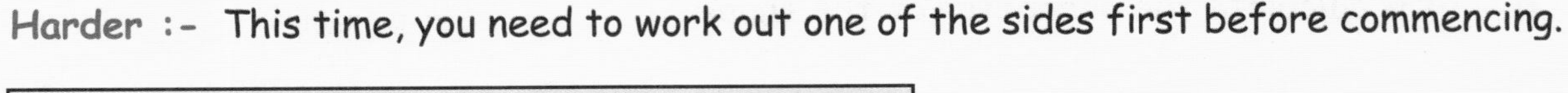

Harder :- This time, you need to work out one of the sides first before commencing.

We need to calculate the missing side (?) first.

Can you see why (?) must = 15 cm - 6 cm = 9 cm ?

Area (A) = $5 \times 6 = 30$ cm^2

Area (B) = $9 \times 18 = 162$ cm^2

=> Area = 30 cm^2 + 162 cm^2 = = 192 cm^2

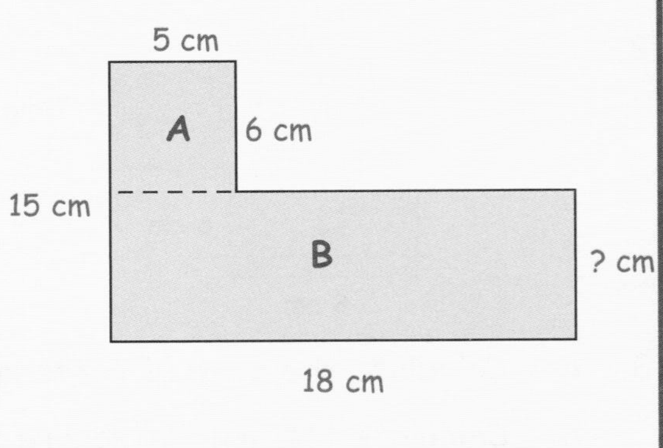

7. In each of these, calculate the length of the missing side (?) first, then calculate the area of each shape :-

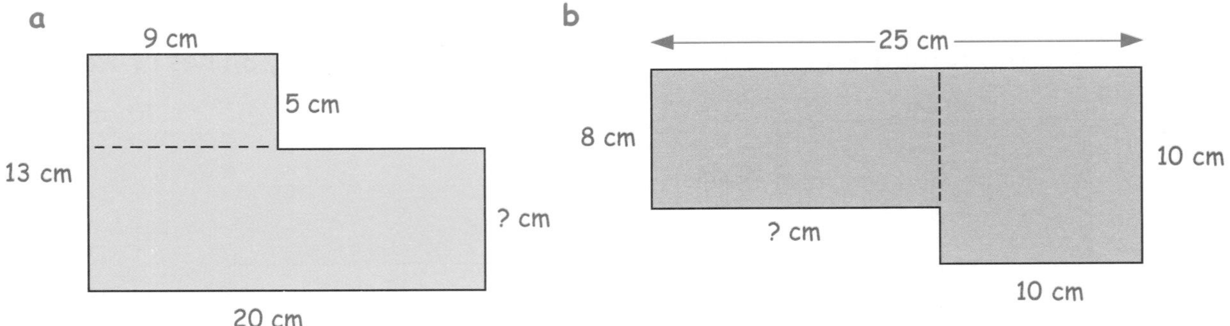

Revisit - Review - Revise

1. Write down the areas (use cm^2) of each of the following shapes :-

a
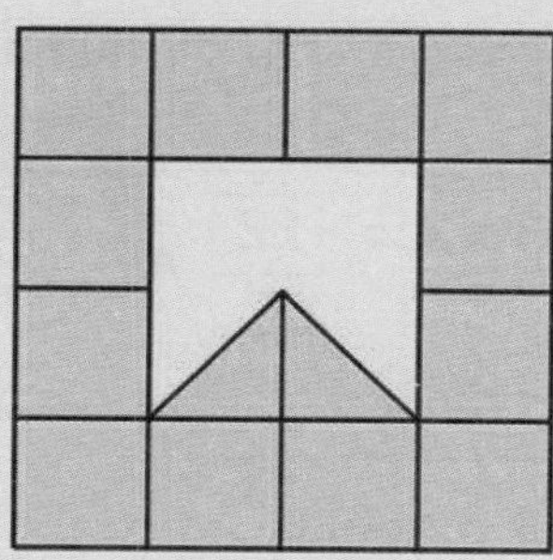

b
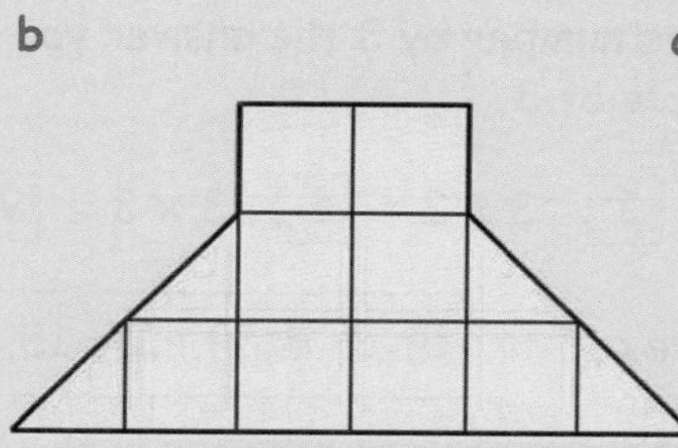

c
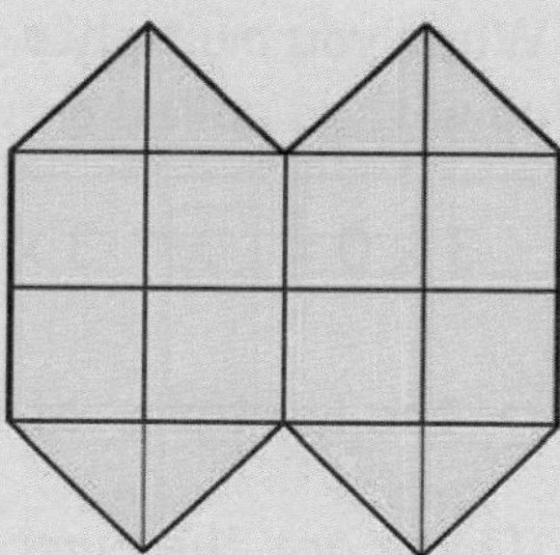

2. Estimate the area of this shape :-

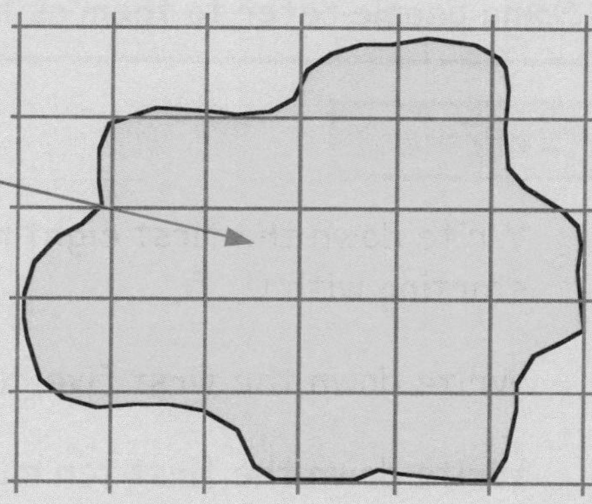

3.
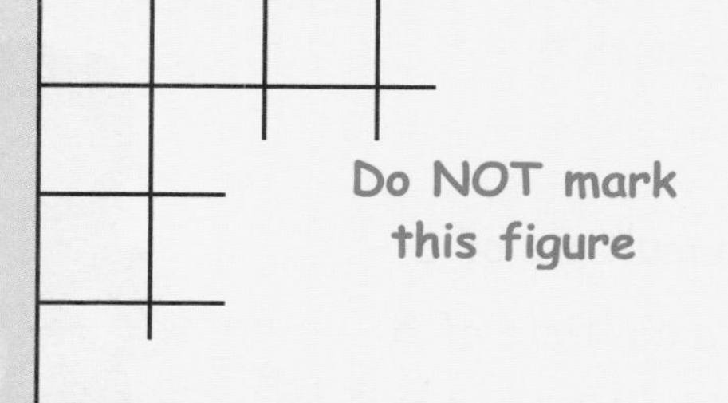

Calculate the area of this rectangle measuring 8 cm by 4 cm.

4. Calculate the areas of these rectangles and squares in cm^2 or in m^2 :-

a
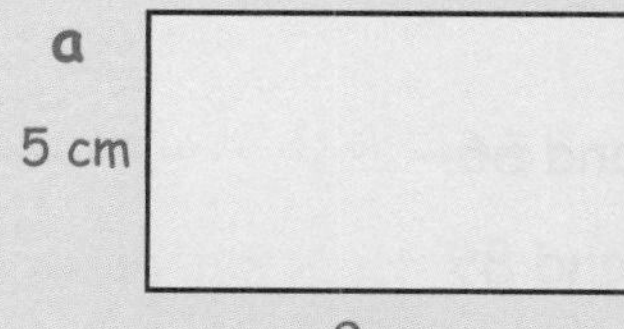

b

c
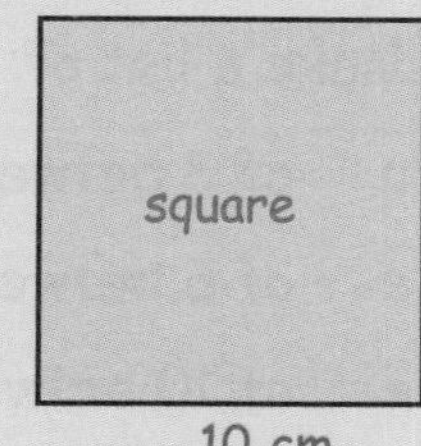

d
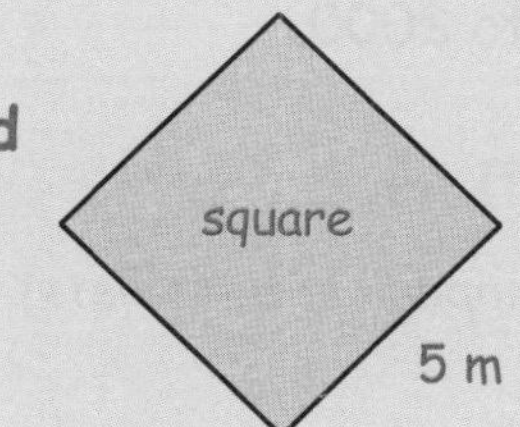

e
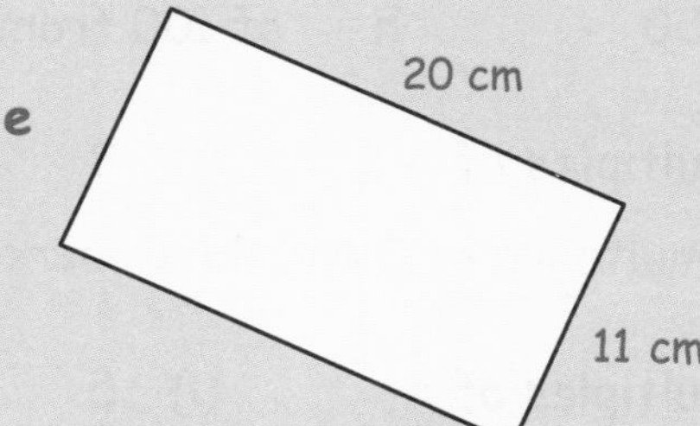

f
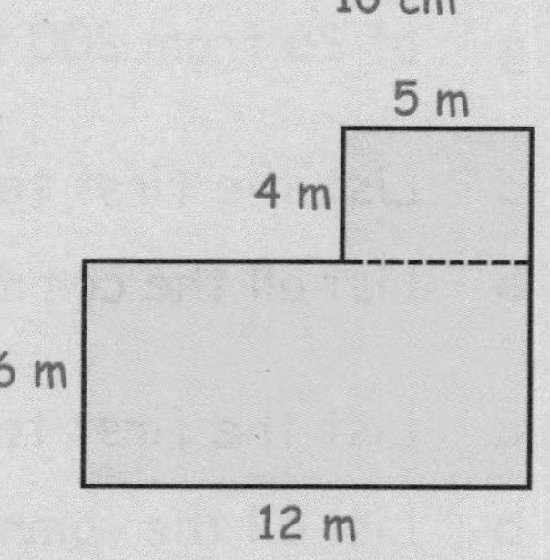

Chapter 7

Special Numbers

Multiples

Understand and be able to find multiples of a number.

When you multiply a whole number by 3 the answer you end up with is called a multiple of 3.

3 x 0 = 0   3 x 1 = 3   3 x 2 = 6   3 x 3 = 9   3 x 4 = 12

=> the multiples of 3 are :-   0, 3, 6, 9, 12, 15, 18, 21, 24 ...

These are the numbers that appear as answers in the times 3 table.

Some people refer to them as the "stations" of 3.

Exercise 1

zero is called the trivial multiple and is generally ignored.

1. Write down the first eight multiples of 5, starting with 0, 5, ...

2. Write down the first five multiples of 8, starting with 8, 16, ...

3. Write down the first ten multiples of 4, starting with 4, ...

4. Write true or false for each statement :-

a	27 is a multiple of 3	b	42 is a multiple of 6
c	54 is a multiple of 7	d	105 is a multiple of 5
e	9 is a multiple of 45	f	121 is a multiple of 11
g	70 is a multiple of 20	h	120 is a multiple of 40.

5. Make a list of the multiples :-

a	of 3 between 23 and 37	b	of 5 between 19 and 66
c	of 6 between 29 and 49	d	of 9 between 44 and 89
e	of 10 between 69 and 169	f	of 50 from 400 to 900
g	of 25 from 200 to 350	h	of 100 from 1200 to 2000.

6. a List the first ten multiples of :-   (i) 3   (ii) 4.

   b List all the common multiples of 3 and 4 (*numbers which appear in both lists*).

7. a List the first ten multiples of :-   (i) 5   (ii) 6.

   b List all the common multiples of 5 and 6 (*numbers which appear in both lists*).

Factors

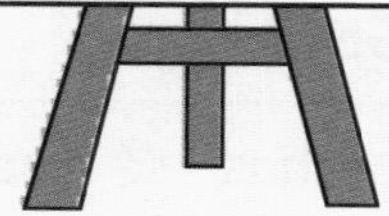

When you can divide a given number by a 2nd number (exactly), with no remainder, then that 2nd number is called a factor of the first number.

Example :- The factors of 12 are 1, 2, 3, 4, 6, 12.

Think of the pairs of numbers that multiply to give 12 => (1 x 12), (2 x 6), (3 x 4).

=> These are called the :- factor pairs of 12.

Exercise 2

1. Write down the :- a two factors of 5 b four factors of 8.

2. Write down the :-

   a two factors of 11 b four factors of 14 c four factors of 10

   d five factors of 16 e six factors of 18 f eight factors of 30.

3. Find all the factors of these numbers :-

   a 6 b 15 c 24 d 36

   e 35 f 50 g 100 h 120.

4. Write down the factor pairs of :-

   a 10 b 20 c 48 d 72.

5. Write true or false for each statement :-

   a 4 is a factor of 32 b 6 is a factor of 38

   c 7 is a factor of 56 d 8 is a factor of 72

   e 9 is a factor of 45 f 5 is a factor of 135

   g 120 is a factor of 30 h 7 is a factor of 128.

6. a List the six factors of 12. b List all six factors of 18.

   c List all the common factors of 12 and 18 - (*numbers that appear in both lists*).

7. List all the common factors of :-

   a 10 and 12 b 12 and 20 c 20 and 40 d 30 and 36

   e 10 and 15 f 20 and 24 g 30 and 50 h 26 and 39

   i 24 and 26 j 17 and 19 k 12, 16 and 20 l 30, 120 and 360.

Prime Numbers

Be able to list all the prime numbers up to 100.

Examine how many factors these two groups of numbers have :-

Group 1 :-

4 has 3 factors {1, 2, 4}
8 has 4 factors {1, 2, 4, 8}
12 has 6 factors {1, 2, 3, 4, 6, 12}
20 has 6 factors {1, 2, 4, 5, 10, 20}
32 has 6 factors {1, 2, 4, 8, 16, 32}

Group 2 :-

5 has 2 factors {1, 5}
7 has 2 factors {1, 7}
11 has 2 factors {1, 11}
19 has 2 factors {1, 19}
23 has 2 factors {1, 23}

There is a special name for the numbers in Group 2 which only have 2 factors :-

They are called PRIME NUMBERS.

Primes are said to be the most important group of numbers in the study of mathematics.

Every number can be divided by itself and 1. but Every prime number can only be divided by itself and 1.

A prime number is a number with exactly 2 factors.

Exercise 3

I've reached my prime.

1. Write all the factors of 10. Why is 10 not a prime number ?
2. Write all the factors of 3. Why is 3 a prime number ?
3. How many factors has the number 14 ? Is 14 a prime number or not ?
4. Explain why the number 1 is not a prime number.
5. For each of the following numbers, list all of its factors, and state whether or not it is a prime number.

a 5	b 16	c 15	d 17	e 23	f 27
g 29	h 35	i 44	j 47	k 51	l 62.

6. A number which is not a prime is called a composite number.

   State which of the following numbers are composite :-

   8, 13, 15, 19, 20, 33, 36, 37, 40, 41, 42, 43, 49, 50, 55, 57, 61.

7. Is 2 a prime number ? Give a reason for your answer.

8. a How long would it take you to write down all the odd prime numbers ?

   b How long would it take you to write down all the even prime numbers ? Try it.

9. a Make a neat large copy of this number square showing all the numbers from 1 to 100.

1	2	3	4	5	6	7	8	9	10
11	12	13	14	15	16	17	18	19	20
21	22	23	24	25	26	27	28	29	30
31	32	33	34	35	36	37	38	39	40
41	42	43	44	45	46	47	48	49	50
51	52	53	54	55	56	57	58	59	60
61	62	63	64	65	66	67	68	69	70
71	72	73	74	75	76	77	78	79	80
81	82	83	84	85	86	87	88	89	90
91	92	93	94	95	96	97	98	99	100

   b On your copy, score out the number 1. It is not a prime number.

   c Don't score out 2 but score out every other multiple of 2 – (4, 6, 8, ... 100).

   d Keep 3. Score out every other multiple of 3 – (6, 9, 12, ... 99).

   e Keep 5. Score out every other multiple of 5 – (10, 15, 20, ... 95).

   f Keep 7. Score out every other multiple of 7 – (14, 21, 28, ... 98).

   g Now draw a circle round every remaining number in the square. You will find that these are all the prime numbers.

   h Make a list of all the primes from 1 to 100. (*Might be a good idea to learn them !*). (*You should have discovered there are exactly 25 primes under 100*).

Squares and Cubes

To square a number means to multiply it by itself.

Example :-

The square of 4 is .. $4 \times 4 = 16$ (*not* 4×2).

This is shortened to 4 squared $= 4 \times 4 = 16$,

or better still $4^2 = 4 \times 4 = 16$. (4^2 is read as four squared).

4^2

To cube a number means to multiply it by itself, then by itself again.

Example :-

The cube of 2 is $2 \times 2 \times 2 = 8$ (*not* 2×3).

This is shortened to 2 cubed $= 2 \times 2 \times 2 = 8$,

or better still $2^3 = 2 \times 2 \times 2 = 8$. ($2^3$ is read as two cubed).

2^3

Exercise 4

1. Copy and complete the following :-

a $3^2 = 3 \times 3 = ...$ b $5^2 = 5 \times 5 = ...$ c $6^2 = 6 \times ... = ...$

d $8^2 = ... \times ... = ...$ e $7^2 =$ f $9^2 =$

g $10^2 =$ h $1^2 =$ i $20^2 =$

2. Copy and complete the following :-

a $4^3 = 4 \times 4 \times 4 = ...$ b $3^3 = 3 \times 3 \times ... = ...$ c $5^3 = ... \times ... \times ... = ...$

d $6^3 = ... \times ... = ...$ e $1^3 =$ f $10^3 =$

g $7^3 =$ h $8^3 =$ i $9^3 =$.

3. Which is bigger :- a 2^3 or 3^2 b 4^3 or 8^2?

4. Find :-

a $4^2 + 5^2$ b $9^2 + 8^2$ c $10^2 + 7^2$

d $9^2 + 2^2$ e $12^2 + 11^2$ f $2^2 + 3^2 + 5^2$.

Mixed Exercise - Problem Solving

Exercise 5

1. From the list of numbers below, write down which of these **multiples** boxes each number could be placed in.
(*Some numbers can go in more than 1 box*).

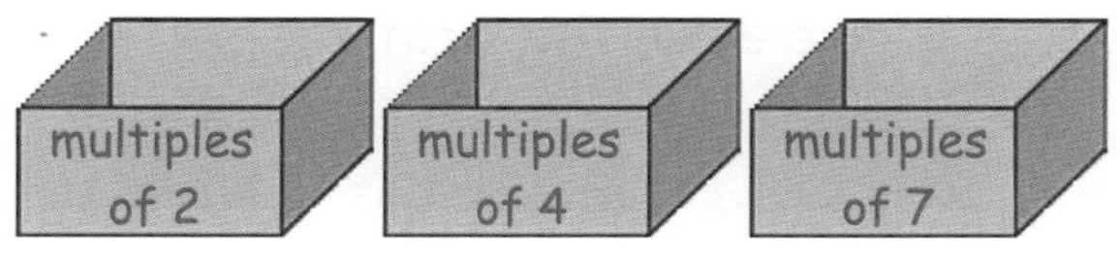

2, 4, 14, 21, 28, 32, 42, 49, 56, 60, 70.

2. Place each of the numbers below in the correct **factor** buckets.

1, 2, 3, 4, 5, 6, 7, 8, 12, 14, 16, 21.

(*Some numbers will go in more than 1 bucket*).

3. Three buses leave Sunderland Bus Station every morning.

- The Newcastle bus leaves every 2 hours.
- The Leeds bus every 3 hours.
- The London bus every 4 hours.

The 3 buses all leave together at 6 am.

a When is the next time all 3 buses leave at the same time ?

b What time after that will another three leave the bus station together ?

4. a Find each of the following :-

$1^2 - 0^2$, $2^2 - 1^2$, $3^2 - 2^2$, $4^2 - 3^2$, $5^2 - 4^2$, $6^2 - 5^2$.

b Did you notice a pattern ? If so, write down the value of :-

$7^2 - 6^2$, $8^2 - 7^2$, $9^2 - 8^2$, $20^2 - 19^2$, $101^2 - 100^2$.

5. Find the unknown number represented by x :-

a $x^2 = 9$ b $x^2 = 25$ c $x^2 = 121$ d $x^2 = 64$.

6. There are obvious reasons why some numbers are not prime.

In each case below, say why the number shown is **not** a prime :-

a 37 495 b 1 264 572 c 89 479 480 d 3 396 303.

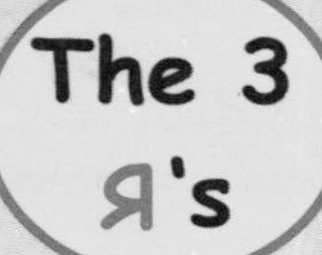

Revisit - Review - Revise

1. Write down the first six **multiples** of :-

   a 3 b 7 c 9 d 12.

2. Write down all the **multiples** of :-

   a 4 between 27 and 49 b 9 from 45 to 81.

3. Write down all the **factors** of :-

   a 6 b 18 c 30 d 48.

4. Write down all the **common factors** of :-

   a 8 and 12 b 20 and 30 c 35 and 45 d 29 and 41.

5. How many **factors** does a **prime** number have ?

6. Write down **all** the **prime** numbers between :-

   a 10 and 20 b 40 and 50 c 50 and 60 d 90 and 110.

7. Find :-

   a 5^2 b 8^2 c 10^2 d 2^3

   e 4^3 f 20^2 g 100^2 h 100^3.

8. Ali is in hospital being treated for a wound which is infected.

   - He receives an injection every 4 hours.
   - He has to take a pill every 5 hours.
   - He has cream rubbed on his wound every 2 hours.

   At 6 am, Ali finds he is given his pill, is injected and has cream rubbed on his wound.

   a When is the next time he takes a pill and has cream rubbed on his wound together ?

   b After 6 am, when is the next time he has all 3 treatments together ?

Chapter 8

Angles 2

Angles Revision

Exercise 1

1. Use right, straight, acute, obtuse or reflex to describe each marked angle below :-

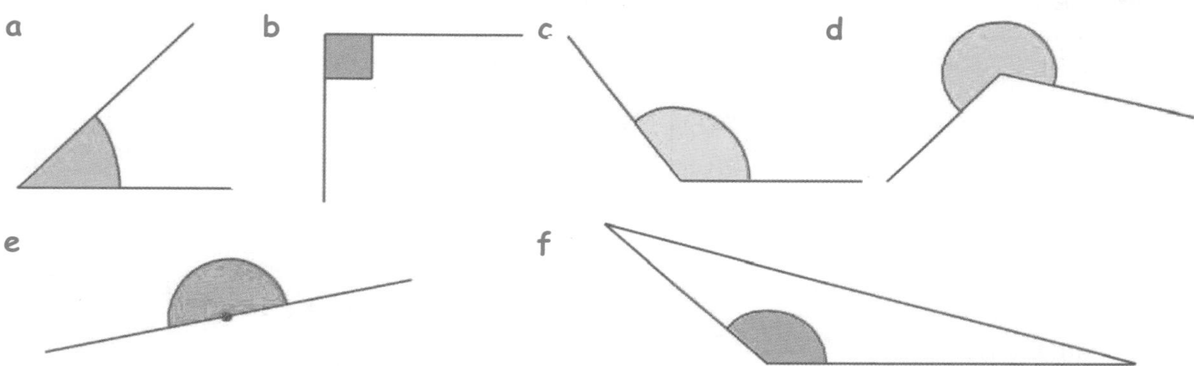

2. Use three letters to name each marked angle below :-

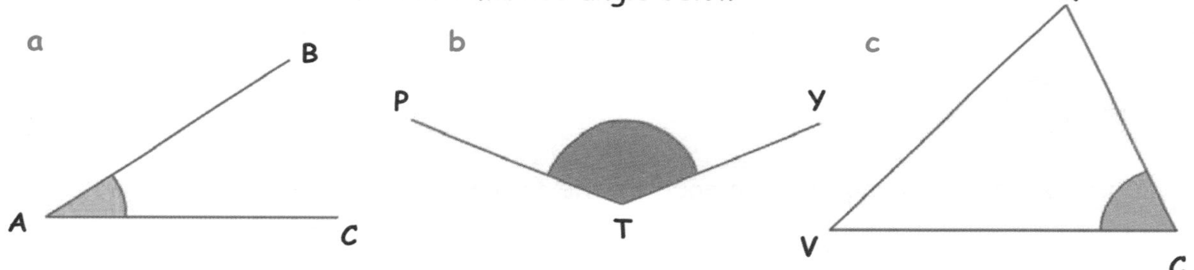

3. a Estimate (in degrees) the size of each marked angle in Question 2.

   b Measure and write down the size of each marked angle in Question 2.

4. Draw each of the following angles :-

   a 40° b 120° c 73° d 147°.

5. How many degrees are there from :-

   a North to West (*clockwise*) b South East to North West (*clockwise*)

   c SW to North (*anti-clockwise*) d North to North (*clockwise*).

6. Jill is facing NE. She makes a three quarter turn anti-clockwise.

   In which direction is she now facing ?

Complementary and Supplementary Angles

Be able to find complementary and supplementary angles.

A 90° angle is called a right angle.

Any two angles that, when added together come to 90°, are called Complementary Angles.

Example :-

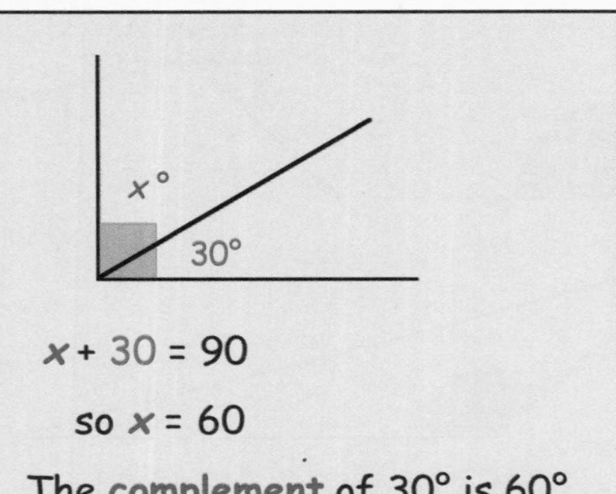

$x + 30 = 90$

so $x = 60$

The complement of 30° is 60°.

A 180° angle is called a straight angle.

Any two angles that, when added together make 180°, are called Supplementary Angles.

Example :-

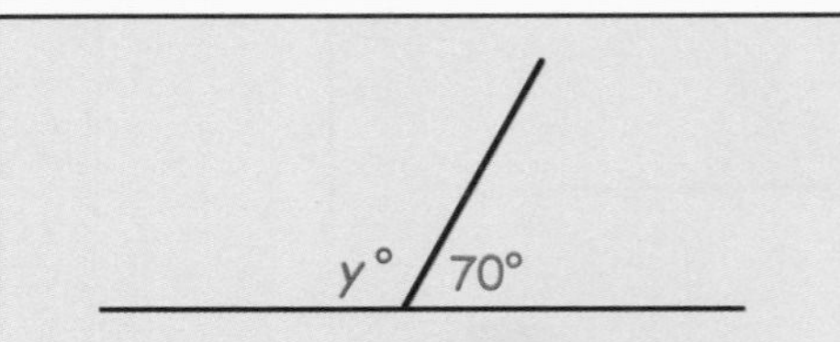

$y + 70 = 180$

so $y = 110$

The supplement of 70° is 110°.

Exercise 2

1. Calculate the missing angle in each of the following :-

a 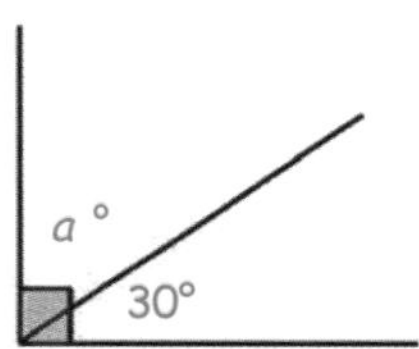

b 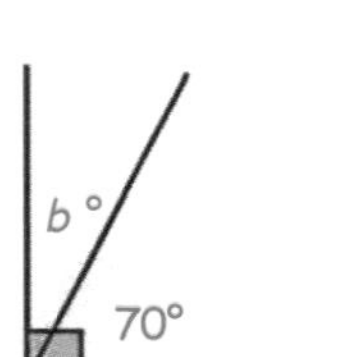

c 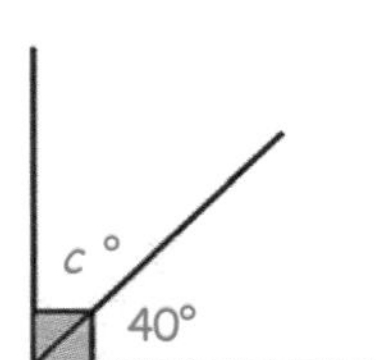

d 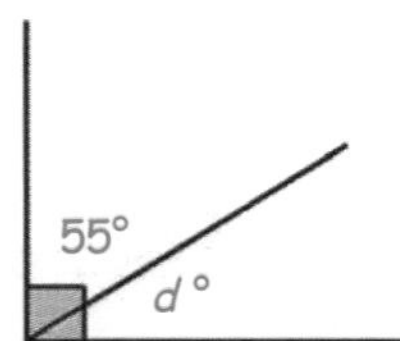

e 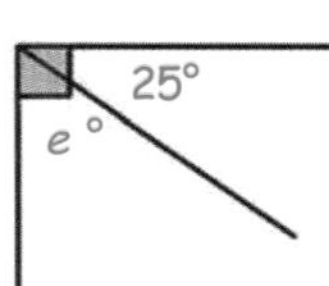

f 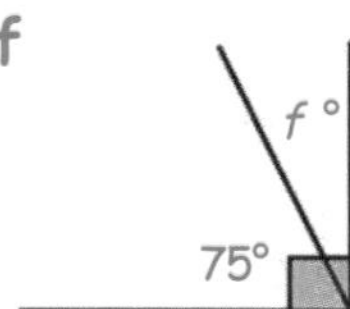

g 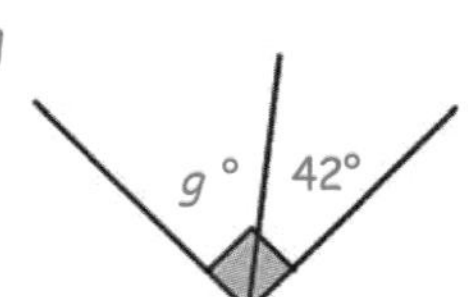

h 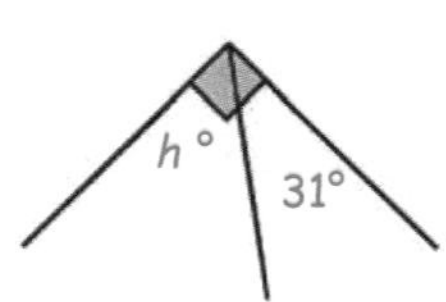

2. Write down the complement (complementary angle) of :-

a	60°	b	10°	c	88°	d	11°
e	19°	f	73°	g	8·5°	h	52·5°.

3. What angle is its own complement ?

4. Calculate the missing angle in each of the following :-

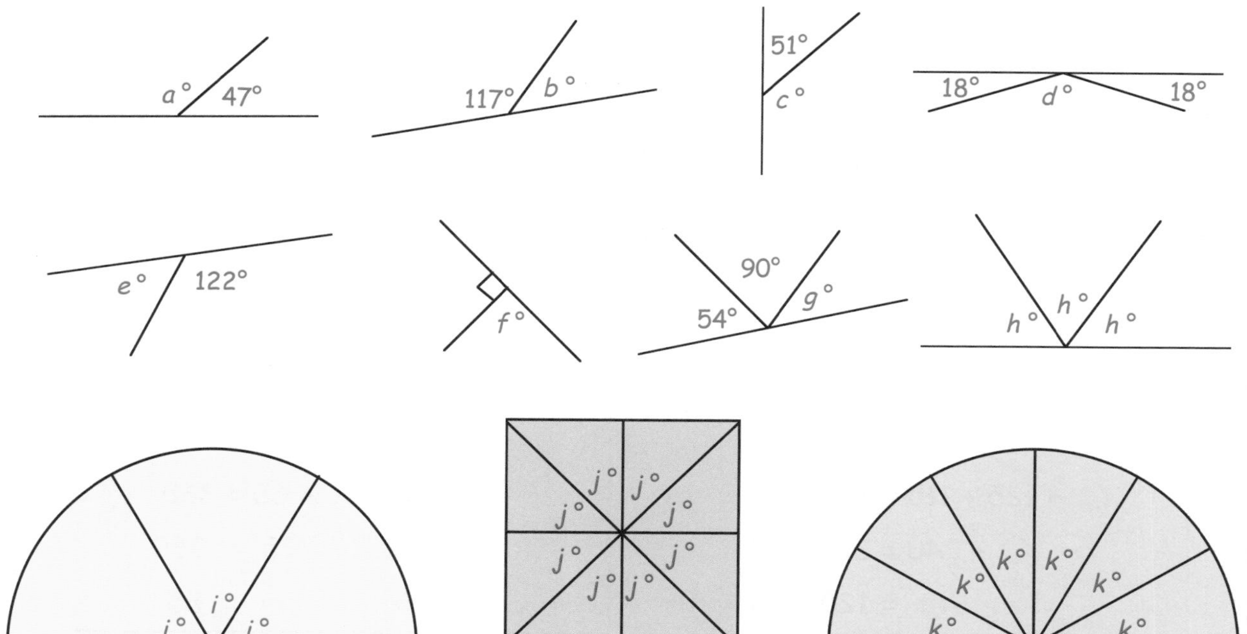

5. Write down the **supplement** (supplementary angle) of :-

a	100°	b	25°	c	137°	d	176°
e	1°	f	111°	g	179·5°	h	87·5°.

6. What angle is its own **supplement** ?

7. An angle is measured and found to be 83°.

   a What is its **complement** ? b What is its **supplement** ?

8. Shown are 4 angles which fit exactly around a point.

   a What answer will you get if you add all 4 angles ? ($p + q + r + s = ?$).

   b In general, what answer will you **ALWAYS** get when you add together all the angles round a point ?

9. a What do you get when you add 130° + 110° ?

   b Calculate the size of the 3rd angle (*).

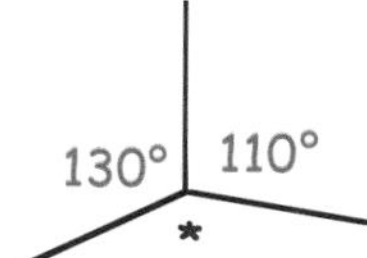

10. a There are 3 angles round a point. One is 120°. The second is a right angle. Calculate the size of the third angle.

    b Four angles round a point are 37°, 111°, 104° and x°. Calculate the value of x.

Angles Round a Point

Be able to calculate a missing angle round a point.

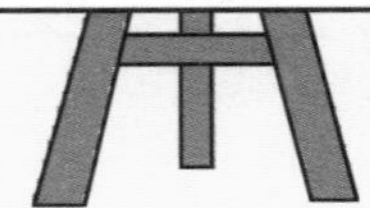

The angles round a point must total 360°. (2 straight angles).

In the diagram shown

$a + b + c + d = 360$.

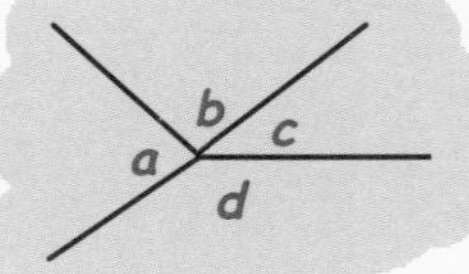

Examples :-

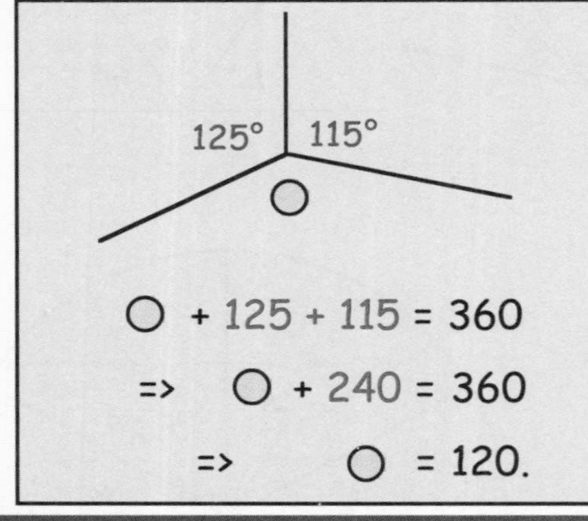

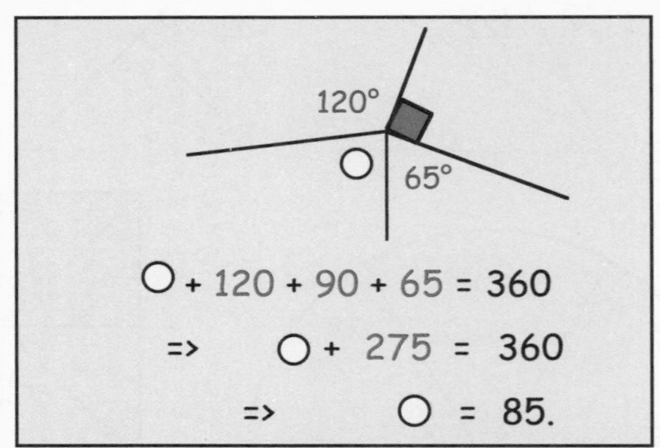

Exercise 3

1. Calculate the value of the angles marked ○ :-

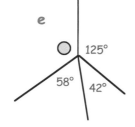

a
125° 125°

b
90° 110°

c
65° 90° 115°

d
180° 40°

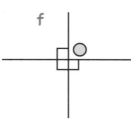

e
125° 58° 42°

f

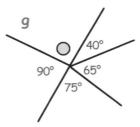

g
40° 90° 65° 75°

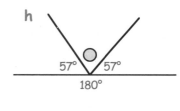

h
57° 57° 180°

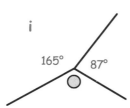

i
165° 87°

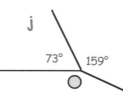

j
73° 159°

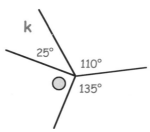

k
25° 110° 135°

l
145° 115°

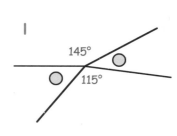

2. Sketch some diagrams similar to Question 1.

   Get your partner to find the missing angles.

Mixed Exercise

Exercise 4

1. Calculate the missing angles :-

a
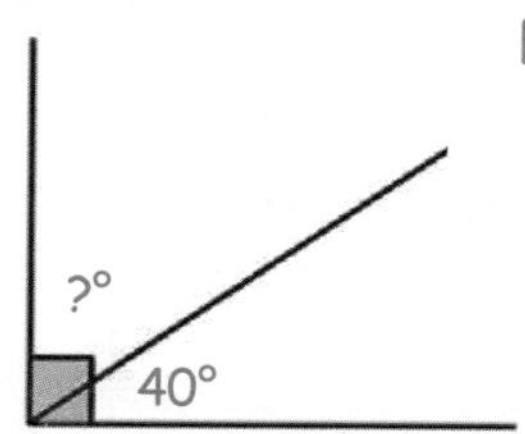

b
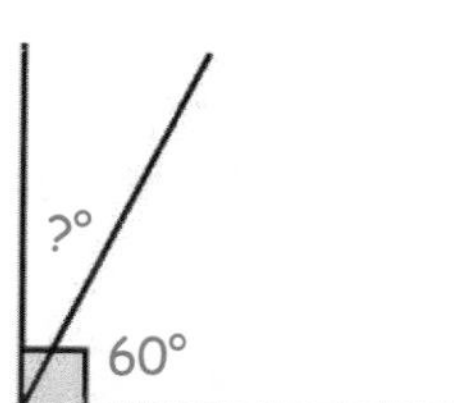

c
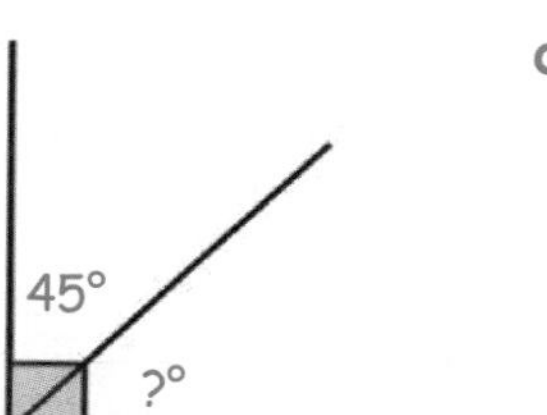

d
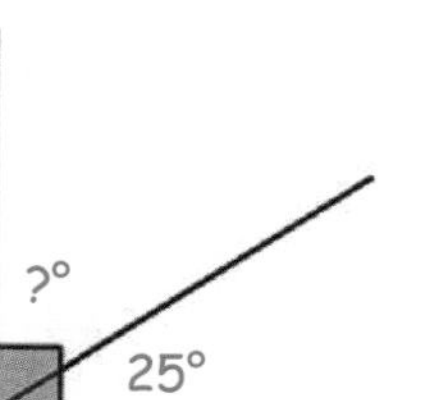

e
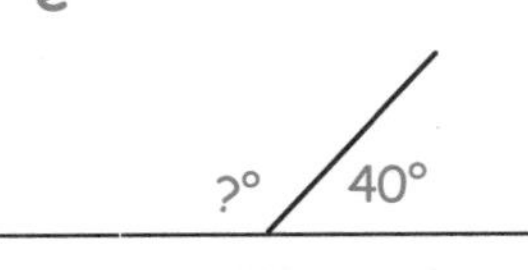

f
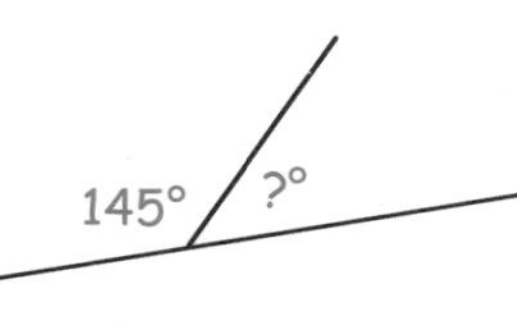

g
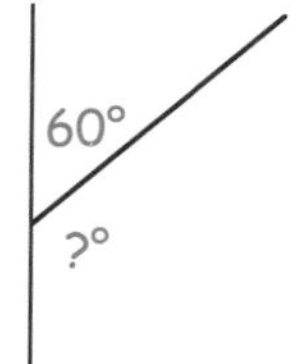

h
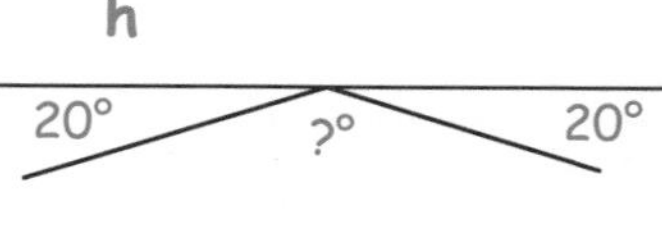

i
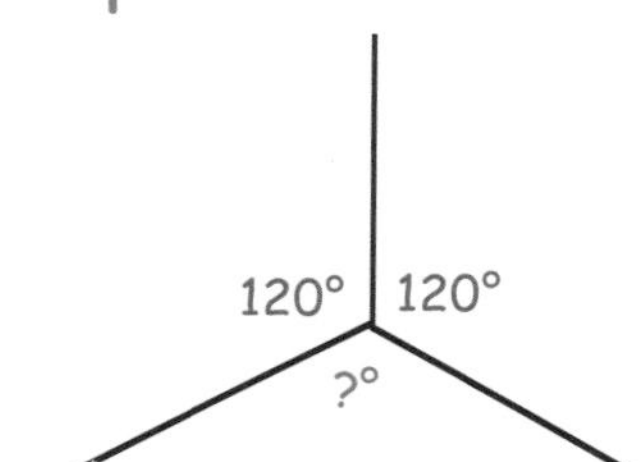

j
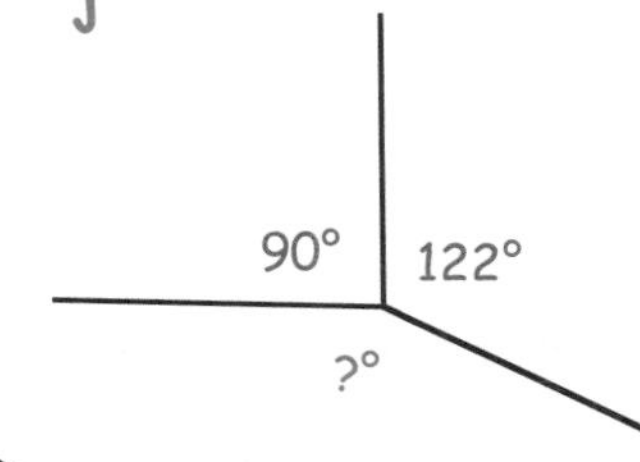

k
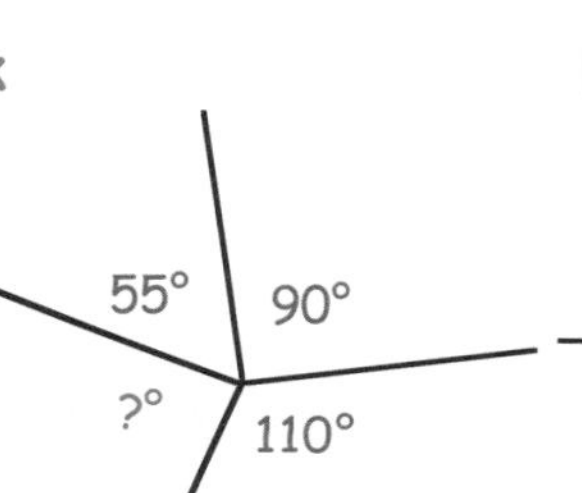

l
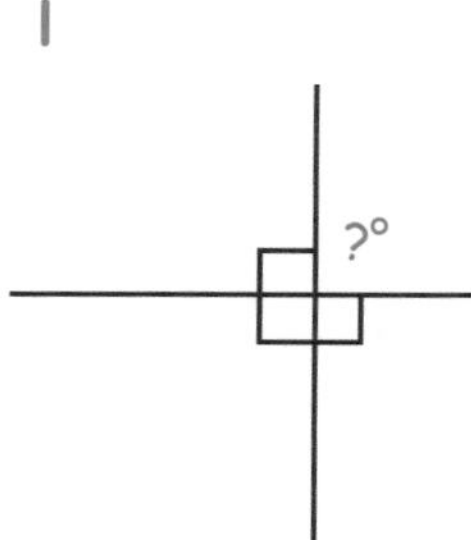

2. Find the **complement** of :-

a 20° b 89° c 42° d 45°.

3. Find the **supplement** of :-

a 100° b 125° c 22° d 124·5°.

4. a Three angles round a point measure 40°, 110° and x°. Find the value of x.

b Angles round a point are 30°, 27°, 90°, 42° and y°. Find the value of y.

c Five angles are drawn round a point.

Three of the angles are 45°, 65° and a right angle.

If the other two angles are the same size, how many degrees is each angle ?

Angles in Shapes

Be able to calculate a missing angle in a shape.

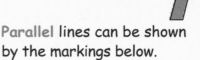

Remember - A rectangle has 4 right angles and has opposite sides which are parallel and of equal length.

Equal sides can be shown by the markings below.

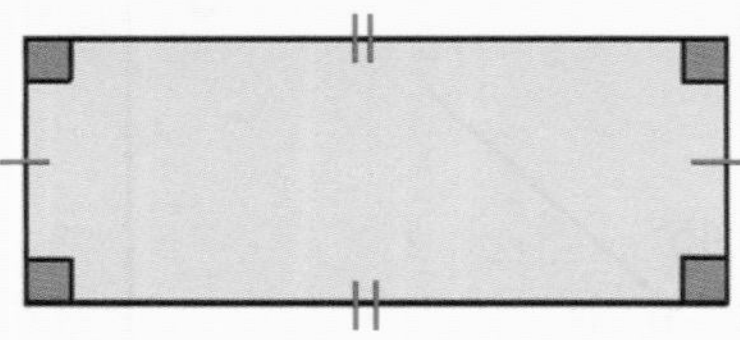

Note :- Lengths are equal, breadths are equal.

Lengths and breadths are NOT equal.

Parallel lines can be shown by the markings below.

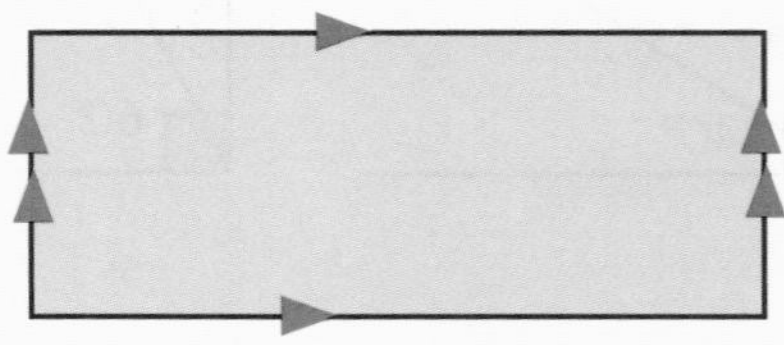

Opposite sides are parallel.

Exercise 5

1. Copy each shape below and show all right angles, equal lengths and parallel lines :-

   a rectangle

   b square

2. A rectangle ABCD is as shown.

   The diagonal line AC is drawn.

   Angle BAC is 60°.

   a Copy ABCD and show all right angles, equal lengths and parallel lines.

   b Write down the size of angle DAC.
   (*Remember that angle DAB is 90°*).

3. Shown is rectangle EFGH.

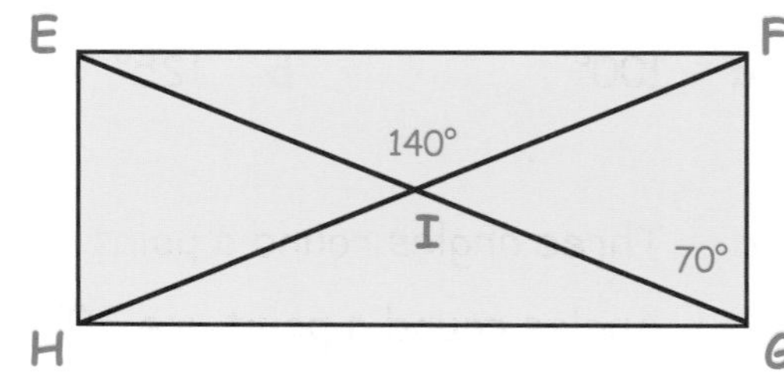

   a Copy EFGH and show all relevant information

   b Write in your diagram the size of angle IGH.
   (*Hint - angle FGH = 90°*)

   c Write in your diagram the size of angle FIG. (*Hint - angle EIG = 180°*)

   d Fill in the sizes of all the other angles. (*Hint - 2 lines of symmetry in a rectangle*).

The 3 Я's

Revisit - Review - Revise

1. Use right, straight, acute, obtuse or reflex to describe each of these angles :-

   a 45° b 180° c 120° d 90° e 300°.

2. Use a protractor to draw each of the angles in Question 1.

3. What is the :- a complement of 40° b supplement of 40° ?

4. Copy and complete each diagram below, filling in all missing angles :-

a

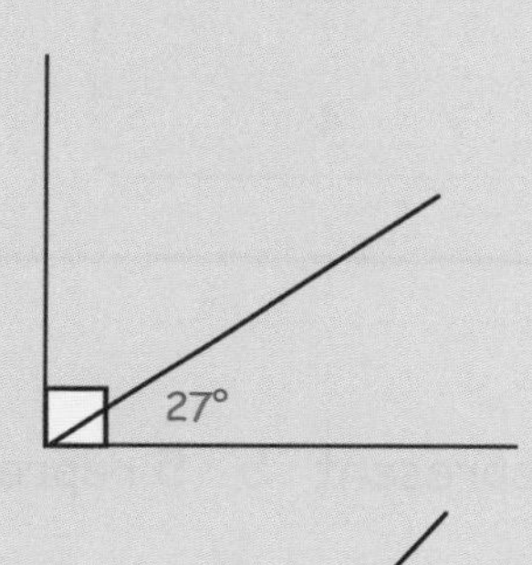

b

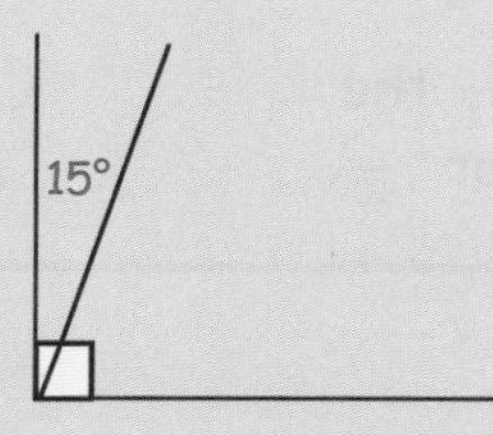

c

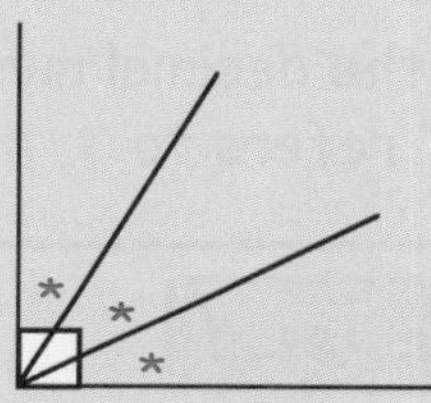

d

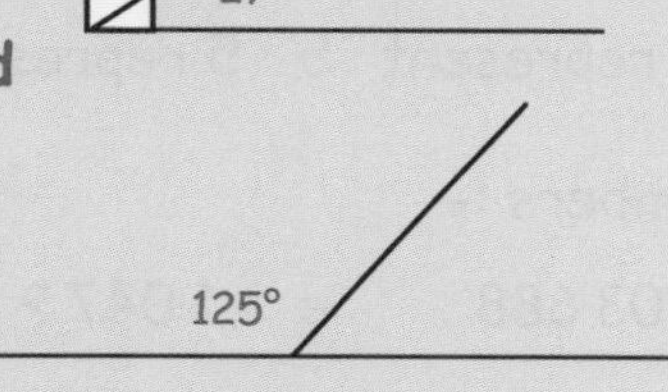

e

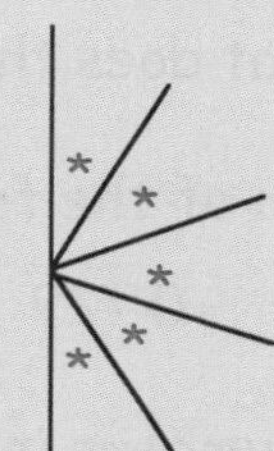

f

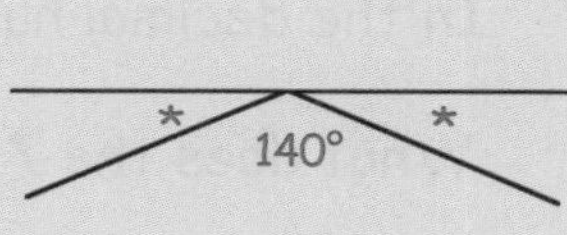

g

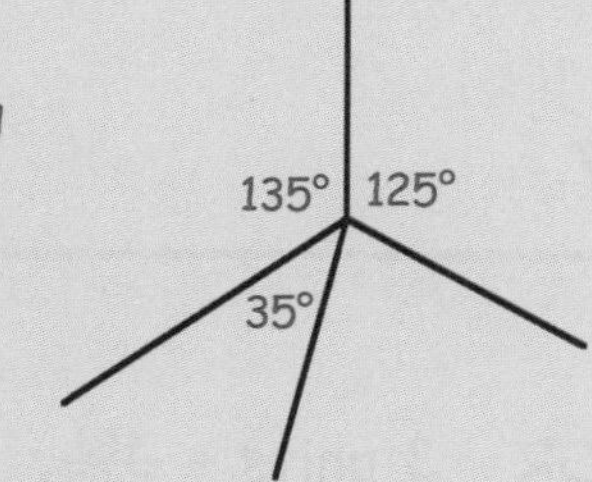

h

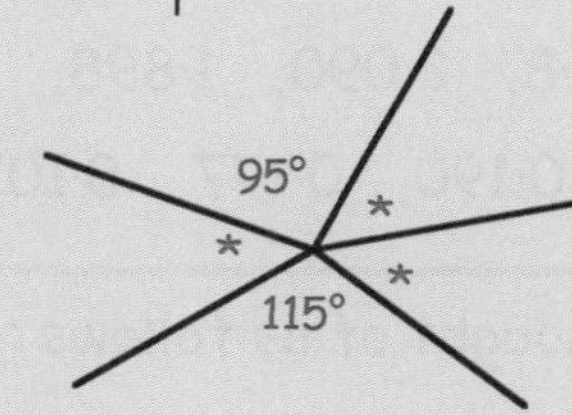

i

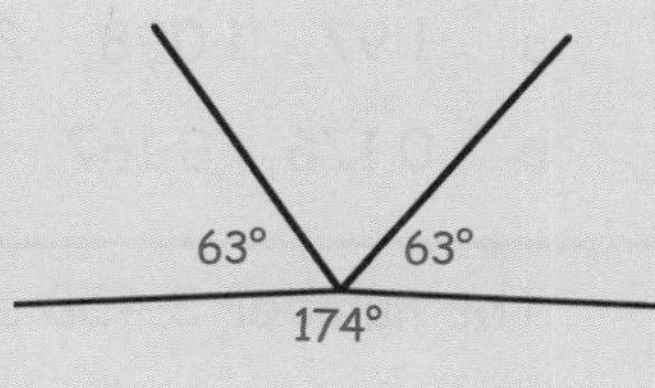

5. Shown is a rectangle ABCD.

   a Make a large sketch of ABCD (*You do NOT need to be accurate*).

   b Use small lines to mark all parallel sides and all equal sides.

   c Fill in the sizes of all the missing angles.

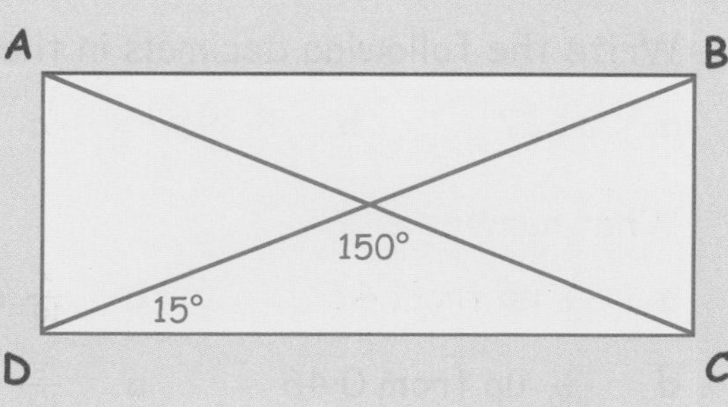

Chapter 9

Decimals

The Third Decimal Place

Be able to deal with decimals up to 3 decimal places.

The Third Decimal Place

Imagine that the small $\frac{1}{100}$ of the chocolate bar, (the ▭), could be cut up into a further 10 equal pieces.

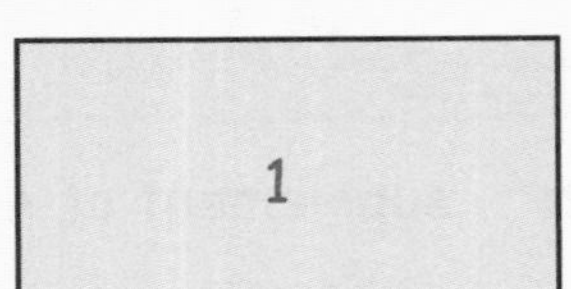

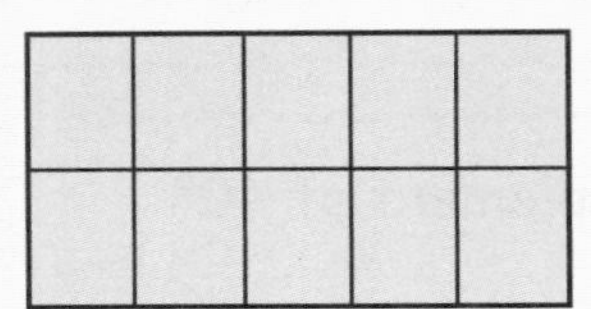

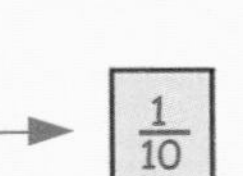

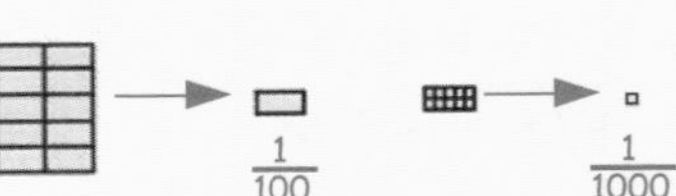

=> Each piece would now be :-

($\frac{1}{10}$ of $\frac{1}{10}$ of $\frac{1}{10}$) = $\frac{1}{1000}$ (a thousandth).

In the decimal number, 5·743, the "3" refers to 3 thousandths or $\frac{3}{1000}$.

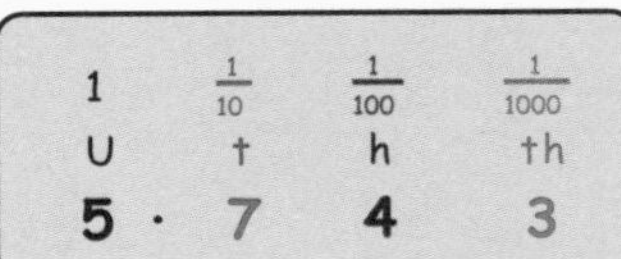

1	$\frac{1}{10}$	$\frac{1}{100}$	$\frac{1}{1000}$
U	t	h	th
5 ·	7	**4**	3

Exercise 1

1. In the decimal number 26·395, what does the :- a 9 represent b 5 represent ?

2. What does the 7 represent in each of the following numbers :-

   a 172·633 b 5·078 c 0·729 d 703·688 e 1·047 ?

3. Arrange the following groups of numbers in order, smallest first :-

   a 1·97, 1·098, 2·001, 1·8, 2·090, 1·898, 1·008

   b 0·176, 0·167, 0·108, 0·190, 0·177, 0·107, 0·207.

The number 3·458 can be thought of as follows :-

3·458 = 3 units + $\frac{4}{10}$ + $\frac{5}{100}$ + $\frac{8}{1000}$ OR 3 units + $\frac{458}{1000}$.

4. Write the following decimals in the same two ways :-

   a 3·627 b 8·396 c 0·351 d 40·409 e 0·087.

5. What number is :-

   a $\frac{3}{10}$ up from 4·5 b $\frac{5}{10}$ down from 6·3 c $\frac{7}{10}$ up from 4·51

   d $\frac{6}{100}$ up from 0·46 e $\frac{8}{100}$ down from 1·54 f $\frac{7}{100}$ up from 2·139

   g $\frac{3}{1000}$ up from 4·578 h $\frac{5}{1000}$ down from 0·821 i $\frac{9}{1000}$ down from 7·901 ?

More on Adding and Subtracting Decimals

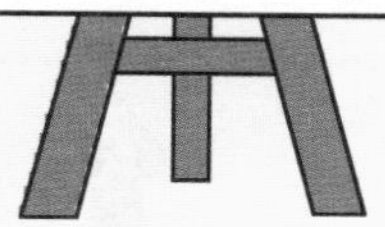

Be able to add or subtract decimal numbers with a varying number of digits.

Remember :-

Whether you are adding decimal numbers or subtracting them, you must line up the decimal points.

Example 1 :-

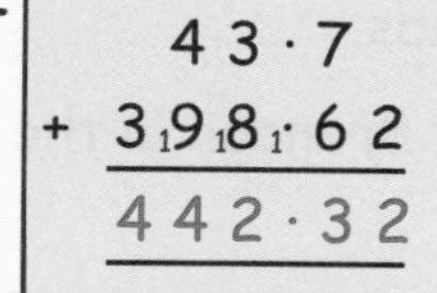

```
    43·7
+ 398·62
  442·32
```

Example 2 :-

```
  24·373
-  9·438
  14·935
```

Exercise 2

1. Set down and work out the following :-

a 39·5 + 48·3 b 38·29 + 27·44 c 624·95 + 38·77 d 9·873 + 16·489

e 5·28 − 3·46 f 50·46 − 29·53 g 532·47 − 68·89 h 25·843 − 7·916

i 9·83 + 7·74 j 8·25 − 3·96 k 133·75 + 219·74

l 45·1 − 8·237 m 160 − 2·714 n 0·952 − 0·097.

Show all your working whilst attempting the following :-

2. Jenny weighs 61 · 83 kilograms and Francis weighs 56 · 49 kilograms.

a What is their combined weight ?

b By how much is Jenny heavier than Francis ?

3. 3 boxes weigh 2 · 813 kg, 4 · 936 kg and 3 · 709 kg.

a What is the combined weight of the 2 lightest boxes ?

b What is the total weight of all 3 boxes ?

c By how much is the heaviest box heavier than the lightest box ?

4. A small truck weighs 450 · 6 kg. It carries washing machines.
Each washing machine weighs 53 · 87 kg.

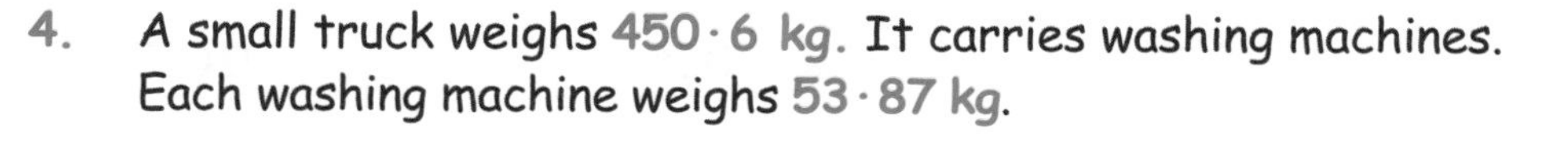

What is the total weight of a truck carrying 2 washing machines ?

5. A metal rod is 1 · 987 metres long.
When heated it expands to 2 · 043 metres.

By how many centimetres does the rod expand ?

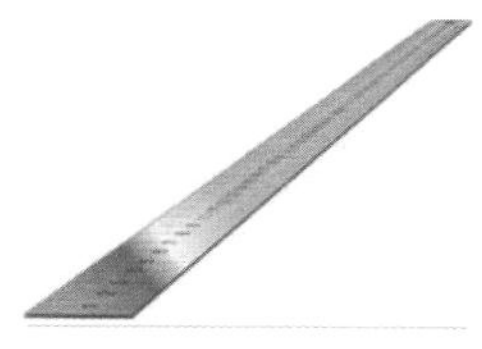

6. A vase contained exactly 3 litres of water. During a hot spell of weather, 0·465 litres of water evaporated.

   How much water was left in the vase ?

7. 

   Brendan ran the 100 metre race in 10·057 seconds. Justin ran it in 9·968 seconds.

   By how much did Justin beat Brendan in the race ?

8. Look at this plan of an L-shaped living room.

   a Calculate the length of the room (marked x metres).

   b Calculate the value of y.

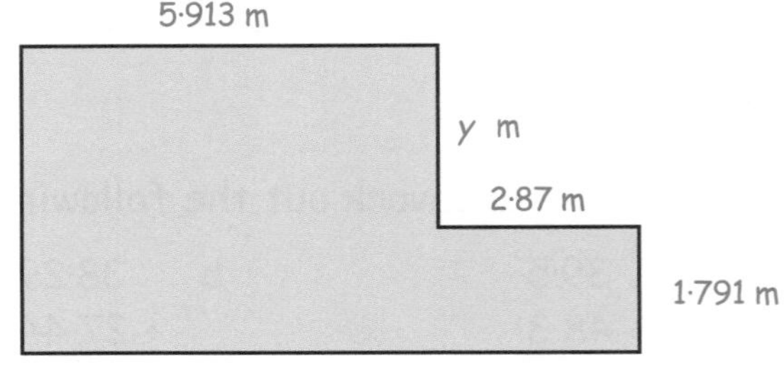

Changing Decimals into Fractions

Be able to change a decimal into a fraction.

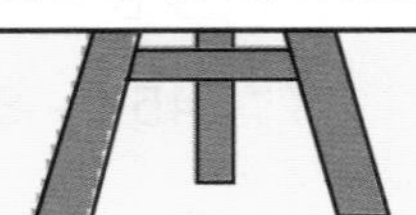

Use the places after the decimal point (*10ths*, *100ths*, *1000ths*) to help convert a decimal to a fraction and simplify, if possible.

Example 1 :-

$0 \cdot \overset{\frac{1}{10}}{6} = \frac{6}{10} = \frac{3}{5}$

Example 2 :-

$0 \cdot 3\overset{\frac{1}{100}}{7} = \frac{37}{100}$

Example 3 :-

$3 \cdot 12\overset{\frac{1}{1000}}{4} = 3\frac{124}{1000}$ or $3\frac{31}{250}$

Exercise 3

1. Change each decimal to a fraction (*in its simplest form*) :-

a 0·1	b 0·01	c 0·001	d 0·3
e 0·03	f 0·003	g 0·4	h 0·02
i 0·004	j 0·7	k 0·15	l 0·057
m 0·8	n 0·25	o 0·12	p 1·2
q 3·75	r 4·25	s 9·5	t 3·03
u 10·05	v 44·4	w 77·77	x 8·04.

Round to Nearest Whole Number or to 1 Decimal Place

Rounding 2 decimal places to the nearest whole number or to 1 decimal place.

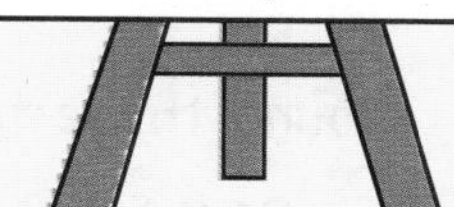

Rounding to the Nearest Whole Number (Mostly Revision)

In Year 4, you saw how to round a number with 1 decimal figure to the nearest whole number.

To round 2 decimal places to the nearest whole number, the same rules are applied.

Look at the first digit which comes just after the decimal point :-

If it is a 5, 6, 7, 8 or 9 => round up to the next whole number.

If it is a 0, 1, 2, 3 or 4 => leave the whole number before the point as it is.

Examples :-

7·<u>3</u>8 = 7 to the nearest whole number.

28·<u>5</u>7 = 29 to the nearest whole number.

Rounding to 1 Decimal Place

3·1<u>7</u>
lies between 3·1 and 3·2
It is closer to 3·2,
(*to 1 decimal place*).

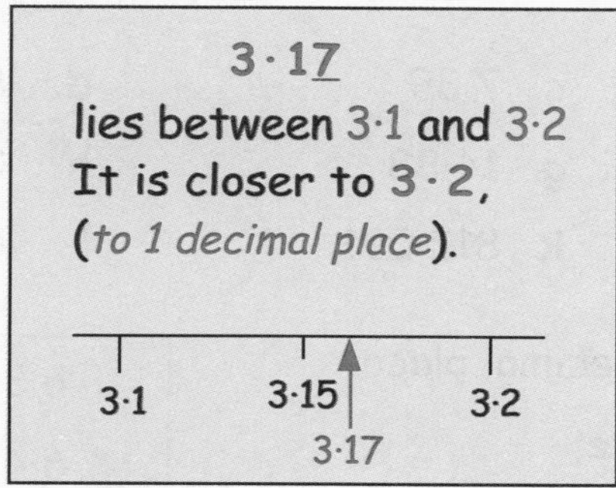

19·8<u>3</u>
lies between 19·8 and 19·9
It is closer to 19·8,
(*to 1 decimal place*).

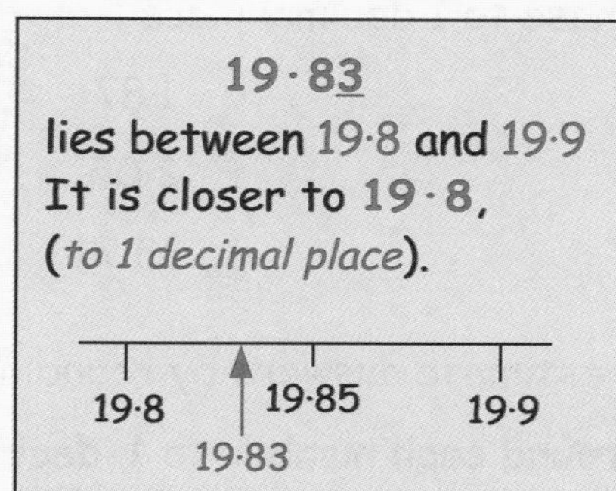

When rounding to 1 decimal place :-

Look at the digit in the 2nd decimal place :-

If it is a 5, 6, 7, 8 or 9 => round your 1st decimal digit up by 1.

If it is a 0, 1, 2, 3 or 4 => leave your 1st decimal digit as it is.

Examples :-

9·8<u>1</u> = 9·8 to one decimal place.

36·4<u>8</u> = 36·5 to one decimal place.

Exercise 4

1. Round each of these numbers to the nearest whole number :-

a 5·36	b 7· 29	c 12·53	d 19·18
e 28·72	f 56·51	g 100·49	h 425·62.

2. Round these to the nearest kilogram :-

a 8·71 kg b 2·46 kg c 14·80 kg d 25·29 kg
e 38·53 kg f 62·45 kg g 112·15 kg h 428·79 kg.

3. Round these to the nearest whole £ :-

a £1·94 b £2·13 c £10·67 d £12·50
e £50·47 f £60·51 g £100·99 h £1230·50.

4. When each number is rounded to 1 decimal place, which of the two values in the brackets is the correct answer :-

a 3·46 (3·4 or 3·5) b 4·72 (4·7 or 4·8)
c 1·07 (1·0 or 1·1) d 0·89 (0·8 or 0·9)
e 12·75 (12·7 or 12·8) f 9·96 (9·9 or 10·0)
g 4·99 (4·9 or 5·0) h 0·07 (0·0 or 0·1) ?

5. Round these to 1 decimal place :-

a 4·42 b 1·87 c 7·39 d 8·43
e 7·04 f 2·05 g 14·88 h 0·34
i 25·17 j 33·71 k 812·091 l 645·909.

6. We can estimate answers by rounding to 1 decimal place.

- round each number to 1 decimal place,
- then find an estimate to :-

6·37 + 5·24
≈ 6·4 + 5·2
≈ 11·6

a 3·298 + 5·528 b 18·601 + 3·288
c 9·742 – 4·199 d 0·886 + 3·631 e 14·877 – 8·616
f 3·398 + 0·765 g 0·943 – 0·676 h 6·83 + 7·291.

Questions 7 and 8 are OPTIONAL (Requires a calculator.)

7. Use a calculator to do the following divisions, then write down the answers correct to 1 decimal place :-

a 90 ÷ 16 b 500 ÷ 27 c 12·6 ÷ 0·95
d 312 ÷ 45·3 e 0·88 ÷ 0·17 f 4000 ÷ 211·6.

8. Use your calculator to change these fractions to decimals and round your answers to 1 decimal place :-

a $\frac{3}{7}$ = (3 ÷ 7) = 0·4285714.... = 0·..... *(to 1 decimal place)*

b $\frac{3}{11}$ = (3 ÷ 11) = 0· c $\frac{7}{9}$ = (7 ÷ ...) = ...

Multiplying Decimals by 10, 100, 1000

Be able to multiply a decimal by 10, 100, 1000.

Yet again, you really must know your tables !!!!!

Learn the following simple rules for multiplying decimals :-

If you multiply by 10,

=> move all the figures ONE place LEFT
(or move the point one place right).

If you multiply by 100,

=> move all the figures TWO places LEFT
(or move the point two places right).

If you multiply by 1000,

=> move all the figures THREE places LEFT
(or move the point three places right).

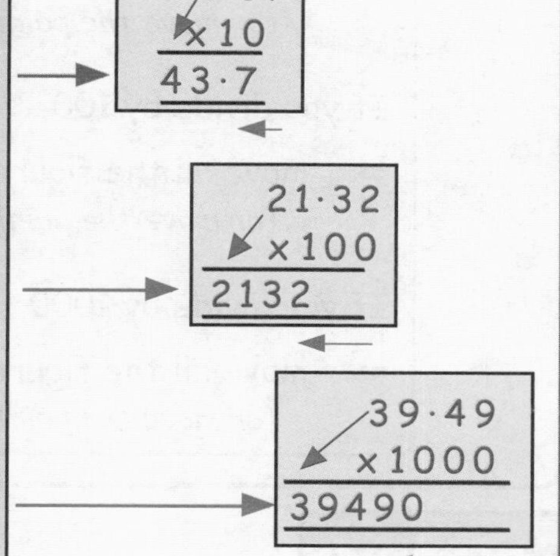

Exercise 5

1. Write down the answers to the following :-

a	3·6 x 10	b	4·8 x 10	c	2·67 x 10	d	10 x 9·17
e	10 x 12·52	f	0·94 x 10	g	10 x 4·08	h	10 x 0·03
i	24·75 x 10	j	9·18 x 10	k	10 x 14·07	l	0·05 x 10.

2. Write down the answers to :-

a	3·82 x 100	b	5·41 x 100	c	100 x 6·09	d	100 x 8·6
e	7·47 x 100	f	100 x 0·71	g	100 x 0·4	h	0·09 x 100.

3. Write down the answers to :-

a	2·94 x 1000	b	3·06 x 1000	c	4·75 x 1000	d	1000 x 19·3
e	1000 x 0·85	f	0·08 x 1000	g	1000 x 2·02	h	1000 x 0·05.

4. A jar of pickles weighs 3·4 pounds. What is the weight of :-

   a 10 jars b 100 jars c 1000 jars ?

5. There are 1000 grams in 1 kilogram. How many grams are there in :-

   a 3·64 kg b 29·7 kg c 0·9 kg d 0·02 kg ?

Dividing Decimals by 10, 100, 1000

Be able to divide a decimal by 10, 100, 1000.

Learn the following simple rules for dividing decimals :-

If you divide by 10,

=> move all the figures ONE place RIGHT
(or move the point one place left).

$10 \overline{)25 \cdot 7}$ → $2 \cdot 57$

If you divide by 100,

=> move all the figures TWO places RIGHT
(or move the point two places left).

$100 \overline{)329}$ → $3 \cdot 29$

If you divide by 1000,

=> move all the figures THREE places RIGHT
(or move the point three places left).

$1000 \overline{)1520}$ → $1 \cdot 52$

Exercise 6

1. Write down the answers to the following :-

a	15·2 ÷ 10	b	37·8 ÷ 10	c	5·9 ÷ 10	d	437·6 ÷ 10
e	17·3 ÷ 10	f	245·8 ÷ 10	g	10·4 ÷ 10	h	13 ÷ 10
i	7 ÷ 10	j	0·9 ÷ 10	k	1·8 ÷ 10	l	20·5 ÷ 10.

2. Do the following :-

a	934 ÷ 100	b	576 ÷ 100	c	75 ÷ 100	d	16 ÷ 100
e	730 ÷ 100	f	1942 ÷ 100	g	108 ÷ 100	h	6 ÷ 100.

3. Do the following :-

a	8470 ÷ 1000	b	39 760 ÷ 1000	c	9370 ÷ 1000	d	1800 ÷ 1000
e	750 ÷ 1000	f	300 ÷ 1000	g	90 ÷ 1000	h	140 ÷ 1000.

4. a When 100 paper clips are weighed, their total weight is 19 grams.
   What is the weight of 1 paper clip ?

   b 10 people formed a syndicate and got 5 numbers up in the lottery.
   If they received a total of £2894·50, how much did each individual receive ?

5. There are 1000 metres in 1 kilometre. How many kilometres are there in :-

   a 2630 metres b 530 metres c 860 metres d 30 metres ?

The 3 R's

Revisit - Review - Revise

1. What does the 3 represent in each of the following numbers :-

   a 531·774   b 25·036   c 100·374   d 312·226   e 13·893 ?

2. What number is :-

   a $\frac{3}{10}$ up from 6·1   b $\frac{6}{100}$ down from 0·46   c $\frac{8}{100}$ down from 12·57

   d $\frac{7}{100}$ up from 0·148   e $\frac{3}{1000}$ down from 19·444   f $\frac{9}{1000}$ up from 7·901 ?

3. Set down and work out :-

   a 273·75 + 59·65   b 240 – 3·998   c 22·174 – 9·258   d 0·875 + 0·215.

4. Tony drinks 0·15 litres of juice from a 1 litre carton.

   a How much juice is left in the carton ?

   b His young sister then pours **two** lots of 0·225 litres from the carton.
   How much juice is left in the carton now ?

5. Change each of these decimal numbers to a fraction in its simplest form :-

   a 0·6   b 0·05   c 0·002   d 6·25.

6. Round these to the nearest whole unit :-

   a 2·81 kg   b 67·24 kg   c £11·18   d £250·50.

7. Round these to 1 decimal place :-

   a 3·64   b 8·05   c 27·49   d 250·019.

8. Round each number to 1 decimal place, then work out :-

   a 1·26 + 3·47   b 9·643 – 7·392   c 31·76 + 19·04   d 0·786 – 0·784.

9. Write down the answers to :-

   a 18·27 × 10   b 0·060 × 100   c 1·409 × 1000   d 1000 × 17·326

   e 1·4 ÷ 10   f 0·9 ÷ 10   g 125 ÷ 100   h 960 ÷ 1000.

10. One thousand adults had paid £40 250 in total for concert tickets.
    What was the price of a ticket ?

Chapter 10

3-D and 2-D Shapes

3-D Shapes

Be able to recognise 3-D shapes and know their properties.

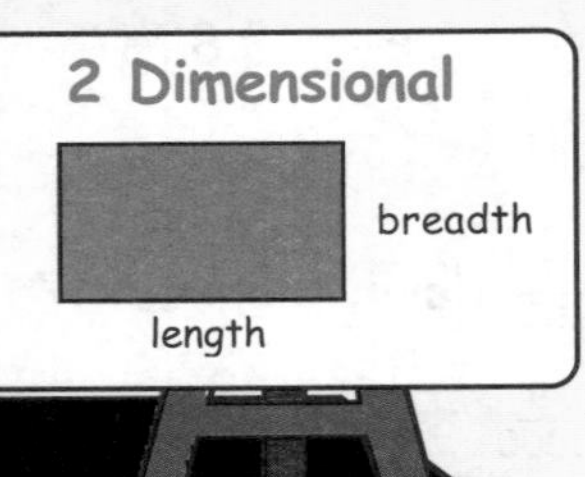

FLAT shapes, drawn on paper, like squares, circles or triangles are called 2-dimensional. They have 2 "dimensions" or 2 sizes :-
(*length* and *breadth*).

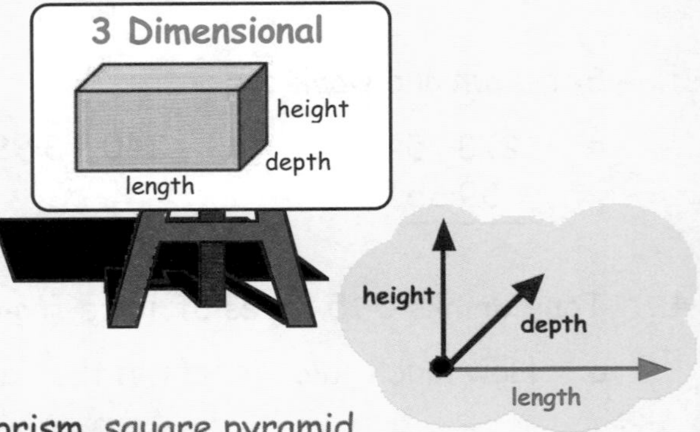

SOLID shapes, like cubes, cones and cylinders are called "3-dimensional".

They have 3 "dimensions" or 3 sizes :-
(*length*, *depth* (or *breadth*) and *height*).

You should recognise these shapes :-

cube, cuboid, cone, cylinder, sphere, triangular prism, square pyramid.

Exercise 1

1. Name the following mathematical shapes :-

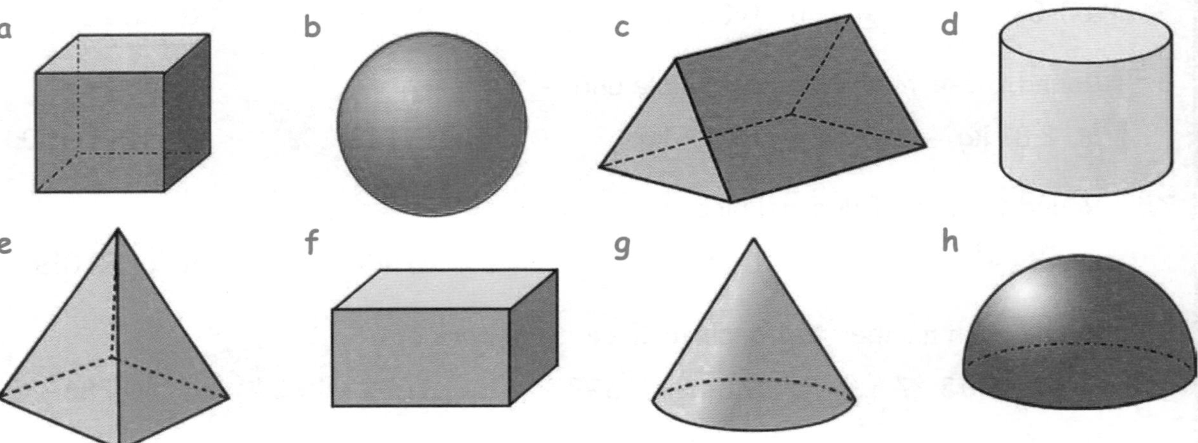

2. The objects below are made up of more than one 3-dimensional shape.

   List the different shapes each time :-

a

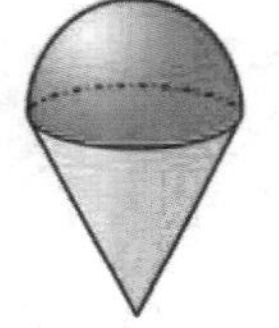

b

c

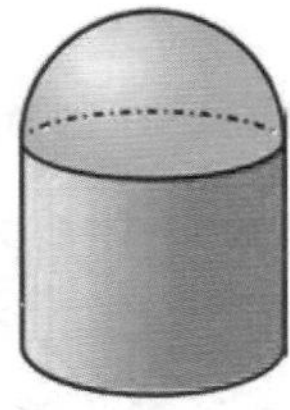

2. d

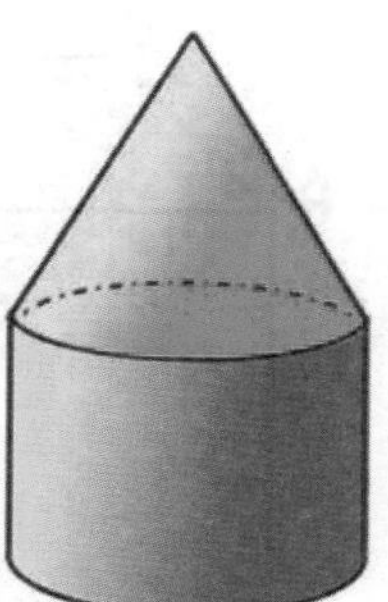

e

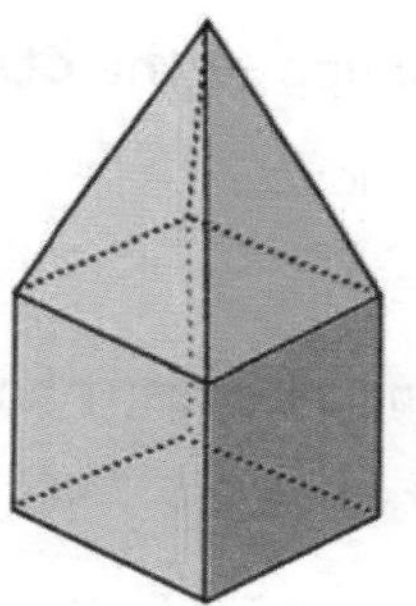

f

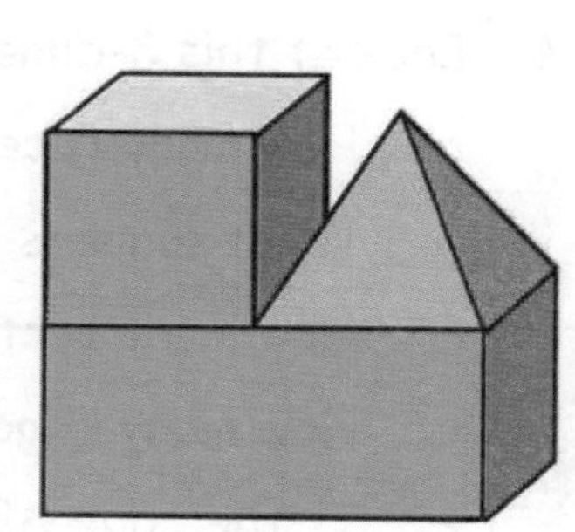

3. Which 3-dimensional shapes will you get if you cut out these shapes and fold them ?

a

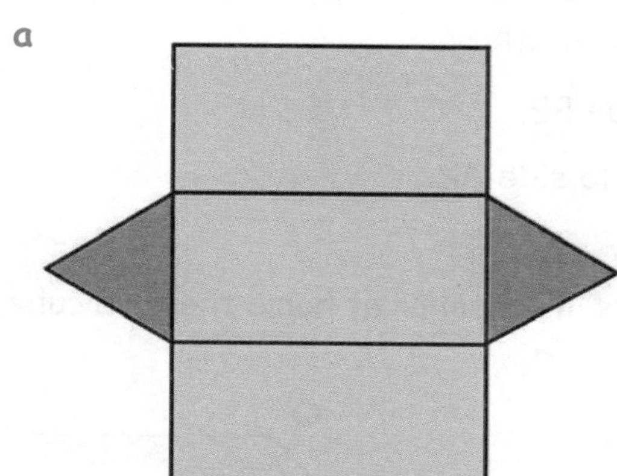

b

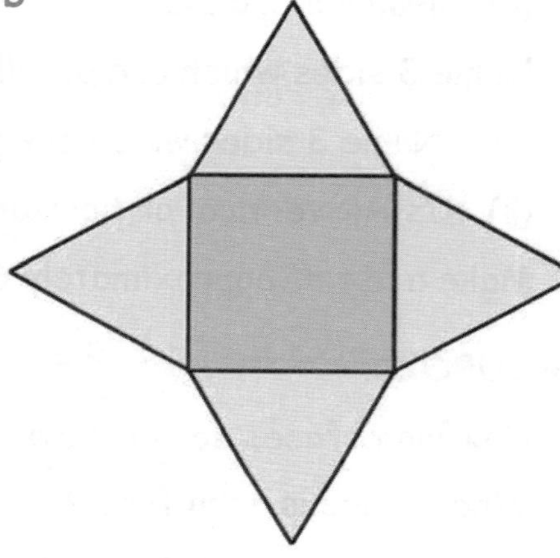

c

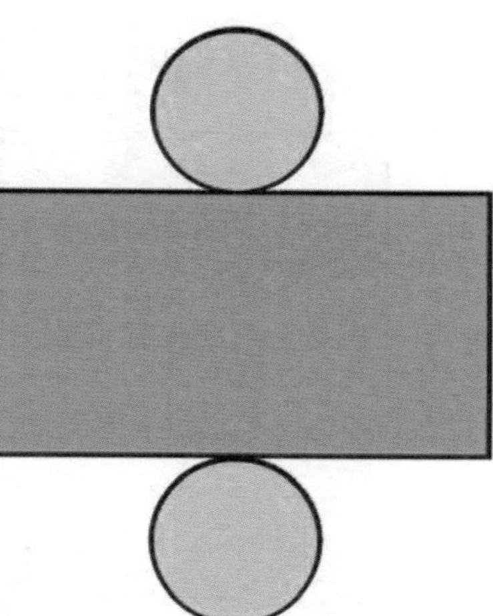

d

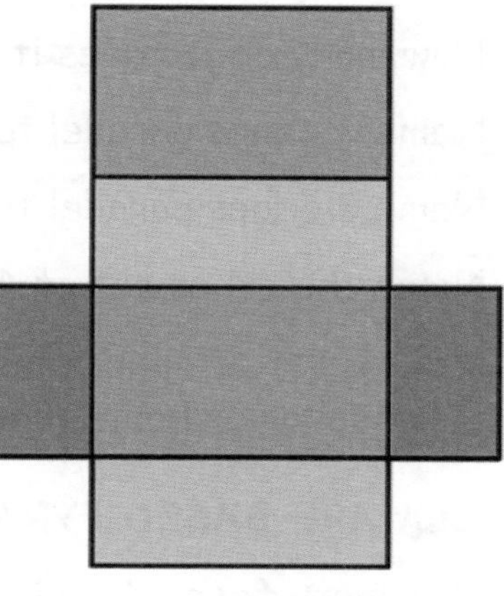

e

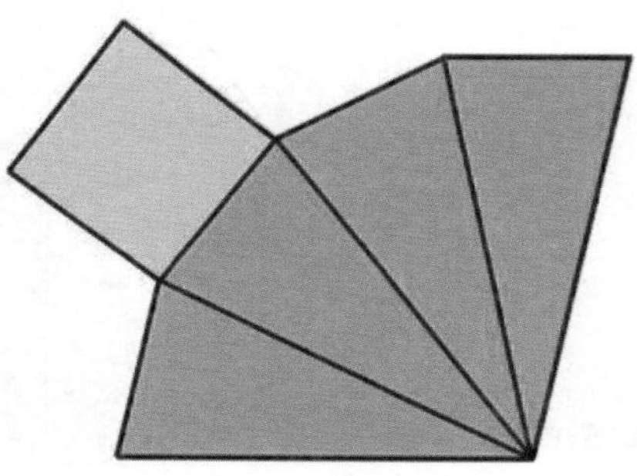

f

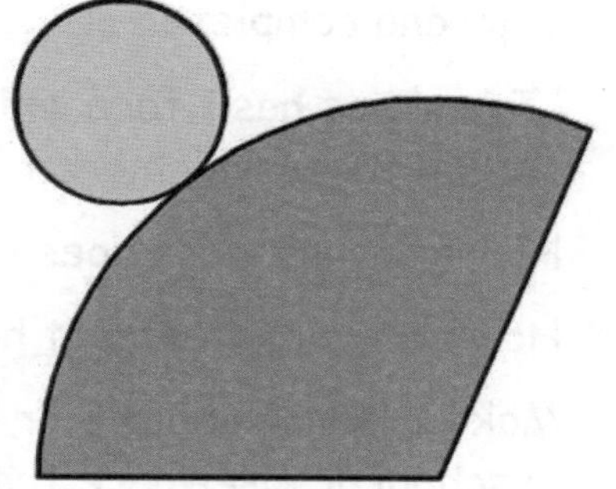

4. Look at this 3-dimensional shape — the CUBE.

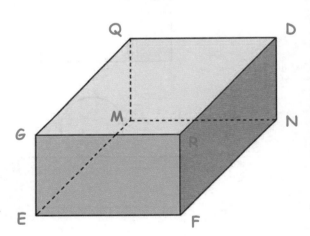

   a How many faces does it have ?

   b What shape is each face ?

   c How many vertices (*corners*) does it have ?

   d How many edges does it have ?

   e Is the edge AB lying "horizontal" or "vertical" ?

   f NE is parallel to AB (*runs in the same direction*).

      (i) Use 2 letters to name another side which is parallel to AB.

      (ii) Name a 3rd side which is parallel to AB.

   g Name 3 sides which are parallel to side BE.

   h (i) Name 3 sides which are parallel to side AR.

      (ii) Is AR vertical or horizontal ?

   i Make a list of approximately 6 objects in school or at home that are cubes.

5. The CUBOID.

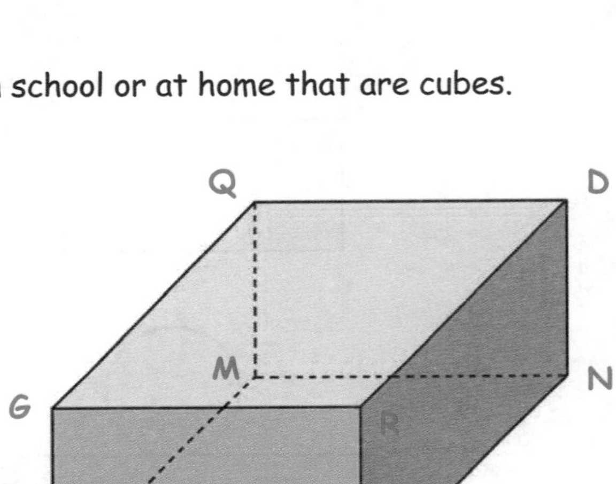

   a How many faces does it have ?

   b What shape is each face ?

   c How many vertices does it have ?

   d How many edges does it have ?

   e Name 3 edges parallel to edge EF.

   f Name 3 edges parallel to edge EG.

   g Name the other set of 4 parallel edges.

   h Make a list of approximately 6 objects in school or at home that are cuboids.

6. The SQUARE BASED PYRAMID.

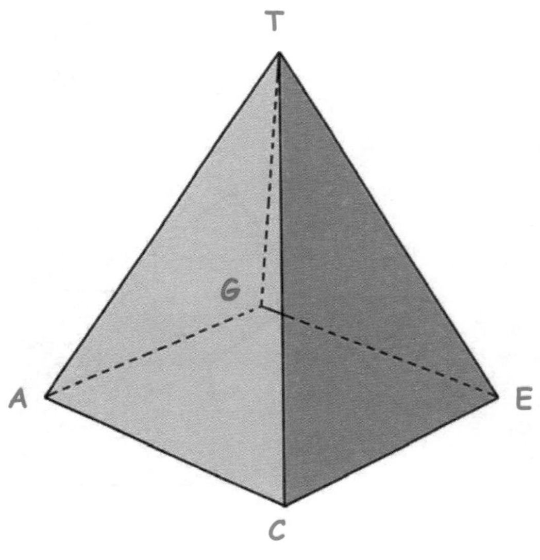

   a How many faces does it have ?

   b Copy and complete :-

      "The shape has 1 face which is a s.............
      and 4 faces which are t...........".

   c How many vertices does it have ?

   d How many edges does it have ?

   e Make a list of about 3 or 4 objects in school or elsewhere that are in the shape of square based pyramids.

7. The TRIANGULAR PRISM.

a How many faces does it have ?

b Copy and complete :-

"It has 2 faces which are .... and .... faces which are ....".

c How many vertices does it have ?

d Name another edge (use 2 letters) parallel to AB.

e Name 2 edges parallel to MN.

f How many edges does it have altogether ?

g Make a list of about 2 or 3 objects in school or elsewhere that are in the shape of triangular prisms.

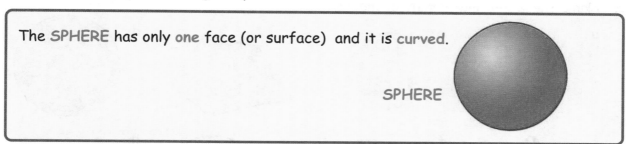

The SPHERE has only one face (or surface) and it is curved.

SPHERE

8. In a similar way, describe the faces (or surfaces) of :-

a

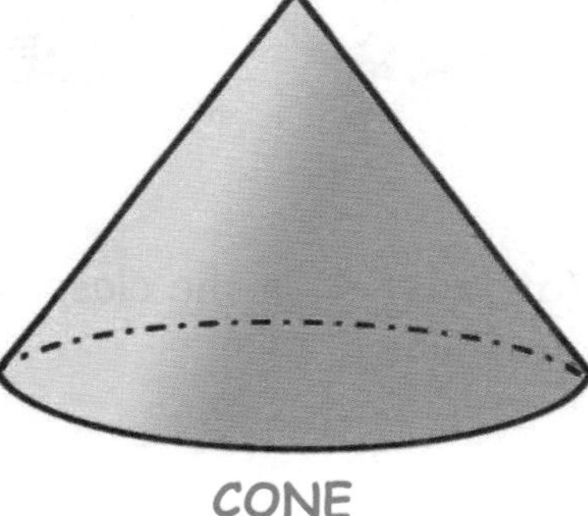

CONE

b

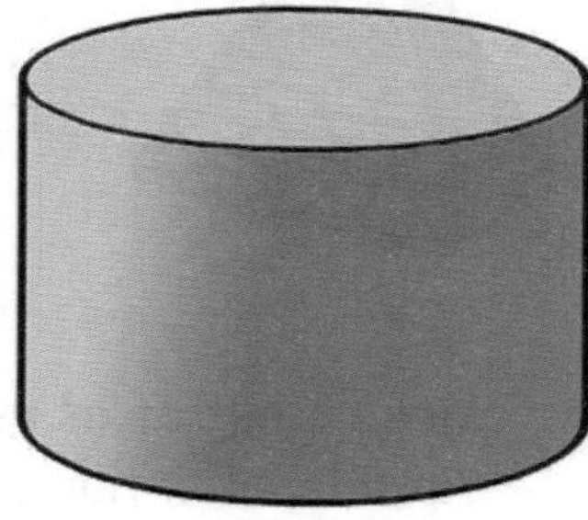

CYLINDER

9. Write down the special name for this shape.

10. Which mathematical 3-D shapes can you see below ?

a

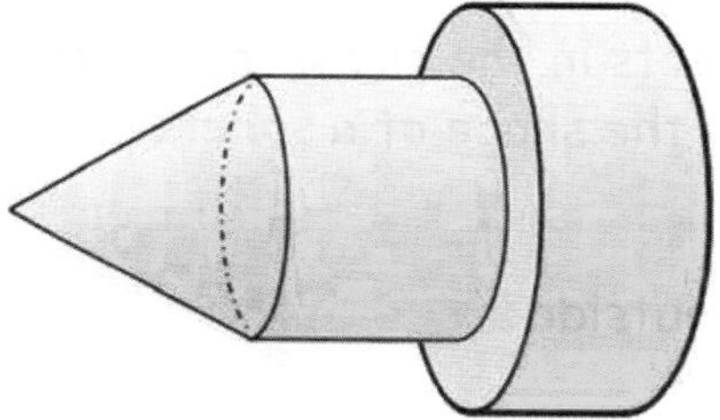

b

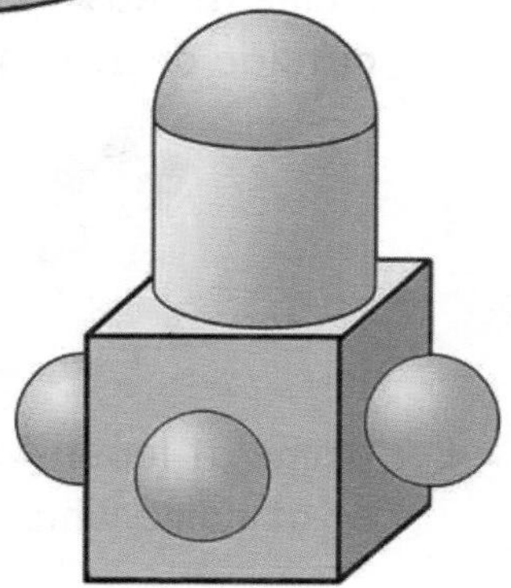

3-D Shapes in the Real World

Be able to recognise 3-D shapes as you look around.

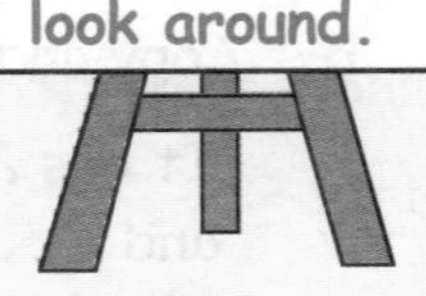

Wherever you go, wherever you are - look around.

3-D shapes are all around us !

cuboid & triangular prism

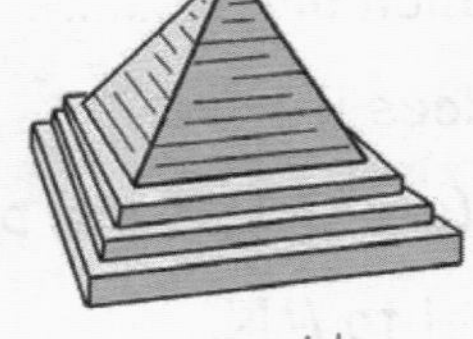

pyramid

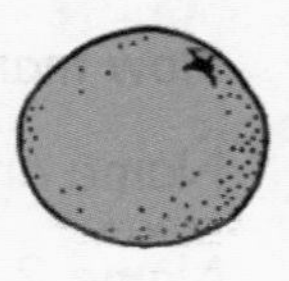

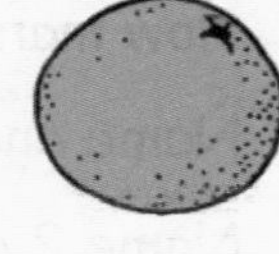

sphere

Exercise 2

1. Name these 3-D mathematical shapes :-

a 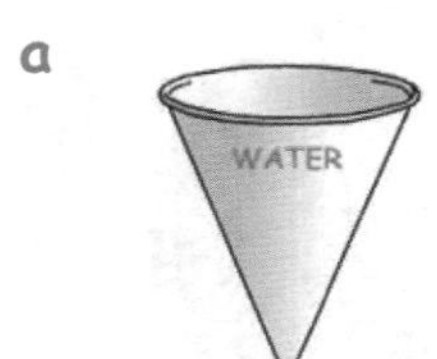

b 

c 

d 

e 

f 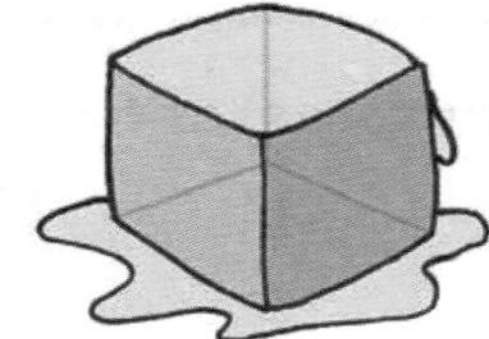

g 

h 

2. a Make a list of as many objects as you can (at least 4) in the classroom, outside or at home which are in the shape of a cube.

b 

Name at least 4 objects in the classroom, outside or at home which are in the shape of a cuboid.

c Name at least 4 objects in the classroom, outside or at home which are in the shape of a cylinder.

d 

Name at least 4 objects in the classroom, outside or at home which are in the shape of a sphere.

e Name at least 4 objects in the classroom, outside or at home which are in the shape of a cone.

Polygons - Regular or Irregular ?

Be able to name and draw regular and irregular polygons.

In Year 4, you learned that a POLYGON is a two dimensional shape with straight sides.

It is REGULAR if all sides and angles are equal.

Otherwise it is IRREGULAR.

Example :- Here are two shapes, each with 4 sides.

This one is a REGULAR polygon.

It is called a square.

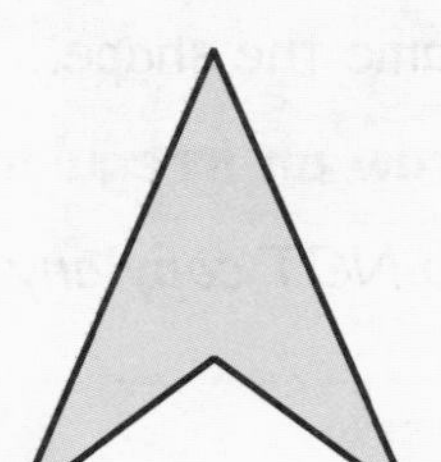

This one does not have its sides or angles equal.

It is an IRREGULAR 4 sided polygon.

Exercise 3

1. Which of these polygons are regular ? Write YES or NO.

a

b
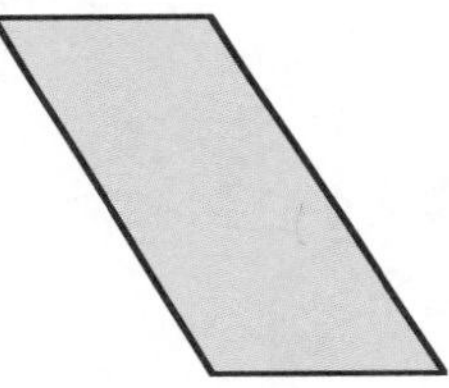

c
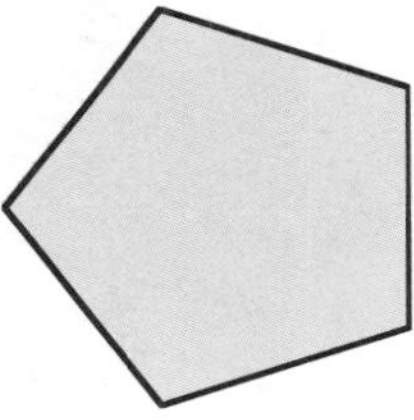

d
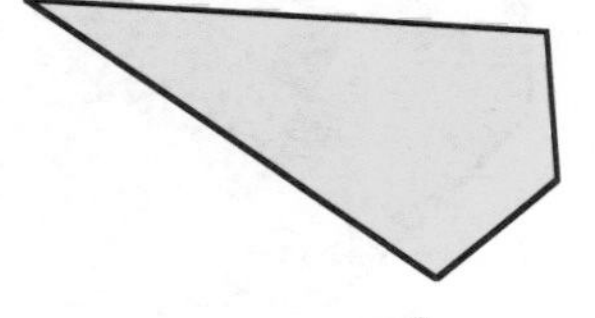

e
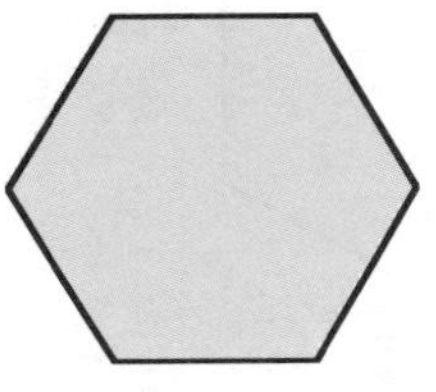

f
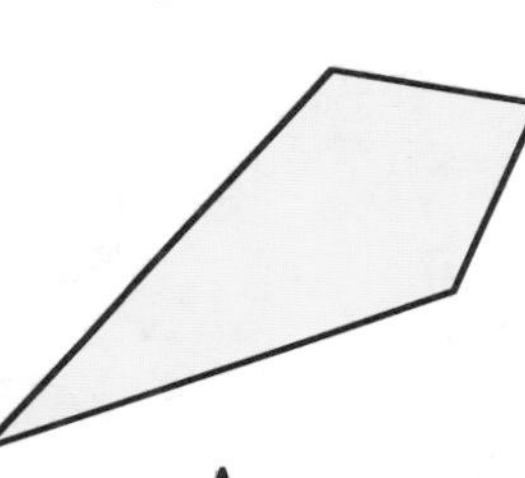

g
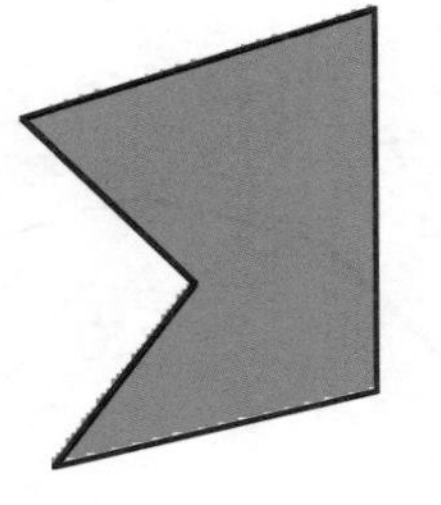

h
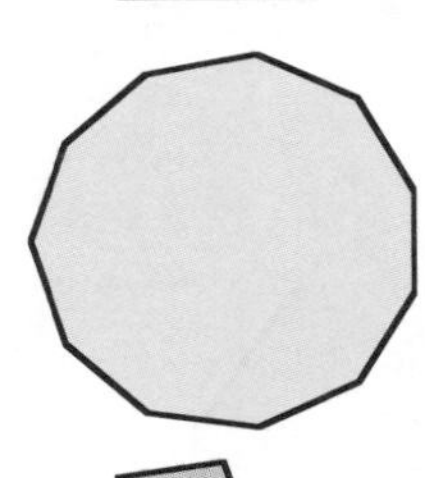

i

j

k
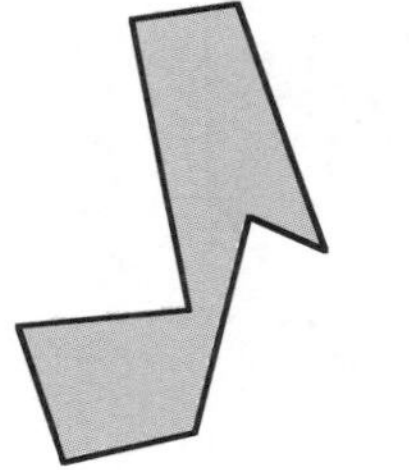

l

2. How many sides do each of these polygons have :-

a pentagon b hexagon c octagon

d nonagon e decagon f dodecagon ?

3. For each of the regular polygons shown below :-

(i) Name the shape.

(ii) Draw an irregular polygon with the same number of sides.

Do NOT copy any of the shapes from Question 1.

a

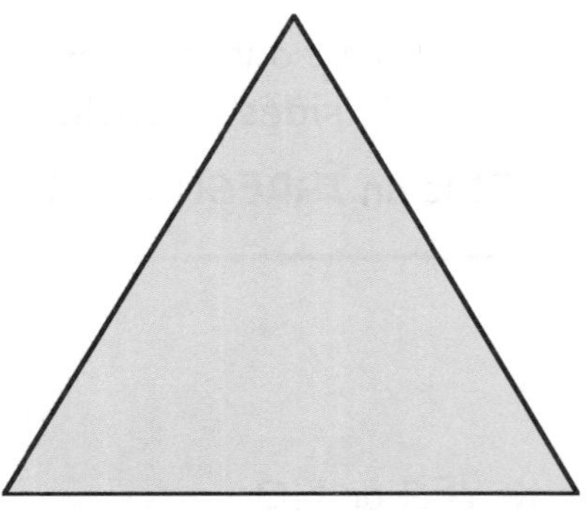

b

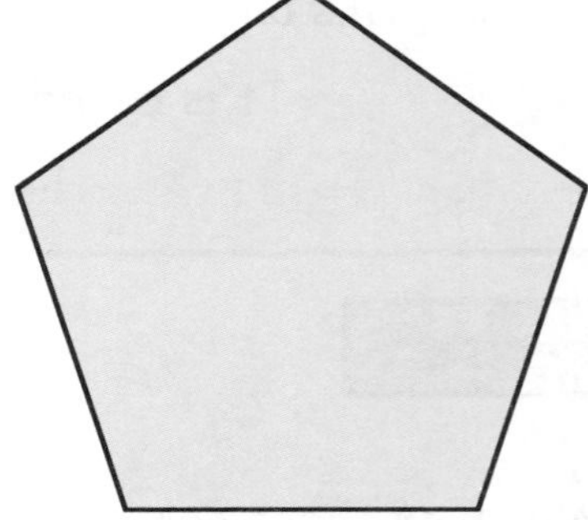

c

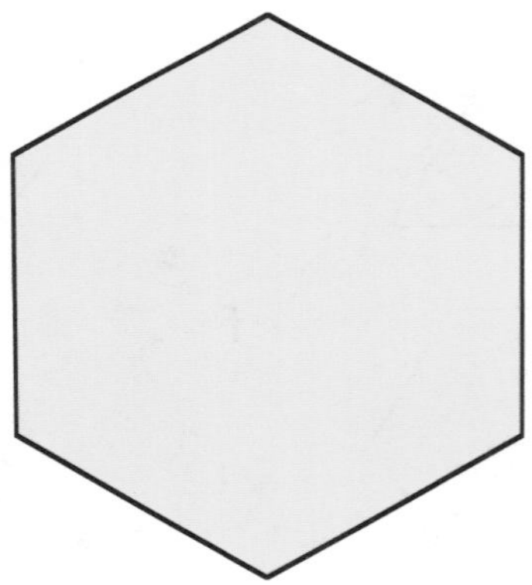

d

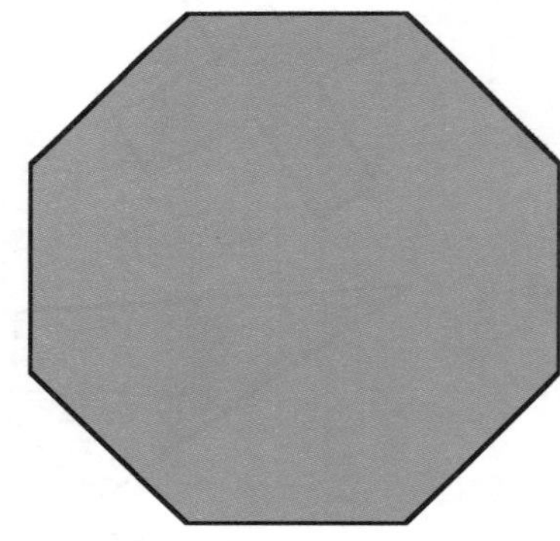

e

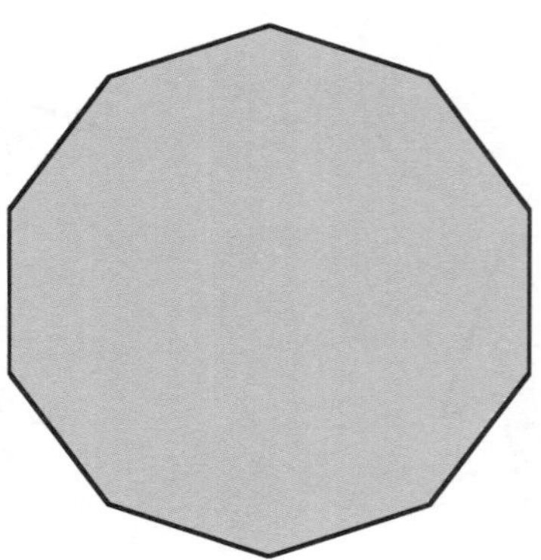

f

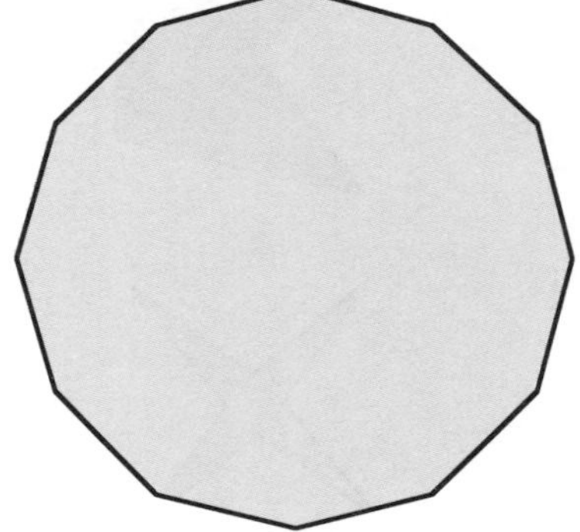

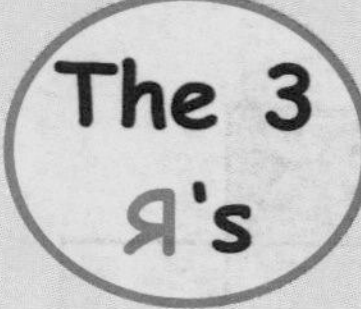

Revisit - Review - Revise

1. Name the 3 dimensional **mathematical** shapes shown below:-

a 

b 

c 

d 

e 

f 

g 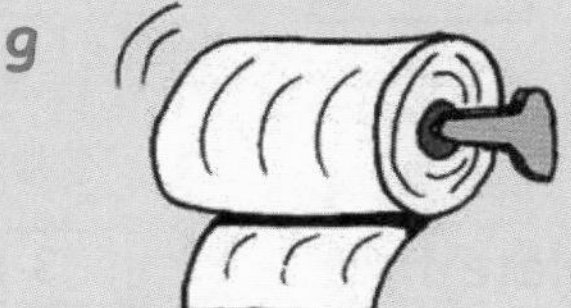

h 

2. The two objects shown below are made up of more than one **3-D** shape.

List the shapes :-

a 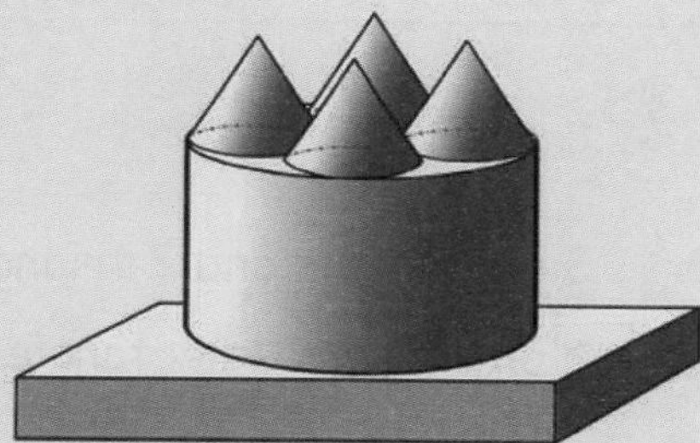

b 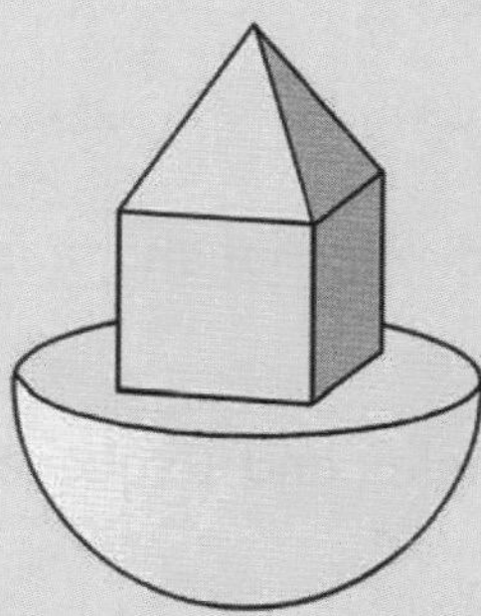

3. This shape is called a **HEXAGONAL** based **PYRAMID**.

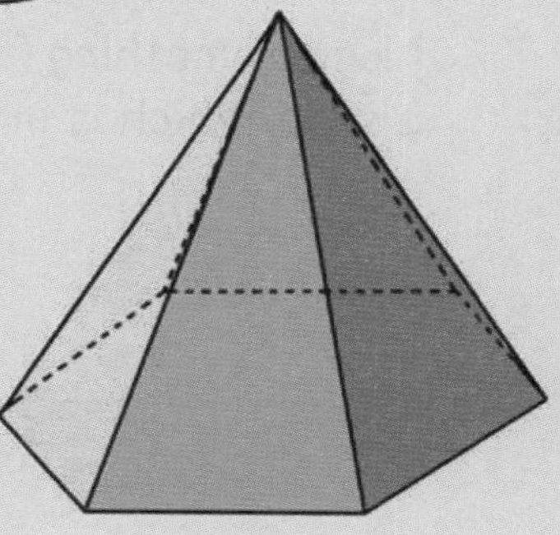

a How many vertices does it have ?

b How many edges does it have ?

c Copy and complete this sentence :-

"This pyramid consists of .... **faces**, one of them being a .... and the others are ....".

4. Which 3 dimensional figure do you get when you cut out each shape and fold it ?

a 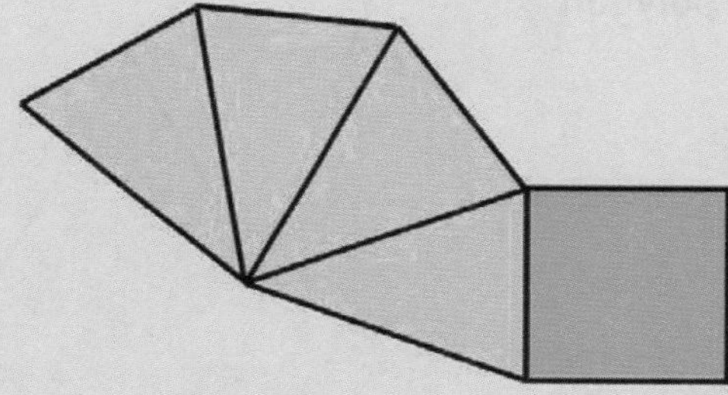

b 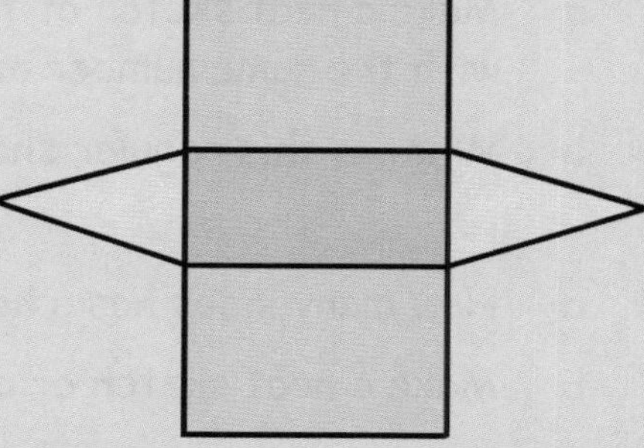

4. c

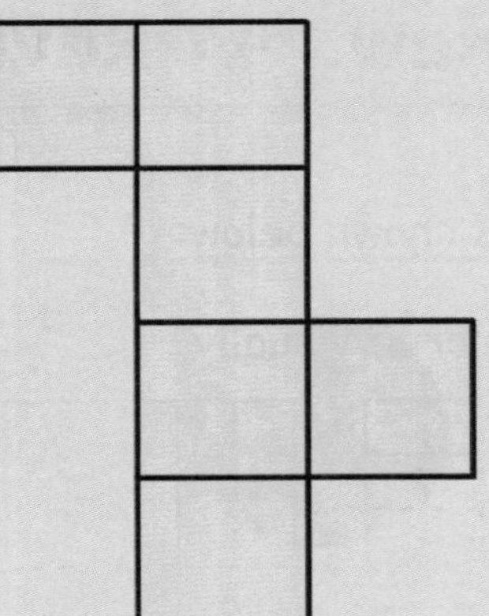

d

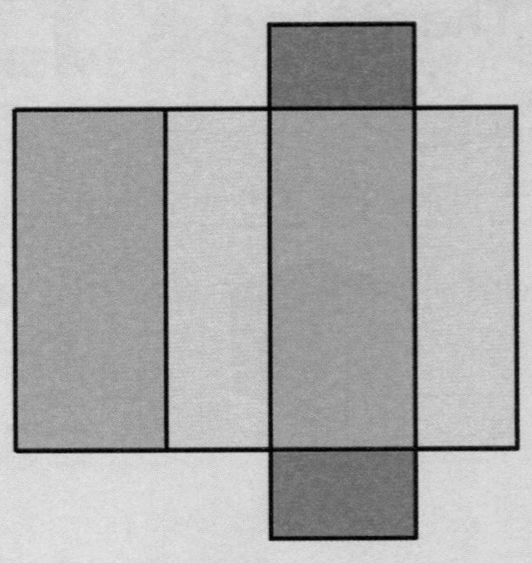

5. **Copy** and complete the table to show the number of edges, faces and vertices which some 3-dimensional shapes have.

3-D Shape	No. Edges	No. Faces	No. Vertices
cube		6	
cuboid			
cone			
cylinder			
Δ prism			
Sq. pyramid			5

6. What **3 dimensional** shape is made from :-

   a 6 squares
   b 3 rectangles and 2 triangles
   c 4 triangles and 1 square
   d 2 circles and 1 rectangle ?

7. Name something (*other than a well known bar of chocolate*), that can be bought in a shop, which is in the shape of a **triangular prism**.

8.

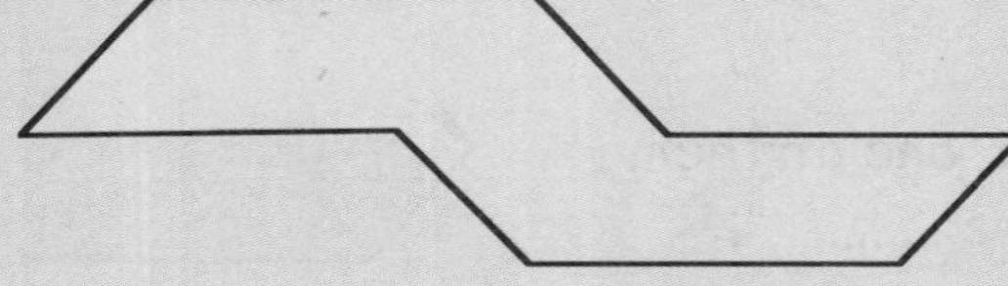

   a Is this polygon **regular** ?
   b Give 2 reasons for your answer.

9. Shown is a sketch of an **irregular polygon**.

   a Make a neat sketch of the regular polygon with the same number of sides.
   b What is this regular shape called ?

10. a How many sides has a **heptagon** ?

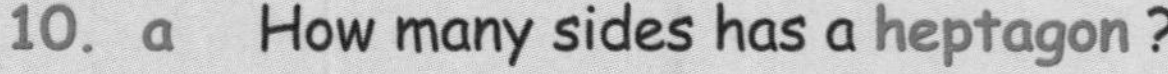

   b Make a neat sketch of a **regular heptagon**.

13/1/21

Chapter 11

Fractions 1

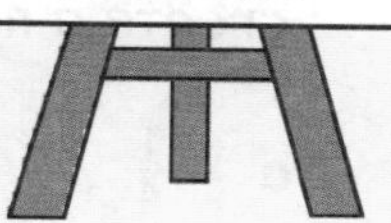

Be able to identify or produce an equivalent fraction.

Equivalent Fractions

Remember :- Equivalent fractions can be compared visually.

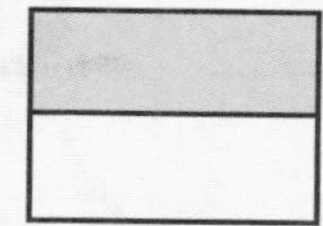
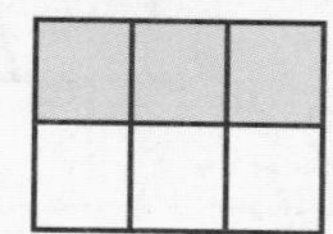
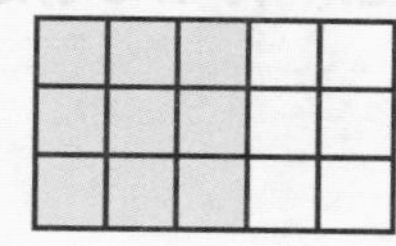
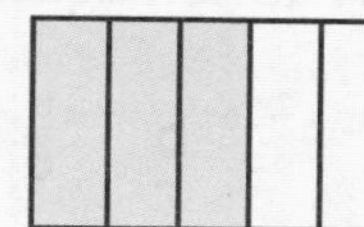

$\frac{1}{2}$ is the same as $\frac{3}{6}$. $\frac{9}{15} = \frac{3}{5}$.

You can also obtain an equivalent fraction by multiplying or dividing the numerator (*top*) and the denominator (*bottom*) of the fraction by the same number.

Examples :-

$\frac{3}{5}$ can become $\frac{3 \times 2}{5 \times 2} = \frac{6}{10}$

$\frac{12}{15}$ simplified is $\frac{12 \div 3}{15 \div 3} = \frac{4}{5}$

Exercise 1

1. Identify each pair of equivalent fractions from the diagrams shown :-

a
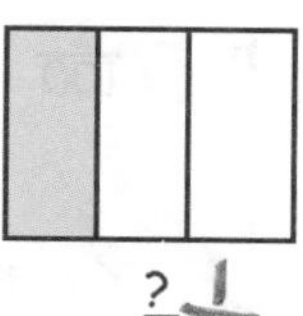
$\frac{?}{?}$ $\frac{1}{3}$ $\frac{?}{9}$ 3

b
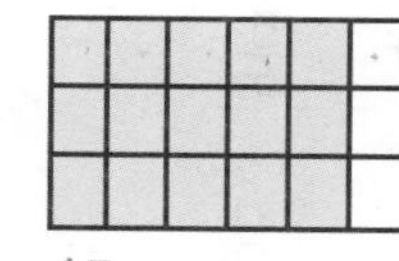
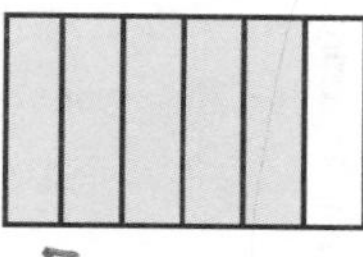
$\frac{15}{18}$ $\frac{5}{6}$

c
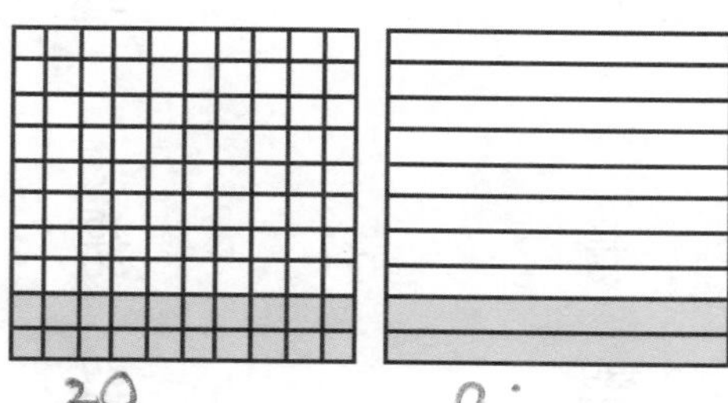
$\frac{20}{100}$ $\frac{2}{10}$

d
$\frac{90}{100}$ $\frac{9}{10}$

e
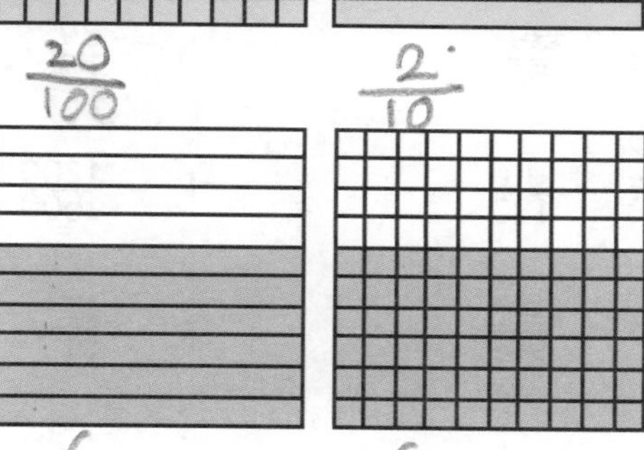
$\frac{6}{10}$ $\frac{60}{100}$

f
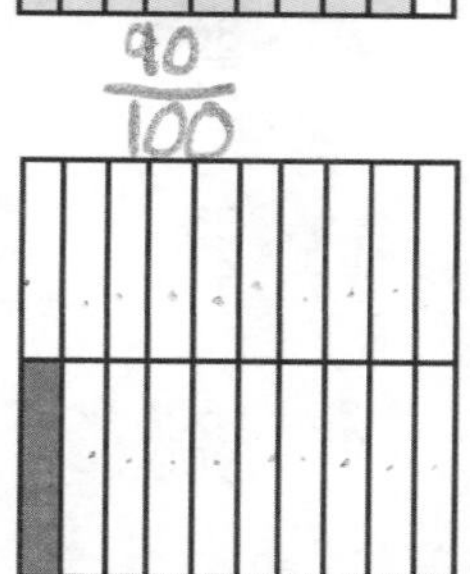
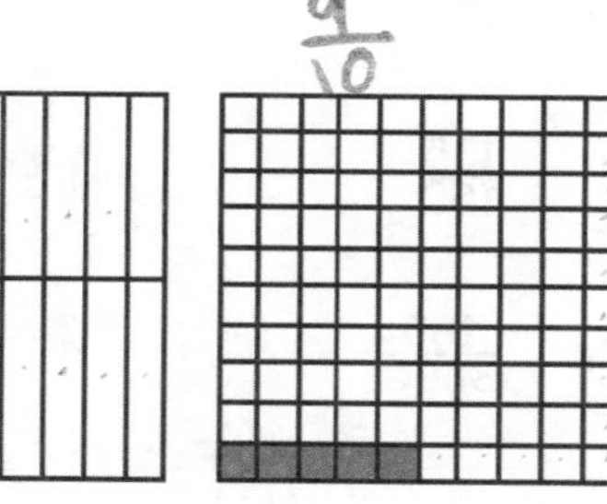

$\frac{1}{20}$ $\frac{5}{100}$

2. Multiply the top and bottom of each fraction by 2 to create a new fraction equivalent to the one given :-

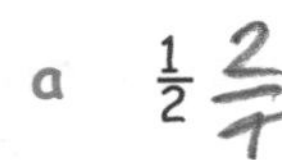

a $\frac{1}{2}$ b $\frac{2}{5}$ c $\frac{3}{7}$

3. 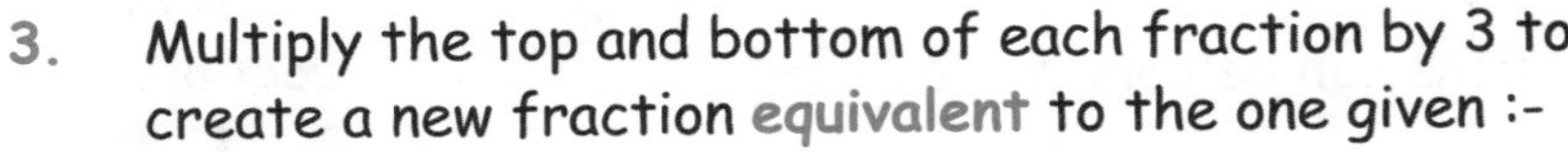Multiply the top and bottom of each fraction by 3 to create a new fraction equivalent to the one given :-

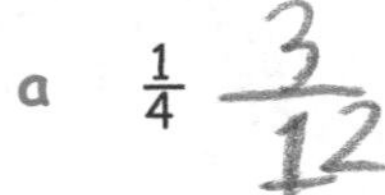

a $\frac{1}{4}$ b $\frac{5}{6}$ c $\frac{3}{8}$

4. 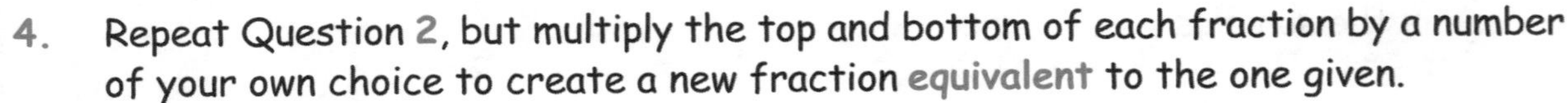Repeat Question 2, but multiply the top and bottom of each fraction by a number of your own choice to create a new fraction equivalent to the one given.

5. Divide the top line and bottom line of each fraction by 2, to simplify each one :-

a $\frac{6}{8}$ b $\frac{2}{12}$ c $\frac{10}{14}$ d $\frac{6}{16}$

6. Divide the top line and bottom line of each fraction by 3, to simplify each one :-

a $\frac{3}{6}$ b $\frac{6}{9}$ c $\frac{9}{12}$ d $\frac{9}{15}$

7. Find two equivalent fractions for each of the following :-

a $\frac{3}{4}$ b $\frac{1}{2}$ c $\frac{1}{3}$ d $\frac{2}{3}$

e $\frac{2}{5}$ f $\frac{5}{6}$ g $\frac{3}{10}$ h $\frac{1}{100}$

i $\frac{7}{9}$ j $\frac{11}{20}$ k $\frac{7}{15}$ l $\frac{9}{25}$

m $\frac{19}{21}$ n $\frac{1}{37}$ o $\frac{111}{157}$ p $\frac{7}{5}$.

8. Simplify fully (where possible) :-

a $\frac{6}{10}$ b $\frac{16}{18}$ c $\frac{12}{15}$ d $\frac{15}{30}$

e $\frac{18}{24}$ f $\frac{36}{72}$ g $\frac{39}{52}$ h $\frac{39}{51}$

i $\frac{135}{150}$ j $\frac{35}{42}$ k $\frac{13}{130}$ l $\frac{1200}{1500}$

m $\frac{180}{3600}$ n $\frac{60}{900}$ o $\frac{108}{909}$ p $\frac{17}{51}$.

Comparing Fractions

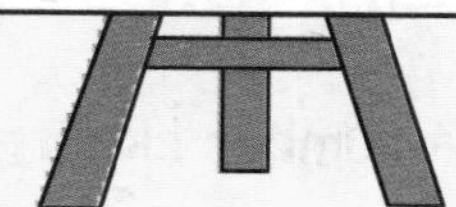

Be able to compare fractions with different denominators.

To decide which is the larger of two fractions, you sometimes need to change one or more of the fractions to an equivalent fraction, (*so that the denominators are equal*).

Example 1 :-

Which is larger $\frac{1}{2}$ or $\frac{3}{8}$?

If we change $\frac{1}{2}$ to $\frac{4}{8}$ we can easily compare the two fractions.

$\frac{4}{8} > \frac{3}{8}$ which means $\frac{1}{2} > \frac{3}{8}$.

Example 2 :-

Write these in order (*smallest first*) :-

$\frac{3}{4}$, $\frac{5}{8}$, $\frac{1}{2}$

Change all to eighths

$\frac{3}{4} = \frac{6}{8}$, $\frac{5}{8}$, $\frac{1}{2} = \frac{4}{8}$

answer $\frac{1}{2}$, $\frac{5}{8}$, $\frac{3}{4}$.

Remember :-

$>$ means greater than.
$<$ means smaller than.

Exercise 2

1. Use $<$, $>$ or $=$ to fill in the missing symbol between each pair of fractions :-

a $\frac{1}{2} \dots \frac{3}{4}$ b $\frac{4}{5} \dots \frac{3}{10}$ c $\frac{3}{4} \dots \frac{8}{12}$ d $\frac{4}{9} \dots \frac{2}{3}$

e $\frac{4}{5} \dots \frac{11}{15}$ f $\frac{8}{10} \dots \frac{17}{20}$ g $\frac{12}{18} \dots \frac{2}{3}$ h $\frac{5}{6} \dots \frac{17}{18}$.

2. Write each set of fractions in order (starting with the smallest) :-

a $\frac{1}{2}$, $\frac{5}{12}$, $\frac{2}{3}$ b $\frac{5}{9}$, $\frac{2}{3}$, $\frac{13}{18}$

c $\frac{5}{6}$, $\frac{11}{12}$, $\frac{3}{4}$, $\frac{2}{3}$ d $\frac{17}{20}$, $\frac{9}{10}$, $\frac{3}{4}$, $\frac{3}{5}$

e $\frac{3}{8}$, $\frac{1}{2}$, $\frac{11}{16}$, $\frac{3}{4}$, $\frac{5}{8}$ f $\frac{3}{5}$, $\frac{1}{2}$, $\frac{13}{20}$, $\frac{7}{10}$, $\frac{3}{4}$.

3. Bill, Ben and Fred share a lottery win.

Since they had put in different amounts Bill suggests they split the money in the following way :-

Bill - $\frac{1}{4}$ Ben - $\frac{5}{12}$ Fred - $\frac{1}{2}$.

Explain why Bill must be wrong !

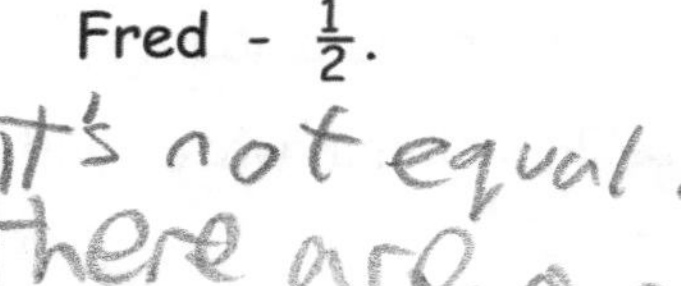

It's not equal!!!
there are onLy 3
PeoPle!

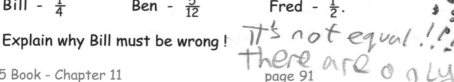

Improper Fractions and Mixed Numbers

Be able to convert between improper fractions and mixed numbers.

A fraction like $\frac{17}{3}$, where the numerator is bigger than the denominator, is called a "top-heavy" or "improper" fraction.

A number like $8\frac{2}{5}$, consisting of a "whole" part and a "fraction" part, is called a "mixed" number.

Examples :- Changing an improper fraction to a mixed number :-

1. $\frac{23}{4}$ really means $23 \div 4$ => $4\overline{)23}$ = 5 (remainder 3) => $5\frac{3}{4}$ (note :- the 3 is divided by the 4)

2. $\frac{25}{7}$ really means $25 \div 7$ => $7\overline{)25}$ = 3 (remainder 4) => $3\frac{4}{7}$ (note :- the 4 is divided by the 7)

Exercise 3

1. Copy and complete the following :-

   a $\frac{17}{2}$ really means $17 \div 2$ => $2\overline{)17}$ (remainder ....) => $8\frac{...}{2}$.

   b $\frac{20}{3}$ really means $20 \div 3$ => $3\overline{)20}$ (remainder ....) => $6\frac{...}{3}$.

   c $\frac{23}{6}$ really means $23 \div ...$ => $...\overline{)23}$ (remainder ....) => $...\frac{...}{6}$.

2. In a similar way, change the following improper fractions to mixed numbers :-

   a $\frac{13}{3}$ b $\frac{27}{4}$ c $\frac{38}{5}$ d $\frac{35}{6}$

   e $\frac{73}{9}$ f $\frac{65}{8}$ g $\frac{87}{10}$ h $\frac{21}{6}$.

3. a 47 kg of apples are packed evenly into 6 plastic bags.
   What weight of apples goes into each bag ?

   b Five boys decide to share 13 bars of chocolate evenly.
   What will each boy receive (as a mixed number) ?

   c 

   A large plastic container holds 25 litres of water.
   The water is poured into 4 jugs such that each holds the same amount.
   How much water will be in each jug ?

3\. d A petrol tanker holds half a million litres of fuel.
It empties this in equal amounts into 3 containers.
How many litres will be in each container ?

e A truck depot petrol pump holds 8450 litres of diesel.
7 trucks use an equal amount of diesel.
How much diesel will each truck receive, if they draw off all the fuel ?

f 
A plumber needs 137 m of pipe to use in 8 identical houses.
He also needs 90 m of plumbers tape.

(i) How much pipe is needed for each house ?

(ii) How much tape will he use for each house ?

4\. Copy and complete :- $\frac{20}{6} = 20 \div 6 = 3\frac{2}{6} = 3\frac{\dots}{3}$ (<— simplified).

5\. Change each of the following to mixed numbers and simplify where possible :-

a	$\frac{27}{6}$	b	$\frac{22}{4}$	c	$\frac{26}{8}$	d	$\frac{34}{10}$
e	$\frac{18}{4}$	f	$\frac{70}{8}$	g	$\frac{75}{30}$	h	$\frac{68}{6}$
i	$\frac{33}{9}$	j	$\frac{40}{16}$	k	$\frac{65}{20}$	l	$\frac{175}{100}$.

6\. This diagram represents $2\frac{3}{4}$ pizzas.

a How many "$\frac{1}{4}$" pizza slices do you get from 1 pizza ?

b How many "$\frac{1}{4}$" pizza slices do you get from 2 pizzas ?

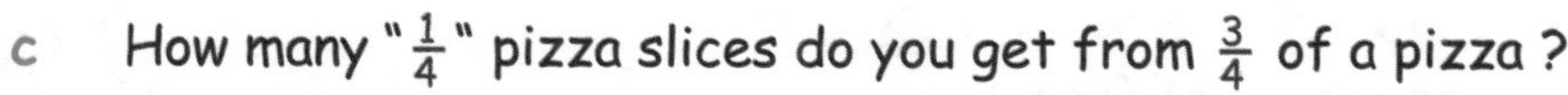

c How many "$\frac{1}{4}$" pizza slices do you get from $\frac{3}{4}$ of a pizza ?

d How many "$\frac{1}{4}$" pizza slices is this altogether from the $2\frac{3}{4}$ pizzas ?

e Write this as $2\frac{3}{4} = \frac{\dots}{4}$.

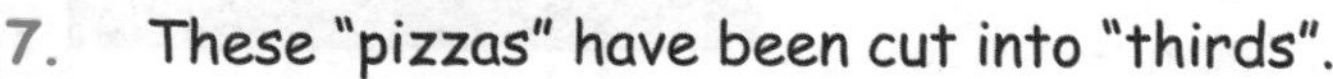

7\. These "pizzas" have been cut into "thirds".

a From the 4 whole pizzas, you get ..... thirds ?

b From the $\frac{2}{3}$ pizza, you get ..... thirds ?

c How many thirds is this altogether ?
Write this as $4\frac{2}{3} = \frac{\dots}{3}$.

Changing a **mixed number** to a **top-heavy fraction** :-

Example 1 :- Change $6\frac{2}{3}$ into "thirds"

- **Step 1** - multiply the 6 by the 3 - (The 6 becomes "18 thirds")
- **Step 2** - now add on the 2 (thirds) - (18 + 2 = "20 thirds").

$6\frac{2}{3}$ = ((6 x 3) + 2) thirds = 20 "thirds" = $\frac{20}{3}$

Example 2 :- Change $2\frac{5}{8}$ into "eighths"

$2\frac{5}{8}$ = ((2 x 8) + 5) eighths = 21 "eighths" = $\frac{21}{8}$

8. Copy and complete :-

   a $3\frac{4}{5}$ = ((3 x 5) + 4) "fifths" = 19 "fifths" = $\frac{...}{5}$.

   b $1\frac{3}{10}$ = ((1 x 10) + 3) "tenths" = 13 "tenths" = $\frac{...}{10}$.

   c $2\frac{5}{8}$ = ((2 x ...) + ...) "eighths" = ... "eighths" = $\frac{...}{...}$.

   d $10\frac{1}{9}$ = ((... x ...) + ...) "ninths" = ... "ninths" = $\frac{...}{...}$.

9. Copy and complete :-

   a $4\frac{1}{5}$ = ... b $2\frac{2}{3}$ = ... c $5\frac{2}{5}$ = ... d $2\frac{7}{10}$ = ...

10. Change each of the following mixed numbers to top heavy fractions :-

    a $1\frac{1}{2}$ b $8\frac{1}{5}$ c $6\frac{2}{3}$ d $7\frac{2}{5}$

    e $10\frac{3}{7}$ f $3\frac{8}{9}$ g $2\frac{9}{10}$ h $6\frac{19}{20}$.

11. How many $\frac{1}{2}$ pizza slices can I get from :-

    a 2 pizzas b 5 pizzas

    c $3\frac{1}{2}$ pizzas d $10\frac{1}{2}$ pizzas ?

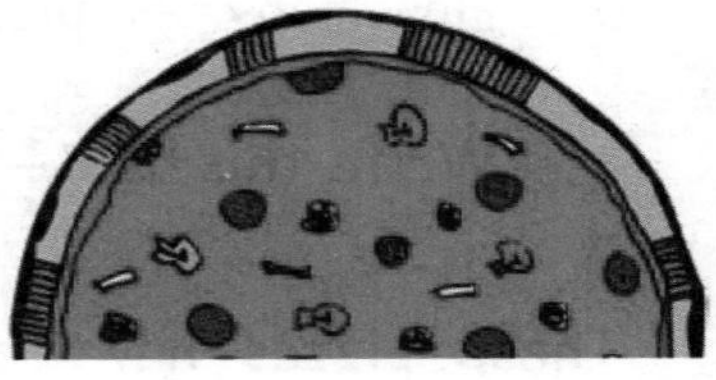

12. How many $\frac{1}{5}$ litre glasses can be filled from :-

    a 3 litres b $1\frac{1}{5}$ litres c $2\frac{2}{5}$ litres d $6\frac{4}{5}$ litres ?

13. Find :-

    a $2\frac{3}{5} + 4\frac{4}{5}$ (Hint - we could change them to "$\frac{1}{5}$'s".) b $3\frac{3}{7} + 1\frac{5}{7}$.

The 3 Я's

Revisit - Review - Revise

1. Write down the fractions indicated by each colour in the diagrams shown and simplify where possible:-

a 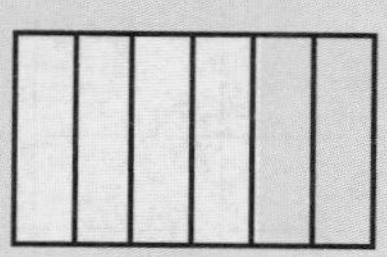

b 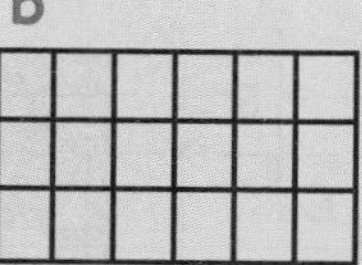

c 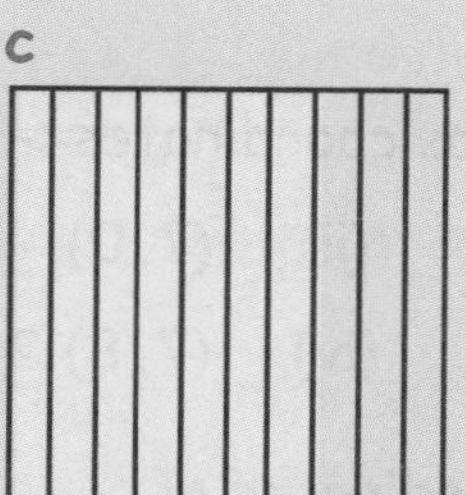

d 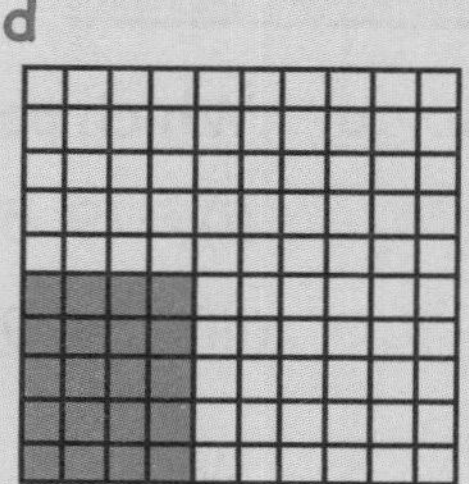

2. Write down three equivalent fractions for :-

a $\frac{1}{4}$ b $\frac{2}{3}$ c $\frac{4}{7}$ d $\frac{1}{15}$.

3. Simplify where possible :-

a $\frac{8}{18}$ b $\frac{3}{18}$ c $\frac{7}{42}$ d $\frac{17}{34}$

e $\frac{15}{65}$ f $\frac{10}{400}$ g $\frac{12}{51}$ h $\frac{11}{111}$.

4. Use $<$, and $>$ or $=$ to fill in the missing symbol between each pair of fractions :-

a $\frac{1}{2}$ ... $\frac{5}{8}$ b $\frac{3}{4}$ ... $\frac{5}{8}$ c $\frac{4}{7}$ ... $\frac{35}{49}$ d $\frac{56}{80}$ ... $\frac{7}{10}$.

5. Write each set of fractions in order (*largest first*) :-

a $\frac{1}{4}$, $\frac{1}{2}$, $\frac{3}{8}$ b $\frac{1}{4}$, $\frac{5}{16}$, $\frac{3}{8}$, $\frac{1}{2}$, $\frac{9}{32}$.

6. Change each of the following to an improper fraction :-

a $1\frac{1}{3}$ b $2\frac{3}{5}$ c $5\frac{3}{8}$ d $10\frac{9}{10}$.

7. Change each of the following to a mixed number :-

a $\frac{7}{4}$ b $\frac{14}{5}$ c $\frac{22}{3}$ d $\frac{100}{13}$.

Chapter 12 Coordinates

Coordinates Revision

Exercise 1

1\. a Which point has coordinates :-

(i) (9, 5) (ii) (7, 0)

(iii) (4, 9) (iv) (7, 8) ?

b Write the coordinates of :-

(i) E (ii) G

(iii) R (iv) P.

c When 4 of the points are joined, a rectangle is formed.

(i) Which 4 points ?

(ii) Write their coordinates.

d Which point lies on the :- (i) x-axis (ii) y-axis ?

e Name any 2 points with :-

(i) the same x-coordinate (ii) the same y-coordinate.

f Which point has the same x *and* y coordinate ?

2\. Copy the 10 by 10 coordinate grid shown below.

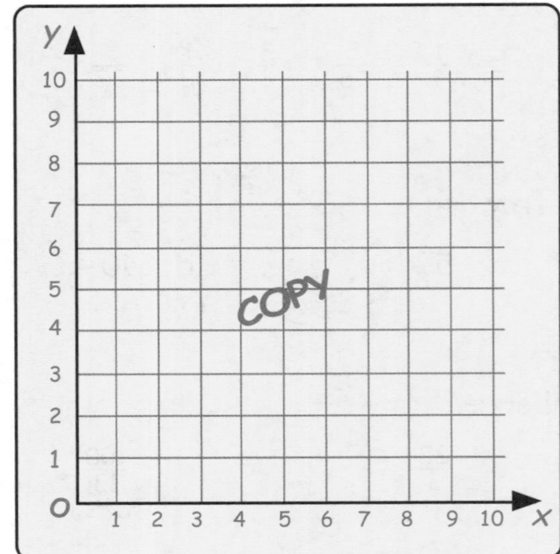

a Plot the points P(2, 7), Q(5, 8) and R(8, 3).

b S is a point to be put on the grid so that figure PQRS is a parallelogram.

On your diagram plot the point S and write down its coordinates.

c Join P to R and join Q to S.

Put a cross where these two diagonals meet and write down the coordinates of this point.

Translation

When you move a shape or a point to another position, this movement is called a translation.

Example :-

The point shown is A(1, 2).

When we translate (move) this point right 2 and up 3 the point becomes B(3, 5).

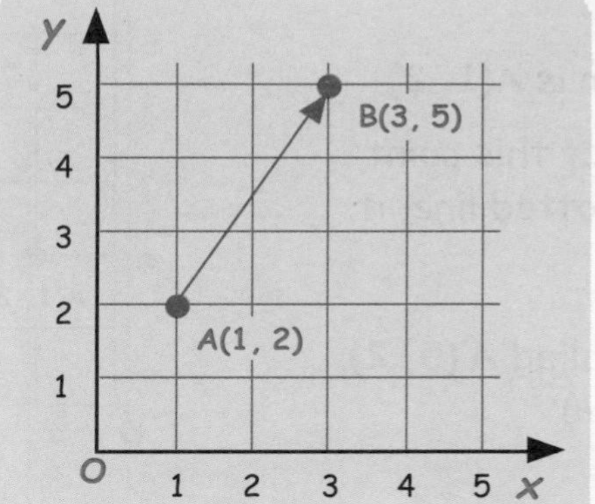

Exercise 2

1. a Copy the grid above and plot the point P(2, 1).
   b Translate this point right 2 and up 1 to a new point Q, and write down the coordinates of Q.

2. Repeat Question 1 for each of the following points :-
   a (3, 2) b (0, 1) c (0, 4) d (3, 3) e (2, 2).

3. a Draw a grid 10 by 10.
   b Plot the point (7, 2) and translate it right 2 and up 3.
   c Plot the point (3, 5) and translate it right 1 and down 3.
   d Plot the point (5, 5) and translate it left 3 and down 1.

4. Describe each translation using left/right and up/down :-
   a (1, 3) moved to (4, 4) b (0, 6) moved to (7, 2)
   c (6, 1) moved to (4, 5) d (8, 11) moved to the origin.

5. a Draw a 10 by 10 grid.
   b Draw the square A(4, 6), B(4, 8), C(6, 8) and D(6, 6).
   c Translate this square left 3 and down 2, (*moving it one point at a time*), and write down the coordinates of the vertices of the new square.

6. Try your own shapes and translations. Test your friend !

Reflection

Be able to reflect a point or a shape over a line.

In symmetry, you learned to reflect a shape or image over a line.
We can do the same with a point or shape on a coordinate grid.

Example :-

The point shown is A(1, 2).

When we reflect this point over the blue dotted line, it becomes (5, 2).

This image is called A′(5, 2).
(*pronounced A dash*)

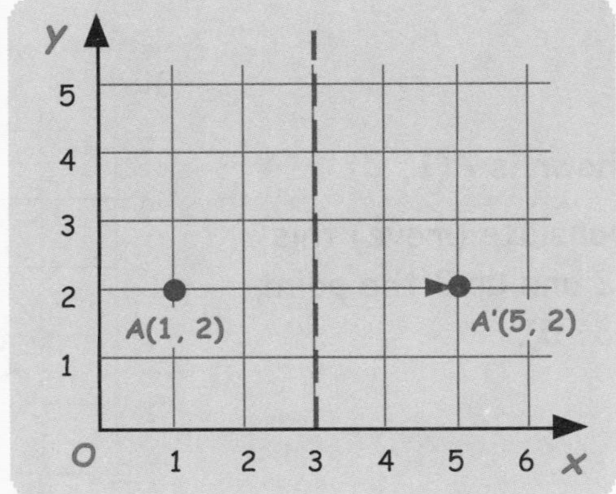

Exercise 3

1. a Copy the diagram shown.
   b Reflect the point A to show its image A′.
   c Reflect the point B to show its image B′.
   d Plot the point C(1, 5).
   e Plot the image of C.
   f Plot the image of D, where D(2, 0).
   g Plot E′ where E(4, 2).
   h In each case write down the coordinates of the new points A′, B′, C′, D′ and E′.

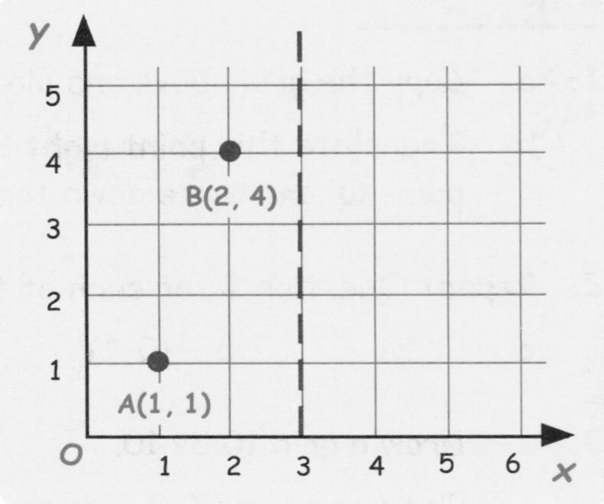

2. 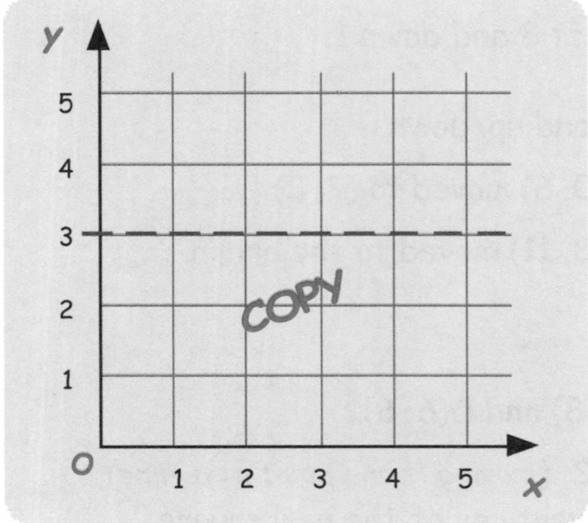

   a Copy the diagram shown.
   b Plot each of these points :-
   A(1, 2), B(4, 1), C(2, 2), D(5, 5).
   c Show A′, B′, C, and D′
   (*the images of A, B, C and D, when reflected over the blue dotted line*).
   d Write down the coordinates of the images of each of these points, when they are reflected over the blue dotted line :-
   (i) E(1, 0), (ii) F(4, 3)
   (iii) G(6, 6) (iv) H(10, 4).

3. a Copy the diagram shown.

   b Plot the six points A(2, 4), B(9, 1), C(5, 3), D(3, 7), E(10, 0) and F(0, 10).

   c Plot the images of these 6 points when they are reflected over the dotted line. (*A′, B′, C′, D′, E′ and F′*). State coordinates.

   d Write down the coordinates of any point (G) that, when reflected over the line, would produce its own image. (*ie G = G′*).

   e Given that H′(4, 3), write down the coordinates of the original point H.

   f Given that I′(8, 6), write down the coordinates of the original point I.

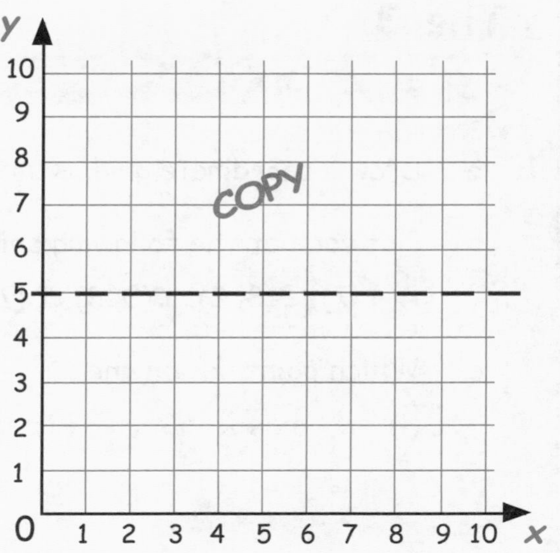

4. a Draw a 10 by 10 grid.

   b Draw a **vertical** dotted line (*parallel to the y-axis*) along the 6 line.

   c Plot the points J(1, 3), K(5, 5), L(9, 7), M(3, 0) and N(6, 9).

   d Show the images of J, K, L, M, and N and write down their coordinates.

5. a Copy the diagram from Question 3.

   b Plot the vertices (corners) of the square A(5, 7), B(5, 9), C(7, 9) and D.

   c Write down the coordinates of the missing vertex (*corner*) D.

   d Show the image of this square reflected over the **blue** dotted line. (*A′, B′, C′, D′*).

6. a Draw a 10 by 10 grid with a **horizontal** dotted line (*parallel to the x-axis*) through the point with coordinates (0, 4).

   b Plot the points P(1, 2), Q(3, 4), R(9, 2) and S(3, 0).

   c State the shape created when P, Q, R and S are joined up.

   d Show the image of PQRS after being reflected over the dotted line

   e Plot the point T, where the diagonals of shape PQRS intersect.

   f Write down the coordinates of T′.

7. Describe where the dotted line of reflection would be each time, given :-

   a T(4, 1) reflects to T′(4, 7)

   b U(9, 3) reflects to U′(9, 7)

   c V(4, 0) reflects to V′(4, 6)

   d W(0, 4) reflects to W′(10, 4).

8. When a figure is reflected or translated, apart from being moved, does the shape of the figure change in any other way ?

The 3 Я's

Revisit - Review - Revise

1. a Draw a coordinate grid as shown.

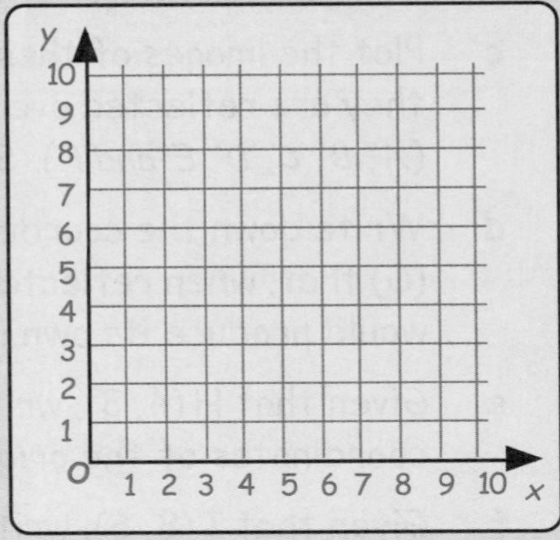

   b Plot each of the following points on your grid :-

   A(4, 7), B(3, 2), C(0, 8), D(7, 0), E(9,9).

   c Which point lies on the :-

   (i) *x* - axis (ii) *y* - axis ?

2. a Draw another coordinate grid similar to that in Question 1.

   b Plot each of the following 4 points and list the coordinates of the 4 new points found after each is given a translation of two right and three down :-

   F(5, 7), G(1, 3), H(10, 4), I(5, 5).

3. Without drawing a diagram, state the coordinates of the new point when :-

   a R(5, 4) is translated right 3 and up 2

   b S(9, 0) is translated left nine and up 1.

4. Describe the translations needed to take the first point to the second :-

   a M(5, 1) -> N(6, 3) b W(7, 6) -> U(0, 3).

5. a Copy the diagram shown.

   b Plot these 4 points on your diagram :-

   K(2, 6), L(9, 5), M(7, 10) and N(0, 3).

   c Plot and write down the coordinates of K', L', M' and N' after K, L, M and N are reflected over the blue dotted line.

6. Describe where each dotted line of reflection must be, given that the first point ends up at the second point :-

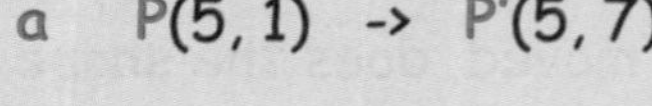

   a P(5, 1) -> P'(5, 7) b Q(6, 3) -> Q'(8, 3).

Chapter 13

Percentages

What is a Percentage ?

Understand what a percentage is and the connection between percentages, decimals and fractions.

When a shape is divided into 100 equal "pieces", each piece is called "1 percent".

We use the symbol " % " for percent.

This square has 38 bits out of 100 coloured **purple**.

This is written as 38%.

There are 6 bits out of a hundred coloured red.

This is written as 6%.

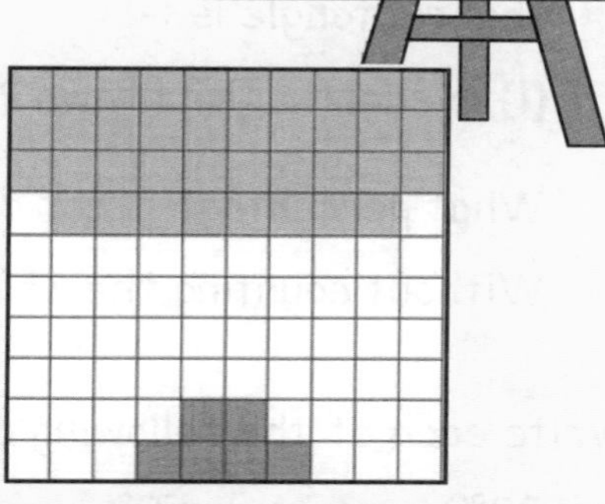

38% means $38 \div 100 = \frac{38}{100} = 0 \cdot 38$

6% means $6 \div 100 = \frac{6}{100} = 0 \cdot 06$

Exercise 1

1. Each of these squares has been divided into 100 bits.

Write down what each coloured section is, as a percentage of the square :-

a

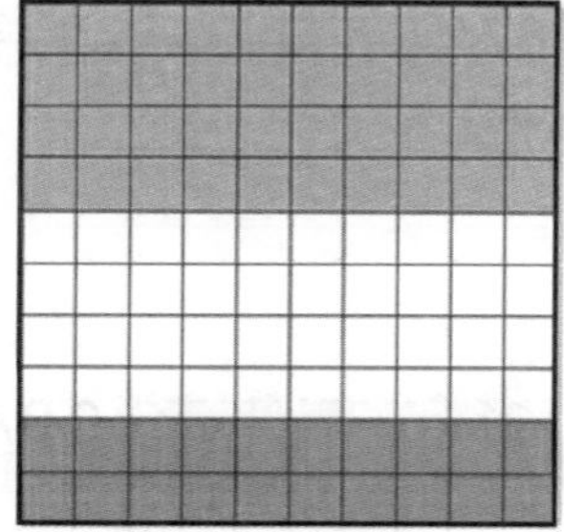

Blue : **40%**

Red : ...%

b

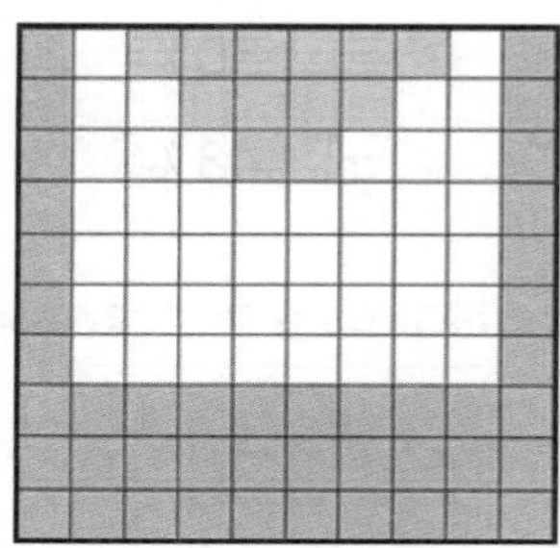

Pink : ...%

Green : ...%

c

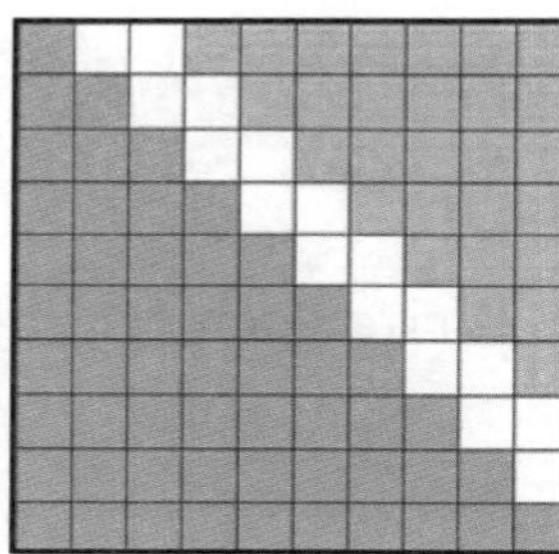

d

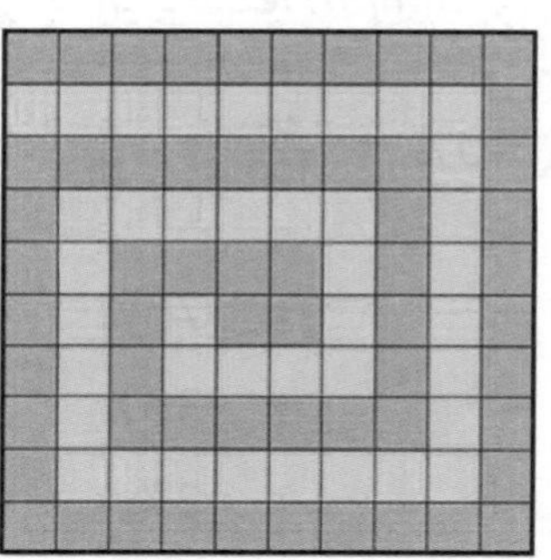

e

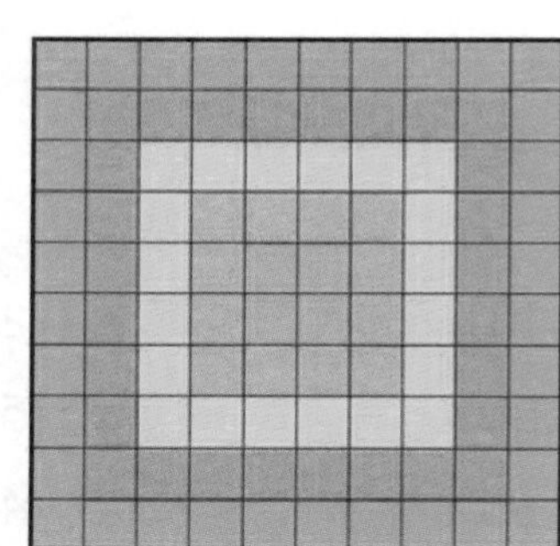

f

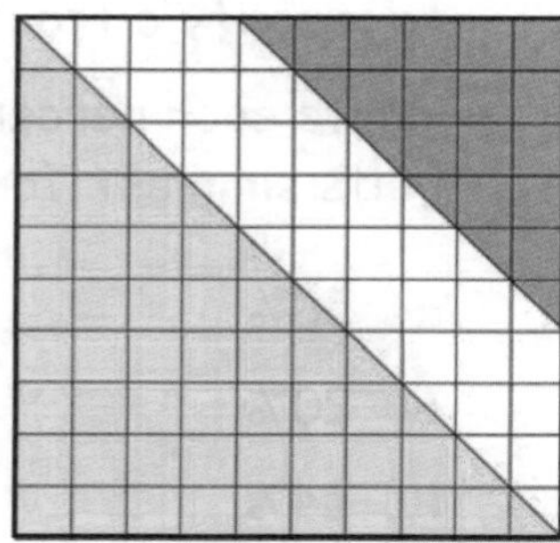

2. a Write down what each coloured section is as a percentage of the rectangle.

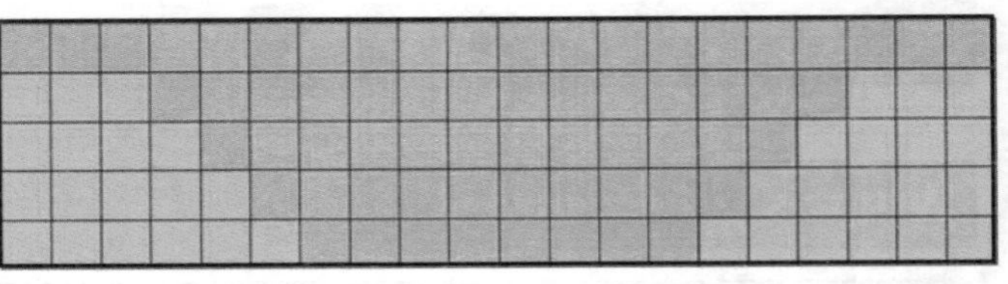

b Add your 3 answers together. (*Did you get 100%*) ?

3. a What percentage of this rectangle is :-

(i) yellow (ii) brown ?

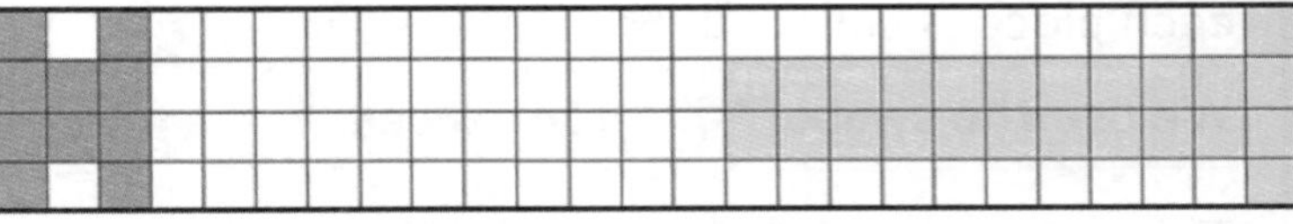

b What percentage is not coloured ?

c Without counting the white squares, explain how you could answer part b ?

4. Write each of the following as a fraction :-

23% means $\frac{23}{100}$

a 33% b 59% c 71% d 6%
e 19% f 49% g 11% h 1%.

5. Write each of the following as a decimal :-

49% means 0·49

a 41% b 37% c 53% d 13%
e 16% f 97% g 7% h 4%.

6. Write each of these as a fraction and as a decimal :-

37% means $\frac{37}{100}$ = 0·37

a 14% b 39% c 50% d 28%
e 20% f 17% g 48% h 9%.

7. Write each fraction or decimal as a percentage :-

a $\frac{17}{100}$ b $\frac{83}{100}$ c $\frac{6}{100}$ d 0·91 e 0·07

f 0·73 g $\frac{5}{100}$ h 0·01 i $\frac{1}{100}$ j $\frac{20}{100}$.

8. Earlier, you found it was often possible to simplify a fraction.

(e.g. $\frac{9}{12}$ *simplifies to give* $\frac{3}{4}$).

Write each percentage as a fraction in its simplest form.

(e.g. 40% = $\frac{40}{100}$ = $\frac{4}{10}$ = $\frac{2}{5}$).

a 50% b 10% c 25% d 75%
e 20% f 80% g 5% h 30%
i 44% j 65% k 4% l 2%.

Linking Fractions, Decimals & Percentages

OPTIONAL - needs a calculator

Be able to change between fractions, decimals and percentages using a calculator.

Remember :- $\frac{27}{100} = 27 \div 100 = 0{\cdot}27 = 27\%$.

We can change any fraction into a decimal then into a percentage.

Examples :-

Change each fraction into a decimal then into a percentage :-

a 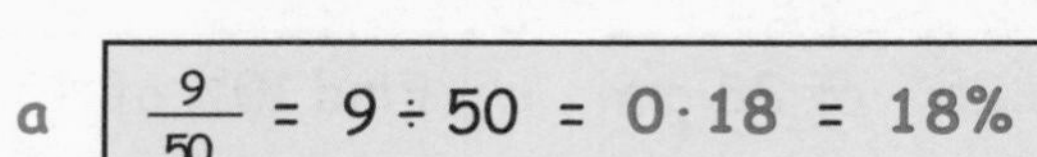
$\frac{9}{50} = 9 \div 50 = 0{\cdot}18 = 18\%$

b 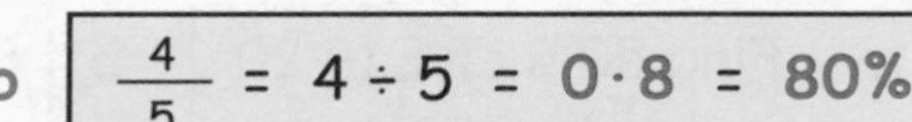
$\frac{4}{5} = 4 \div 5 = 0{\cdot}8 = 80\%$

Exercise 2 *(A calculator is required for this exercise).*

1. Copy and complete each of the following :-

   a $\frac{3}{25} = 3 \div 25 = 0{\cdot}\ldots = \ldots\%$ b $\frac{6}{10} = 6 \div \ldots = 0{\cdot}\ldots = \ldots\%$

   c $\frac{1}{40} = \ldots \div \ldots = 0{\cdot}\ldots = \ldots\%$ d $\frac{36}{80} = \ldots \div \ldots = 0{\cdot}\ldots = \ldots\%$.

2. Change each of the fractions shown to a decimal, then to a percentage :-

   a $\frac{6}{24}$ b $\frac{36}{48}$ c $\frac{7}{20}$ d $\frac{72}{300}$ e $\frac{60}{250}$ f $\frac{9}{180}$.

You must be careful with answers like 0·1. (This is NOT 1%).
The "1" is in the tenths column so $0{\cdot}1 = 0{\cdot}1\underline{0} = 10\%$.

3. Carefully, change each of these fractions to percentages :-

   a $\frac{3}{5}$ b $\frac{9}{45}$ c $\frac{18}{20}$ d $\frac{55}{110}$ e $\frac{3}{30}$ f $\frac{444}{5550}$.

4. Hazel scored $\frac{30}{40}$ in a Geography test.
   Change her score to a percentage.

5. 

   Of the 20 sausages being cooked on the barbecue, chef burned 8 of them.

   What percentage did he burn ?

6. Sidney got $\frac{39}{60}$ for Maths, $\frac{49}{70}$ for English and $\frac{34}{50}$ for Science.

   a Change each mark to a percentage.

   b In which subject did he score the highest test mark ?

Finding a (Simple) Percentage of a Quantity

Be able to find a simple percentage of a quantity.

Some percentages are used quite frequently in mathematics.

It is often quicker and easier to use their **fractional values** instead.

$50\% = \frac{50}{100} = \frac{1}{2}$ $\quad$ $25\% = \frac{25}{100} = \frac{1}{4}$ $\quad$ $10\% = \frac{10}{100} = \frac{1}{10}$

Examples :-

a Find 50% of £18·20
$= \frac{1}{2}$ of £18·20
$=$ £9·10

b Find 25% of 28 cm
$= \frac{1}{4}$ of 28 cm
$=$ 7 cm

c Find 10% of 45 kg
$= \frac{1}{10}$ of 45 kg
$=$ 4·5 kg

Exercise 3

1. Copy and complete the following :-

a Find 50% of £80
$= \frac{1}{2}$ of £80
= ....

b Find 25% of 36p
$= \frac{1}{4}$ of 36p
= ......

c Find 10% of 30 m
$= \frac{1}{10}$ of 30 m
= ......

2. Calculate each of the following :-

a	50% of £16	b	50% of 58 m	c	50% of 146 g
d	25% of 4p	e	25% of 44 kg	f	25% of 600 mm
g	10% of 200 ml	h	10% of 700 cm	i	10% of 3000 miles
j	50% of £750	k	10% of £820	l	25% of £18.

3. a Tony had £360. He spent 50% on a hotel weekend break.
How much did Tony pay for the holiday ?

b Abbie weighed 72 kilograms.
She went on a diet and lost 25% of her weight.
How many kilograms did she lose ?

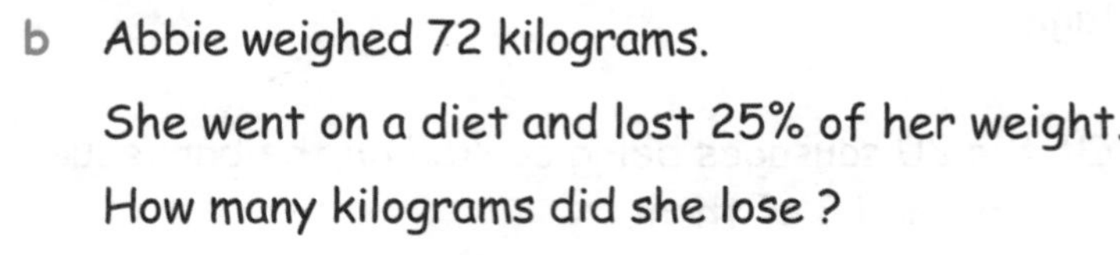

c Coleen weighed 60 kg. On a diet, she lost 10% of her weight.
What was her **new** weight ?

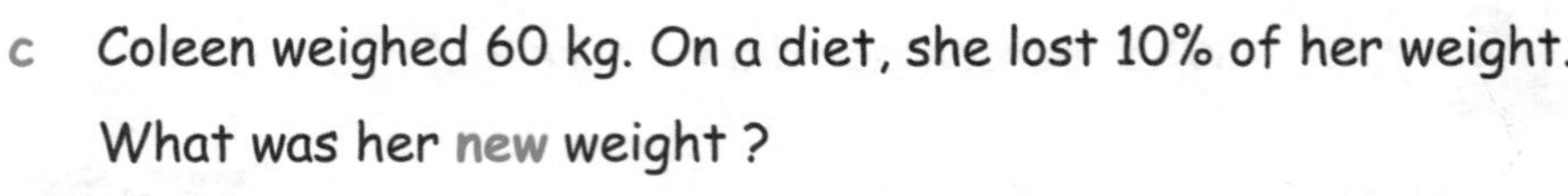

4. A sale in a sport's shop offers "**25% off**".

a How much would you get off £76 trainers ?

b What is the price of the trainers in the sale ?

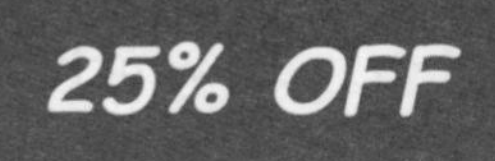

2/03/2021 

Finding a (more difficult) Percentage of a Quantity

Be able to find a percentage of a quantity without a calculator.

Remember – Many Percentages can be reduced to simple fractions.

To find 25% of something you divide by 4.
20% of something you divide by 5, etc.....

To find 75% of £80 = $\frac{3}{4}$ of £80 = (80 ÷ 4) x 3 = £60

Try to learn these

percentage	50%	25%	75%	$33\frac{1}{3}$%	$66\frac{2}{3}$%	20%	40%	60%	80%	10%	30%	70%	90%
fraction	$\frac{1}{2}$	$\frac{1}{4}$	$\frac{3}{4}$	$\frac{1}{3}$	$\frac{2}{3}$	$\frac{1}{5}$	$\frac{2}{5}$	$\frac{3}{5}$	$\frac{4}{5}$	$\frac{1}{10}$	$\frac{3}{10}$	$\frac{7}{10}$	$\frac{9}{10}$

Examples :-

To find 3% .....
- first, find 1%, (÷ 100)
- then times by 3. (x 3)

To find 90% .....
- first find 10%, (÷ 10)
- then times by 9. (x 9)

To find 13% .....
- first find 10%, (÷ 10)
- then find 3% (*see opp.*)
- then add them both.

Exercise 4

1. Find the following :-

a 10% of £15	b 70% of £50	c 20% of £5·50
d 80% of 400 kg	e 25% of 1260 kg	f $33\frac{1}{3}$% of 48 kg
g 75% of £6·40	h 1% of 120 cm	i 60% of 12 000 km
j 50% of £$\frac{1}{2}$million	k $66\frac{2}{3}$% of 18 ml	l 10% of 7 m
m 2% of £800	n 3% of 500 mm	o 5% of £5.

2. *Difficult* Find the following :- (*You may wish to set down ALL your working*).

a 11% of £200	b 15% of £60	c 3% of £32
d 8% of 3000 m	e 5% of 1200 ml	f 2% of 45 000 mm
g 11% of 50 000 g	h 12% of £1200	i 90% of 40 000 kg
j $12\frac{1}{2}$% of £1600	k 4% of £1150	l 150% of $800
m 0·5% of 8600 ml	n 1·5% of £600	o 2·5% of 1600 km.

3. There are 360 employees in a factory. 10% of them are women.

   a What percentage of employees are men ?

   b How many men work in the factory ?

4. A shop, selling a new bike costing £120, gives a 20% discount.

   a How much is the discount ?

   b How much will the bike now cost ?

   Discount means money off.

   A bicycle helmet priced at £30 is given a 30% discount.

   c How much will the helmet cost now ?

5. Heather puts £450 into a bank which gives an interest of 5% every year.

   Interest is money usually added on.

   How much interest will she get after one year ?

6. Alicia has £850 to invest in a bank.

   How much more interest will she get by putting her money into Colford Bank ?

   (*p.a. means per annum - per year*).

   Colford Bank
   5% interest p.a.

   Ainslie Bank
   3% interest p.a.

7. a A University noticed that twelve and a half percent of new students dropped out in their first year.

   If there were 1600 first year students, how many dropped out ?

   b Of a group of 800 people surveyed :-

   30% read the Sun, 45% read the Mail, 15% read the Guardian and the rest read the Express.

   How many of the 800 people read the :-

   (i) Sun (ii) Mail (iii) Guardian (iv) Express ?

8. 

   The diameter of Mars is only 55% of the Earth's diameter.

   If the diameter of Earth is 14000 km, what is the diameter of Mars ?

9. In a school election, only 22·5% voted for the Head Boy.

   If 1000 pupils voted, how many voted for the Head Boy ?

3/03/21 TH (test)

The 3 Я's

Revisit - Review - Revise

1. Write down each colour as a percentage of each shape :-

a

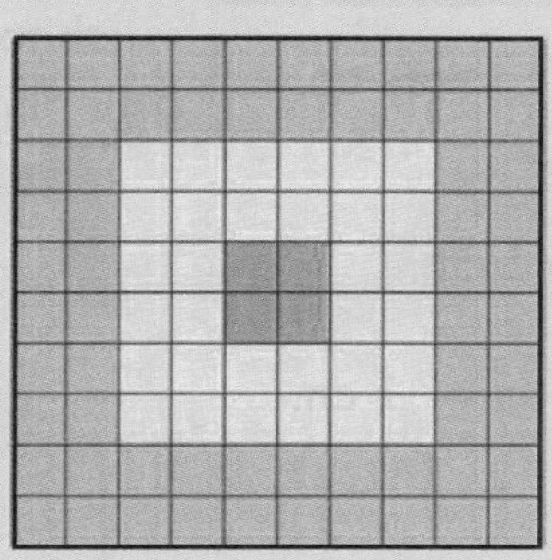

b

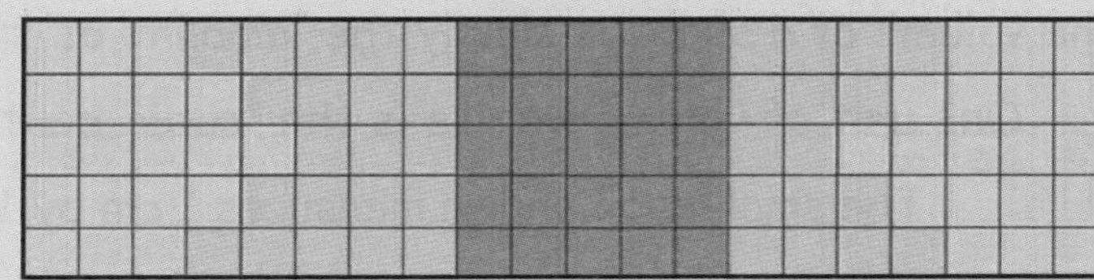

2. Write each of the following as a fraction :-

a 77%   b 51%   c 19%   d 7%.

3. Write each of the following as a decimal :-

a 61%   b 38%   c 125%   d 4%.

4. Write each of the following as a fraction and as a decimal :-

a 17%   b 69%   c 8%   d 30%.

5. Write each fraction or decimal as a percentage :-

a $\frac{33}{100}$ b 0·98   c $\frac{3}{100}$ d 0·01.

6. Change each of these fractions to a percentage :-

a $\frac{4}{5}$ b $\frac{16}{20}$ c $\frac{6}{60}$ d $\frac{22}{550}$.

7. Sandy scored 8 out of 10 in his English test.

What was his percentage mark ?

8. Work out :-

a 30% of £20   b 25% of 1800 cm   c 3% of 500 grams

d $33\frac{1}{3}$% of 54 kg   e 15% of £2400   f $12\frac{1}{2}$% of £5600.

9. Mazdo was offering 10% off the price of a new sports car.

a What was the new price of a car which originally cost £20000 ?

b Mazdo is also offering 5% off that new discounted price.

What's the final price of the sports car ?

Chapter 14

Measure 2

Volumes by Counting Cubes

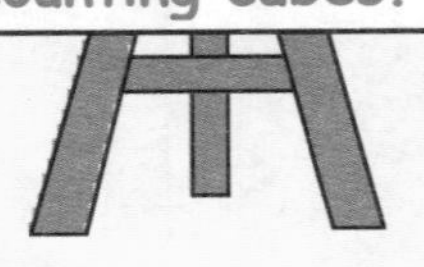

Be able to find the volume of a shape by counting cubes.

The volume of a shape is simply the "amount of space" it takes up.

One unit of volume we use is the "cubic centimetre".

The small cube shown measures 1 cm by 1 cm by 1 cm.

It has a volume of 1 cubic centimetre,

or for short :- 1 cm^3

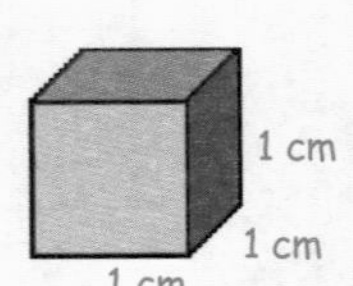

Exercise 1

1. State the volume of each of the following shapes, (*in* cm^3) :-

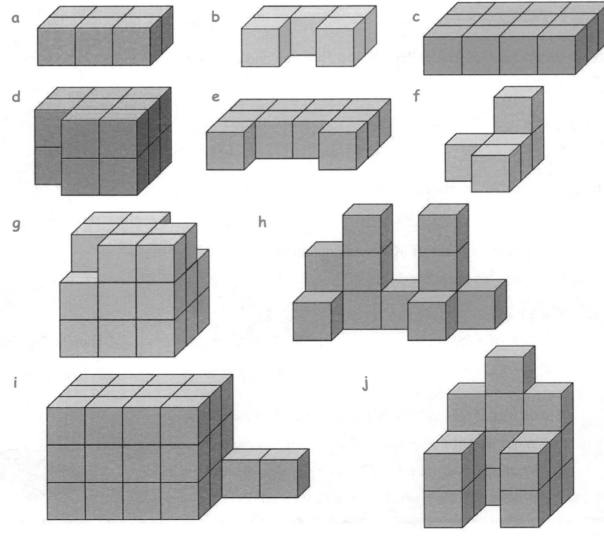

a

b

c

d

e

f

g

h

i

j

2. a How many cubes are on the top layer of this shape ?

   b How many layers does it have ?

   c What is its total **volume** ?

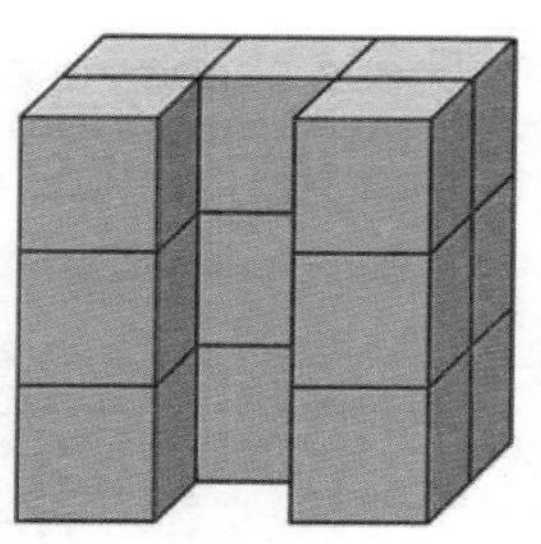

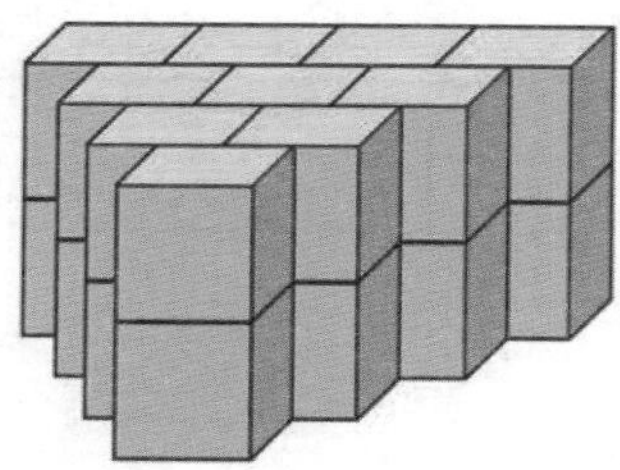

3. a How many cubes are on the top layer of this shape ?

   b How many layers does it have ?

   c What is its total **volume** ?

4. What is the total **volume** of this shape ?

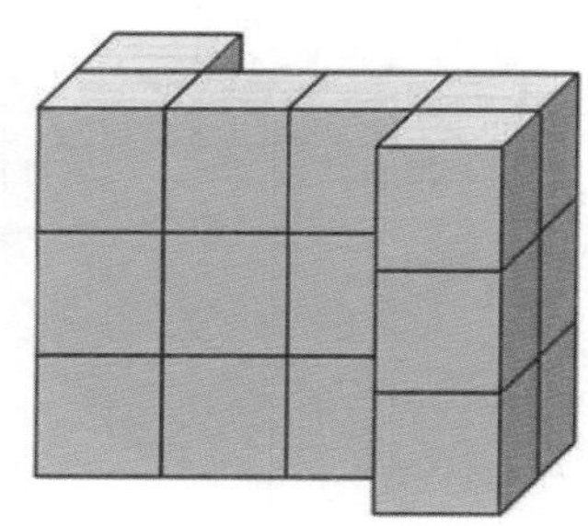

5. By working out the volume of the top layer first, calculate the total **volume**, (*in* cm^3), of each of the following shapes :-

a

b

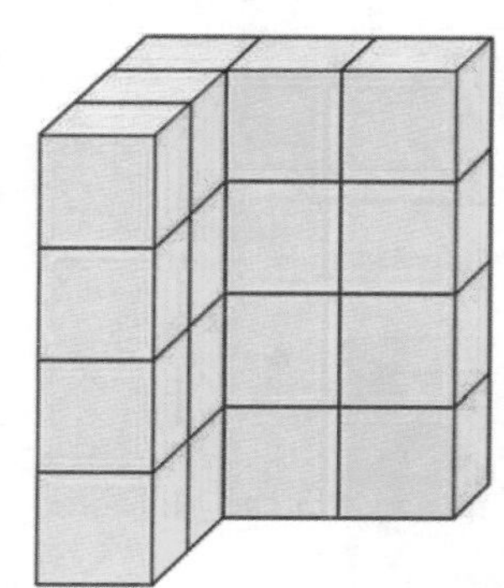

c

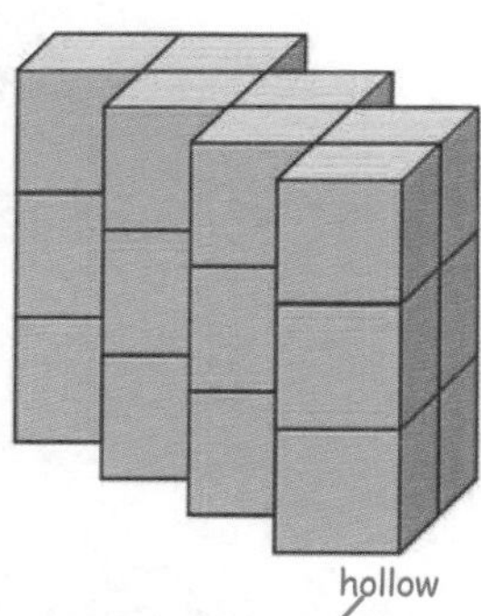

d

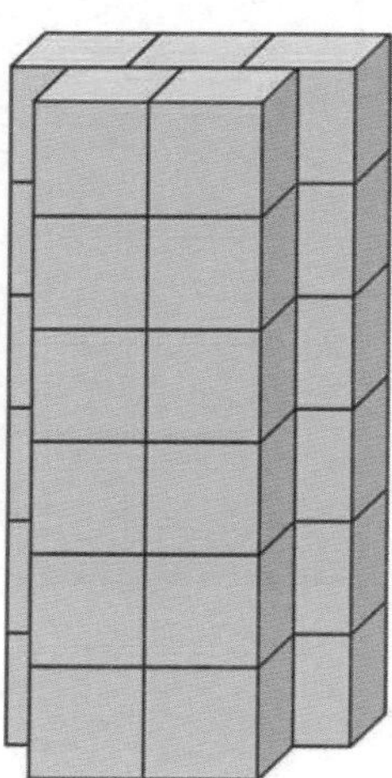

e

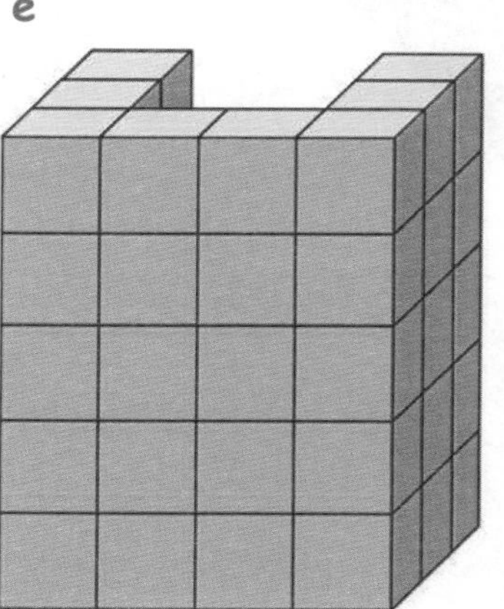

f

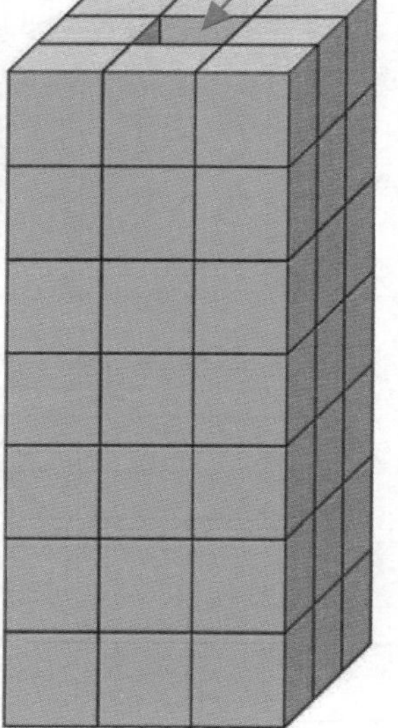

6. These shapes are cuboids made up using 1 cm cubes.

Find the number of cubes in 1 layer and then calculate the **volume** of each cuboid :-

a

b

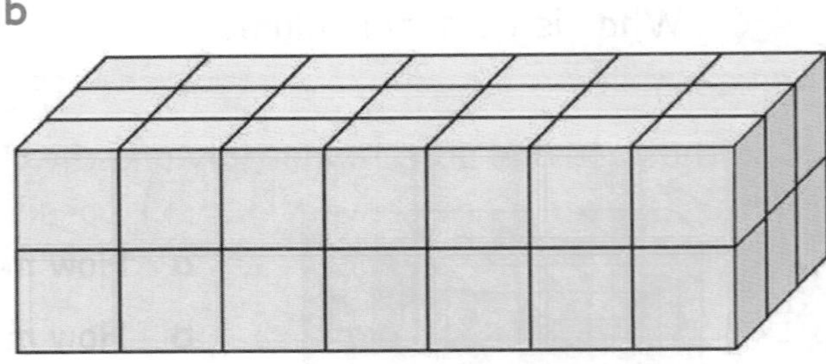

7. Calculate the **volume** of each cuboid :-

a

b

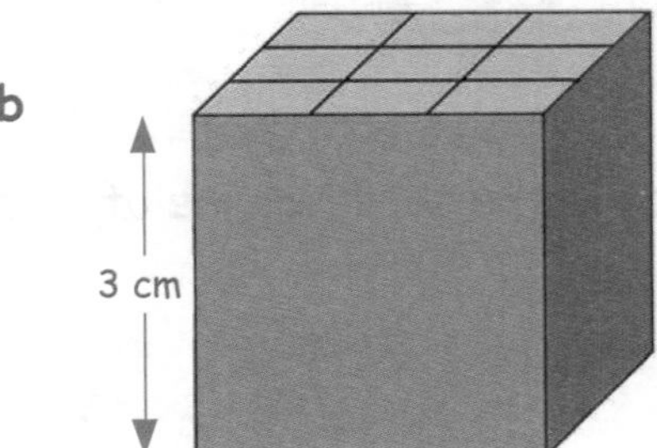

c

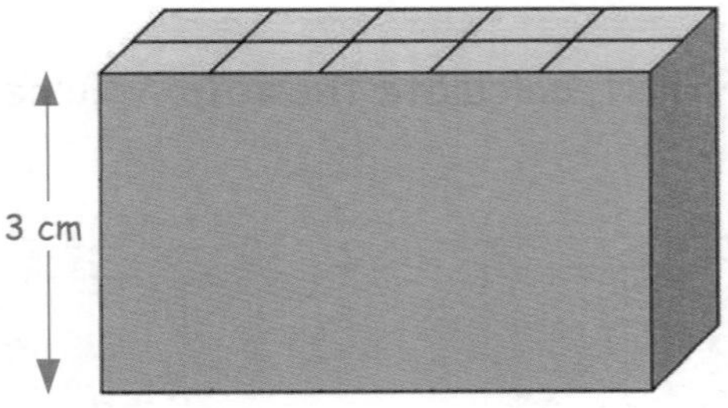

d

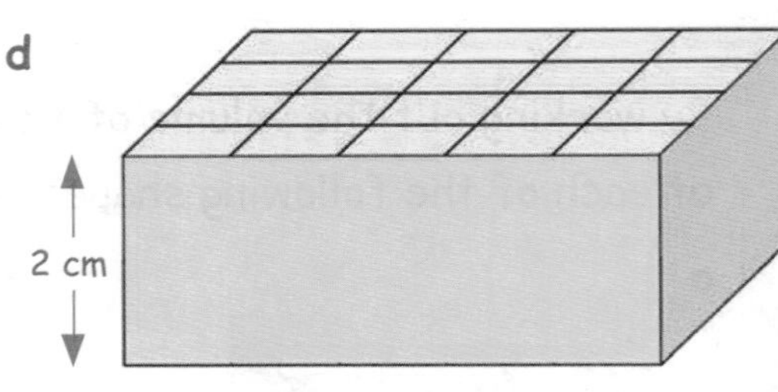

e

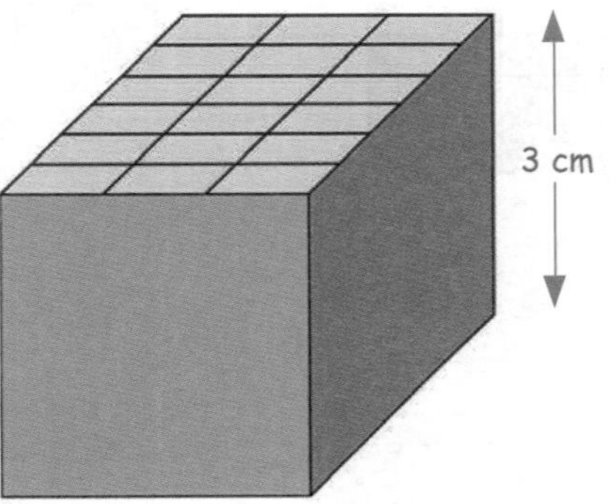

f

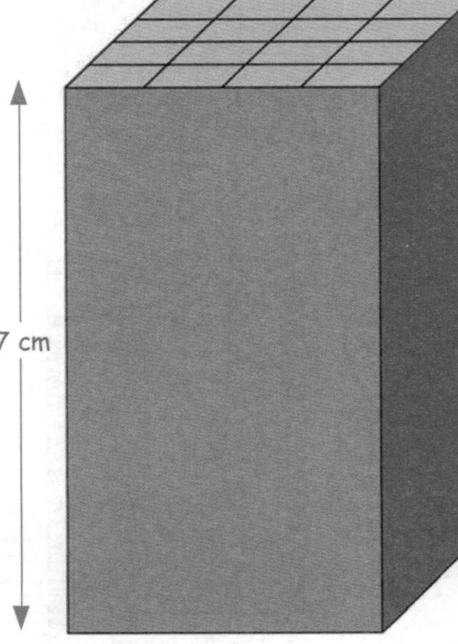

g

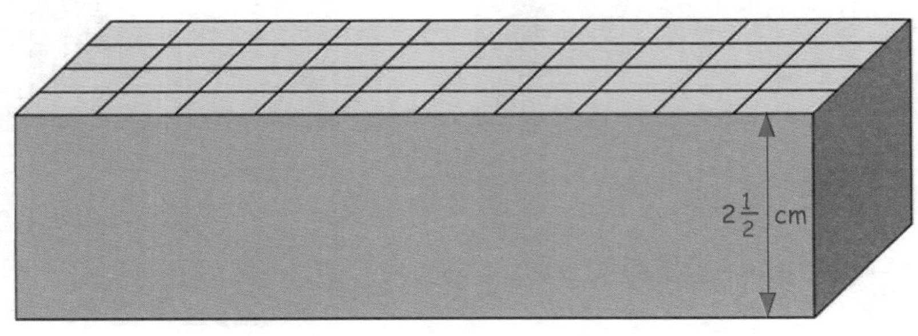

Converting Units of Measurement

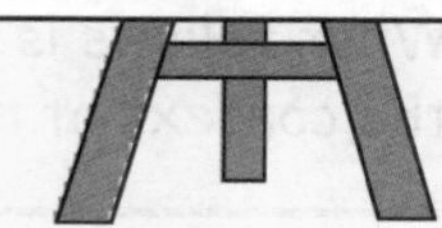

Be able to convert between different units of measurement.

In Year 4, you learned to change from one unit to another.

For example :- 7 cm = 70 mm or 5000 grams = 5 kg.

Now that you are able to multiply and divide decimals by 10, 100 and 1000, even more conversions are possible.

Examples :-

0·4 cm = (*0·4 x 10*) mm = 4 mm

3820 m = (*3820 ÷ 1000*) km = 3·82 km

0·85 *L* = (*0·85 x 1000*) ml = 850 ml

20 g = (*20 ÷ 1000*) kg = 0·02 kg

Exercise 2

1 cm = 10 mm
1 m = 100 cm
1 km = 1000 m
1 kg = 1000 g
1 litre = 1000 ml

Change :-

1. 0·7 centimetres to millimetres
2. 63 millimetres to centimetres
3. 5·5 centimetres to millimetres
4. 9 millimetres to centimetres
5. 0·4 metres to centimetres
6. 23 centimetres to metres
7. 15·91 metres to centimetres
8. 7 centimetres to metres
9. 0·2 kilometres to metres
10. 400 metres to kilometres
11. 12·85 kilometres to metres
12. 10 metres to kilometres
13. 5·75 metres to millimetres
14. 3000 millimetres to metres
15. 7500 millimetres to metres
16. 1·2 kilometres to centimetres
17. 20·05 kilometres to metres
18. 25 000 millimetres to metres
19. 5·2 litres to millilitres
20. 0·03 litres to millilitres
21. 800 millilitres to litres
22. 90 millilitres to litres
23. 5 millilitres to litres
24. 0·125 litres to millilitres
25. 4·8 kilograms to grams
26. 672 grams to kilograms
27. 300 grams to kilograms
28. 81 grams to kilograms.

Money & Measurement - Problems

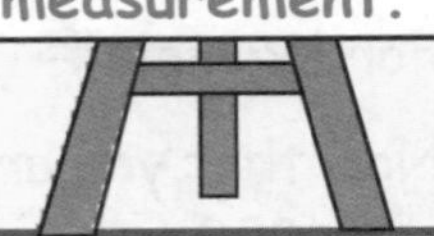

By now, you should be able to add and subtract decimal numbers.

What follows is more on addition and subtraction - this time in the context of **money** and **measurement**.

Exercise 3 *Show all working for the following examples.*

1. 
Mrs Taylor took her two daughters to the ballet.
It cost £25·50 for herself and £12·85 for each of her daughters.
What was the **total** cost ?

2. Mr Boyd received two quotes from a building company.
A conservatory was to cost £16 602·50.
A house extension was priced at £18 211·95.
By how much is the house extension more expensive ?

3. 
If three bottles, holding 0·944, 0·87 and 1·078 litres of flavoured water are poured into a punchbowl, how much will there be **altogether** in the punchbowl ?

4. Helen pours 0·25 litres of water from a 1 litre kettle.
   a How much water is left in the kettle ?
   b Her young brother then pours two lots of 0·17 litres from the kettle.
   How much water is left now ?

5. 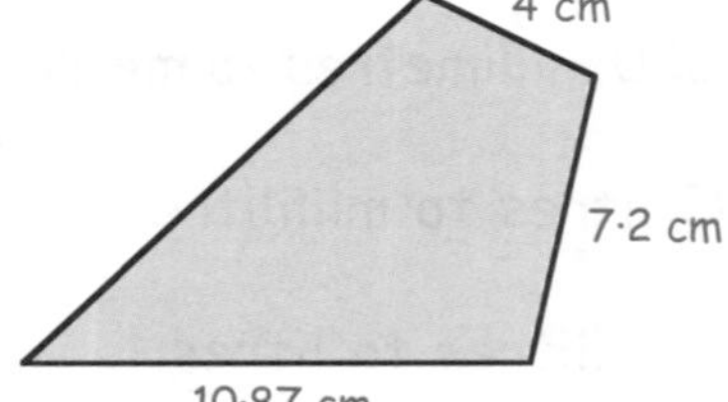

The **perimeter** of this shape is 34·43 centimetres.
Calculate the length of the remaining side.

6. An empty barrel weighs 8·621 kilograms.
7·799 kilograms of apples are put into the barrel.
What is the combined weight ?

7. Bill collects his paper round money on a Monday.

He collects £9·75 from Calder Lane, £12·80 from Palm Grove and £19·90 from Cherry Street.

a How much should he collect altogether ?

b He collected £51, including tips. How much did he get in tips ?

8. 

Drew cycles 8·9 kilometres of a 12 kilometre journey.

Tara jogs 5·72 kilometres of an 8·5 kilometre run.

Who has further still to travel, and by how much ?

9. A joiner has a 4·75 metre plank of wood.

He cuts off a 2·9 m and a 0·87 m piece.

How much of the plank is remaining ?

10. 

A bug crawls along a telephone wire.

He crawls 5·2 metres, then turns and crawls back 3·84 metres.

He turns again and crawls forward 1·77 metres.

How far is the bug from its starting point ?

11. Ally has a square garden of side 8·52 metres.

Julie has a rectangular garden with length 8·95 m and breadth 7·2 m.

They calculate the perimeters of their gardens.

Who has the larger perimeter and by how much ?

12. The table below shows how much money four girls raised for charity by holding a sponsored stay awake sleepover.

Sponsor	Erin	Alison	Fiona	Helen
Neighbours	£9·20	£7·00	£8·94	£12·82
Friends	£9·00	£10·20	£4·30	£7·80
Family	£13·57	£12·75	£17·38	£9·10
Others	£0·99	£2·87	£2·47	£0·28

a How much did each of the children raise individually ?

b Who raised the most and who raised the least ?

c By how much was the lowest total smaller than the second lowest total ?

Metric and Imperial Measure Investigation

Exercise 4

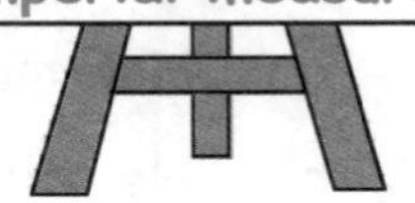

In Britain, a mixture of imperial and metric measurements is used.

We have recently been using metric measurements such as metres, kilograms and litres, etc.

We still at times use imperial measurement, such as feet, inches, gallons, ounces, etc.

Length - millimetre, centimetre, metre, kilometre. *(inch, foot, yard, furlong, mile.)*

1. Find one item for each imperial length that you know is measured in that unit.

   For example "my house door is 7 feet in height".

2. "A yard is a bit shorter than a metre". Write a sentence linking each of the 5 imperial units of length with their nearest equivalent in metric measure.

3. Find out how many :-

   a inches are in 1 foot b feet are in 1 yard c yards are in 1 chain

   d chains are in 1 furlong e furlongs are in 1 mile f inches are in 1 mile.

Weight - gram, kilogram and tonne. *(ounce, pound, stone, ton.)*

4. Find one item for each imperial weight that you know is measured in that unit.

   For example "the bag of potatoes I am carrying weighs 3 pounds".

5. "A pound is about half a kilogram". Write a sentence linking each of the 4 imperial units of weight with their nearest equivalent in metric units.

6. Find out how many :-

   a ounces in 1 pound b pounds are in 1 stone c stones are in 1 ton.

Volume (capacity) - millilitre and litre. *(pint and gallon.)*

7. Find one item for each imperial volume that you know is measured in that unit.

   For example "a pint of milk".

8. "2 pints is about 1 litre". Write a sentence linking both imperial units of volume with their nearest equivalent in metric units.

9. Find out how many pints are in 1 gallon.

Something else for you to find out :-

10. How many :-

   a millimetres = 1 inch b centimetres = 1 inch c yards = 1 metre

   d kilometres = 1 mile e pints = 1 litre f litres = 1 gallon

   g grams = 1 ounce h pounds = 1 kilogram i tons = 1 tonne ?

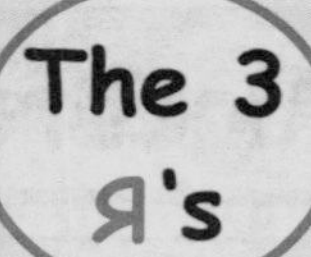

Revisit - Review - Revise

1. Write down the volume of each shape, in cm^3.

a

b

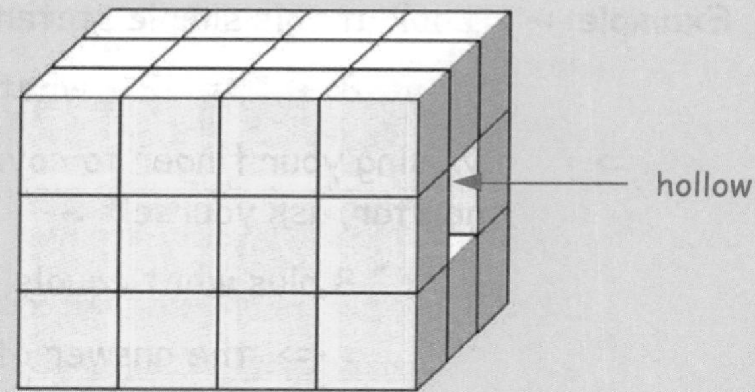

2. Change :-

a 0·9 centimetres to millimetres
b 71·5 millimetres to centimetres
c 1·65 kilometres to metres
d 25 400 metres to kilometres
e 23·05 litres to millilitres
f 6800 millilitres to litres
g 0·321 kilograms to grams
h 9 grams to kilograms.

3. Mary ran the 200 metre race in 20·072 seconds.
Sally ran it in 18·979 seconds.
Who finished in front and by how many seconds ?

4.

A plant pot had exactly 4 kg of compost in it.
During a rainy spell, 0·555 kg of compost was washed away.
How much was left ?

5. Mavis walked 2·86 km from her home to the Post Office.
She then walked 1·7 km to the chiropodist before catching the bus for the 4·99 km journey back home.
How far had Mavis travelled altogether ?

6. Mr Johnson has a PC shop voucher worth £300 to exchange for goods.

He wants :-

a memory card	@	£90·50
a sound card	@	£77·99
PC speakers	@	£35·80
20 inch screen	@	£66·85
PC game	@	£35·79.

How much extra must he pay, along with all his vouchers ?

Chapter 15 An Introduction to Algebra

Basic Equations Extension

Know what equations are and be able to solve them.

Example :- Look at this simple statement (an equation).

$8 + * = 12$ what does the " * " stand for ?

=> By using your finger to cover up the star, ask yourself :-

$8 + \quad = 12$

=> $* = 4$

" 8 plus what equals 12 ?"

=> the answer of course is "4".

3 further examples :-

$13 - * = 6$ => $* = 7$	$6 \times * = 18$ => $* = 3$	$\frac{*}{5} = 14$ => $* = 70$

3 different examples :-

Which of the 4 symbols, + , − × or ÷ should replace the ☐ box each time ?

15 ☐ 7 = 8 => ☐ is "−"	4 ☐ 7 = 11 => ☐ is "+"	3 ☐ 9 = 27 => ☐ is "x"

Exercise 1

1. Copy each of the following and find what * stands for each time :-

a $6 + * = 9$ => $* = ...$

b $12 - * = 3$ => $* = ...$

c $* \times 7 = 42$ => $* = ...$

2. Find the value of * in each of the following :-

a $5 + * = 19$ b $6 + * = 6$ c $17 + * = 29$

d $* + 12 = 20$ e $13 - * = 4$ f $21 - * = 9$

g $7 - * = 0$ h $13 - * = 13$ i $* - 5 = 8$

j $* - 11 = 20$ k $* - 5 = 0$ l $* - 6 = 5$

m $4 \times * = 28$ n $7 \times * = 63$ o $* \times 6 = 30$

p $21 \times * = 0$ q $\frac{*}{4} = 8$ r $\frac{*}{8} = 7$

s $\frac{70}{*} = 10$ t $54 \div * = 6$ u $63 \div * = 9$.

3. In each of the following, ☐ stands for +, −, × or ÷.

Decide which symbol is needed each time here :-

a	9 ☐ 7 = 16		b	14 ☐ 5 = 9		c	6 ☐ 4 = 24	
d	40 ☐ 8 = 5		e	7 ☐ 1 = 6		f	9 ☐ 1 = 9	
g	11 ☐ 1 = 12		h	22 ☐ 2 = 11		i	60 ☐ 3 = 57	
j	10 ☐ 2 = 20		k	10 ☐ 10 = 0		l	10 ☐ 10 = 1.	

4. Look at the scales shown below and find the weight of one coloured box each time :-

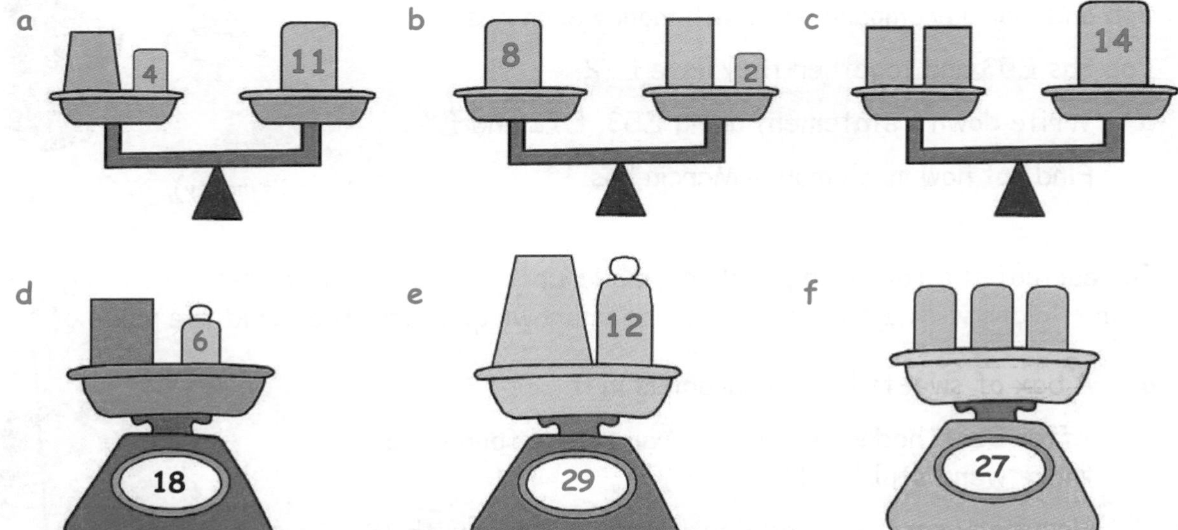

5. Which of the 2 sweetie jars is heavier and by how much is it heavier than the other ?

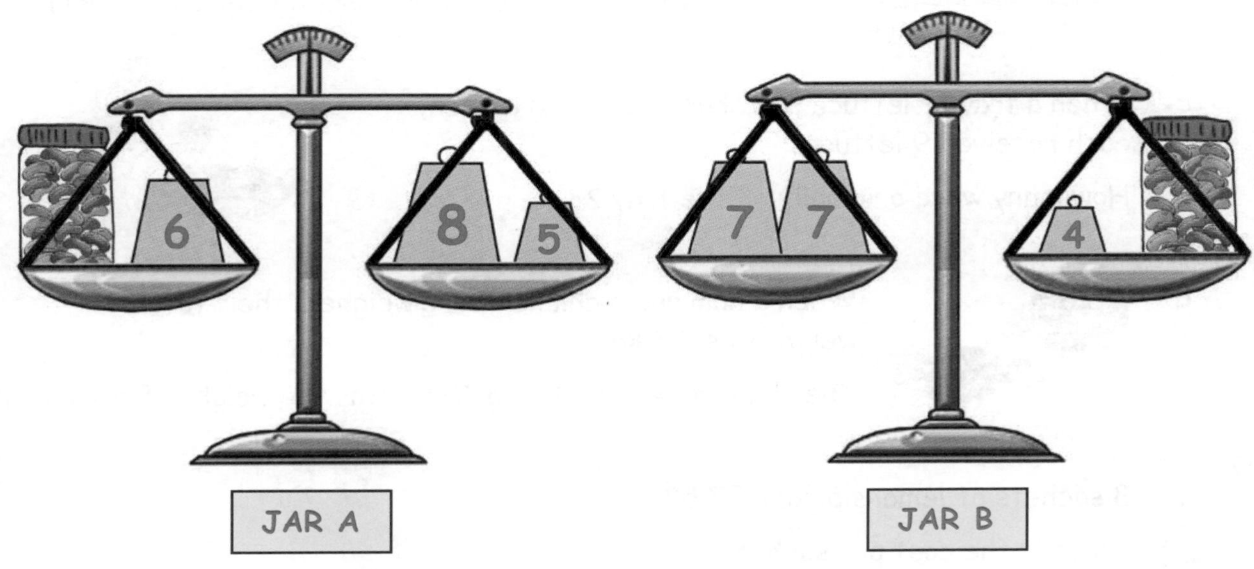

6. What must the length of the red strip of paper be each time here ?

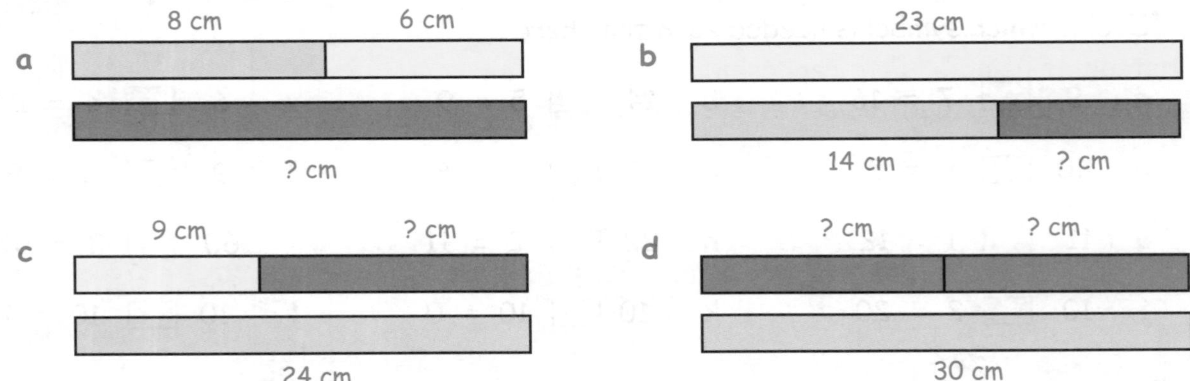

7. Bob and Marcia compare how much money each has.

Bob has £53 and together they have £72.

a Write down a statement using £53, £72 and £*.

b Find out how much money Marcia has.

(*Marcia's money*).

8. For each of the following problems, make up a statement (equation) involving +, −, × or ÷ along with a * to stand for the unknown quantity, then find the value of *.

a A box of sweets had 18 caramels in it .

After Berti had eaten some caramels, he found that there were still 3 left.

How many caramels had Berti eaten ? (start with 18 − * = ...)

b 7 euro coins weigh 52·5 grams.

What does 1 euro coin weigh ? (Form an equation first).

c When a tray of lettuce was shared among 8 women, each received 9 lettuces.

How many were originally on the tray ?

d 

When a ham and a chicken were weighed, their total weight was 3·2 kg.

The chicken weighed 1·4 kg. What was the weight of the ham ?

e 8 sachets of lemonsip cost £7·52.

What is the cost per sachet ?

Algebra Equations

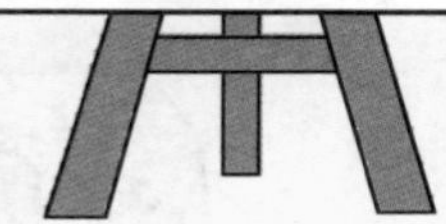

Solve basic equations involving letters instead of symbols.

Instead of using " * " to represent a missing value, mathematicians tend to use letters instead.

"x" is the most popular letter used by mathematicians.

Examples :-

$x + 7 = 13$ => $x = 6$	$x - 7 = 11$ => $x = 18$	$2 \times x = 26$ => $x = 13$	$\frac{x}{10} = 8$ => $x = 80$

Use the cover up method shown on page 116.

These are examples of what are called mathematical equations.

Exercise 2

1. Copy each equation and solve it to find the value of x :-

a $x + 5 = 12$ b $x + 11 = 15$ c $8 + x = 23$

d $x + 9 = 9$ e $x - 7 = 3$ f $x - 15 = 1$

g $x - 8 = 8$ h $17 - x = 4$ i $23 - x = 9$

j $6 \times x = 30$ k $5 \times x = 45$ l $10 \times x = 70$

m $x \times 30 = 90$ n $\frac{x}{2} = 4$ o $\frac{x}{7} = 6$

p $x \div 8 = 8$ q $x \div 11 = 7$ r $64 \div x = 4$.

2. Though x is a firm favourite, any letter can be used to stand for a missing quantity.

Copy each of the following and find the missing value each time :-

a $p + 8 = 14$ b $q - 4 = 12$ c $3 \times r = 27$

d $\frac{s}{4} = 9$ e $t + 12 = 12$ f $g - 40 = 60$

g $h \times 8 = 32$ h $j \div 9 = 1$ i $1{\cdot}3 + k = 8{\cdot}3$

j $34 - m = 8$ k $9 \times n = 54$ l $56 \div v = 7$

m $18 + a = 18$ n $b - 5 = 0$ o $9 \times c = 0$.

3. For each of the following :-

   (i) make up an equation using the letter shown.

   (ii) solve the equation to find the value of the letter.

a 

b 

c 

d 

e 

f 

4. The combined age of two architects Douglas and Donald is 63.

   Douglas is 25.

   Make up an equation and solve it to find Donald's age.

5. 

   The **total** cost for 4 adults flying on a weekend break to Prague is £1000.

   Make up an equation and solve it to find the cost for each of them.

6. Professor Banquet was asked to count how many octopuses were in the vicinity.

   He counted the tentacles instead and found there were 56 tentacles.

   Make up an equation and solve it to find how many octopuses there were.

7. 

   When 240 grams of soup was served from a pot into a bowl, there were still 965 grams left in the pot.

   Make up an equation and solve it to find how much soup was in the pot to begin with.

The 3 Я's

Revisit - Review - Revise

1. Find the value of * in each of the following :-

a $6 + * = 13$ b $8 + * = 8$ c $22 + * = 35$

d $* - 5 = 7$ e $10 - * = 3$ f $20 - * = 0$

g $* + 10 = 20$ h $5 \times * = 40$ i $3 \times * = 120$

j $* \times 8 = 96$ k $\frac{*}{4} = 5$ l $66 \div * = 6$.

2. In each of the following, ◎ stands for +, −, × or ÷.

Decide which symbol is needed each time here :-

a 6 ◎ 4 = 2 b 5 ◎ 5 = 25 c 12 ◎ 3 = 15

d 12 ◎ 3 = 4 e 10 ◎ 10 = 0 f 15 ◎ 15 = 1.

3. Copy each **equation** and solve it to find the value of x :-

a $x + 4 = 15$ b $x + 15 = 20$ c $9 + x = 30$

d $x - 5 = 6$ e $x - 13 = 12$ f $x + 5 = 5$

g $12 - x = 2$ h $7 \times x = 42$ i $8 \times x = 88$

j $10 \times x = 200$ k $\frac{x}{3} = 7$ l $\frac{x}{5} = 5$.

4. Copy each of the following and find the missing value each time :-

a $m + 7 = 19$ b $t - 5 = 13$ c $4 \times d = 32$

d $\frac{w}{4} = 10$ e $p + 16 = 16$ f $r - 30 = 70$

g $f \times 7 = 84$ h $s \div 7 = 1$ i $2{\cdot}5 + q = 9{\cdot}5$.

5. The combined weight of two boys, Alf and Balbir, is 95 kg.

Alf weighs 46 kg.

Let x kg represent Balbir's weight.

Make up an equation involving x and solve it to find how heavy Balbir is.

Chapter 16

Fractions 2

Adding and Subtracting (basic) Fractions

Be able to add or subtract basic mixed fractions.

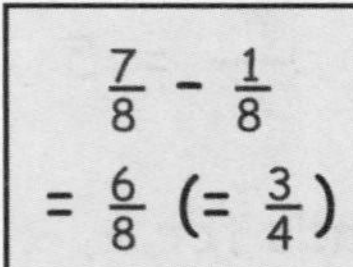

Simple Rule :- You can only add (or subtract) two fractions if

BOTH HAVE THE SAME DENOMINATOR.

Example 1 :-

$\frac{3}{7} + \frac{2}{7}$

$= \frac{5}{7}$

Example 2 :-

$\frac{7}{8} - \frac{1}{8}$

$= \frac{6}{8}$ $(= \frac{3}{4})$

$\frac{7}{8}$ - $\frac{1}{8}$

= $\frac{6}{8} = \frac{3}{4}$

Example 3 :-

$2\frac{3}{5} + 1\frac{4}{5}$

$= 3\frac{7}{5}$

$= 4\frac{2}{5}$

Example 4 :-

$5\frac{5}{6} - 1\frac{1}{6}$

$= 4\frac{4}{6}$

$= 4\frac{2}{3}$

Exercise 1

1. Copy and complete the following :-

a $\frac{3}{5} + \frac{1}{5} = \frac{...}{5}$

b $\frac{7}{9} - \frac{5}{9} = \frac{...}{9}$

c $\frac{7}{10} - \frac{3}{10} = \frac{...}{10} = \frac{...}{5}$

d $\frac{3}{8} + \frac{3}{8} = \frac{...}{8} = \frac{...}{4}$.

2. Copy the following and simplify where possible :-

a $\frac{3}{7} + \frac{1}{7}$ b $\frac{5}{9} + \frac{3}{9}$ c $\frac{7}{9} - \frac{1}{9}$ d $\frac{3}{4} + \frac{3}{4}$

e $\frac{7}{12} - \frac{5}{12}$ f $\frac{11}{12} + \frac{11}{12}$ g $\frac{8}{15} + \frac{7}{15}$ h $\frac{15}{16} - \frac{7}{16}$.

3. Copy the following and simplify where possible :-

a $2\frac{1}{3} + 3\frac{1}{3}$ b $5\frac{3}{5} - 1\frac{2}{5}$ c $4\frac{1}{7} + 3\frac{1}{7}$ d $2\frac{1}{2} + 1\frac{1}{2}$

e $6\frac{4}{5} - 6\frac{1}{5}$ f $4\frac{5}{9} + 3\frac{5}{9}$ g $5\frac{5}{9} - 1\frac{1}{9}$ h $10\frac{4}{11} + 3\frac{2}{11}$.

4. Of the $\frac{9}{10}$ kilometre journey to his school, David had walked $\frac{3}{10}$ km.
How much further had he to go ?

5. Hat sizes go up in $\frac{1}{8}$'s of an inch at a time.

Pauline wears a hat size $6\frac{7}{8}$. Alexis is 5 sizes bigger than this.

What is Alexis' hat size ?

6. 

John mixes $23\frac{3}{5}$ kg of sand with $24\frac{4}{5}$ kg of cement.

What is the total weight of the mixture ?

7. a A piece of rope is $6\frac{3}{5}$ metres long.

A piece measuring $3\frac{2}{5}$ is cut off.

What length of rope remains ?

b  

Two jugs of juice were poured into an empty basin.

The first jug held $2\frac{3}{4}$ litres, the second $1\frac{3}{4}$ litres.

How much juice in total was in the basin ?

c Of the $10\frac{5}{6}$ kilometres journey from his house to the shops,

Alan had cycled $7\frac{1}{6}$ kilometres.

How much further had Alan to travel to reach the shops ?

d George ate $\frac{4}{5}$ of his pizza, Billy ate $\frac{3}{5}$ of his and Amanda ate $\frac{2}{5}$ of hers.

How much pizza had they eaten altogether ?

e 

Bunty weighed $72\frac{7}{9}$ kilograms.

She went on a diet and lost $4\frac{4}{9}$ kilograms.

What is Bunty's new weight ?

8. A table measures $6\frac{7}{10}$ feet long by $4\frac{3}{10}$ feet wide.

a By how much is the length bigger than the width ?

b Calculate the perimeter of the table top.

9. People used to measure lengths in inches.
An inch was divided into eighths.

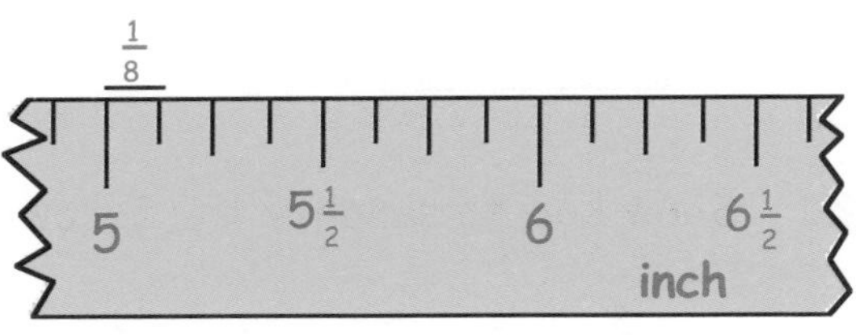

Davie cut a piece of wood $6\frac{1}{8}$ inches

from a piece measuring $11\frac{5}{8}$ inches.

What was the length of the remaining piece ?

Adding and Subtracting (Harder) Fractions

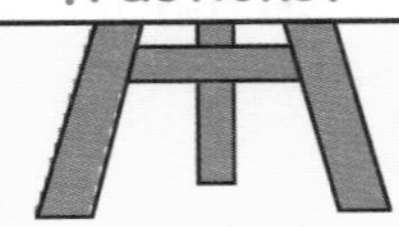
Be able to add or subtract harder fractions.

Remember the Golden Rule :-

The denominators MUST be the same if you wish to add or subtract.

Question :- What do we do if the denominators are not the same ?

Answer :- Change one or more fraction so that they do have the same denominator.

Example 1 :- Find $\frac{5}{6} + \frac{1}{2}$. [they do not add to give $\frac{6}{8}$ X]

- the denominators 6 and 2 are not the same.
- we must change the $\frac{1}{2}$ to $\frac{1}{6}$'s.

$$\frac{5}{6} + \frac{1}{2}$$
$$\frac{5}{6} + \frac{3}{6}$$
$$= \frac{8}{6} = 1\frac{2}{6} = 1\frac{1}{3}$$

note $(\frac{1}{2} = \frac{?}{6}) \rightarrow ? = 3$

Example 2 :-

(Change $\frac{1}{5}$ to $\frac{?}{10}$)

$$\frac{7}{10} - \frac{1}{5}$$
$$\frac{7}{10} - \frac{?}{10}$$
$$= \frac{7}{10} - \frac{2}{10}$$
$$= \frac{5}{10} = \frac{1}{2}$$

Example 3 :-

(Change $\frac{3}{4}$ to $\frac{?}{12}$)

$$\frac{7}{12} + \frac{3}{4}$$
$$\frac{7}{12} + \frac{?}{12}$$
$$= \frac{7}{12} + \frac{9}{12}$$
$$= \frac{16}{12} = 1\frac{4}{12} = 1\frac{1}{3}$$

Exercise 2

1. Copy each of the following and complete :-

a
$$\frac{3}{4} + \frac{1}{2}$$
$$= \frac{3}{4} + \frac{?}{4}$$
$$= \frac{?}{4} = 1\frac{?}{4}$$

b
$$\frac{11}{12} - \frac{2}{3}$$
$$= \frac{11}{12} - \frac{?}{12}$$
$$= \frac{?}{12} = \frac{?}{4}$$

c
$$\frac{7}{8} - \frac{3}{4}$$
$$= \frac{7}{8} - \frac{?}{8}$$
$$= \frac{?}{8}$$

d
$$\frac{4}{15} + \frac{2}{3}$$
$$= \frac{4}{15} + \frac{?}{15}$$
$$= \frac{?}{15}$$

2. Show how to simplify the following :-

a $\frac{4}{5} + \frac{3}{20}$ b $\frac{3}{4} - \frac{1}{2}$ c $\frac{5}{8} + \frac{3}{4}$ d $\frac{2}{3} + \frac{8}{9}$

2. e $\frac{5}{6} - \frac{1}{3}$ f $\frac{3}{4} - \frac{3}{16}$ g $\frac{7}{10} + \frac{2}{5}$ h $\frac{27}{40} - \frac{1}{2}$.

3. Show your working here :-

a $\frac{1}{2} + \frac{1}{4} + \frac{1}{8}$ *(Hint change the $\frac{1}{2}$ and the $\frac{1}{4}$ to $\frac{?}{8}$).*

b $\frac{5}{6} - \frac{1}{2} - \frac{1}{3}$ c $\frac{3}{10} + \frac{3}{5} - \frac{1}{20}$ d $\frac{1}{2} + \frac{3}{8} + \frac{1}{16} - \frac{3}{4}$.

Harder Addition and Subtraction *(Extension)*

Mixed Fractions :- Deal with the whole numbers first - then the fractions.

Example 4 :-

$2\frac{1}{2} + 3\frac{1}{6}$
$= 5(\frac{1}{2} + \frac{1}{6})$
$= 5 + (\frac{3}{6} + \frac{1}{6})$
$= 5\frac{4}{6}$
$= 5\frac{2}{3}$

Example 5 :-

$7\frac{7}{8} - 4\frac{1}{4}$
$= 3 + (\frac{7}{8} - \frac{1}{4})$
$= 3 + (\frac{7}{8} - \frac{2}{8})$
$= 3\frac{5}{8}$

Example 6 :-

$4\frac{3}{4} + 3\frac{7}{12}$
$= 7 + (\frac{3}{4} + \frac{7}{12})$
$= 7 + (\frac{9}{12} + \frac{7}{12})$
$= 7\frac{16}{12}$
$= 8\frac{4}{12} = 8\frac{1}{3}$

4. Copy and complete the following :-

a $1\frac{1}{10} + 2\frac{2}{5}$ b $16\frac{1}{3} + \frac{7}{9}$ c $5\frac{7}{8} - 3\frac{1}{4}$

d $14\frac{11}{12} + 10\frac{3}{4}$ e $2\frac{5}{6} - 1\frac{2}{3}$ f $9\frac{1}{4} + 11\frac{5}{8}$

g $17\frac{1}{5} + 12\frac{3}{10}$ h $51\frac{9}{10} - 50\frac{1}{2}$ i $11\frac{1}{7} + 3\frac{5}{28}$.

5. Copy and complete :-

a
$7 - 4\frac{1}{3}$
$= 3 - \frac{1}{3}$ (7 - 4)
$= 2\frac{...}{3}$

b
$15 - 13\frac{2}{5}$
$= 2 - \frac{2}{5}$
$= 1\frac{...}{5}$

6. Use the above method to find :-

a $4 - 1\frac{1}{5}$ b $6 - 3\frac{4}{7}$ c $10 - 5\frac{5}{6}$

d $6 - 4\frac{3}{5}$ e $5 - 4\frac{7}{10}$ f $35 - 29\frac{3}{8}$.

7. 

From a 6 metre length of garden hose, the gardener cut off a piece which was $3\frac{3}{8}$ metres long.

What was the length of the piece of hose remaining ?

Multiply a Fraction or Mixed Number by a Whole Number

Be able to multiply a fraction or mixed number by a whole number.

Example 1 :-

Shown is an eighth of a pizza.

If I had five of these pieces

I could write it as $\frac{1}{8} + \frac{1}{8} + \frac{1}{8} + \frac{1}{8} + \frac{1}{8} = \frac{5}{8}$.

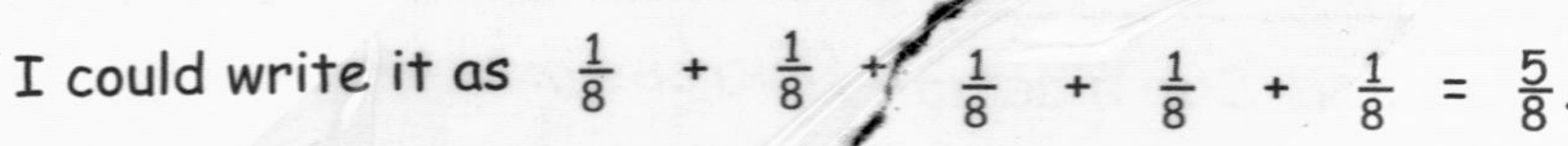

or I could write it as $5 \times \frac{1}{8} = \frac{5}{8}$ (*notice only the numerator (top) is multiplied by the 5*).

Example 2 :-

If I had four $\frac{7}{8}$'s pizza's,

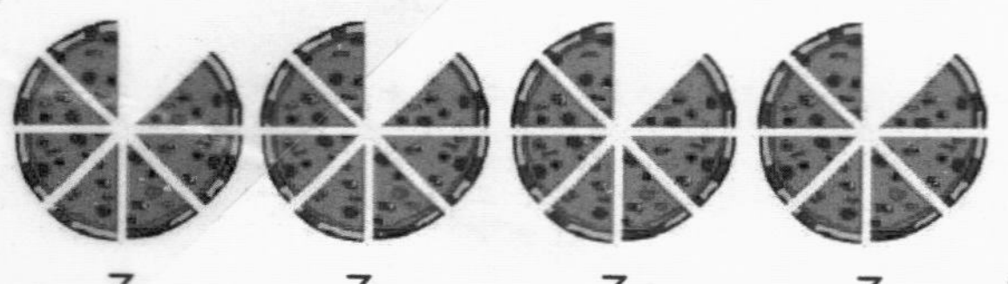

=> $\frac{7}{8} + \frac{7}{8} + \frac{7}{8} + \frac{7}{8} = \frac{28}{8} = 3\frac{4}{8} = 3\frac{1}{2}$

It is quicker to write as $4 \times \frac{7}{8} = \frac{28}{8} = 3\frac{4}{8} = 3\frac{1}{2}$.

Example 3 :-

Find a $7 \times 3\frac{1}{2}$ b $8 \times 4\frac{4}{5}$.

a
- **step 1** $7 \times 3 = 21$
- **step 2** $7 \times \frac{1}{2} = \frac{7}{2} = 3\frac{1}{2}$
- **step 3** $21 + 3\frac{1}{2} = 24\frac{1}{2}$

b
- **step 1** $8 \times 4 = 32$
- **step 2** $8 \times \frac{4}{5} = \frac{32}{5} = 6\frac{2}{5}$
- **step 3** $32 + 6\frac{2}{5} = 38\frac{2}{5}$

Exercise 3

1. Copy each of the following and complete :-

a
$\frac{1}{3} + \frac{1}{3} + \frac{1}{3} + \frac{1}{3} + \frac{1}{3}$
$= 5 \times \frac{1}{3}$
$= \frac{\dots}{3}$
$= 1\frac{\dots}{3}$

b
$\frac{5}{8} + \frac{5}{8} + \frac{5}{8} + \frac{5}{8} + \frac{5}{8} + \frac{5}{8}$
$= 6 \times \dots$
$= \frac{\dots}{8}$
$= 3\frac{\dots}{8} = 3\frac{\dots}{4}$

c $\frac{1}{4} + \frac{1}{4} + \frac{1}{4} + \frac{1}{4} + \frac{1}{4} + \frac{1}{4} + \frac{1}{4} =$

d $\frac{5}{12} + \frac{5}{12} + \frac{5}{12} + \frac{5}{12} + \frac{5}{12} =$.

2. Find :-

a $7 \times \frac{1}{5}$ b $9 \times \frac{3}{4}$ c $5 \times \frac{5}{8}$ d $8 \times \frac{4}{5}$

e $3 \times \frac{7}{10}$ f $6 \times \frac{5}{6}$ g $10 \times \frac{5}{8}$ h $8 \times \frac{13}{20}$.

3. Find :-

a $3 \times 2\frac{1}{5}$ b $5 \times 2\frac{3}{4}$ c $8 \times 7\frac{5}{8}$ d $4 \times 6\frac{4}{5}$

e $9 \times 1\frac{7}{10}$ f $7 \times 3\frac{5}{6}$ g $10 \times 3\frac{5}{8}$ h $6 \times 6\frac{13}{20}$.

4. Half pizzas can be ordered in Pizza Place.
Jake orders nine half pizzas.
Write Jake's order as a mixed number.

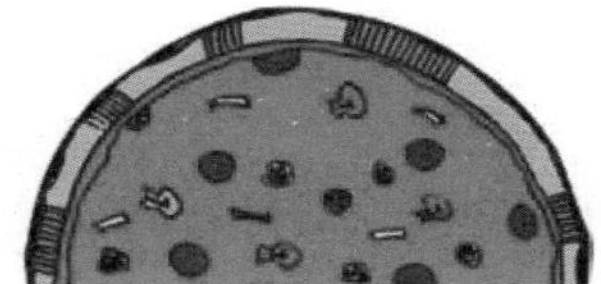

5. 

Marcus the magician has a trick where he uses ten $\frac{3}{4}$ metre strips of rope.

What is the total length of rope Marcus needs to perform his trick ?

6. A path is made using slabs which are $\frac{7}{8}$ of a metre square.

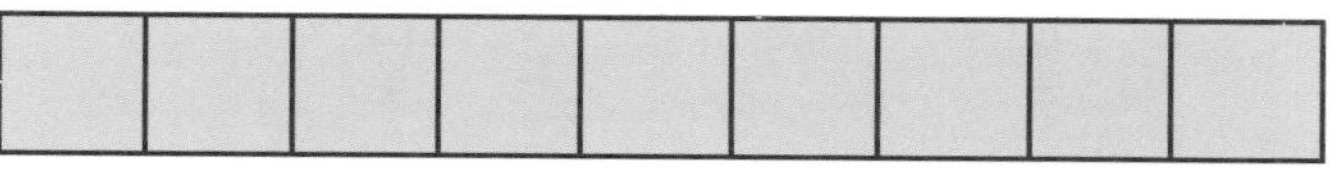

How long is the path if nine slabs are used ?

7. 

Bricks are $9\frac{4}{5}$ cm high.

How high is a wall that is seven bricks high ?

8. An average African elephant weighs $5\frac{2}{3}$ tonnes (*1 tonne = 1000 kg*).

What should this herd of 4 elephants weigh, in tonnes ?

9. 

Eight pencils, each of length $12\frac{1}{5}$ cm, and four pens, each of length $15\frac{3}{5}$ cm, are laid end to end in a straight line.

How long will this line of pens and pencils be ?

The 3 Я's

Revisit - Review - Revise

1. Write down three **equivalent** fractions for :-

a $\frac{1}{2}$ b $\frac{2}{3}$ c $\frac{5}{6}$ d $\frac{1}{12}$.

2. Find and **simplify** where possible :-

a $\frac{3}{8} + \frac{1}{8}$ b $\frac{7}{10} - \frac{3}{10}$ c $\frac{1}{3} + \frac{1}{3}$ d $\frac{1}{6} + \frac{1}{3}$

e $\frac{1}{6} + \frac{1}{2}$ f $\frac{1}{4} - \frac{1}{8}$ g $\frac{2}{3} + \frac{5}{6}$ h $\frac{3}{4} - \frac{1}{2}$

i $\frac{9}{10} - \frac{2}{5}$ j $\frac{7}{8} - \frac{3}{4}$ k $\frac{9}{10} - \frac{4}{5}$ l $\frac{11}{16} - \frac{3}{8}$.

3. Find :- a $\frac{1}{2} + \frac{1}{3} + \frac{1}{6}$ b $\frac{3}{4} + \frac{1}{2} + \frac{1}{8}$ c $\frac{4}{5} - \frac{3}{4} - \frac{1}{20}$.

4. Change each of the following to an **improper fraction** :-

a $1\frac{1}{4}$ b $3\frac{2}{3}$ c $7\frac{5}{8}$ d $10\frac{3}{10}$.

5. Change each of the following to a **mixed number** :-

a $\frac{9}{4}$ b $\frac{19}{3}$ c $\frac{29}{5}$ d $\frac{147}{12}$.

6. Find each of the following, leaving your answer as a **mixed number** :-

a $\frac{4}{3} + \frac{1}{3}$ b $1\frac{1}{5} + 2\frac{3}{5}$ c $6\frac{7}{8} - 2\frac{3}{8}$ d $2\frac{1}{2} + 3\frac{1}{4}$

e $5\frac{1}{4} + 1\frac{5}{8}$ f $6\frac{5}{6} - 4\frac{1}{3}$ g $10\frac{3}{4} - 7\frac{1}{2}$ h $3\frac{3}{7} + 1\frac{13}{14}$

i $4\frac{1}{3} - 1\frac{1}{6}$ j $7\frac{7}{12} - 3\frac{1}{2}$ k $6 - 2\frac{2}{7}$ l $11 - 7\frac{3}{10}$.

7. Find :-

a $8 \times \frac{1}{3}$ b $6 \times \frac{4}{5}$ c $3 \times \frac{9}{10}$ d $10 \times \frac{2}{5}$

e $2 \times 3\frac{2}{5}$ f $3 \times 2\frac{3}{8}$ g $5 \times 4\frac{2}{3}$ h $4 \times 6\frac{4}{5}$.

8. After a party, I was left with $3\frac{3}{4}$ cold pizzas.
Next morning my friends and I ate $1\frac{5}{8}$ of them.
The rest, we threw out. How much pizza was thrown out ?

Chapter 17

Time

Revision

Exercise 1

1. How many :-
   a minutes in 2 hours b seconds in 6 minutes
   c seconds in ten minutes d days in a leap year e weeks in a year ?

2. How many days are in :- a October b July ?

3. Write each time in 24 hour notation :-

   a 4:15 am b 7:10 pm c 10:20 am
   d 10:20 pm e 1:11 pm f noon.

4. Write each time in 12 hour notation (using am or pm) :-
   a 1415 b 1935 c 0510
   d 1100 e 1205 f 0001.

5. Change each of these to minutes and seconds :-
   a 130 secs b 305 secs c 800 secs.

6. Change each of these to hours and minutes :-
   a 85 mins b 215 mins c 541 mins.

7. Change each of these from minutes and seconds to seconds :-
   a 2 mins 20 secs b 10 mins 10 secs c 8 mins 15 secs.

8. Change each of these from hours and minutes to minutes :-
   a 3 hrs 35 mins b 9 hrs 5 mins c 5 hrs 17 mins.

9. Copy and complete :-

a		b		c	
	6 mins 20 secs		9 mins 40 secs		5 hrs 15 mins
	+ 2 mins 15 secs		− 6 mins 25 secs		− 4 hrs 30 mins

10. Write these in order, shortest time first :-

2·3 secs,	0·9 secs,	2·04 secs,	2·11 secs,	2 seconds.

Short Time Intervals Revision

Be able to calculate short time intervals.

Exercise 2

1. How many hours is it from :-

a 1 o'clock to 4 o'clock
b 8 o'clock to 12 o'clock
c 12 o'clock to 5 o'clock
d 1400 hours to 1700 hours
e half past 5 to half past 6
f half past 2 to half past 11
g quarter past 1 to quarter past 6
h 8:10 am to 10:10 am
i 0330 to 1130
j 1315 to 1915 ?

2. How many minutes is it from :-

a 2.15 pm to 3 pm
b 4.45 am to 5.10 am
c 3.55 pm to 4:35 pm
d 11.25 am to 12.05 pm
e 1520 to 1605
f 1840 to 2000
g 1115 to 1205
h 1642 to 1737 ?

3. The time on the bus station clock is shown opposite.

a What time does the clock read ?

b My bus leaves at quarter past four. How many minutes until my bus leaves ?

c Abel's bus leaves in 45 minutes time. At what time does his bus leave ?

d The bus to town leaves in 1 hour and 30 minutes time.
At what time does the bus to town leave ?

4. a Fiona arrives at 1635. Her bus is not till 1705.
How long will she have to wait for her bus ?

b If her bus is delayed until 1800, what will be her total wait time now ?

Longer Time Intervals

Be able to calculate more difficult time intervals.

Counting on :- The easiest way of finding how long something lasts is by counting on.

Example :- A TV programme started at 7.45 pm and ended at 10.25 pm.

How long did it last ?

Answer :-

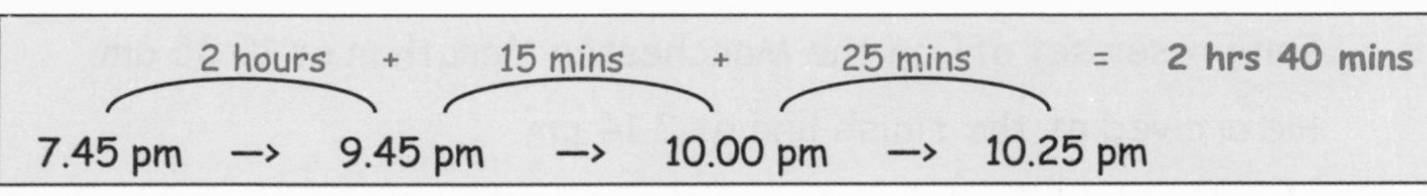

or

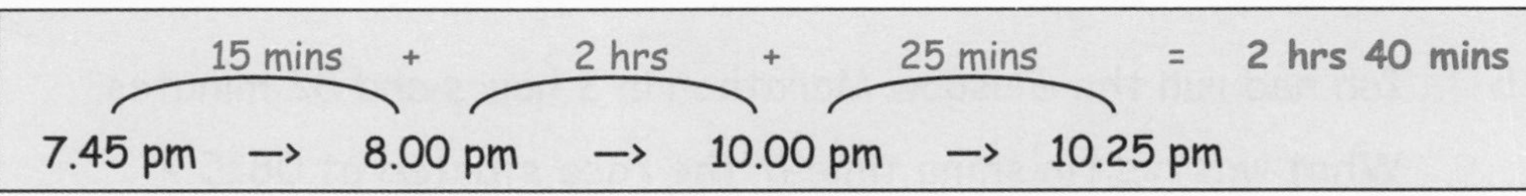

Discuss the above two methods of counting on.

Exercise 3

(*Show which method you used to "count on" in obtaining your answer*).

1. How long is it from :-

a 3.05 pm to 6.05 pm
b 10.00 am to 12.30 am
c midday to 5.30 pm
d 8.30 pm to 11.35 pm
e 7.55 am to 9.25 am
f 4.40 am to 6.15 am
g 0820 to 1025
h 1855 to 2020
i 1950 to 2105
j 2240 to 0300 (*next day*)
k Saturday 1645 to Sunday 1845
l Monday 1400 to Tuesday noon.

2. Calculate the finishing times for the following films :-

	Film A	Film B	Film C	Film D	Film E
Start Time	3.30 pm	5.45 pm	8.35 pm	11.35 am	11.30 pm
Film lasted	2 hr 30 mins	2 hr 40 mins	2 hr 45 mins	55 mins	3 hr 45 mins

3. The two clocks show when a gig started and finished one Saturday evening.

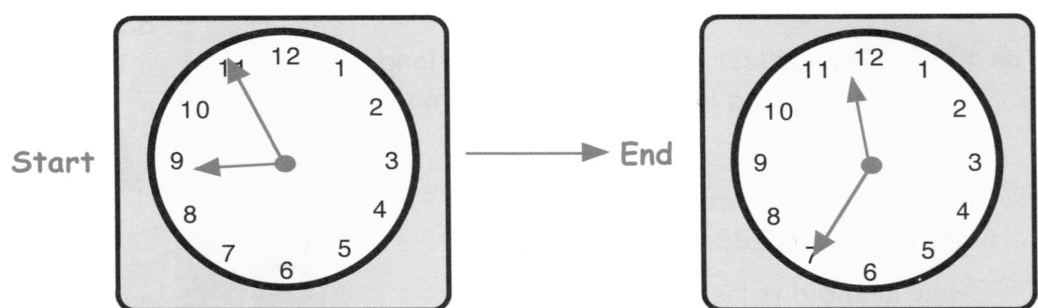

For how long did the gig last ?

4. a Ian Fraser set off on the Manchester Marathon at 10.35 am.
He arrived at the finish line at 2.14 pm.
How long had Ian taken to run the marathon ?

b Ian had run the Glasgow Marathon in 3 hours and 52 minutes.
What was his finishing time if the race started at 0815 ?

5. Shown is part of the bus timetable from Malton to Highrose.

	Malton ➤	*Lugton* ➤	*Blythe* ➤	*Fenton* ➤	*Highrose*
Early Bus	7.10 am	8.20 am	10.30 am	11.15 am	2.00 pm
Late Bus	11.05 am	12.15 am			5.55 pm

a How long does the early bus take to travel from :-

(i) Malton to Lugton

(ii) Blythe to Fenton

(iii) Malton to Highrose ?

b Assuming that the late bus travels at the same speed as the early bus, when would it be expected to arrive at :-

(i) Blythe (*Hint ! Notice how long the early bus takes from Lugton to Blythe*).

(ii) Fenton ?

c On a Sunday, the buses leave Malton at 8.45 am and at noon.
Use the same time intervals above to write out a new timetable for Sunday.

6. 

A cargo ship leaves Plymouth at 4.40 am and does not reach its destination till quarter to 6 at night.

For how long has the ship been at sea ?

7. A plane left Heathrow Airport at 2250 on Thursday.

It touched down in Mexico at 0735 (British time) on Friday.

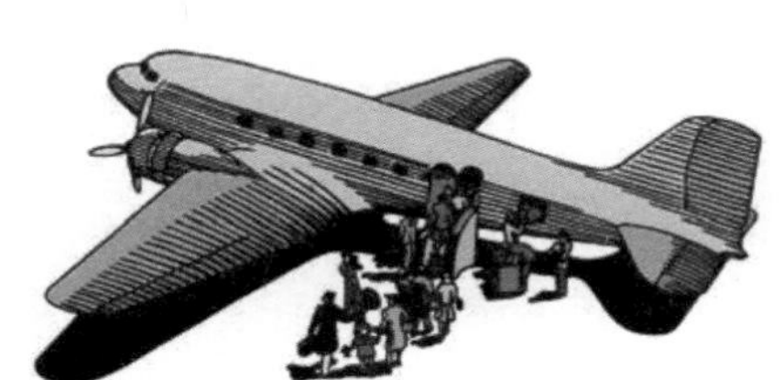

a How long did the flight take ?

On the flight back the plane took the same flight time and left at 0840 (*British Time*).

b At what time did the plane arrive at Heathrow ?

8. A satellite circles the earth. At 0350 it is directly above Newcastle.

It is then found to be above Newcastle again at 0730.

a Calculate the time taken for 1 complete orbit of the earth.

b When would you next expect the satellite to be over Newcastle ?

c How many times did it pass over Newcastle that day ?

9. 

Joe challenged Penny to see who could paint one side of the fence surrounding the village green quicker.

Joe started his side at 1045 and completed his task at 1305.

Penny began to paint the other side at 1350 and finished at 1605.

Who was quicker and by how many minutes ?

10. How long is it from :-

a 11 am Sunday to 6 pm Monday

b 2:40 pm Friday to 4:50 pm Sunday

c noon Monday to midnight Friday

d 3:20 pm Sunday to 5:50 pm Tuesday ?

11. Roz and her friends went to watch their favourite bands play at the "G in the Park" concert last weekend.

They arrived on Friday morning at 0930 and went home on Sunday night at 2230.

How long had they spent at the concert ?

More About Timetables

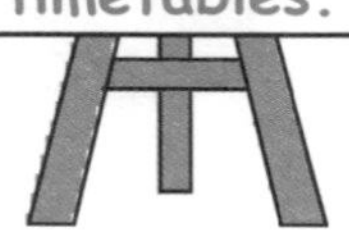

Exercise 4

1. A Sunday train service timetable is shown below.

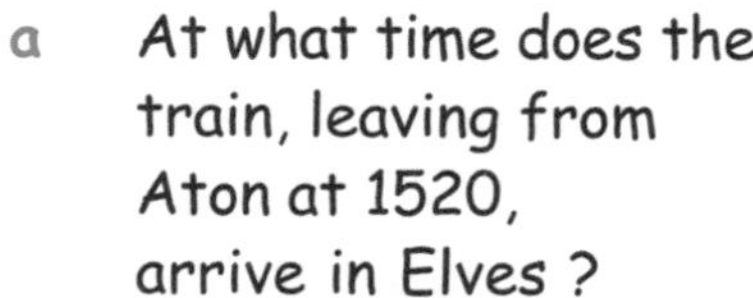

a At what time does the train, leaving from Aton at 1520, arrive in Elves ?

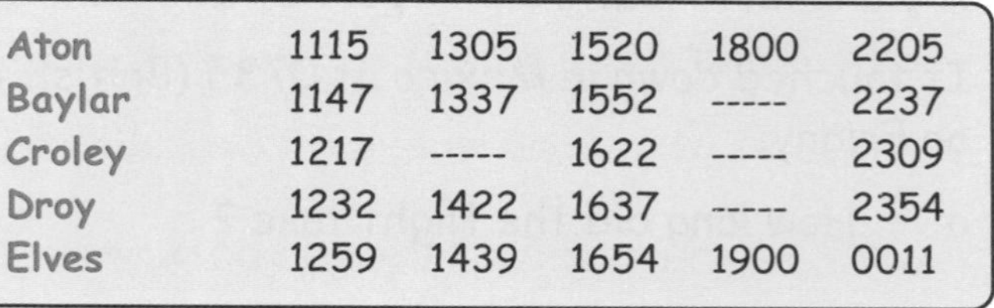

Aton	1115	1305	1520	1800	2205
Baylar	1147	1337	1552	-----	2237
Croley	1217	-----	1622	-----	2309
Droy	1232	1422	1637	-----	2354
Elves	1259	1439	1654	1900	0011

b At what time does the 1337 Baylar train arrive in Droy ?

c How long does the 1232 Droy train take to reach Elves ?

d What do you think ---- indicates on the timetable ?

e I arrive in Croley at 3:50 pm.

How long do I have to wait for a train to Elves ?

f It takes me 22 minutes to walk from my uncle's house in Croley to the station. If I want to catch the 1217 to Elves, what is the latest time I can leave his house ?

g Use the timetable to make up 3 questions of your own.

2. A scheduled executive helicopter flies from :-

Liverpool to Manchester to Leeds to Birmingham, then back to Liverpool.

The timetable is as shown :-

a When the helicopter departs at 10.10, at what time does it arrive at :-

(i) Manchester

(ii) Leeds

(iii) Birmingham ?

Liverpool		Manchester		Leeds		Birmingham	
Arrive	**Depart**	**Arrive**	**Depart**	**Arrive**	**Depart**	**Arrive**	**Depart**
	10.10	10.20	10.25	10.50	10.55	11.25	11.35
12.05	12.10	12.20	12.25	12.50	12.55	13.25	13.35
14.05	14.10	14.20	14.25	14.50	14.55	15.25	15.35
16.05	16.10	16.20	----	----	----	----	----
----	----	----	17.25	17.50	17.55	18.25	----

2. b The helicopter arrives in Leeds at 17.50.

Can you see that it did not depart from Liverpool ?

(i) Where did it depart from ?

(ii) At what time did it leave ?

c A managing director arrived at the helipad in Manchester at 2.10 pm.

(i) How long did he have to wait for the helicopter to Birmingham ?

(ii) At what time will he arrive in Birmingham ?

d Why is there a 5 minute gap between the arrival and departure times ?

e Using the timetable, make up questions where each of the following are the answers :-

(i) 16.05 (ii) 12.25 (iii) 25 minutes (iv) 18.25.

3. Here are train timetables for "London to Perth" and "Perth to London".

London <—> Perth				Perth <—> London			
London	leave	0525	2115	Perth	leave	0910	1922
Watford	arrive	0544	2133	Gleneagles	arrive	0930	1941
	leave	0545	2134		leave	0932	1943
Crewe		0805	2355	Dunblane		0945	1957
Preston	arrive	0903	0052	Stirling	arrive	0956	2008
	leave	0908	0057		leave	1000	2009
Stirling		1323	0454	Preston		1415	0032
Dunblane		1334	0504	Crewe		1514	0132
Gleneagles	arrive	1349	0520	Watford	arrive	1730	0353
	leave	1351	0522		leave	1732	0355
Perth	arrive	1410	0541	London	arrive	1749	0410

Write the following times in 12 hour time with am or pm :-

a When did the overnight train from London to Perth leave Preston ?

b At what time did the overnight train from Perth to London pass through Preston ?

3. c At what times do the trains leave Watford for London ?

d For how long do all trains stop at Gleneagles ?

e On the daytime London to Perth train, how long is the journey from Stirling to Dunblane ?

f On the daytime Perth to London train, how long is the journey from Dunblane to Stirling ?

g On the overnight London to Perth train, how long is the journey from Preston to Stirling ?

h On the overnight Perth to London train, how long is the journey from Stirling to Preston ?

i You were hoping to board the London bound train at Stirling Station, but arrived 10 minutes too late for the morning train.

How long was it till the next one ?

j I leave London on the early train for a meeting in Gleneagles at 2.30 pm. The train pulls out of London 35 minutes late.

Am I still likely to be on time for my meeting ?

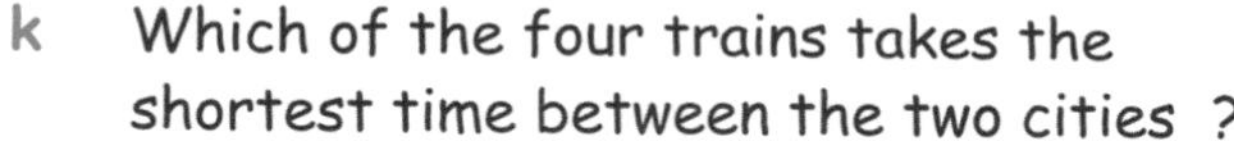

k Which of the four trains takes the shortest time between the two cities ?

4. The London to Perth timetable (*on the previous page*) is to be updated.

The morning train will now leave London **one hour and ten minutes later** than the original time.

All train times after that will also change by the same length of time.

Write out the new daytime train timetable.

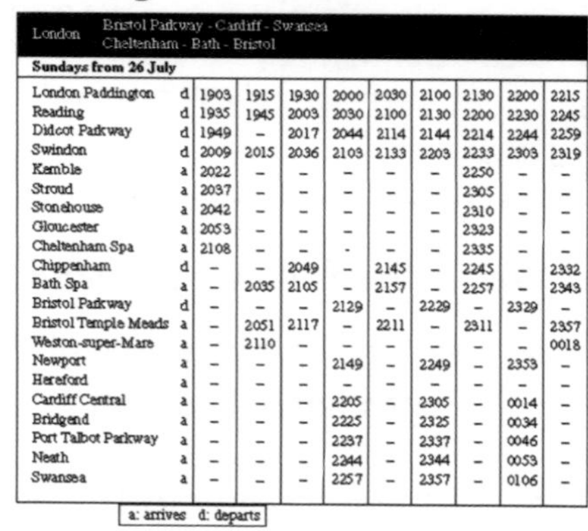

London — Bristol Parkway - Cardiff - Swansea / Cheltenham - Bath - Bristol

Sundays from 26 July

London Paddington	d	1903	1915	1930	2000	2030	2100	2130	2200	2215
Reading	d	1935	1945	2003	2030	2100	2130	2200	2230	2245
Didcot Parkway	d	1949	–	2017	2044	2114	2144	2214	2244	2259
Swindon	d	2009	2015	2036	2103	2133	2203	2233	2303	2319
Kemble	a	2022	–	–	–	–	–	2250	–	–
Stroud	a	2037	–	–	–	–	–	2305	–	–
Stonehouse	a	2042	–	–	–	–	–	2310	–	–
Gloucester	a	2053	–	–	–	–	–	2323	–	–
Cheltenham Spa	a	2108	–	–	-	–	–	2335	–	–
Chippenham	d	–	–	2049	–	2145	–	2245	–	2332
Bath Spa	a	–	2035	2105	–	2157	–	2257	–	2343
Bristol Parkway	d	–	–	–	2129	–	2229	–	2329	–
Bristol Temple Meads	a	–	2051	2117	–	2211	–	2311	–	2357
Weston-super-Mare	a	–	2110	–	–	–	–	–	–	0018
Newport	a	–	–	–	2149	–	2249	–	2353	–
Hereford	a	–	–	–	–	–	–	–	–	–
Cardiff Central	a	–	–	–	2205	–	2305	–	0014	–
Bridgend	a	–	–	–	2225	–	2325	–	0034	–
Port Talbot Parkway	a	–	–	–	2237	–	2337	–	0046	–
Neath	a	–	–	–	2244	–	2344	–	0053	–
Swansea	a	–	–	–	2257	–	2357	–	0106	–

a: arrives d: departs

5. a Investigate some local timetables.

b Write down some of the information given in your timetable.

c Make up some questions about your timetable and get your friend to answer them.

6. **Project.**

Pick 4 or 5 cities in England and plan a circular bus/train trip using the internet that will allow you to visit all your chosen cities.

The 3 R's — Revisit - Review - Revise

1. Write these times as **24 hour times** :- a 8:17 am b 11:29 pm.

2. Change the following into **minutes** and **seconds** :-
   a 70 secs b 132 secs c 201 secs d 390 secs.

3. Write these in **hours** and **minutes** :-
   a 86 mins b 150 mins c 193 mins d 423 mins.

4. Here are the times of two wine & dine cruises down the west coast of Scotland.

	Ullapool	Mallaig	Fort William	Oban	Greenock	Ayr	Stranraer
Early dep.	0845	1135	1520	1725	1958	2112	2245
Late dep.	1330	1620	2005				

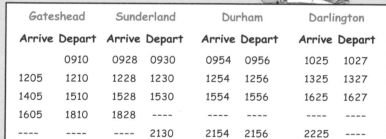

   a How long does it take from Mallaig to Oban ?
   b How long does the Early sail take altogether ?
   c Assuming both take the same time, at what time would the Late sail pass Ayr ?

5. A timetable for a special Senior Citizens' Minibus is shown.

Gateshead Arrive	Gateshead Depart	Sunderland Arrive	Sunderland Depart	Durham Arrive	Durham Depart	Darlington Arrive	Darlington Depart
	0910	0928	0930	0954	0956	1025	1027
1205	1210	1228	1230	1254	1256	1325	1327
1405	1510	1528	1530	1554	1556	1625	1627
1605	1810	1828	----	----	----	----	----
----	----	----	2130	2154	2156	2225	----

   a When the Minibus leaves Gateshead at 0910, at what time does it arrive at Darlington ?

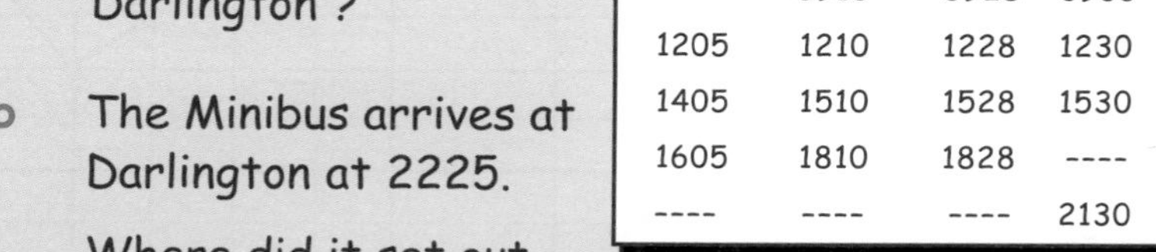

   b The Minibus arrives at Darlington at 2225.
   Where did it set out from and when did it leave ?

   c I am at the bus stop in Sunderland at 6:15 pm.
   How long do I have to wait for the next Darlington bus to come along ?

   d How long does the journey take from :-
   (i) Gateshead to Sunderland (ii) Gateshead to Durham
   (iii) Sunderland to Durham (iv) Gateshead to Darlington ?

Chapter 18

Statistics

Line Graphs Revision

Exercise 1

1. This line graph shows the daily noon temperatures recorded in a school.

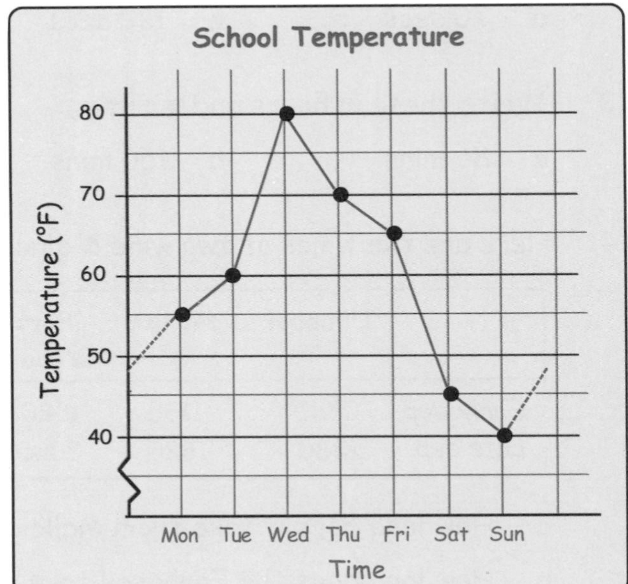

   a What was the noon temperature on :-
      (i) Monday
      (ii) Friday ?

   b One day was particularly hot.
      Which day do you think this was ?

   c On what day was the lowest recorded temperature ?

   d Why do you think this day had the lowest temperature ?

2. A hospital patient's temperature was taken every hour and recorded on the graph opposite.

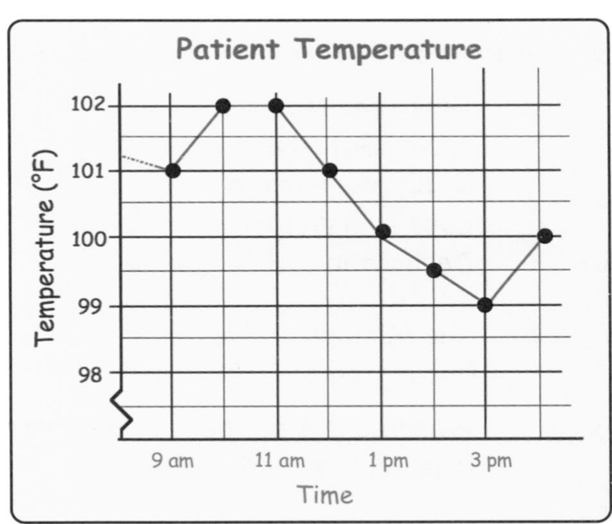

   a What was the patient's :-
      (i) highest temperature
      (ii) lowest temperature ?

   b By how many degrees did it fall between 11 am and 3 pm ?

   c State the patient's temperature :-
      (i) at 9 am (ii) at noon
      (iii) at 2 pm (iv) at 4 pm.

   d Estimate the patient's temperature at half past one.

3. Bob runs an ice cream van from February to November.

He records the number of ice-creams sold each month and plots these on a line graph.

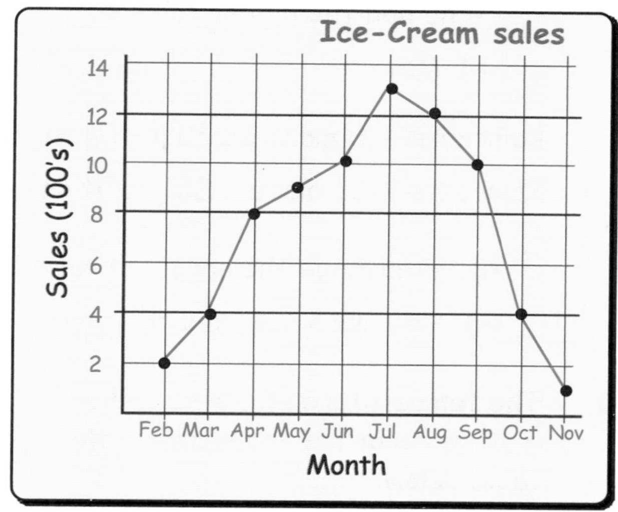

a How many ice-creams were sold in :-

(i) March (*not just 4*

(ii) August

(iii) October ?

b How many ice-creams were sold in :-

(i) April (ii) May (iii) July ?

c Bob buys a bigger van and estimates he will sell double the amount next year.

How many ice-creams is Bob expecting to sell next year altogether ?

d Why do you think Bob does not take his van out in December and January ?

e (i) Between which 2 months was the biggest change in sales ?

(ii) Describe what happened to the sales in these two months.

4. Two rain coat companies

- Raincoats-4-U (in red) and
- RainCoats-R-Us (in green)

compare sales.

The comparative line graph gives the sales in thousands of units.

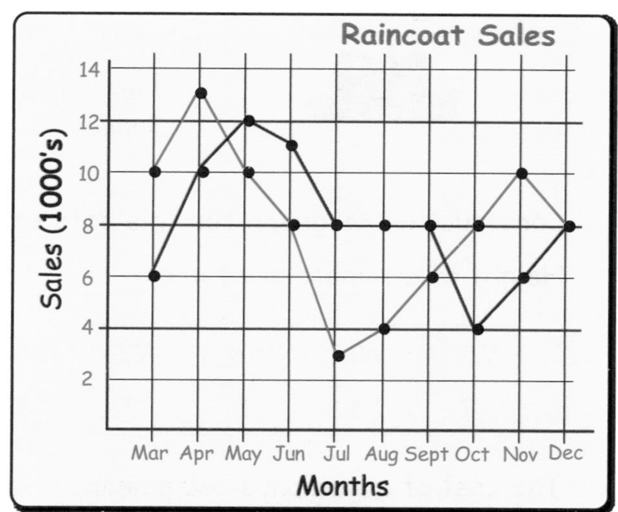

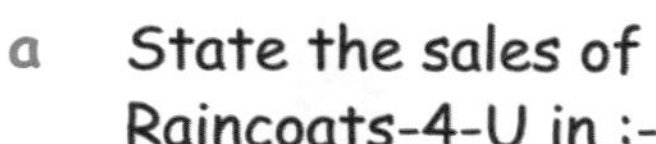

a State the sales of Raincoats-4-U in :-

(i) March

(ii) August

(iii) July.

b State the sales of Raincoats-R-Us in :-

(i) April (ii) August (iii) June.

4. c Who had the higher sales in :-

(i) May (ii) December ?

Raincoats-4-U made a £10 profit on each coat.

Raincoats-R-Us made a £6 profit on each coat.

d (i) Who made the greater profit in August ?

(ii) How much more did they make ?

5. The temperature of a wine chiller, in °C, is recorded and shown in the table below.

Mon	Tue	Wed	Thu	Fri	Sat
4	5	4·5	6	8	7·5

Copy and complete the line graph to show this information.

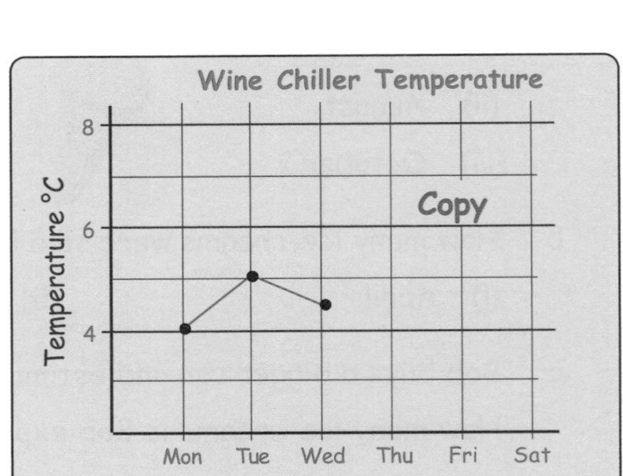

6.

The temperature (°C) in a pharmacist's medicine cooler is recorded and shown in the table below.

Mon	Tue	Wed	Thu	Fri	Sat
6	7	4	5	8·5	7·5

Draw a line graph to show this information. (*Similar to the one above*).

7. Construct a line graph for this data set :-

Height of a tomato plant in cm.

Wk 1	Wk 2	Wk 3	Wk 4	Wk 5	Wk 6
2	3	5	7	10	12

8. The cost of a medium sized pineapple varies at different times of the year.

This table shows the cost in pence of a pineapple from June (2013) to June (2014).

Jun	Aug	Oct	Dec	Feb	Apr	Jun
40	50	70	90	85	60	45

Construct a line graph for this set of prices.

Misleading Graphs

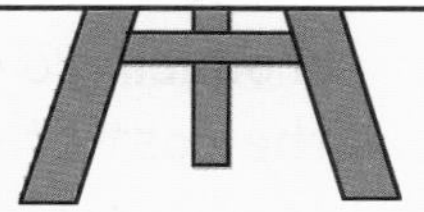

Sometimes, graphs can be misleading. This might be because of a bad scale or because of a lack of information.

At other times, the errors are used to deliberately mislead the person looking at the graph.

The graph below on the left shows the price of a litre of petrol over a 2 year period.

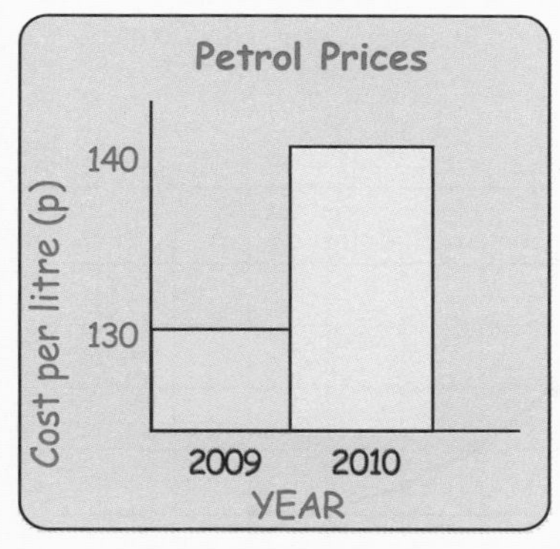

The graph is very misleading.

It looks as if the price of petrol in 2010 was nearly 3 times that in 2009.

In fact, it was only 10p more, which is only about 8% greater than the 2009 price.

The graph on the right gives a better indication of the prices.

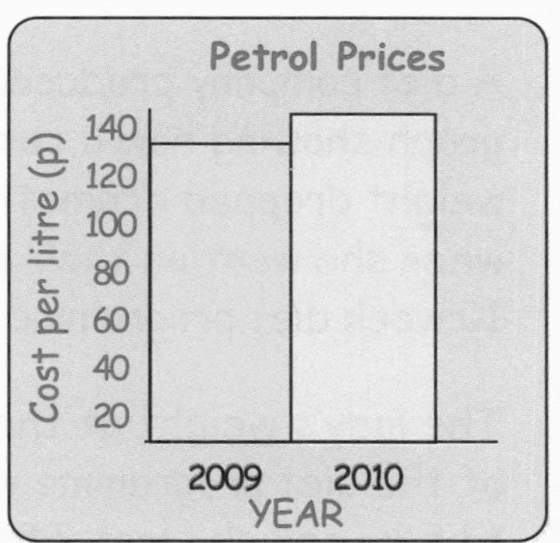

Exercise 2

1. Discuss with your teacher and the rest of the class the two graphs shown above.
   - a Why do you think the graph on the left (above) is drawn this way, and who do you think might have deliberately produced it like this ?
   - b The oil companies who sell petrol would prefer the right hand graph. Say why you think they would prefer it.

2. Discuss or write down other ways in which graphs or charts can be misleading.

   Explain why companies or businesses might want to show information in a misleading way.

3. This graph shows the average price of a small loaf of bread in 2005 and 2010.

   - a Explain why the graph is misleading.
   - b Draw a bar graph that gives a better picture of the comparison of prices in 2005 and 2010.

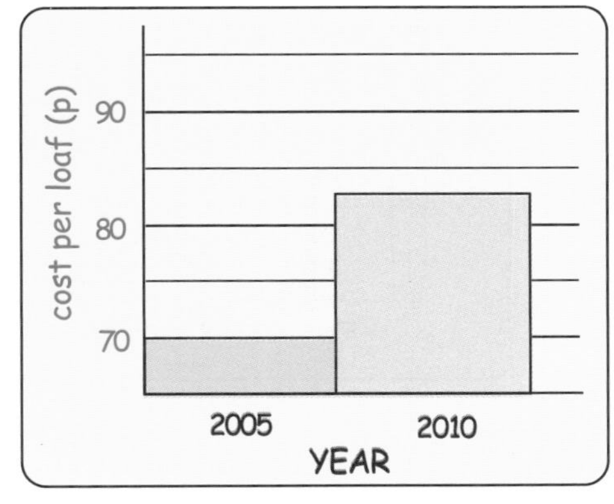

4. Adsco supermarket advertised how good their prices were compared to their rivals, Tesca and Rainburys by producing a graph showing the cost of a 250 g pack of vine tomatoes.

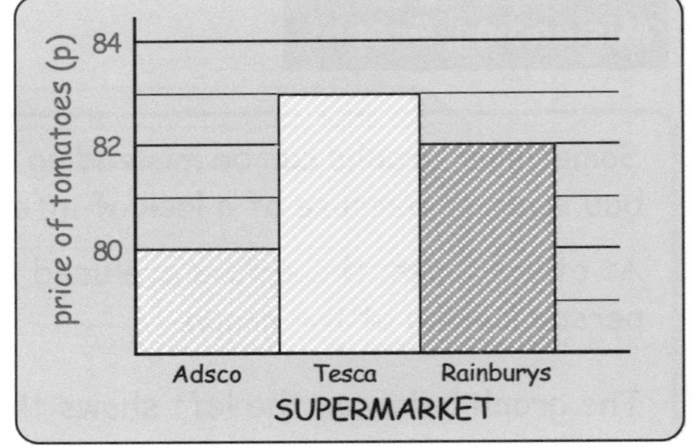

a Explain why Adsco's graph is unfair.

b Draw a new graph showing more clearly the prices of the tomatoes in all 3 stores.

5. A diet company produced a line graph showing how a customer's weight dropped dramatically (?) when she went on their new 10 week diet programme.

The lady's weight at the start of the diet programme was 61·5 kg and she lost 2·5 kg over the 10 weeks.

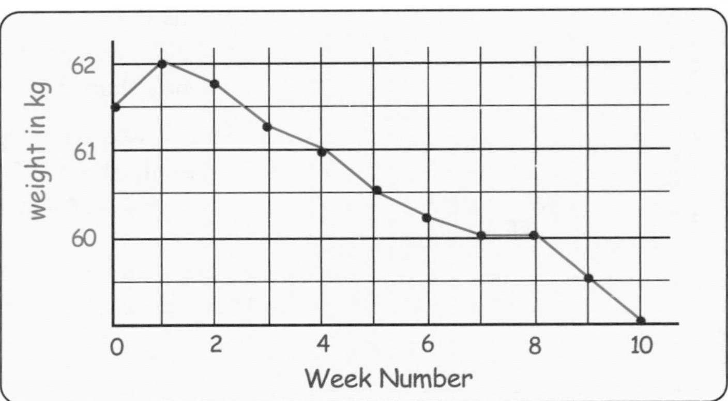

a Explain why the graph is misleading.

b Draw a new line graph showing her weight loss more accurately.

6. Many graphs are poor or misleading because of bad scales or no scales at all, or because vital information, including labels, are missing.

Say what is wrong with the following graphs (possibly several points) and indicate how the graphs could be improved.

a

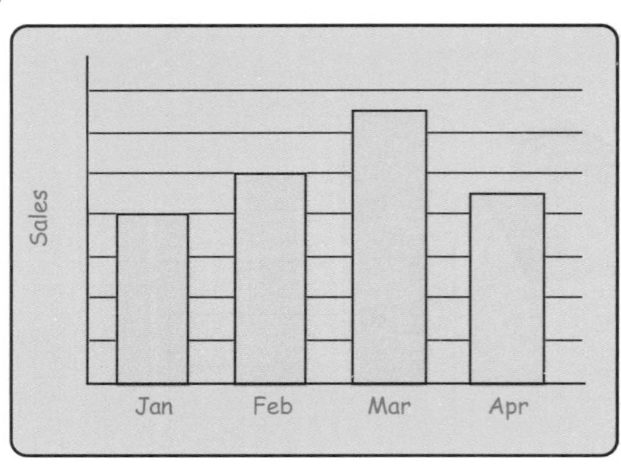

b

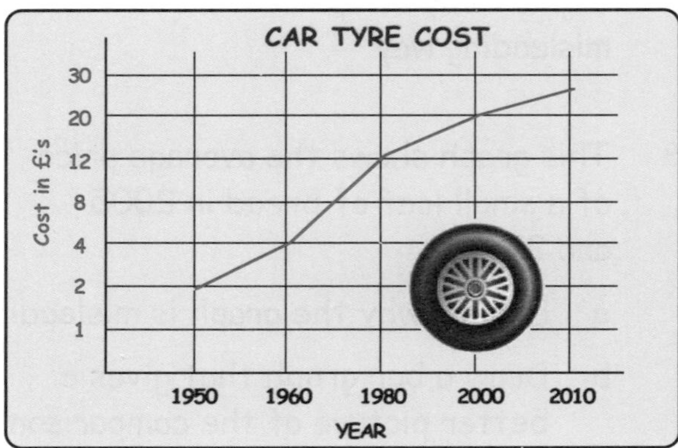

6. c

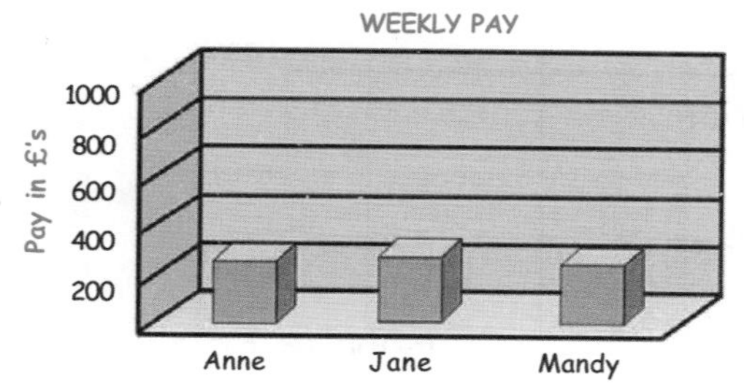

d

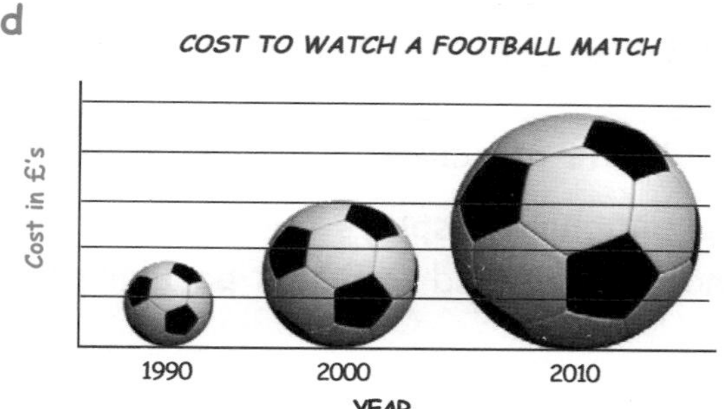

e

CRIME RATES

Crimes

Crime has dropped drastically over the last 5 years

2007 2008 2009 2010 2011

f

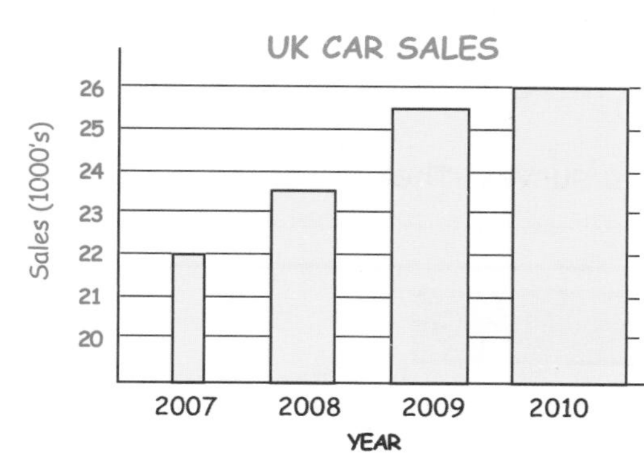

7. Two companies, A and B, were asked to conduct a survey into which brand of coffee - *Kwik Koffee* or *Rich Coffee* - people prefer.

Company A

9/10 of people surveyed preferred *Kwick Koffee.*

100 people in survey

Company B

7/10 of people surveyed preferred *Rich Coffee.*

ten thousand people in survey

Which of the two surveys do you think is more valid.

Explain your answer.

8. Try to draw some of your own misleading graphs.

9. Try to find examples of graphs that are badly drawn or misleading from newspapers, magazines or books and bring them in to form a classroom display.

Interpreting Pie Charts

Pie Charts are useful for displaying information.

This pie chart displays the result of a survey conducted to find the most popular pet in a class.

The chart shows that the dog was the most popular.

The cat is shown to be liked by $\frac{1}{4}$ of the class.

If there were 28 pupils in the class at the time of the survey, then $\frac{1}{4}$ of 28 = 7 pupils voted for the cat.

Favourite Pets

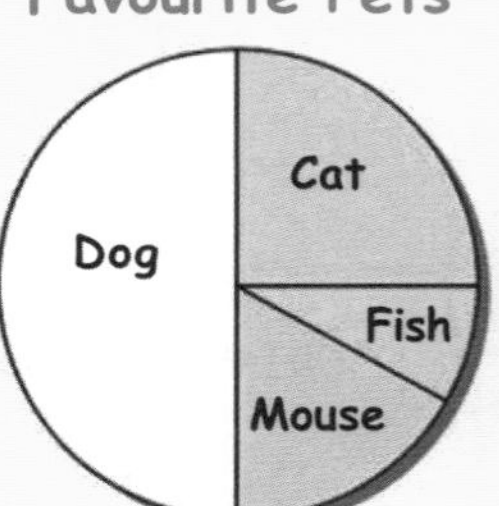

Exercise 3

Favourite Drinks

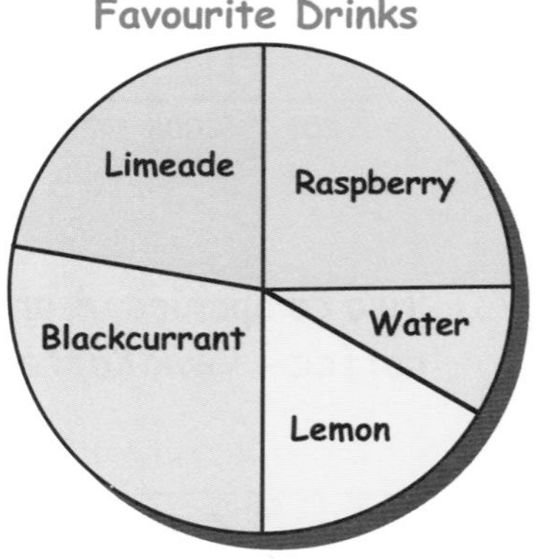

1. The class also surveyed the most popular drink.
   - a Write down the class' favourite drink.
   - b List the drinks in order, from most popular.

2. This pie chart has been divided into 10 equal sectors.

   How many tenths are shown in the :-
   - a **green** sector (A)
   - b pink sector (B)
   - c **blue** sector (C) ?

Favourite Restaurant

3. The pie chart shows the results of a survey of favourite restaurant food.
   - a Write the fraction ($\frac{?}{10}$) of those who chose :-
     - (i) Chinese
     - (ii) Thai
     - (iii) Italian
     - (iv) Indian.
   - b List the foods in order, from most popular to least popular.
   - c 50 people took part in this survey,

     How many of them preferred :- (i) Italian (ii) Indian ?

4. 200 people were asked to name their favourite holiday destination.

The results are shown in the pie chart.

Calculate how many people chose :-

a USA b Tenerife
c Spain d Greece.

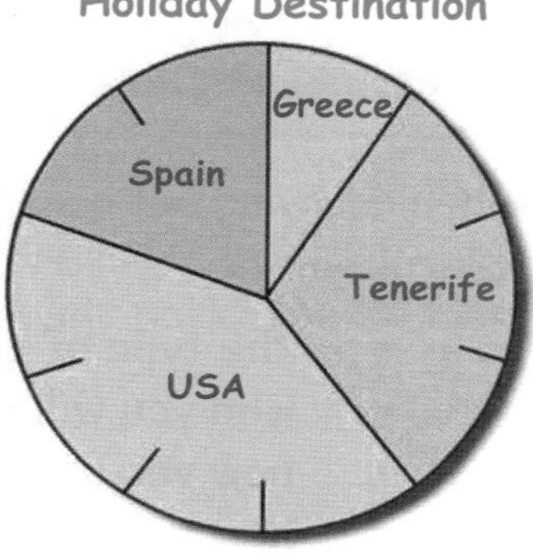

5. TRANSPORT to SCHOOL

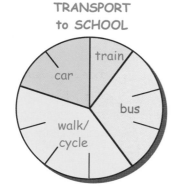

train
car
bus
walk/ cycle

This pie chart was constructed showing the results of a survey into how children got to school.

a What fraction of pupils walked/cycled to school ?

b What fraction took a bus ?

c If the whole school population (800) was surveyed, how many :-

(i) took the train to school

(ii) were driven by car to school ?

6. During a police traffic survey, the number of faults which each car had was recorded.

The least common fault was a faulty brake light.

The most common fault was bald tyres.

Of the rest, no tax discs were more common than broken exhaust pipes.

Write down which letter represents which type of fault.

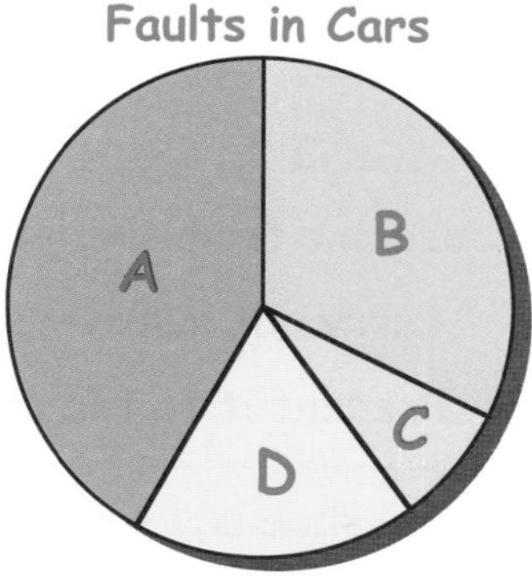

7. This pie chart has been divided into 20 equal parts.

a What fraction does each part stand for ?

b What fraction represents :-

(i) Dinner (ii) Supper
(iii) Lunch (iv) Breakfast ?

400 people were asked in the survey :-

c What is $\frac{1}{20}$ of 400 ?

d How many people chose :-

(i) Dinner (ii) Supper (iii) Lunch (iv) Breakfast ?

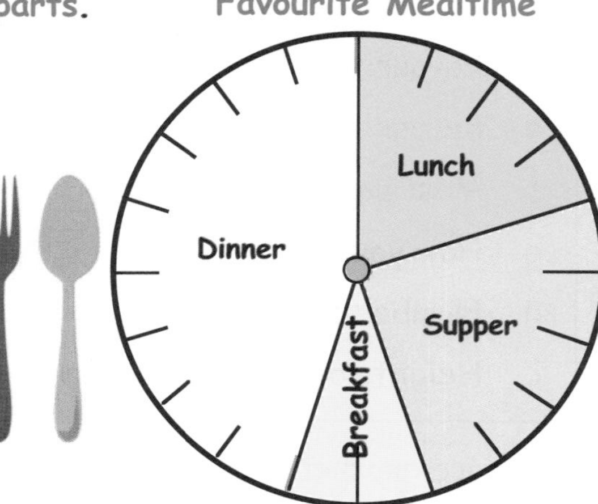

Conducting a Survey

Conduct a survey, write & present a report and discuss the results.

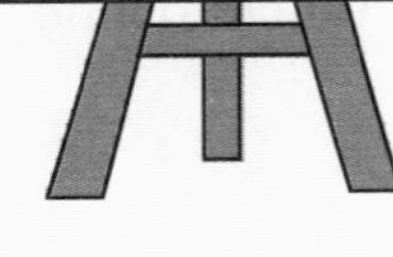

When carrying out a survey you need to consider several points :-

- the type of questions you will ask
- who you will ask
- how you will organise your answers
- how you will display your answers.

When deciding how to present or display the results of your survey, you may wish to use a frequency table, bar graph, line graph or pie chart.

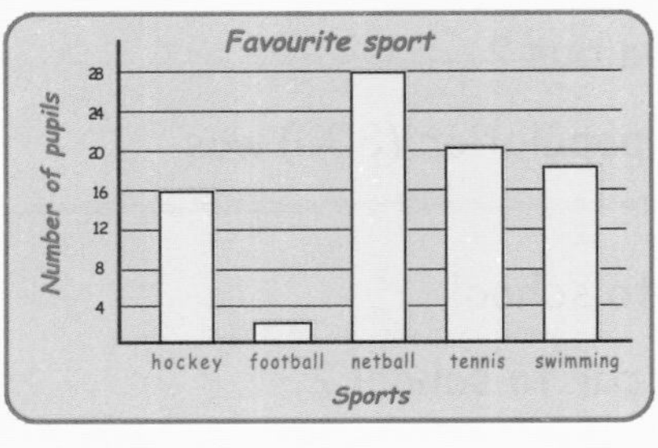

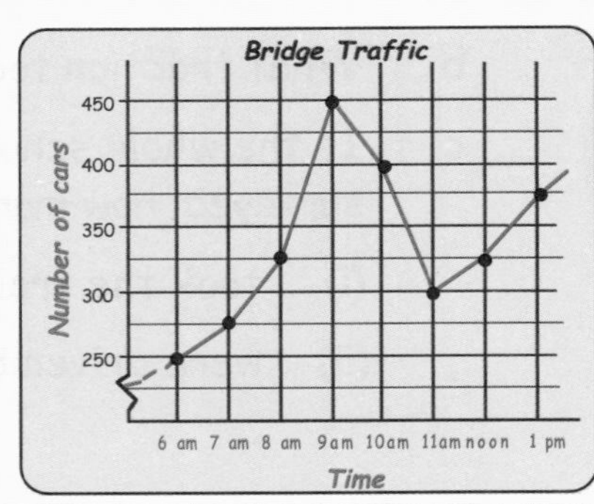

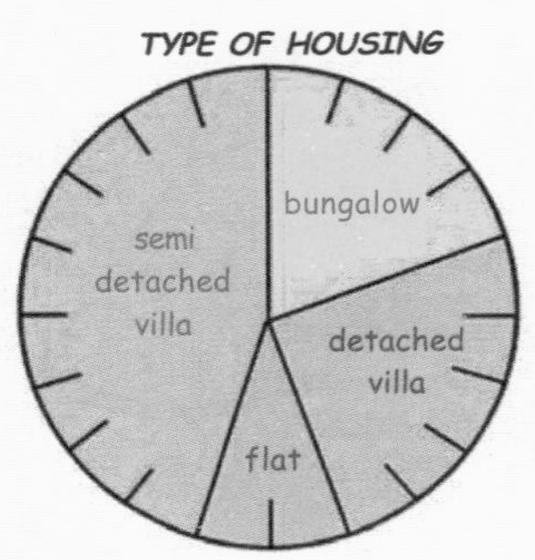

Exercise 4

1. Choose one from the list shown in the yellow box below, then :-
   - Carry out a survey;
   - Write a report;
   - Present it to the class;
   - Discuss your results with the class.

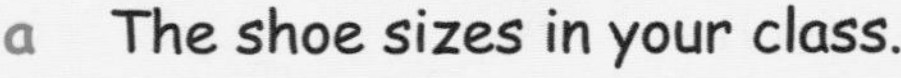

a The shoe sizes in your class.

b Which month of the year were the members of your class born ?

c Favourite class cartoon character.

d Favourite international football team.

e Favourite pop star.

f Most popular breakfast.

g How you get to school

h Number of words each member of your class can write neatly in 30 seconds.

i Heights of each pupil in your class.

2. Choose another from the list - or make one up for yourself - and conduct a survey.

   (Make sure that this survey is different from your first. You could work in groups and display your graphs and charts).

The 3 Я's

Revisit - Review - Revise

1. The line graph shows the average temperatures in a warehouse over a 10 month period.

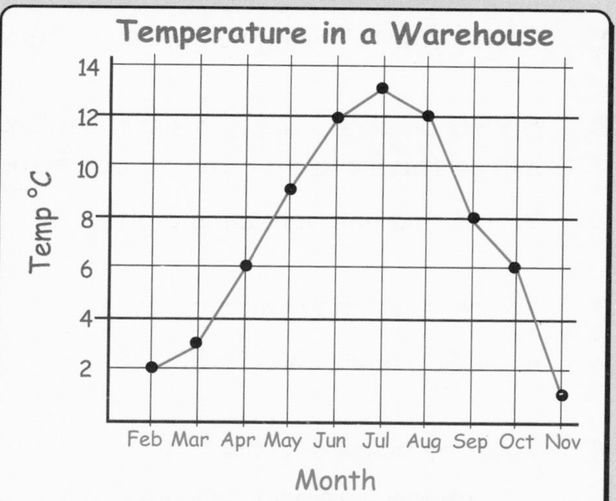

   a What was the average temperature in :-

      (i) February (ii) April

      (iii) May (iv) November ?

   b What was the highest average temperature ?

   c Why do you think the temperatures go up and down in this way ?

2. The sales of Halibut in a fish shop over one week are as follows :-

   Mon - 30 **Tue** - 20 **Wed** - 10 **Thu** - 25 **Fri** - 45 **Sat** - 35.

   Draw a line graph to show this information.

3. a Draw an example of a misleading graph with scales and heading included.

   b Explain why your graph is misleading.

4. The pie chart shows the results of a survey asking people what their favourite weekend activities were.

Favourite Activity

TV

Golf

Swimming

Football

   a Write the fraction ($\frac{?}{10}$) of those who chose :-

      (i) TV (ii) Swimming

      (iii) Football (iv) Golf.

   b List the activities in order, from **most** popular to **least** popular.

   c If 200 people took part in this survey, **how many** of them preferred :-

      (i) Football (ii) Golf (iii) Swimming ?

Chapter 19

Revision - Year 5

1. Write the following numbers out fully in words :- a 53 006 b 320 800.

2. Six hundred and eight thousand five hundred and eleven motorists drove over the Golden Gate Bridge last month.

   Write this number using digits.

3. Write down the number that is :-

   a 3000 more than 28 500 b 30 000 less than 850 000.

4. Find the missing numbers :-

   a 17 200, 15 200, 13 200, ... b 1 000 000, ..., 900 000 ... .

5. a Round to the nearest 1000 :- (i) 6589 (ii) 34 812.

   b Round to the nearest 10 000 :- (i) 48 320 (ii) 276 500.

   c Round to the nearest 100 000 :- (i) 572 000 (ii) 849 999.

6. Round both numbers to the nearest 1000, then estimate :- 39 740 + 8199.

7. What Roman Numerals are used to write the number :-

   a 123 b 360 c 849 d 950 ?

8. What numbers do these Roman symbols represent :-

   a CXXI b CCCLXVII c CDXCII d CMLIII ?

9. Try these mentally. Write down the answers to :-

   a 370 + 530 b 6000 - 1300 c 65 000 + 25 000

   d 54 300 - 13 300 e 152 013 + 301 704 f 1 000 000 - 699 999.

10. Copy each example and work out the answer :-

    a $\begin{array}{r} 69\,837 \\ -\ 28\,475 \\ \hline \end{array}$ b $\begin{array}{r} 306\,524 \\ +\ 75\,387 \\ \hline \end{array}$ c $\begin{array}{r} 463\,938 \\ -\ 163\,085 \\ \hline \end{array}$

11. Milandy Bakeries sold 517 000 loaves last month.

    186 500 of them were white - the rest were brown.

    How many brown loaves did Milandy Bakers sell ?

12. Name each of the angles below using 3 letters and the "∠" sign, and state what type of angle each is :-

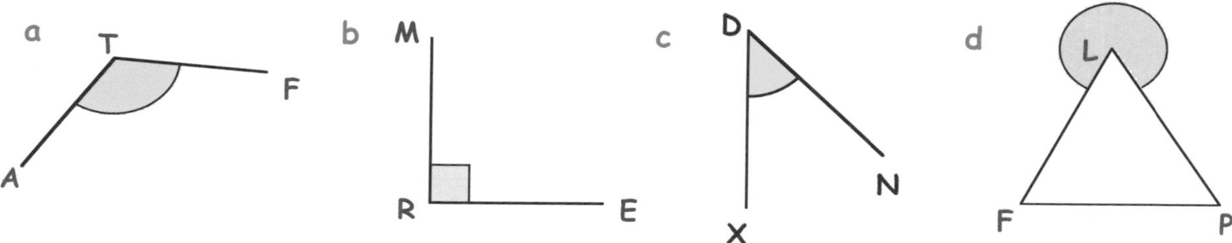

13. Use a protractor to measure each of these angles :-

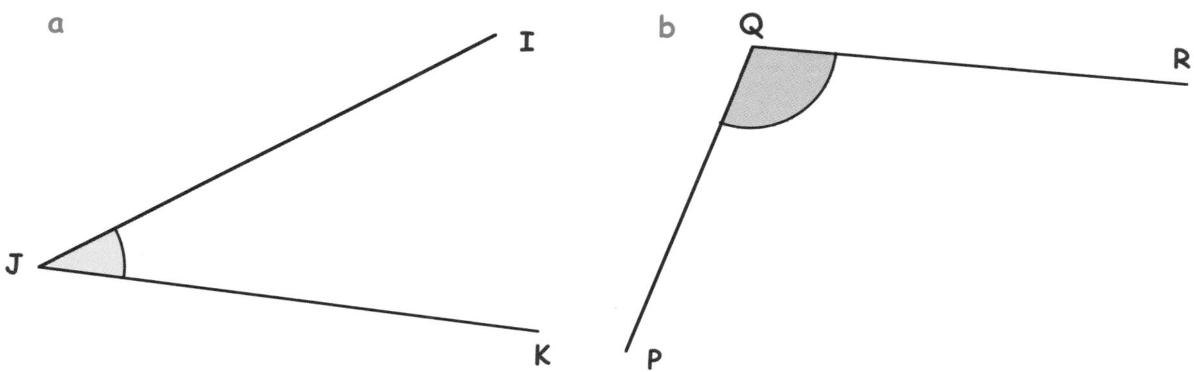

14. Draw and label these two angles :- a ∠DEF = 75° b ∠WYZ = 155°.

15. How many degrees will I turn through if I rotate clockwise from SE to West ?

16. Copy the following and work out the answers :-

a
```
   93
 x 7
 ____
 ____
```

b
```
  264
  x 9
 ____
 ____
```

c 6 x 1387

d 5079 x 8.

17. Set down and work out :-

a
```
   5 3
 x 3 2
 ______
 ........
 ........
 ........
```

b
```
  2 8 5
   x 7 3
 ______
 ........
 ........
 ........
```

c
```
 1 3 0 7
   x 5 4
 ______
 ........
 ........
 ........
```

18. Write down the answer to each of these :-

a 10 x 5365 b 432 x 1000 c 49 200 ÷ 10 d 520 000 ÷ 100.

19. Set down the following, show your working and complete each calculation :-

a 5124 ÷ 6 b 34 047 ÷ 9 c $\frac{2352}{8}$ d $\frac{53\,900}{7}$.

20\. a Do these, expressing the remainder as a fraction :- (i) 134 ÷ 3 (ii) 2874 ÷ 8.

b Do these, expressing the remainder as a decimal :- (i) 347 ÷ 2 (ii) 3267 ÷ 5.

21\. State what temperature is represented on this thermometer :-

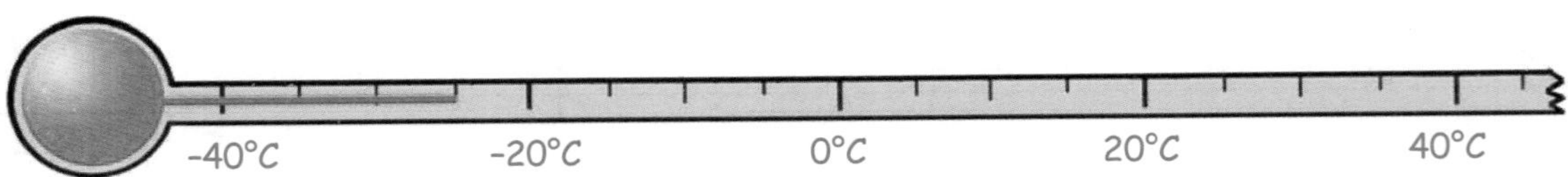

22\. Write down the missing numbers :-

a 11, 8, 5, ..., ..., -4, ..., -10

b -30, -23, -16, ..., ..., 5, ...

23\. What is :-

a 11°C down from 7°C

b 7°C up from -1°C

c 25° up from -10°C

d 13°C down from -67°C ?

24\. Write down the area in cm^2 of this shape :-

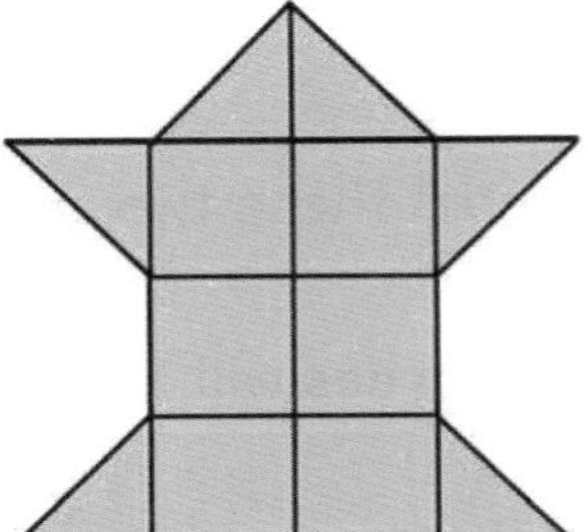

25\. Calculate the areas of these shapes in cm^2 or in m^2 :-

a

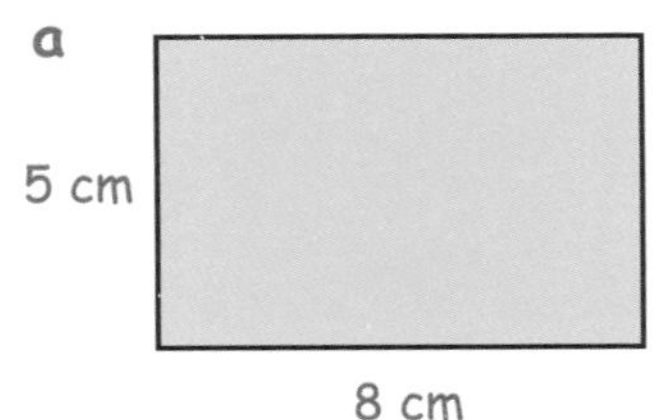

b

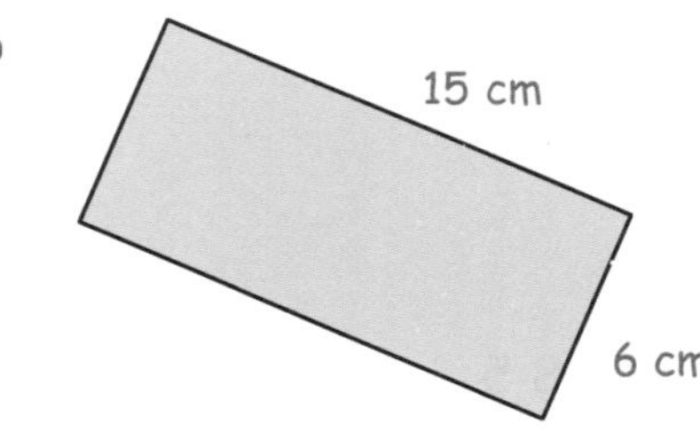

c

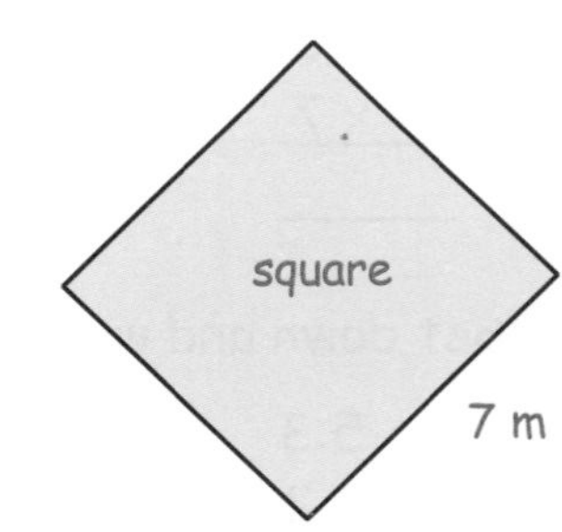

26\. Write down the first six multiples of :- a 5 b 11.

27\. Write down all the factors of :- a 18 b 50.

28\. Write down all the common factors of :- a 18 and 24 b 80 and 100.

29\. List all the prime numbers between :- a 0 and 10 b 30 and 40.

30. Find :-

a 5^2 b 11^2 c 4^3 d 10^3.

31. Of the 5 angles, 55°, 210°, 90°, 107° and 180°, one is a right angle, one an acute angle, one an obtuse angle, one a reflex angle and one a straight angle. Which is which ?

32. What is the :- a complement of 70° b supplement of 70° ?

33. Copy and complete each diagram below, filling in all missing angles :-

a

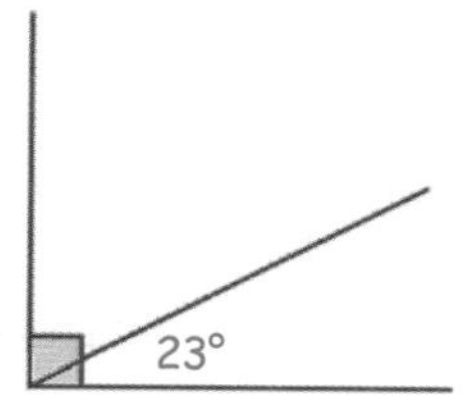

b

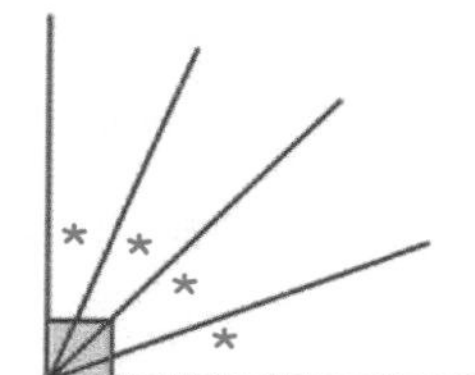

c

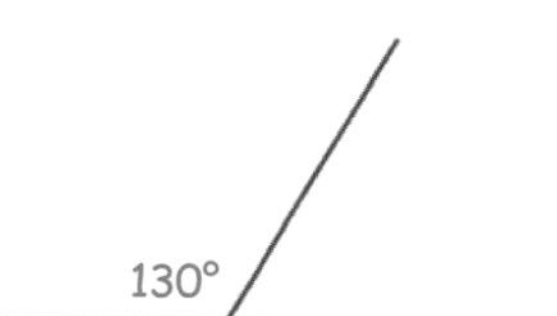

d

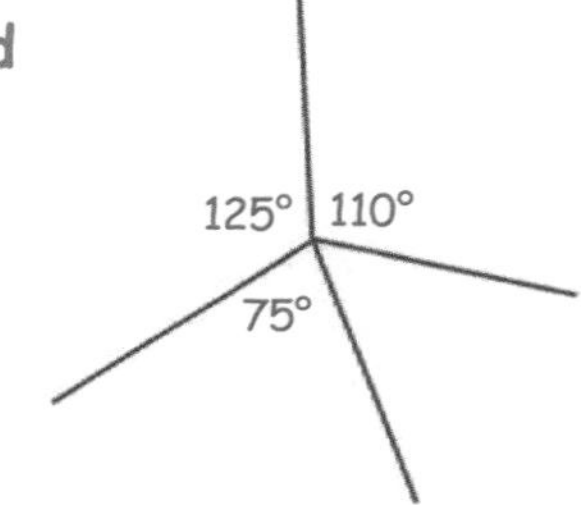

e

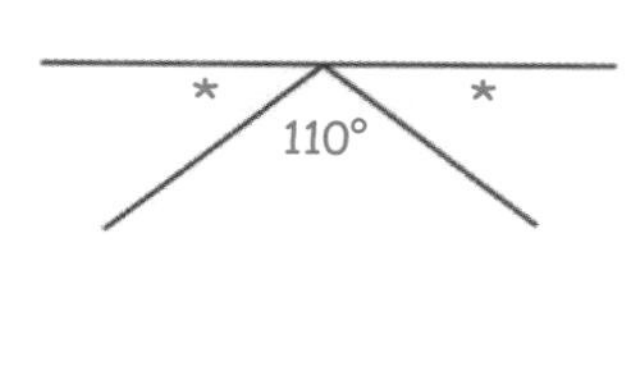

f

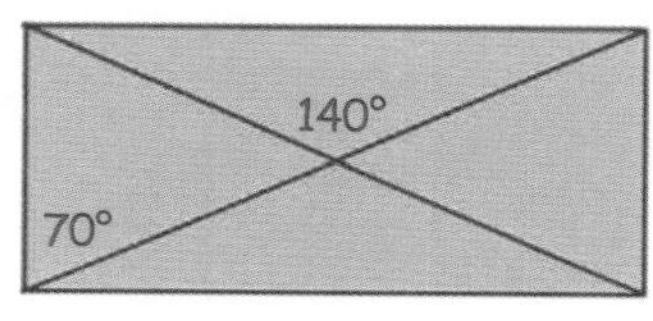

34. What does the 6 represent in :- a 0·619 b 15·056 ?

35. What number is :-

a $\frac{9}{10}$ up from 8·2 b $\frac{7}{100}$ down from 0·99 c $\frac{3}{1000}$ down from 1·673 ?

36. Set down and work out :-

a $\begin{array}{r} 384{\cdot}86 \\ +\ 69{\cdot}77 \\ \hline \end{array}$ b 100 – 19·99 c $\begin{array}{r} 32{\cdot}285 \\ -\ 8{\cdot}369 \\ \hline \end{array}$ d 0·625 + 0·375.

37. Write as a fraction in its simplest form :- a 0·8 b 0·75.

38. Round to the nearest whole number :- a 23·409 b 39·888.

39. Round to 1 decimal place :- a 8·741 b 0·651.

40. Write down the answers to :-

a 10·83 × 10 b 0·020 × 1000 c 13·4 ÷ 10 d 870 ÷ 100.

41. List all the mathematical shapes that make up this figure :-

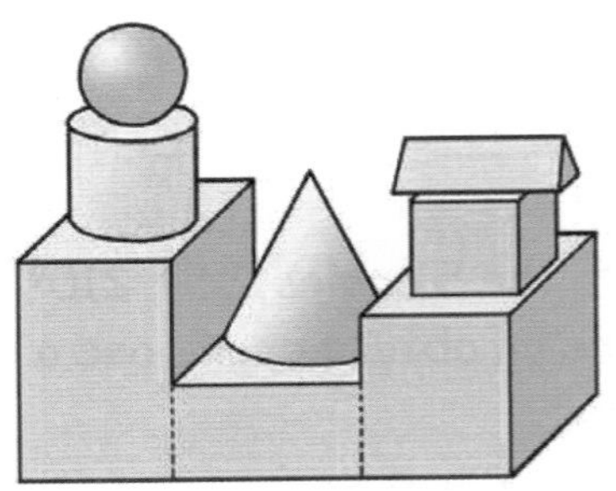

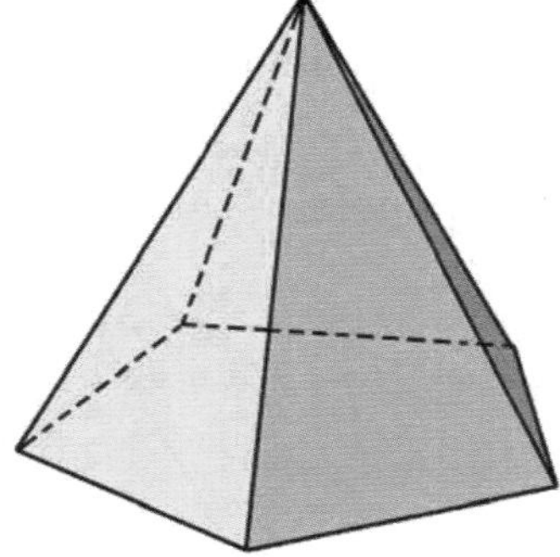

42. This shape is called a PENTAGONAL based PYRAMID.

a How many faces does it have ?

b How many edges does it have ?

c How many vertices does it have ?

43. Which 3-D figures do you get when you cut out these two shapes and fold them ?

a

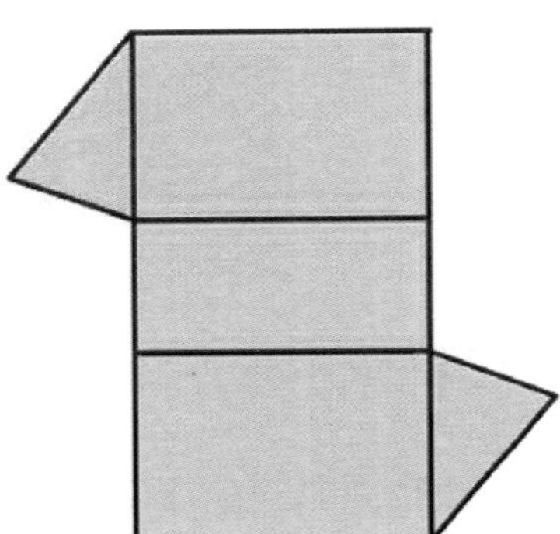

b

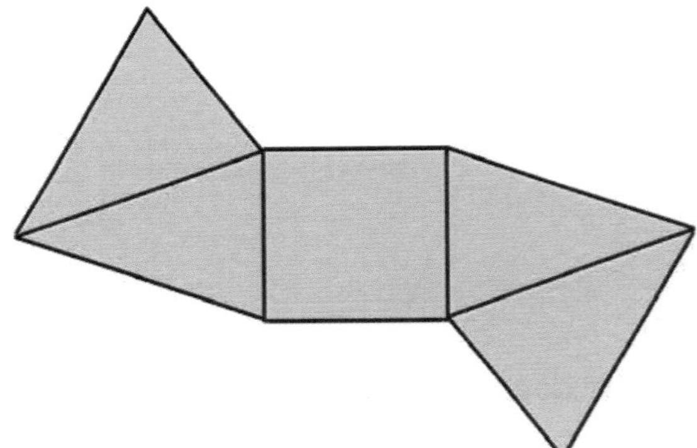

44. Make a neat sketch of a regular octagon.

45. Simplify these fractions as far as possible :-

a $\frac{6}{15}$ b $\frac{10}{65}$ c $\frac{22}{99}$ d $\frac{13}{52}$.

46. Write these fractions in order (*smallest first*) :- $\frac{3}{4}$, $\frac{11}{16}$, $\frac{7}{8}$, $\frac{1}{2}$, $\frac{17}{32}$.

47. Change to an improper fraction :- a $3\frac{2}{3}$ b $4\frac{5}{6}$.

48. Change to a mixed number :- a $\frac{11}{4}$ b $\frac{17}{5}$.

49. Imagine you have a set of coordinate axes with the point P(2, 7) plotted on it. Write down the coordinates of point P', when P is translated 4 right and 5 down.

50. a Copy the diagram shown.

b Plot these 4 points on your diagram :-
A(1, 6), B(3, 4), C(8, 6) and D(3, 8).

c What shape is ABCD ?

d Plot and write down the coordinates of A', B', C' and D' after A, B, C and D are reflected over the blue dotted line.

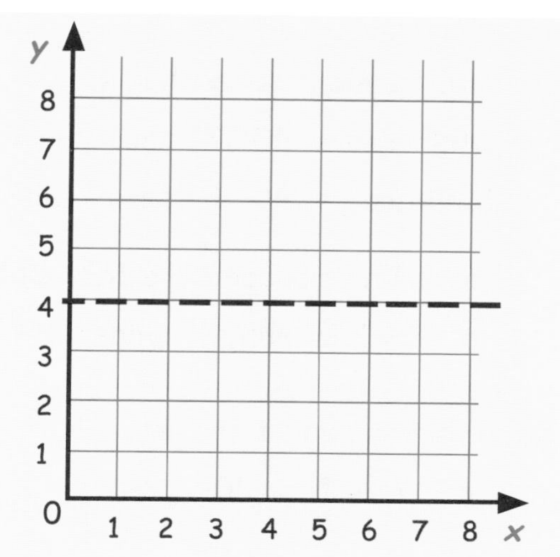

51. Write each of the following as a fraction and simplify where possible :-

a 39% b 80% c 24% d 5%.

52. Change each of these fractions to a percentage :-

a $\frac{3}{4}$ b $\frac{7}{10}$ c $\frac{47}{50}$ d $\frac{13}{20}$.

53. Work out :-

a 30% of £80 b 25% of 140 cm c 5% of 800 g d 15% of $120.

54. Fergusons were offering 20% off in their sale. This jacket was £45.

a How much would Sara save if she bought the jacket in the sale ?

b How much would the jacket actually cost her ?

55. Write down the volume of each shape, in cm^3.

a

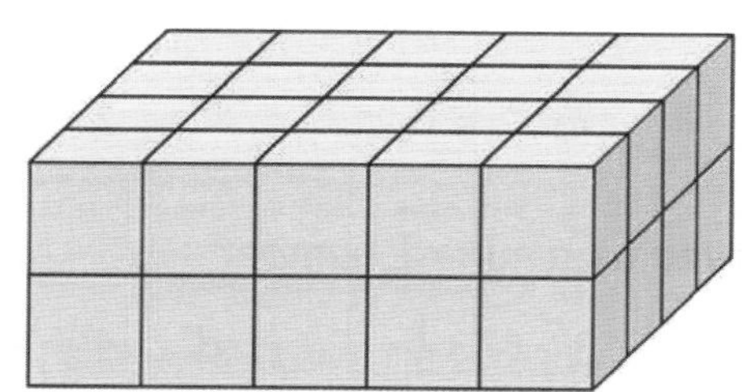

b

56. Change :-

a 3·7 centimetres to millimetres

b 18·5 millimetres to centimetres

c 3·05 kilometres to metres

d 65 800 metres to kilometres

e 23·05 litres to millilitres

f 6800 grams to kilograms.

57. Here are the times of the fastest 4 laps in the Le Mans speed trials.

Alphonso - 40·376 secs	Badrido - 39·978 secs
Callibra - 40·087 secs	Dunhill - 39·899 secs

a Who managed the fastest time in the trials ?

b By how many seconds did Dunhill beat Alphonso ?

58. Find the value of * in each of the following :-

a 7 + * = 20 b * - 2 = 11 c 8 - * = 1

d 4 x * = 32 e 12 x * = 132 f 36 ÷ * = 9.

59. In each of the following, ☆ stands for +, −, x or ÷.

Decide which symbol is needed each time here :-

a 9 ☆ 3 = 3 b 9 ☆ 3 = 6 c 9 ☆ 3 = 12

d 9 ☆ 3 = 27 e 8 ☆ 8 = 0 f 8 ☆ 8 = 1.

60. Copy each equation and solve it to find the value of the x each time :-

a $x + 5 = 13$ b $7 + x = 20$ c $x - 8 = 2$

d $15 - x = 1$ e $8 \times x = 56$ f $x \times 9 = 108$

g $2{\cdot}5 + x = 10$ h $\frac{x}{5} = 9$ i $\frac{x}{6} = 1$.

j $x \div 10 = 2{\cdot}5$ k $x - 61 = 39$ l $20 \div x = 5$.

61. Find and simplify where possible :-

a $\frac{5}{8} - \frac{1}{8}$ b $\frac{9}{10} - \frac{7}{10}$ c $\frac{5}{7} + \frac{2}{7}$ d $\frac{1}{3} - \frac{1}{6}$

e $\frac{5}{6} + \frac{1}{2}$ f $\frac{3}{4} - \frac{3}{8}$ g $\frac{9}{10} - \frac{3}{5}$ h $\frac{1}{4} + \frac{1}{2} - \frac{3}{8}$.

62. Find each of the following, leaving your answer as a mixed number :-

a $1\frac{1}{5} + 2\frac{2}{5}$ b $1\frac{5}{8} + 2\frac{5}{8}$ c $8\frac{7}{9} - 3\frac{1}{9}$ d $4\frac{1}{2} + 5\frac{1}{4}$

e $2\frac{3}{4} + 1\frac{7}{8}$ f $3\frac{5}{6} - 1\frac{2}{3}$ g $10 - 7\frac{2}{5}$ h $4\frac{7}{12} + 1\frac{3}{4}$.

63. Find :-

a $10 \times \frac{1}{6}$ b $5 \times \frac{2}{3}$ c $3 \times 2\frac{3}{8}$ d $4 \times 3\frac{3}{5}$.

64. Write these times as 24 hour times :- a 3:40 am b 5:55 pm.

65. Write these times using am and pm :- a 1945 b 0805.

66. Change the following into mins and secs :- a 145 secs b 301 secs.

67. Change these to minutes :- a 1 hr 35 mins b $3\frac{1}{4}$ hours.

68. I caught the 1023 train from London Euston, arriving in Newcastle at 1233.

a How long did my train journey take ?

The train left Newcastle 10 minutes later and took another 2 hours and 24 minutes to reach Glasgow Central station.

b At what time did I arrive at Glasgow Central ?

69. Between 10 am and 11 am, the elevator in an office block made ten trips to different floors.

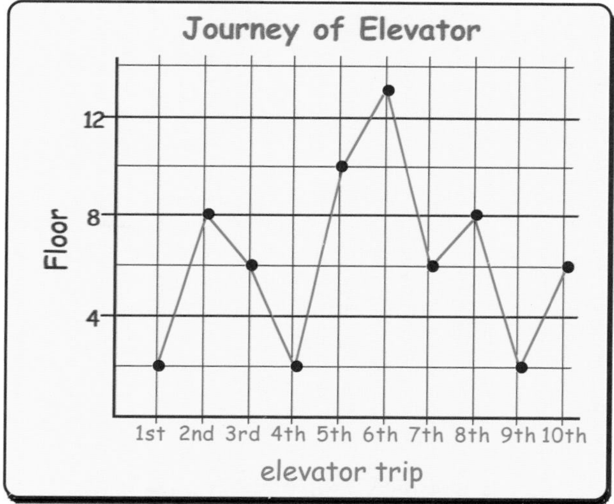

a Which floor did the elevator reach on its :-

(i) 1st trip (ii) 5th trip

(iii) 8th trip (iv) final trip ?

b On one of the trips, the elevator reached the 2nd top floor of the office building.

How many floors must there be in the building ?

70. Various types of trees were found in a small wood.

The pie chart shows the distribution of trees.

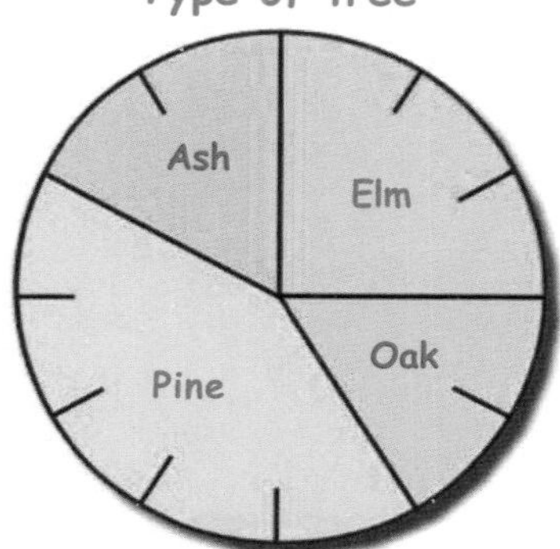

a Write down and simplify the fraction ($\frac{?}{12}$) of the trees that are :-

(i) Elm (ii) Oak

(iii) Ash (iv) Pine.

b There were in fact 240 trees altogether in the wood.

How many of the 240 were :-

(i) Elm (ii) Pine (iii) Oak or Ash ?

Answers to Year 5 Book

Ch 0 - Revision - Page 1

eight thousand and fifty six
7401
6051, 6688, 7001, 7018, 7040, 7051
P = 860 Q = 1020 R = 5950 S = 6080
5200
5100
a 960, 955 b 540, 560
c 6200, 5900 d 3500, 2000
a (i) 26 (ii) 69 (iii) 94
b (i) XXIX (ii) LVII (iii) XCIX
a 4 b 5 c 0 d 1
.

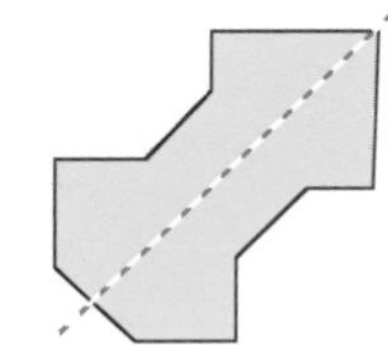

. a 9313 b 4474 c 8895 d 7525
. a 2463 miles b 9379 miles
. a 84 b 448 c 9800 d 63
e 4150 f 3600 g 6145 h 4981
. a (i) 70 (ii) 300 (iii) 630
b (i) 500 (ii) 3000 (iii) 9800
c (i) 4000 (ii) 8000 (iii) 7000
. a 0740 b 2310 c 1640
. a 8.55 am b 1.50 pm
c 11.35 am d 10.40 pm
. a 90 b 70 c 45
. a (i) 30 (ii) 31 b 60 c 13
. a 54 b 55 c 64
d 120 e 63 f 70
. a 7 b 50 c 9
d 10 e 12 f 100
. a 585 b 1656 c 2709
d 2030 e 890 f 2070
. 1032 km
. a -8°C b -8°C
. a 13°C b -6°C c -1°C d -10°C
. a 24 b 0 c -5
. a 7 b 12 c 14 d 23
e 23 f 66 g 32 h 25
. a 13 b 53 c 18 d 13
e 49 f 15 g 470 h 45
. £47 each
. £1650
. a A(7, 2) b/c S(4, 3)
. 2·35
. a b

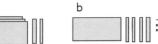

33. tenths b units c hundredths
34. 8·0 b 2·39 c 6·1
35. a 0·5 b 6·8 c 0·36
36. a 3·23, 3·28, 3·3, 3·67, 3·9, 4
    b 7·9, 6·62, 6·18, 6·05, 5·8, 5·77
37. a 15·48 b 12·6
38. a Triangle IJH is a right angled scalene triangle
    b Triangle STV is an acute angled isosceles triangle
39. a 9 b 12 c 33 d 88
40. a 11·8 b 17·77 c 6·2 d 0·04
41. a 6·31 b 42·26 c 4·5 d 5·78
    e £8·82 b £29·80 c £2·76 h 12·10
    i 35·69 j 27·55 k 47·21 l 86·01
42. £2·52 change
43. a a closed shape made up of straight lines with all its angles the same size and all its sides the same length
    b pentagon, hexagon, heptagon, octagon, nonagon, decagon, etc ...
44. a F b T c T
    d F e F
45. all 4 angles of a rectangle are right angles and it has 2 lines of symmetry
46. rhombus
47. £2·07 b £0·63 c £12·75
48. a £65·04 b £89·24
    c £8·74 d £200·00
49. a £12·11 b £23·05
50. 300 b 180 c 104
51. a 31 b 31 c 30
52. a 1 min 40 sec b 6 min 0 secs
    c 16 mins 40 secs
53. a 1 hr 10 mins b 3 hrs 30 mins
    c 10 hrs 0 mins
54. a 135 b 220 c 355
55. a 170 b 361 c 1220
56. a 7 min 55 sec b 3 min 35 sec
    c 1 hr 20 min
57. a 32500 b 4300 c 7000 d 82
    e 90 f 3 g 72 h 150
    i 7 j 10 k 16 l 20
58. 2500
59. 132 players
60. 13 shillings
61. a 56 mm b 200 cm
    c 12 cm 5 mm d 375 cm
    e 5 m 60 cm f 2900 m
    g 8 km 250 m h 3000 mm
    i 2250 m
62. a 3800 ml b 5 L 200 ml
    c 4500 ml
63. a 5650 g b 9 kg 50 g
    c 10250 g
64. square by 2·2 cm
65. 15 cm²
66. a $\frac{2}{3}$ b $\frac{3}{4}$ c $\frac{1}{7}$ d $\frac{4}{5}$
67. a 7 b 80 c 1400 d 8
68. a $\frac{4}{7}$ b $\frac{1}{2}$ c $6\frac{2}{5}$ d $5\frac{1}{2}$
69. a 0·25 b 0·77 c 0·9
70. a

Item	Tally marks	Number
buck/spade	𝍸 𝍸	10
ball	𝍸 III	8
costume	𝍸 I	6
towel	IIII	4
suncream	II	2

b

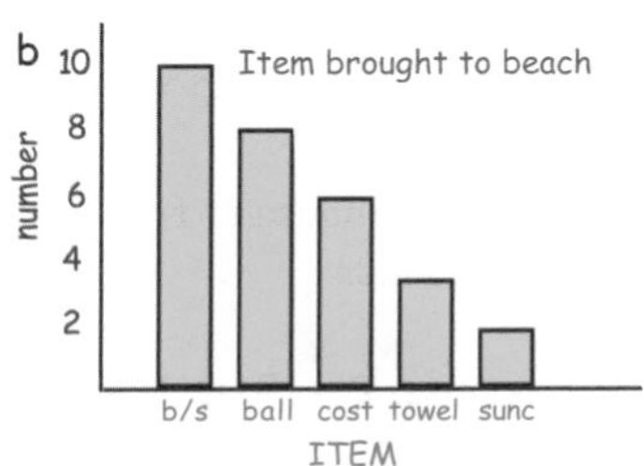

71. a (i) 20 (ii) 50
    b 12.00 c 1.00 and 2.00
    d getting colder/darker etc

Ch 1 - Whole Numbers - Page 9

Ch 1 - Exercise 1 - Page 9

1. a 2 hundred b 7 thousand
   c 80000 d 400000
2. a 7 hundred b 70
   c 7 thousand d 700000
3. a four thousand and eighty
   b twenty one thousand nine hundred
   c seventy one thousand three hundred and fifty
   d two hundred and thirty five thousand and eighty
   e seven hundred and three thousand four hundred and sixty
   f eight hundred and seventy thousand
   g four hundred and ninety three thousand and seventy
   h seven hundred and fifty thousand and sixty two
4. a 4201 b 17050
   c 230004 d 407080
   e 100007 f 560040
5. a 6786, 6867, 6876, 7008, 7068, 7080, 7086

b 90887, 98999, 99924, 100076, 100086, 100870

6. a 370 b 3170 c 1190 d 700
   e 12300 f 6200 g 120000
   h 90000 i 950000 j 400000
7. A = 480 B = 7900
   C = 9100 D = 1660
   E = 1840 F = 1500
   G = 2200 H = 13900
   I = 14700 J = 30000
   K = 45000 L = 125000
   M = 250000 N = 650000
   O = 780000 P = 25500
   Q = 26800 R = 28300
   S = 200000 T = 460000
   U = 720000
8. a 975 b 3450
   c 44250 d 850000
   e 730500 f 950000
9. a 1000000 b 500000
   c 250000 d 750000
10. a £98500
    b ninety eight thousand five hundred pounds

Ch 1 - Exercise 2 - *Page 11*

1. a 120, 130 b 200, 190
   c 1000, 1100 d 1900, 1800
   e 10000, 11000 f 20000, 19000
   g 70000, 80000 h 120000, 110000
   i 900000, 1000000 j 100000, 0
2. a 65, 85 b 92, 62
   c 420, 720 d 910, 890
   e 1400, 4400 f 7100, 5100
   g 47000, 67000 h 79000, 59000
   i 1220, 1200 j 5400, 5420
   k 3520, 3220 l 9125, 11125
   m 49600 n 42910
   o 541000 p 1000000

Ch 1 - Exercise 3 - *Page 12*

1. a 70 b 30 c 180 d 380
   e 430 f 2770 g 9800 h 25680
2. a 800 b 800 c 4700 d 9500
   e 26300 f 29900 g 16100 h 212500
3. a 9000 b 48000 c 38000 d 92000
   e 84000 f 358000 g 436000 h 800000
4. a 10000 b 30000
   c 30000 d 60000
   e 90000 f 120000
   g 250000 h 990000
5. a 200000 b 500000
   c 600000 d 900000
   e 600000 f 800000
   g 600000 h 900000

Ch 1 - Exercise 4 - *Page 13*

1. 4836
2. a 2379 b 3204 c 34998
   d 33988 e 1024
3. a 2100 b 2000 c 7200 d 24000
   e 24000 f 160000 g 40 h 100
   i 30 j 200 k 100 l 50
4. a 16000 grams b £500
   c 2400000 miles

Ch 1 - Exercise 5 Intro - *Page 14*

1	I	21	XXI	41	XLI	61	LXI	81	LXXXI
2	II	22	XXII	42	XLII	62	LXII	82	LXXXII
3	III	23	XXIII	43	XLIII	63	LXIII	83	LXXXIII
4	IV	24	XXIV	44	XLIV	64	LXIV	84	LXXXIV
5	V	25	XXV	45	XLV	65	LXV	85	LXXXV
6	VI	26	XXVI	46	XLVI	66	LXVI	86	LXXXVI
7	VII	27	XXVII	47	XLVII	67	LXVII	87	LXXXVII
8	VIII	28	XXVIII	48	XLVIII	68	LXVIII	88	LXXXVIII
9	IX	29	XXIX	49	XLIX	69	LXIX	89	LXXXIX
10	X	30	XXX	50	L	70	LXX	90	XC
11	XI	31	XXXI	51	LI	71	LXXI	91	XCI
12	XII	32	XXXII	52	LII	72	LXXII	92	XCII
13	XIII	33	XXXIII	53	LIII	73	LXXIII	93	XCIII
14	XIV	34	XXXIV	54	LIV	74	LXXIV	94	XCIV
15	XV	35	XXXV	55	LV	75	LXXV	95	XCV
16	XVI	36	XXXVI	56	LVI	76	LXXVI	96	XCVI
17	XVII	37	XXXVII	57	LVII	77	LXXVII	97	XCVII
18	XVIII	38	XXXVIII	58	LVIII	78	LXXVIII	98	XCVIII
19	XIX	39	XXXIX	59	LIX	79	LXXIX	99	XCIX
20	XX	40	XL	60	LX	80	LXXX	100	C

Ch 1 - Exercise 5 - *Page 14*

1. a XL b VIII c L, XLV
   d XXXVIII e XCV, XLIX
2. a CI b CX
   c CXXV d CL
   e CLV f CLXXXVIII
   g CXC h CC
   i CCV j CCXXX
   k CCXXXIX l CCXLIX
   m CCL n CCLXXV
   o CCXC p CCXCIX
3. a 103 b 109 c 115 d 126
   e 139 f 166 g 180 h 220
   i 245 j 259 k 276 l 295
4. a CCCLX b CDI
   c CDXXX d CDL
   e CDLXXX f DXX
   g DLXX h DCXXXV
   i DCLXXXIV j DCXCIX
   k DCCLX l DCCCXLV
   m DCCCLXIX n CMXXXVII
   o CMLXVI p CMXCV
5. a 380 b 445 c 491 d 526
   e 550 f 610 g 850 h 890
   i 910 j 956 k 971 l 991
6. DCCCLXXXVIII
7. Investigation

Ch 2 - Add & Subtract - *Page 17*

Ch 2 - Exercise 1 - *Page 17*

1. a 880 b 546 c 9044
   d 3218 e 33690 f 33627
   g 34156 h 537207 i 628241
   j 113653 k 9718 l 611985
   m 335979 n 901186 o 154568
2. a 12923 b 23550 c 2350
   d 1805 e 4900 f 26492
   g 1950 h 8001 i 100710
   j 379901 k 1000000 l 525000
3. 50000
4. 8450
5. 46450
6. a £711000 b £439800
7. £172275
8. 37322

Ch 2 - Exercise 2 - *Page 19*

1. a 106 b 24 c 180
   d 68 e 200 f 27
   g 630 h 380 i 900
   j 150 k 1220 l 770
   m 1270 n 466 o 1153
   p 1110 q 9100 r 1400
   s 9899 t 5900 u 10000
2. a 28000 b 14000 c 81200
   d 48000 e 71000 f 15000
   g 19500 h 96000 i 50200
3. a 40000 b 380000 c 240000
   d 810000 e 150000 f 835000
   g 441000 h 899000 i 1000
4. a 395972 b 541116 c 695897
   d 100112 e 757599 f 9
5. 43000
6. 311600
7. 840500 square km
8. 130000
9. £658000

Ch 2 - Exercise 3 - *Page 21*

1. a 15000 b 30000 c 80000
   d 200000 e 80000 f 500000
2. a 12000 b 87000 c 530000
   d 770000 e 520000 f 500000
3. 340000
4. 90000
5. 400000
6. 20000

Ch 2 - Exercise 4 - *Page 22*

1. 12 games
2. 625 ml
3. 287
4. 3300
5. £127000

Ch 3 - Angles 1 - *Page 24*

Ch 3 - Exercise 1 - *Page 24*

1. a right b obtuse c acute
   d reflex e straight f acute
   g obtuse h reflex i acute

2. a right b obtuse c acute
   d obtuse e acute f reflex
3. a acute b obtuse c reflex
4.

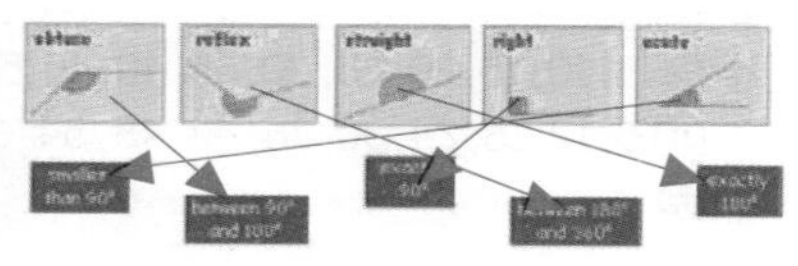

5. a 88°, 17°, 60°, 31°
   b 110°, 176°, 91°, 169°
   c 180°
   d 90°
   e 210°, 335°

Ch 3 - Exercise 2 - Page 26.

a ∠TAP b ∠LPV c ∠ISB
d ∠HJK e ∠POD f ∠KVU

a ∠GCB is a right angle
b ∠RTH is an acute angle
c ∠EBO is an obtuse angle
d ∠POY is an acute angle
e ∠SWT is a straight angle
f ∠CBS is a reflex angle
g ∠BUT is an acute angle
h ∠BAC is a reflex angle
i ∠ITN is an obtuse angle

a ∠PGY, ∠RVS, ∠MVB
b ∠GPY, ∠RSV, ∠MBV
c ∠PYG, ∠SRV, ∠VMB

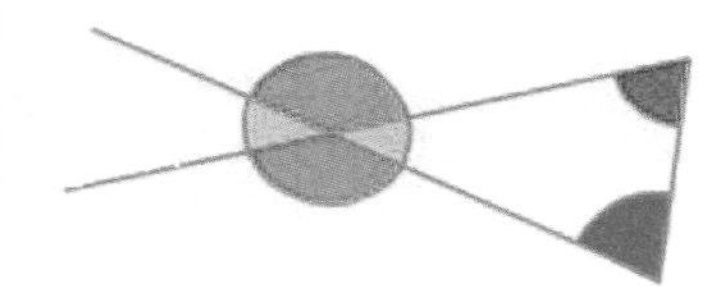

Ch 3 - Exercise 3 - Page 28.

a 70° b 160° c 90°
d 65° e 115° f 95°
g 100° h 65° i 120°

a 60° b 30° c 110°
d 140° e 50° f 150°

a 27° b 108° c 115°
d 41° e 136° f 102°
g 12° h 175° i 75°
j 45° k 48°, 42° l 70°, 110°

Ch 3 - Exercise 4 - Page 30.

Practical - check diagrams
Practical - check diagrams
Practical - check diagrams

Ch 3 - Exercise 5 - Page 31.

1.

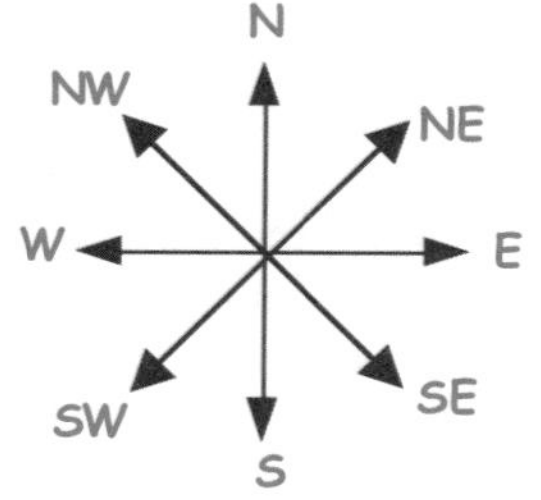

2. a 90° b 90° c 90° d 270°
   e 45° f 180° g 135° h 135°
   i 180° j 270°
3. a North b East c North West
   d (i) 135° (ii) 45° (iii) 180° (iv) 315°
   e South f East g 135°
4. a (i) N (ii) E (iii) SW (iv) NW
   b (i) W (ii) N (iii) S (iv) SW
   c Moves NW, then SW, then South
   d Domed Theatre

Ch 4 - Multiply & Divide - Page 35

Ch 4 - Exercise 1 - Page 35

1. a 210 b 348 c 672 d 783
   e 2244 f 1480 g 3663 h 2596
   i 41736 j 21182 k 54420 l 88884
2. a 472 b 365 c 609 d 864
   e 2226 f 3025 g 7281 h 2928
   i 4948 j 57204 k 32640 l 10824
   m 43778 n 10185 o 11484 p 29961
3. Checking answers
4. 1428
5. 3105
6. 1392
7. 2495
8. £13110
9. 25200
10. 18864
11. 5400
12. 68778 km

Ch 4 - Exercise 2 - Page 37

1. 8892
2. a 848 b 1728 c 73968 d 30580
   e 20592 f 163674 g 349095 h 75764
3. a 315 b 1610 c 3886 d 3276
   e 4012 f 20150 g 20313 h 53196
   i 237916 j 497728 k 3905981 l 81539

Ch 4 - Exercise 3 - Page 38

1. a 150 b 110 c 560 d 980
   e 1250 f 3020 g 4570 h 19200
   i 30800 j 82630 k 65430 l 461800
2. a 5400 b 7700
   c 15500 d 70000
   e 702000 f 200400
   g 860000 h 905000
3. a 16000 b 72000
   c 750000 d 870000
   e 900000 f 246000
   g 534000 h 480000
4. a 1500 b 2800 c 25000
5. a 6000 b 37000 c 620000 d 701000

Ch 4 - Exercise 4 - Page 39

1. a 25 b 37 c 59 d 345
   e 890 f 9010 g 5420 h 4800
   i 4000 j 18600 k 70000 l 33030
2. a 6 b 12 c 46 d 210
   e 90 f 3080 g 500 h 4900
3. a 9 b 36 c 84 d 50
   e 415 f 390 g 400 h 625
4. a 17 b 450 c 2600
5. a 23 b 49 c 160 d 2000

Ch 4 - Exercise 5 - Page 40

1. 360 2. 1260 3. 700 4. 1080
5. 1260 6. 990 7. 1500 8. 2480
9. 9 10. 9 11. 50 12. 90
13. 420 14. 330 15. 40 16. 70
17. 6000 18. 10000 19. 30000 20. 28700
21. 40000 22. 12000 23. 60000 24. 45000
25. 3000 26. 3000 27. 500 28. 700
29. 4 30. 60 31. 70 32. 70
33. 300 34. 450 35 550 36. 3500
37. 6 38. 8 39. 100 40. 300
41. 693 42. 2412 43. 1995 44. 4422

Ch 4 - Exercise 6 - Page 41

1. a 9 b 179 c 127 d 68
   e 1083 f 2356 g 11623 h 9874
2. a 16 b 297 c 159 d 87
   e 108 f 1149 g 2238 h 2247
   i 128 j 1597 k 709 l 698
   m 1248 n 329 o 3417 p 13649
3. a 69 b 357 c £379 d 892
4. a 2684 b 792

Ch 4 - Exercise 7 - Page 42

1. a 7r1 b 11r3 c 16r1 d 12r7
   e 172r2 f 452r3 g 74r5 h 631r4
   i 740r4 j 228r3 k 628r3 l 2057r1
2. a $2\frac{1}{3}$ b $5\frac{1}{2}$ c $4\frac{2}{7}$ d $5\frac{7}{8}$
   e $19\frac{1}{2}$ f $14\frac{4}{5}$ g $15\frac{2}{3}$ h $11\frac{5}{9}$
   i $138\frac{1}{3}$ j $120\frac{5}{6}$ k $203\frac{1}{2}$ l $130\frac{6}{7}$
   m $767\frac{2}{5}$ n $4565\frac{1}{2}$ o $815\frac{7}{9}$ p $1121\frac{1}{4}$
3. a 1·6 b 7·5 c 17·5 d 11·5

e 4·75 f 20·6 g 76·5 h 12·5
i 19·5 j 48·25 k 24·4 l 58·5
m 456·4 n 4565·5 o 426·5 p 248·25

4. a 4 b 7 c 18 d 17
e 35 f 43 g 75 h 523
i 196 j 874 k 1822 l 148

5. a $64\frac{1}{2}$ b 51·4 ml c 165 tonne

Ch 5 - Negative Numbers - Page 45

Ch 5 - Exercise 1 - Page 45

1. a 3°C b -6°C c -17°C
d 36°C e -80°C
2. a -1, -3, -5 b -3, -1, 0
c -15, -17 d -6, -2, 0
e -70, -10, 10 f -101, -95, -89

Ch 5 - Exercise 2 - Page 46

1. a see diagram b -9°C
2. a 19°C b 12°C c 21°C d 6°C
e 10°C f 2°C g -10°C h 5°C
i -7°C j -18°C k -19°C l -21°C
m -3°C n -1°C
3. a 6°C up b 5°C down
c 15°C down d 9°C up
e 9°C down f 15°C up
g 7°C down h 13°C down
i 80°C up j 12°C down
k 28°C up l 158°C up
4. -16°C 5. 44°C 6. 77°C
7. a 1°C b -3°C c -7°C d -31°C
8. a -21°C, -2°C, -1°C, 0°C, 1°C, 18°C
b -58°C, -36°C, -17°C, -9°C, -2°C, 2°C
9. a (i) -1 (ii) -2 (iii) 1
(iv) -3 (v) 3 (iii) -1
b (i) 5 (ii) 3 (iii) 1 (iv) 6
10. a (i) +30 (ii) +15 (iii) -15 (iv) +55
(v) -35 (vi) -40 (vii) +45 (viii) -25
b 30 m c 80 m
11. 5 levels
12. a 10 b 35 c 1
d 2 e -6 f -7
g -12 h -27 i -185
13. Money you have in the bank is +ve
If overdrawn, your money is -ve

Ch 6 - Measure 1 - Page 50

Ch 6 - Exercise 1 - Page 50

1. a 12 b 12 cm²
2. a 6 cm² b 12 cm² c 8 cm²
d 12 cm² e 16 cm² f 8 cm²
g 8 cm² h 9cm² i 8 cm²
j 12 cm² k 16 cm²
l 10 cm² m $16\frac{1}{2}$ cm²
3. a 11-12 cm² b 24 cm²
c 12 cm² d 19 cm²

Ch 6 - Exercise 2 - Page 52

1. a/b/c 18 cm²
2. 45 cm²
3. a 32 cm² b 63 cm² c 36 cm²
d 120 cm² e 110 cm² f 54 cm²
4. a 35 m² b 36 m² c 52 m²
d 126 m² e 160 m²
5. £4090
6. a 408 m² b 224 m² c 532 m²
d 2800 m² e 960 m²
7. £1050
8. a 600 m² b 10 c £170
9. a Area = 15 cm², Perimeter = 16 cm
Perimeter is numerically bigger
b Area = 12 cm², Perimeter = 16 cm
Perimeter is numerically bigger
c No - consider rect 6 cm by 5 cm
Area = 30 cm², Perimeter = 22 cm
Area is numerically bigger
Possibly draw up a table
d For a square of side less than 4 cm, area is smaller than perimeter
For a square of side more than 4 cm, area is bigger than perimeter

Ch 6 - Exercise 3 - Page 55

1. a 66 cm² b 50 cm² c 116 cm² d 54cm
2. a 140 cm² b 48 cm² c 188 cm² d 66cm
3. a 200 cm² b 81 cm² c 281 cm² d 84cm
4. a 384 cm² b 190 cm²
5. Area large rectangle = 84 cm²
Area of hole = 18 cm²
Yellow area = 66 cm²
6. a 126 cm² b 800 cm²
7. a 205 cm² b 220 cm²

Ch 7 - Special Numbers - Page 58

Ch 7 - Exercise 1 - Page 58

1. 0, 5, 10, 15, 20, 25, 30, 35
2. 8, 16, 24, 32, 40
3. 4, 8, 12, 16, 20, 24, 28, 32, 36, 40
4. a T b T c F d T
e F f T g F h T
5. a 24, 27, 30, 33, 36
b 20, 25, 30, 35, 40, 45, 50, 55, 60, 65
c 30, 36, 42, 48
d 45, 54, 63, 72, 81
e 70, 80, 90, 100, 110, 120, 130, 140, 150, 160
f 400, 450, 500, 550, 600, 650, 700, 750, 800, 850, 900
g 200, 225, 250, 275, 300, 325, 350
h 1200, 1300, 1400, 1500, 1600, 1700, 1800, 1900, 2000
6. a (i) 3, 6, 9, 12, 15, 18, 21, 24, 27, 30
(ii) 4, 8, 12, 16, 20, 24, 28, 32, 36, 40
b 12, 24
7. a (i) 5, 10, 15, 20, 25, 30, 35, 40, 45, 50
(ii) 6, 12, 18, 24, 30, 36, 42, 48, 54, 60
b 30

Ch 7 - Exercise 2 - Page 59

1. a 1 and 5 b 1, 2, 4 and 8
2. a 1, 11 b 1, 2, 7, 14
c 1, 2, 5, 10 d 1, 2, 4, 8, 16
e 1, 2, 3, 6, 9, 18
f 1, 2, 3, 5, 6, 10, 15, 30
3. a 1, 2, 3, 6 b 1, 3, 5, 15
c 1, 2, 3, 4, 6, 8, 12, 24
d 1, 2, 3, 4, 6, 9, 12, 18, 36
e 1, 5, 7, 35
f 1, 2, 5, 10, 25, 50
g 1, 2, 4, 5, 10, 20, 25, 50, 100
h 1, 2, 3, 4, 5, 6, 8, 10, 12, 15, 20, 24, 30, 40, 60, 120
4. a 1 x 10, 2 x 5
b 1 x 20, 2 x 10, 4 x 5
c 1 x 48, 2 x 24, 3 x 16, 4 x 12, 6 x 8
d 1 x 72, 2 x 36, 3 x 24 4 x 18, 6 x 12, 8 x 9
5. a T b F c T d T
e T f T g F h F
6. a 1, 2, 3, 4, 6, 12 b 1, 2, 3, 6, 9, 18
c 1, 2, 3, 6
7. a 1, 2 b 1, 2, 4
c 1, 2, 4, 5, 10, 20 d 1, 2, 3, 6
e 1, 5 f 1, 2, 4
g 1, 2, 5, 10 h 1, 13
i 1, 2 j 1
k 1, 2, 4
l 1, 2, 3, 5, 6, 10, 15, 30

Ch 7 - Exercise 3 - Page 60

1. 1, 2, 5, 10. It has more than 2 factors
2. 1, 3. It has exactly 2 factors
3. Four. No it is not
4. It has only one factor (1)
5. a 1, 5 Yes b 1, 2, 4, 8, 16 No
c 1, 3, 5, 15 No d 1, 17 Yes
e 1, 23 Yes f 1, 3, 9, 27 No
g 1, 29 Yes h 1, 5, 7, 35 No
i 1,2,4,11,22,44 No j 1, 47 Yes
k 1, 3, 17, 51 No l 1, 2, 31, 62 No
6. 8, 15, 20, 33, 36, 40, 42, 49, 50, 55, 57
7. yes - Has exactly two factors (1, 2)
8. a Forever
b one second (2 is only even prime)

9. a/b/c/d/e/f

1	2	3	4	5	6	7	8	9	10
11	12	13	14	15	16	17	18	19	20
21	22	23	24	25	26	27	28	29	30
31	32	33	34	35	36	37	38	39	40
41	42	43	44	45	46	47	48	49	50
51	52	53	54	55	56	57	58	59	60
61	62	63	64	65	66	67	68	69	70
71	72	73	74	75	76	77	78	79	80
81	82	83	84	85	86	87	88	89	90
91	92	93	94	95	96	97	98	99	100

h 2, 3, 5, 7, 11, 13, 17, 19, 23, 29, 31, 37, 41, 43, 47, 53, 59, 61, 67, 71, 73, 79, 83, 89, 97.

Ch 7 - Exercise 4 - Page 62

1. a 9 b 25 c 36
   d 64 e 49 f 81
   g 100 h 1 i 400
2. a 64 b 27 c 125
   d 216 e 1 f 1000
   g 343 h 512 i 729
3. a 3^2 b same
4. a 41 b 145 c 149
   d 85 e 265 f 38

Ch 7 - Exercise 5 - Page 63

1. Multiples of 2 - 2, 4, 14, 28, 32, 42, 56, 60, 70
   Multiples of 4 - 4, 28, 32, 56, 60
   Multiples of 7 - 14, 28, 42, 49, 56, 70
2. Factors of 16 - 1, 2, 4, 8, 16
   Factors of 24 - 1, 2, 3, 4, 6, 8, 12
   Factors of 42 - 1, 2, 3, 6, 7, 14, 21
3. a 6 pm b 6 am next morning
4. a 1, 3, 5, 7, 9, 11
   b 13, 15, 17, 39, 201
5. a 3 b 5 c 11 d 8
6. a ends in a 5 - can be divided by 5
   b ends in a 2 - is even
   c ends in a 0 - can be divided by 10
   d all digits can be divided by 3 so whole number can be divided by 3

Ch 8 - Angles 2 - Page 65

Ch 8 - Exercise 1 - Page 65

1. a acute b right c obtuse
   d reflex e straight f obtuse
2. a ∠BAC b ∠PTY c ∠VCQ
3. a 35° b 135° c 65°
4. See angles
5. a 270° 180° c 135° d 360°
6. South East

Ch 8 - Exercise 2 - Page 66

1. a 60° b 20° c 50° d 35°
   e 65° f 15° g 48° h 59°
2. a 30° b 80° c 2° d 79°
   e 71° f 17° g 81·5° h 37·5°
3. 45°
4. a 133° b 63° c 129° d 144°
   e 58° f 90° g 36° h 60°
   i 60° j 45° k 30°
5. a 80° b 155° c 43° d 4°
   e 179° f 69° g 0·5° h 92·5°
6. 90°
7. a 7° b 97°
8. a $p + q + r + s = 360$
   b Angles will always add to 360°
9. a 240 b 120°
10. a 150° b 108°

Ch 8 - Exercise 3 - Page 68

1. a 110° b 160° c 90° d 140°
   e 135° f 90° g 90° h 66°
   i 108° j 128° k 90° l 50°
2. Practical

Ch 8 - Exercise 4 - Page 69

1. a 50° b 30° c 45° d 65°
   e 140° f 35° g 120° h 140°
   i 120° j 148° k 105° l 90°
2. a 70° b 1° c 48° d 45°
3. a 80° b 55° c 158° d 55·5°
4. a 210° b 171° c 80° each

Ch 8 - Exercise 5 - Page 70

1.

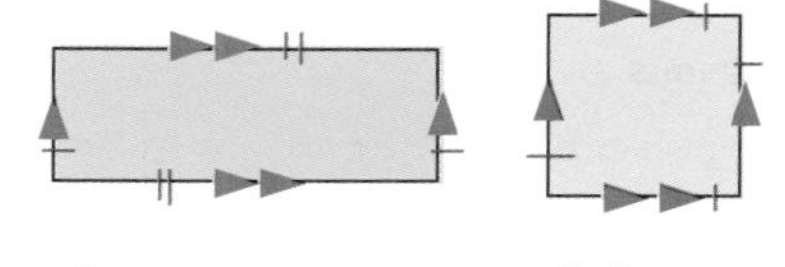

2. a/b 3. a/b/c

A B C D: 60°, 30°, 30°, 60°

E F G H: 70°, 20°, 140°, 40°, 40°, 140°, 70°, 20°, 20°, 70°, 20°, 70°

Ch 9 - Decimals - Page 72

Ch 9 - Exercise 1 - Page 72

1. a hundredths b thousandths
2. a 7 tens b 7 hundredths
   c 7 tenths d 7 hundreds
   e 7 thousandths
3. a 1·008, 1·098, 1·8, 1·898, 1·97, 2·001, 2·909
   b 0·107, 0·108, 0·167, 0·176, 0·177, 0·190, 0·207
4. a 3 units + $\frac{6}{10}$ + $\frac{2}{100}$ + $\frac{7}{1000}$ = $3\frac{627}{1000}$
   b 8 units + $\frac{3}{10}$ + $\frac{9}{100}$ + $\frac{6}{1000}$ = $3\frac{396}{1000}$
   c 0 units + $\frac{3}{10}$ + $\frac{5}{100}$ + $\frac{1}{1000}$ = $3\frac{351}{1000}$
   d 40 units + $\frac{4}{10}$ + $\frac{0}{100}$ + $\frac{9}{1000}$ = $40\frac{409}{1000}$
   e 0 units + $\frac{0}{10}$ + $\frac{8}{100}$ + $\frac{7}{1000}$ = $\frac{87}{1000}$
5. a 4·8 b 5·8 c 5·21
   d 0·52 e 1·46 f 2·209
   g 4·581 h 0·816 i 7·892

Ch 9 - Exercise 2 - Page 73

1. a 87·8 b 65·73 c 663·72 d 26·362
   e 1·82 f 20·93 g 463·58 h 17·927
   i 17·57 j 4·29 k 353·49
   l 36·863 m 157·286 n 0·855
2. a 118·32 kg b 5·34 kg
3. a 6·522 kg b 11·458 kg
   c 2·123 kg
4. 558·34 kg
5. 0·056 m
6. 2·535 litres
7. 0·089 second
8. a 8·783 m b 3·831 m

Ch 9 - Exercise 3 - Page 74

1. a $\frac{1}{10}$ b $\frac{1}{100}$ c $\frac{1}{1000}$ d $\frac{3}{10}$
   e $\frac{3}{100}$ f $\frac{3}{1000}$ g $\frac{2}{5}$ h $\frac{1}{50}$
   i $\frac{1}{250}$ j $\frac{7}{10}$ k $\frac{3}{20}$ l $\frac{57}{1000}$
   m $\frac{4}{5}$ n $\frac{1}{4}$ o $\frac{3}{25}$ p $1\frac{1}{5}$
   q $3\frac{3}{4}$ r $4\frac{1}{4}$ s $9\frac{1}{2}$ t $3\frac{3}{100}$
   u $10\frac{1}{20}$ v $44\frac{2}{5}$ w $77\frac{77}{100}$ x $8\frac{1}{25}$

Ch 9 - Exercise 4 - Page 75

1. a 5 b 7 c 13 d 19
   e 29 f 57 g 100 h 426
2. a 9 kg b 2 kg c 15 kg d 25 kg
   e 39 kg f 62 kg g 112 kg h 429kg
3. a £2 b £2 c £11 d £13
   e £50 f £61 g £101 h £1231
4. a 3·5 b 4·7 c 1·1 d 0·9
   e 12·8 g 10·0 g 5·0 h 0·1
5. a 4·4 b 1·9 c 7·4 d 8·4
   e 7·0 f 2·1 g 14·9 h 0·3
   i 25·2 j 33·7 k 812·1 l 645·9
6. a 8·8 b 21·9
   c 5·5 d 4·5 e 6·3
   f 4·2 g 0·2 h 14·1
7. a 5·6 b 18·5 c 13·3
   d 6·9 e 5·2 f 18·9
8 a 0·4 b 0·3 c 0·8

Ch 9 - Exercise 5 - Page 77

1. a 36 b 48 c 26·7 d 91·7
   e 125·2 f 9·4 g 40·8 h 0·3
   i 247·5 j 91·8 k 140·7 l 0·5
2. a 382 b 541 c 609 d 860
   e 747 f 71 g 40 h 9
3. a 2940 b 3060 c 4750 d 19300
   e 850 f 80 g 2020 h 50
4. a 34 pounds b 340 pounds
   c 3400 pounds
5. a 3640 b 29700 c 900 d 20

Ch 9 - Exercise 6 - Page 78

1. a 1·52 b 3·78 c 0·59 c 43·76
   e 1·73 f 24·58 g 1·04 h 1·3
   i 0·7 j 0·09 k 0·18 l 2·05
2. a 9·34 b 5·76 c 0·75 d 0·16
   e 7·30 f 19·42 g 1·08 h 0·06
3. a 8·47 b 39·76 c 9·37 d 1·80
   e 0·75 f 0·3 g 0·09 h 0·14
4. a 0·19 g b £289·45 each
5. a 2·63 b 0·53 c 0·86 d 0·03

Ch 10 - 3-Dimensions - Page 80

Ch 10 - Exercise 1 - Page 80

1. a cube b sphere
   c triangular prism d cylinder
   e square pyramid f cuboid
   g cone h hemisphere
2. a cone and hemisphere
   b cuboid and triangular prism
   c hemisphere and cylinder
   d cone and cylinder
   e square pyramid and cube
   f cube, cuboid and square pyramid
3. a triangular prism b square pyramid
   c cylinder d cuboid
   e square pyramid f cone
4. a 6 b square c 8 d 12
   e horiz f (i) RT (ii) VU
   g AN, RV and TU
   h (i) NV, BT and EU (ii) Vertical
   i various
5. a 6 b rectangle c 8
   d 12 e GR, QD and MN
   f FR, ND and MQ
   g EM, GQ, RD and FN
   h various
6. a 5 b square ... triangles
   c 5 d 8 e various
7. a 5 b triangles ... rectangles
   c 6 d TD e BD and AT
   f 9 g various
8. a the cone has 1 curved face and 1 flat circular face
   b The cylinder has 1 curved face and 2 flat circular faces
9. A hemisphere
10. a cone, and 2 cylinders b cube, cylinder, 1 hemisphere & 4 spheres

Ch 10 - Exercise 2 - Page 84

1. a cone b cylinder
   c triangular prism d sphere
   e square pyramid f cube
   g sphere h cuboid
2. a/b/c/d/ various

Ch 10 - Exercise 3 - Page 85

1. a no b no c yes
   d no e yes f no
   g no h yes i no
   j no k no l yes
2. a 5 b 6 c 8
   d 9 e 10 f 12
3. a equilateral triangle
   b pentagon c hexagon
   d octagon e decagon
   f dodecagon

Ch 11 - Fractions 1 - Page 89

Ch 11 - Exercise 1 - Page 89

1. a $\frac{1}{3} = \frac{3}{9}$ b $\frac{15}{18} = \frac{5}{6}$
   c $\frac{20}{100} = \frac{2}{10}$ d $\frac{90}{100} = \frac{9}{10}$
   e $\frac{6}{10} = \frac{60}{100}$ f $\frac{1}{20} = \frac{5}{100}$
2. a $\frac{2}{4}$ b $\frac{4}{10}$ c $\frac{6}{14}$
3. a $\frac{3}{12}$ b $\frac{15}{18}$ c $\frac{9}{24}$
4. various
5. a $\frac{3}{4}$ b $\frac{1}{6}$ c $\frac{5}{7}$ d $\frac{3}{8}$
6. a $\frac{1}{2}$ b $\frac{2}{3}$ c $\frac{3}{4}$ d $\frac{3}{5}$
7. various answers
8. a $\frac{3}{5}$ b $\frac{8}{9}$ c $\frac{4}{5}$ d $\frac{1}{2}$
   e $\frac{3}{4}$ f $\frac{1}{2}$ g $\frac{3}{4}$ h $\frac{13}{17}$
   i $\frac{9}{10}$ j $\frac{5}{6}$ k $\frac{1}{10}$ l $\frac{4}{5}$
   m $\frac{1}{20}$ n $\frac{1}{15}$ o $\frac{12}{101}$ p $\frac{1}{3}$

Ch 11 - Exercise 2 - Page 91

1. a $<$ b $>$ c $>$ d $<$
   e $>$ f $<$ g = h $<$
2. a $\frac{5}{12} < \frac{1}{2} < \frac{2}{3}$ b $\frac{5}{9} < \frac{2}{3} < \frac{13}{18}$
   c $\frac{2}{3} < \frac{3}{4} < \frac{5}{6} < \frac{11}{12}$ d $\frac{3}{5} < \frac{3}{4} < \frac{17}{20} < \frac{9}{10}$
   e $\frac{3}{8} < \frac{1}{2} < \frac{5}{8} < \frac{11}{16} < \frac{3}{4}$ f $\frac{1}{2} < \frac{3}{5} < \frac{13}{20} < \frac{7}{10} < \frac{3}{4}$
3. $\frac{1}{4} + \frac{5}{12} + \frac{1}{2} = \frac{3}{12} + \frac{5}{12} + \frac{6}{12} = \frac{14}{12}$ which is > 1

Ch 11 - Exercise 2 - Page 92

1. a $8\frac{1}{2}$ b $6\frac{2}{3}$ c $3\frac{5}{6}$
2. a $4\frac{1}{3}$ b $6\frac{3}{4}$ c $7\frac{3}{5}$ d $5\frac{5}{6}$
   e $8\frac{1}{9}$ f $8\frac{1}{8}$ g $8\frac{7}{10}$ h $3\frac{1}{2}$
3. a $7\frac{5}{6}$ kg b $2\frac{3}{5}$ bars
   c $6\frac{1}{4}$ litres d $166666\frac{2}{3}$ litres
   e $1207\frac{1}{7}$ litres
   f (i) $17\frac{1}{8}$ metres (ii) $11\frac{1}{4}$ metres
4. $3\frac{1}{3}$
5. a $4\frac{1}{2}$ b $5\frac{1}{2}$ c $3\frac{1}{4}$ d $3\frac{2}{5}$
   e $4\frac{1}{2}$ f $8\frac{3}{4}$ g $2\frac{1}{2}$ h $11\frac{1}{3}$
   i $3\frac{2}{3}$ j $2\frac{1}{2}$ k $3\frac{1}{4}$ l $1\frac{3}{4}$
6. a 4 b 8 c 3 d 11
   e $2\frac{3}{4} = \frac{11}{4}$
7. a 12 b 2 c 14, $4\frac{2}{3} = \frac{14}{3}$
8. a $\frac{19}{5}$ b $\frac{13}{10}$ c $\frac{21}{8}$ d $\frac{91}{9}$
9. a $\frac{21}{5}$ b $\frac{8}{3}$ c $\frac{27}{5}$ d $\frac{27}{10}$
10. a $\frac{3}{2}$ b $\frac{41}{5}$ c $\frac{20}{3}$ d $\frac{37}{5}$
    e $\frac{73}{7}$ f $\frac{35}{9}$ g $\frac{29}{10}$ h $\frac{139}{20}$
11. a 4 b 10 c 7 d 21
12. a 15 b 6 c 12 d 34
13. a $7\frac{2}{5}$ b $5\frac{1}{7}$

Ch 12 - Coordinates - Page 96

Ch 12 - Exercise 1 - Page 96

1. a (i) D (ii) A (iii) Q (iv) R
   b (i) (4,2) (ii) (0,8) (iii) (7,8) (iv) (6,4)
   c (i) KEQB
   (ii) K(2,2), E(4,2), Q(4,9), B(2,9)
   d (i) A (ii) G
   e (i) B & K, etc (ii) K & E etc
   f K
2.

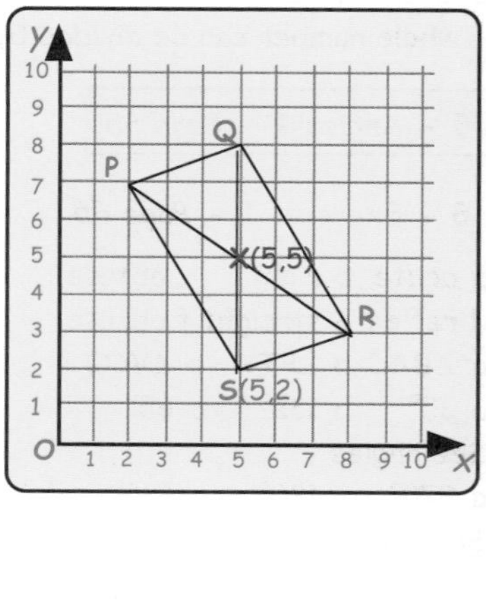

Ch 12 - Exercise 2 - *Page 97*

1. a/b/c

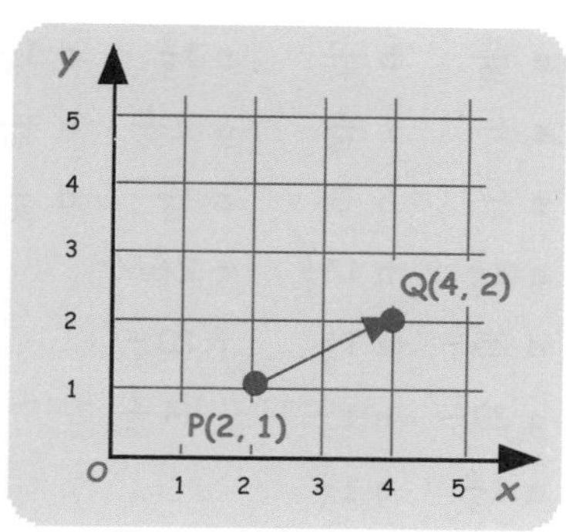

. a (5, 3) b (2, 2) c (2, 5)
  d (5, 4) e (4, 3)
. A See diagram
  b (9, 5) c (4, 2) d (2, 4)
. a 3 right 1 up b 7 right 4 down
  c 2 left 4 up d 8 left 11 down
. A'(1, 4), B'(1, 6), C'(3, 6), D'(3, 4)
. Practical

Ch 12 - Exercise 3 - *Page 98*

a/b/c/d/e/f/g/h

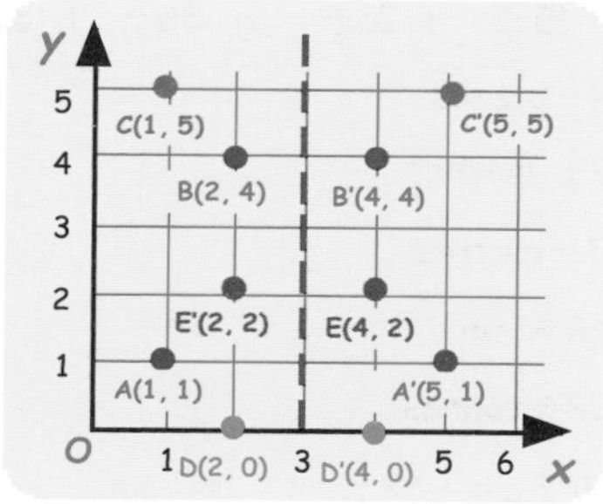

a/b/c

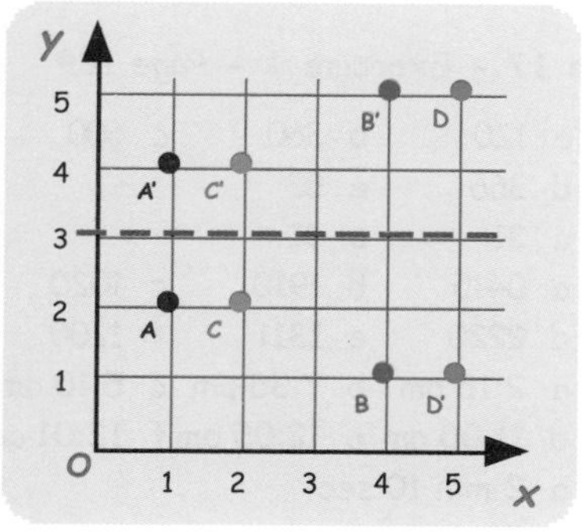

d E'(1, 6), F'(4, 3), G'(6, 0), H'(10, 2)
a/b s see diagram
c A'(2, 6), B'(9, 9), C'(5, 7), D'(3, 3), E'(10, 10), F'(0, 0)
d various (1, 5), (2, 5), etc
e H(4, 7) f I(8, 4)
a/b/c see diagram
d J'(11, 3), K'(7, 5), L'(3, 7), M'(9, 0), N'(6, 9)

5. a/b See diagram
   c D(7, 7)
   d A'(5, 3), B'(5, 1), C'(7, 1), D'(7, 3)
6. a/b c kite d/e

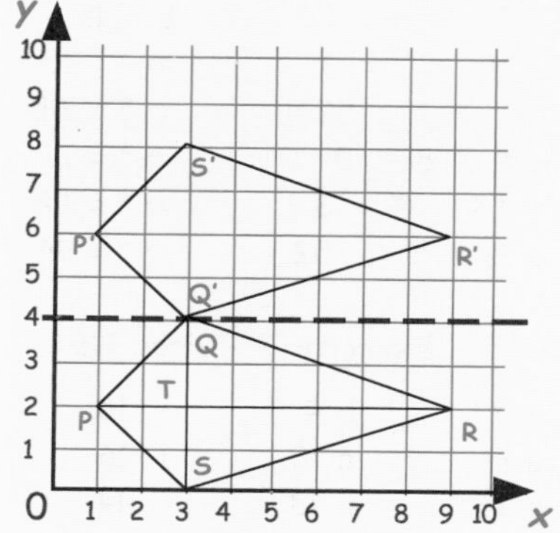

   f T(3, 6)
7. a horizontal line through (0, 4)
   b horizontal line through (0, 5)
   c horizontal line through (0, 3)
   d vertical line through (5, 0)
8. No

Ch 13 - Percentages - *Page 101*

Ch 13 - Exercise 1 - *Page 101*

1. a blue-40%, white-40%, pink-20%
   b green-44%, white-44%, pink-12%
   c brown-55%, white-17%, blue-28%
   d blue-60%, brown-40%
   e pink-36%, blue-28%, yellow-20%, green-12%, violet-4%
   f yellow-50%, white-32%, green-18%
2. a pink-44%, blue-20%, green-36%
   b 44 + 20 + 36 = 100
3. a (i) yellow-24% (ii) brown-10%,
   b white-66%
   c 100 - 24 - 10 = 66
4. a $\frac{33}{100}$ b $\frac{59}{100}$ c $\frac{71}{100}$ d $\frac{6}{100}$
   e $\frac{19}{100}$ f $\frac{49}{100}$ g $\frac{11}{100}$ h $\frac{1}{100}$
5. a 0·41 b 0·37 c 0·53 d 0·13
   e 0·16 f 0·97 g 0·07 h 0·04
6. a $\frac{14}{100}$ = 0·14 b $\frac{39}{100}$ = 0·39
   c $\frac{50}{100}$ = 0·50 d $\frac{28}{100}$ = 0·28
   e $\frac{20}{100}$ = 0·20 f $\frac{17}{100}$ = 0·17
   g $\frac{48}{100}$ = 0·48 h $\frac{9}{100}$ = 0·09
7. a 17% b 83% c 6% d 91%
   e 7% f 73% g 5% h 1%
   i 1% j 20%
8. a $\frac{1}{2}$ b $\frac{1}{10}$ c $\frac{1}{4}$ d $\frac{3}{4}$
   e $\frac{1}{5}$ f $\frac{4}{5}$ g $\frac{1}{20}$ h $\frac{3}{10}$
   i $\frac{11}{25}$ j $\frac{13}{20}$ k $\frac{1}{25}$ l $\frac{1}{50}$

Ch 13 - Exercise 2 - *Page 103*

1. a 12% b 60% c 2·5% d 45%
2. a 0·25 = 25% b 0·75 = 75%
   c 0·35 = 35% d 0·24 = 24%
   e 0·24 = 24% f 0·05 = 5%
3. a 60% b 20% c 90%
   d 50% e 10% f 8%
4. 75%
5. 40%
6. a Maths-65%, Eng-70%, Science-68%
   b English

Ch 13 - Exercise 3 - *Page 104*

1. a £40 b 9p c 3 m
2. a £8 b 29 m c 73 g
   d 1p e 11 kg f 150 mm
   g 20 ml h 70 cm i 300 miles
   j £375 k £82 l £4·50
3. a £180 b 18 kg c 54 kg
4. a £19 b £57

Ch 13 - Exercise 4 - *Page 105*

1. a £1·50 b £35 c £1·10
   d 320 kg e 315 kg f 16 kg
   g £4·80 h 1·2 cm i 7200 km
   j £250000 k 12 ml l 70 cm
   m £16 n 15 mm o 25p
2. a £22 b £9 c 96p
   d 240 m e 60 ml f 900 mm
   g 5500 g h £144 i 36000 kg
   j £200 k £46 l $1200
   m 43 ml n £9 o 40 km
3. a 90% b 324 men
4. a £24 b £96 c £21
5. £22·50 6. £17
7. a 200
   b (i) 240 (ii) 360 (iii) 120 (iv) 80
8. 7700 km
9. 225

Ch 14 - Measure 2 - *Page 108*

Ch 14 - Exercise 1 - *Page 108*

1. a 6 cm^3 b 5 cm^3 c 12 cm^3
   d 16 cm^3 e 10 cm^3 f 5 cm^3
   g 25 cm^3 h 12 cm^3
   i 38 cm^3 j 18 cm^3
2. a 5 b 3 c 15 cm^3
3. a 10 b 2 c 20 cm^3
4. 18 cm^3
5. a 15 cm^3 b 20 cm^3 c 21 cm^3

d 30 cm^3 e 40 cm^3 f 56 cm^3

6. a 18 cm^3 b 42 cm^3

7. a 24 cm^3 b 27 cm^3 c 30 cm^3
   d 40 cm^3 e 54 cm^3 f 112 cm^3
   g 100 cm^3

Ch 14 - Exercise 2 - Page 111

1. 7 mm   2. 6·3 cm   3. 55 mm
4. 0·9 cm   5. 40 cm   6. 0·23 m
7. 1591 cm   8. 0·07 m   9. 200 m
10. 0·4 km   11. 12850 m   12. 0·01 km
13. 5750 mm   14. 3 m   15. 7·5 m
16. 120000   17. 20050 m   18. 25 m
19. 5200 ml   20. 30 ml   21. 0·8 L
22. 0·09 L   23. 0·005 L   24. 125 ml
25. 4800 g   26. 0·672 kg   27. 0·3 kg
28. 0·081 kg

Ch 14 - Exercise 3 - Page 112

1. £51·20
2. £1609·45
3. 2·892 litres
4. a 0·75 litres   b 0·41 litres
5. 12·36 cm
6. 16·42(0) kg
7. a £42·45   b £8·55
8. Drew - 3·1 km, Tara - 2·78 km
   Drew has further to go by 0·32 km
9. 0·98 m
10. 3·13 m
11. Ally - 34·08 m, Julie - 32·3 m
    Ally has greater by 1·78 m
12. a Erin - £32·76   Alison - £32·82
    Fiona - £33·09   Helen - £30·00
    b Fiona most, Helen least
    c £2·76

Ch 14 - Exercise 4 - Page 114

Various answers/investigation.

Ch 15 - Algebra - Page 116

Ch 15 - Exercise 1 - Page 116

1. a 3   b 9   c 6
2. a 14   b 0   c 12
   d 8   e 9   f 12
   g 7   h 0   i 13
   j 31   k 5   l 11
   m 7   n 9   o 5
   p 0   q 32   r 56
   s 7   t 9   u 7
3. a +   b -   c x
   d ÷   e -   f x or ÷
   g +   h ÷   i -
   j x   k -   l ÷
4. a 7   b 6   c 7
   d 12   e 17   f 9
5. Jar B weighs 10 - 3 heavier than A
6. a 14 cm   b 9 cm
   c 15 cm   d 15 cm
7. a 53 + * = 72   b £19
8. a 18 - * = 3   => * = 15
   b 7 x * = 52·5   => * = 7·5
   c * ÷ 8 = 9   => * = 72
   d 1·4 + * = 3·2   => * = 1·8
   e 8 x * = 752   => * = 94

Ch 15 - Exercise 2 - Page 119

1. a 7   b 4   c 15
   d 0   e 10   f 16
   g 16   h 13   i 14
   j 5   k 9   l 7
   m 3   n 8   o 42
   p 64   q 77   r 16
2. a 6   b 16   c 9
   d 36   e 0   f 100
   g 4   h 9   i 7
   j 26   k 6   l 8
   m 0   n 5   o 0
3. a $a + 6 = 13$ => $a = 7$
   b $b + 7 = 22$ => $b = 15$
   c $2 \times c = 20$ => $c = 10$
   d $4 \times d = 36$ => $d = 9$
   e $3 \times e = 120$ => $e = 40$
   f $f + 25 = 45$ => $f = 20$
4. $x + 25 = 63$ => Donald is 38
5. $4 \times x = 1000$ => ticket costs £250
6. $8 \times x = 56$ => 7 octopuses
7. $x - 240 = 965$ => 1205 grams at start

Ch 16 - Fractions 2 - Page 122

Ch 16 - Exercise 1 - Page 122

1. a $\frac{4}{5}$ b $\frac{2}{9}$ c $\frac{2}{5}$ d $\frac{3}{4}$
2. a $\frac{4}{7}$ b $\frac{8}{9}$ c $\frac{2}{3}$ d $1\frac{1}{2}$
   e $\frac{1}{6}$ f $1\frac{5}{6}$ g 1   h $\frac{1}{2}$
3. a $5\frac{2}{3}$ b $4\frac{1}{5}$ c $7\frac{2}{7}$ d 4
   e $\frac{3}{5}$ f $8\frac{1}{9}$ g $4\frac{4}{9}$ h $13\frac{6}{11}$
4. $\frac{3}{5}$ km
5. size $7\frac{1}{2}$
6. $48\frac{2}{5}$ kg
7. a $3\frac{1}{5}$ m   b $4\frac{1}{2}$ L   c $3\frac{2}{3}$ km
   d $1\frac{4}{5}$ e $68\frac{1}{3}$ kg
8. a $2\frac{2}{5}$ feet   b 22 feet
9. $5\frac{1}{2}$ inches

Ch 16 - Exercise 2 - Page 124

1. a $1\frac{1}{4}$ b $\frac{1}{4}$ c $\frac{1}{8}$ d $\frac{14}{15}$
2. a $\frac{19}{20}$ b $\frac{1}{4}$ c $1\frac{3}{8}$ d $1\frac{5}{9}$
   e $\frac{1}{2}$ f $\frac{9}{16}$ g $1\frac{1}{10}$ h $\frac{7}{40}$
3. a $\frac{7}{8}$ b 0   c $\frac{17}{20}$ d $\frac{3}{16}$
4. a $3\frac{1}{2}$ b $17\frac{1}{9}$ c $2\frac{5}{8}$
   d $25\frac{2}{3}$ e $1\frac{1}{6}$ f $20\frac{7}{8}$
   g $29\frac{1}{2}$ h $1\frac{2}{5}$ i $14\frac{9}{28}$
5. a $2\frac{2}{3}$ b $1\frac{3}{5}$
6. a $2\frac{4}{5}$ b $2\frac{3}{7}$ c $4\frac{1}{6}$
   d $1\frac{2}{5}$ e $\frac{3}{10}$ f $5\frac{5}{8}$
7. $2\frac{5}{8}$ metres

Ch 16 - Exercise 3 - Page 126

1. a $1\frac{2}{3}$ b $3\frac{3}{4}$ c $1\frac{3}{4}$ d $2\frac{1}{12}$
2. a $1\frac{2}{5}$ b $6\frac{3}{4}$ c $3\frac{1}{8}$ d $6\frac{2}{5}$
   e $2\frac{1}{10}$ f 5   g $6\frac{1}{4}$ h $5\frac{1}{5}$
3. a $6\frac{3}{5}$ b $13\frac{3}{4}$ c 61   d $27\frac{1}{5}$
   e $15\frac{3}{10}$ f $26\frac{5}{6}$ g $36\frac{1}{4}$ h $39\frac{9}{10}$
4. $4\frac{1}{2}$ pizzas
5. $7\frac{1}{2}$ metres
6. $7\frac{7}{8}$ metres
7. $68\frac{3}{5}$ cm
8. $22\frac{2}{3}$ tonnes
9. $97\frac{3}{5}$ cm + $62\frac{2}{5}$ cm = 160 cm

Ch 17 - Time - Page 129

Ch 17 - Exercise 1 - Page 129

1. a 120   b 360   c 600
   d 366   e 52
2. a 31   b 31
3. a 0415   b 1910   c 1020
   d 2220   e 1311   f 1200
4. a 2:15 pm   b 7:35 pm   c 5:10 am
   d 11:00 am   e 12:05 pm   f 12:01 am
5. a 2 min 10 sec
   b 5 min 5 sec
   c 13 min 20 sec
6. a 1 hr 25 min
   b 3 hr 35 min
   c 9 hr 1 min
7. a 140 sec   b 610 sec   c 495 sec
8. a 215 min   b 545 min   c 317 min
9. a 8 min 35 sec
   b 3 min 15 sec
   c 45 min

). 0·9sec, 2sec, 2·04sec, 2·11sec, 2·3sec

Ch 17 - Exercise 2 - *Page 130*

a 3 hrs b 4 hrs c 5 hrs d 3 hrs
e 1 hr f 9 hrs g 5 hrs h 2 hrs
i 8 hrs j 6 hrs
a 45 min b 25 min c 40 min d 40 min
e 45 min f 80 min g 50 min h 55 min
a 3:50 b 25 min c 4:35 d 5:20
a 30 min b 85 min

Ch 17 - Exercise 3 - *Page 131*

a 3 hrs b 2 hr 30 min
c 5 hr 30 min d 3 hr 5 min
e 1 hr 30 min f 1 hr 35 min
g 2 hr 5 min h 1 hr 25 min
i 1 hr 15 min j 4 hr 20 min
k 26 hours l 22 hours

a 6 pm b 8.25 pm
c 11.20 pm d 12.30 pm
e 3.15 am
2 hrs 40 mins
a 3 hrs 39 mins b 1207
a (i) 1 hr 10 min (ii) 45 min
(iii) 6 hr 50 min
b (i) 2:25 pm (ii) 3:10 pm
c 8:45->9:55->12:05->12:50->3:35
12:00->1.10->3:20->4:05->6:50
13 hrs and 5 minutes
a 8 hr 45 min b 1725
a 3hr 40 min b 1110
c 0010 -> 0350 -> 0730 -> 1110 ->
1450 -> 1830 -> 2210 = 7 times
Joe - 2 hr 20 mins
Penny - 2 hr 15 mins
Penny quicker by 5 mins
). a 31 hrs b 50 hrs 10 mins
c 108 hrs d 50 hrs 30 mins
. 61 hours

Ch 17 - Exercise 4 - *Page 134*

a 1654 b 1422 c 27 mins
d does not stop e 32 mins
f 1155 g practical
a (i) 1020 (ii) 1050 (iii) 1125
b (i) Manchester (ii) 1725
c (i) 15 minutes (ii) 1525
d refuelling/allow passenger on/off
e various
a 12.57 am b 12.32 am
c 5.32 pm and 3.55 am
d 2 mins e 11 mins
f 11 mins g 3 hr 57 min
h 4 hr 23 min i 10 hr 2 min
j possibly - should arrive at 2.24 pm
k night train from London takes
8 hours 26 minutes

4.

London	<—>	Perth
London	leave	0635
Watford	arrive	0654
	leave	0655
Crewe		0915
Preston	arrive	1013
	leave	1018
Stirling		1433
Dunblane		1444
Gleneagles	arrive	1459
	leave	1501
Perth	arrive	1520

5. Investigation
6. Project

Ch 18 - Statistics - *Page 138*

Ch 18 - Exercise 1 - *Page 138*

1. a (i) 55°F (ii) 65°F
   b Wed c Sun d no heating
2. a (i) 102°F (ii) 99°F
   b 3°F
   c (i) 101°F (ii) 101°F
   (iii) 99·5°F (iv) 100°F
   d 99·75°F
3. a (i) 400 (ii) 1200 (iii) 400
   b (i) 800 (ii) 900 (iii) 1300
   c 14600
   d Not many people buy in winter
   e (i) Sept-Oct (ii) dropped
4. a (i) 10000 (ii) 4000 (iii) 3000
   b (i) 10000 (ii) 8000 (iii) 11000
   c (i) Raincoats-R-Us
   (ii) same
   d (i) Raincoats-R-Us (ii) £4000
5.

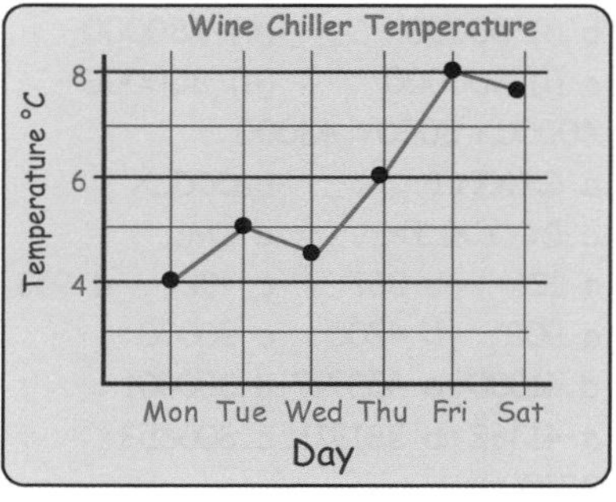

6.

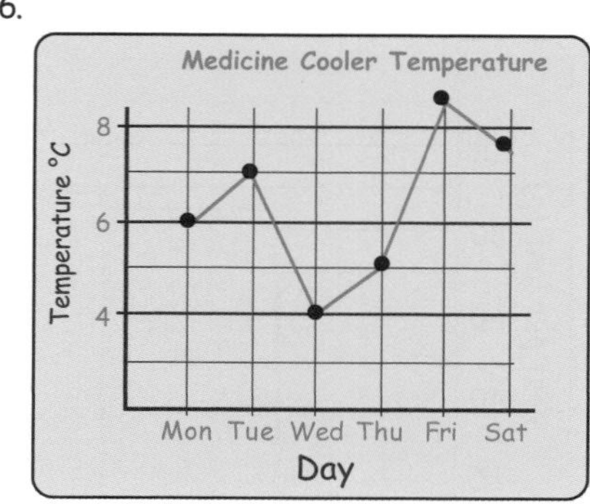

7.

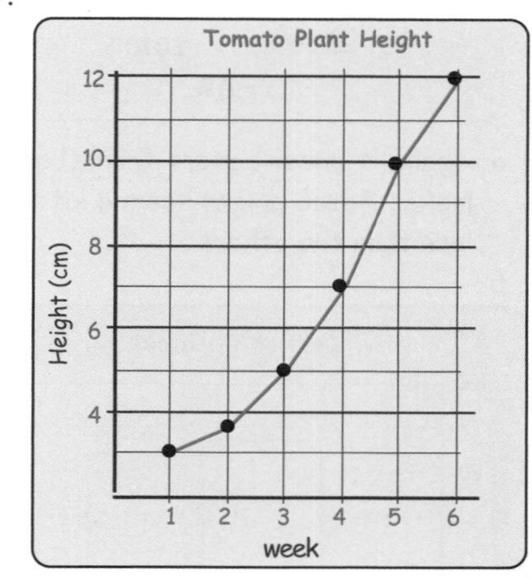

8.

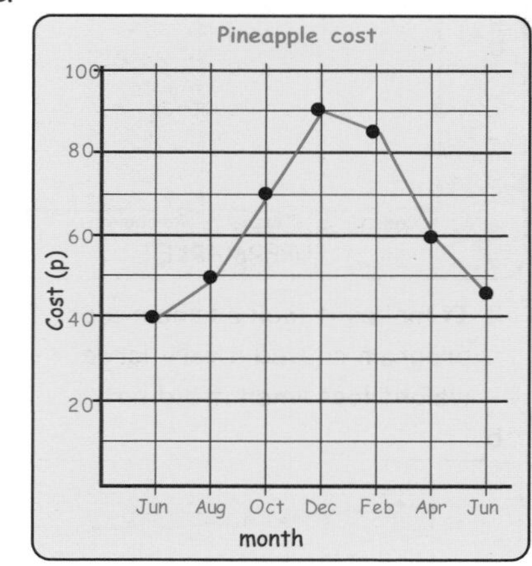

Ch 18 - Exercise 2 - *Page 141*

1. a To make people think there has been an amazing rise in the price
   b To make it look like the petrol firms are making lots of profit
2. Various
3. a Does not start at 0 so makes difference in price look greater than it is.

b

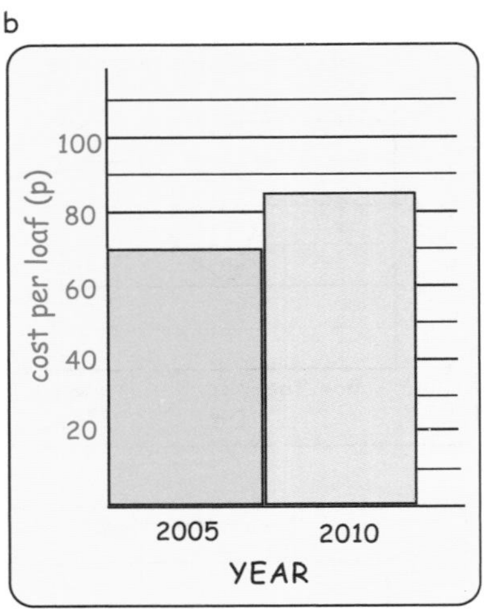

4. a Again, it doesn't start from 0 and makes Adsco prices seem a lot lot less than the others

b

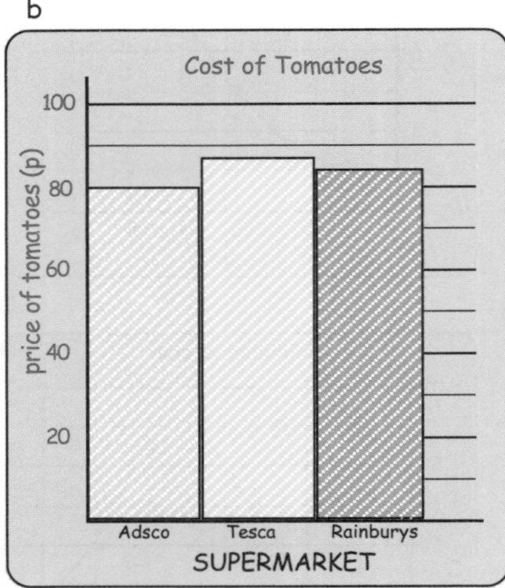

5. a It makes it look as their diet program caused a very large weight loss when it did not

b

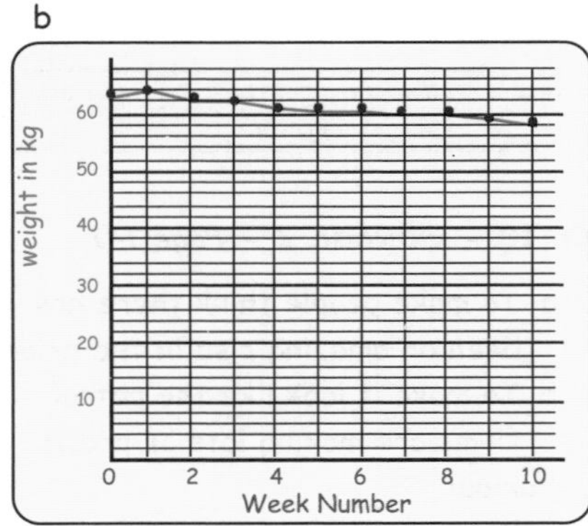

6. a No scale given. No titles.
   b Vertical scale should go up in steady amounts.
   Year along the bottom should increase by the same value.
   c Scale to big - Can't see clearly the differences in pay
   d No Scale. The width and height of balls together distort the actual numbers
   e No proper scale to judge
   f Vertical scale should start at 0
   Columns should have then same width.
7. Company B with a larger sample size
8. Practical
9. Project/Investigation

Ch 18 - Exercise 3 - *Page 144*

1. a blackcurrant
   b blackcurrant, raspberry, limeade lemon, water
2. a 5 b 3 c 2
3. a (i) $\frac{4}{10}$ (ii) $\frac{2}{10}$ (iii) $\frac{1}{10}$ (iv) $\frac{3}{10}$
   b Chinese, Indian, Thai, Italian
   c (i) 5 (ii) 15
4. a 80 b 60 c 40 d 20
5. a $\frac{4}{10}$ b $\frac{3}{10}$
   c (i) 80 (ii) 160
6. A - Bald tyres B - No Tax Disc
   C - Brake light D - Broken exhaust
7. a $\frac{1}{20}$
   b (i) $\frac{9}{20}$ (ii) $\frac{5}{20}$ (iii) $\frac{4}{20}$ (iv) $\frac{2}{20}$
   c 20
   d (i) 180 (ii) 100 (iii) 80 (iv) 40

Ch 18 - Exercise 4 - *Page 146*

Practical

Ch 19 - Revision - *Page 148*

1. a fifty three thousand and six
   b three hundred and twenty thousand eight hundred
2. 608511
3. a 31500 b 820000
4. a 11200 b 950000, 850000
5. a (i) 7000 (ii) 35000
   b (i) 50000 (ii) 280000
   c (i) 600000 (ii) 800000
6. 40000 + 8000 = 48000
7. a CXXIII b CCCLX
   c DCCCXLIX d CML
8. a 121 b 367 c 492 d 953
9. a 900 b 4700 c 90000
   d 41000 e 453717 d 300001
10. a 41362 b 381911 c 300853
11. 330500
12. a ∠ATF is obtuse b ∠MREis right
    c ∠XDN is acute d ∠FLP is reflex
13. a 35° b 106°
14. see drawings
15. 135°
16. a 651 n 2376 c 8322 d 40632
17. a 1696 b 20805 c 70587
18. a 53650 b 432000 c 4920 d 5200
19. a 854 b 3783 c 294 d 7700
20. a (i) $44\frac{2}{3}$ (ii) $359\frac{1}{4}$
    b (i) 173·5 (ii) 653·4
21. -25°C
22. a 2, -1, -7 b -9, -2, 12
23. a -4°c b 6°C c 15°C d -80°C
24. 9 cm^2
25. a 40 cm^2 b 90 cm^2 c 49 m^2
26. a (0), 5, 10, 15, 20, 25, 30
    b (0), 11, 22, 33, 44, 55, 66
27. a 1, 2, 3, 6, 9, 18 b 1, 2, 5, 10, 25, 5
28. a 1, 2, 3, 6 b 1, 2, 4, 5, 10, 20
29. a 2, 3, 5, 7 b 31, 37
30. a 25 b 121 c 64 d 1000
31. 55° - acute, 210° - reflex, 90° - righ
    107° - obtuse, 180° - straight
32. a 20° b 110°
33. a 67° b 22·5° c 50°
    d 50° e 35°
    f

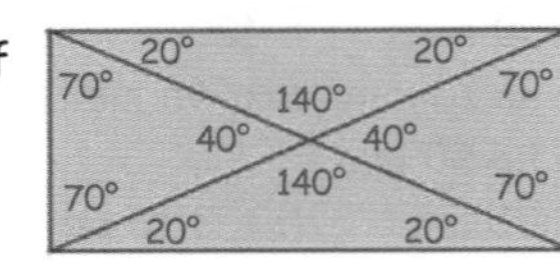

34. a 6 tenths b 6 thousandths
35. a 9·1 b 0·92 c 1·67(0)
36. a 454·63 b 80·01 c 23·916 d 1
37. a $\frac{4}{5}$ b $\frac{3}{4}$
38. a 23 b 40
39. a 8·7 b 0·7
40. a 108·3 b 20 c 1·34 d 8·7
41. cuboid - 3 cube - 1 cylinder -
    cone - 1 sphere - 1 prism - 1
42. a 6 b 10 c 6
43. a triangular prism b square pyrami
44.

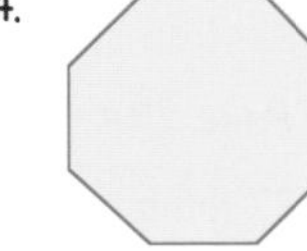

45. a $\frac{2}{5}$ b $\frac{2}{13}$ c $\frac{2}{9}$ d $\frac{1}{4}$
46. $\frac{1}{2}$, $\frac{17}{32}$, $\frac{11}{16}$, $\frac{3}{4}$, $\frac{7}{8}$
47. a $\frac{11}{3}$ b $\frac{29}{6}$
48. a $2\frac{3}{4}$ b $3\frac{2}{5}$
49. P'(6, 2)

0. a/b c kite

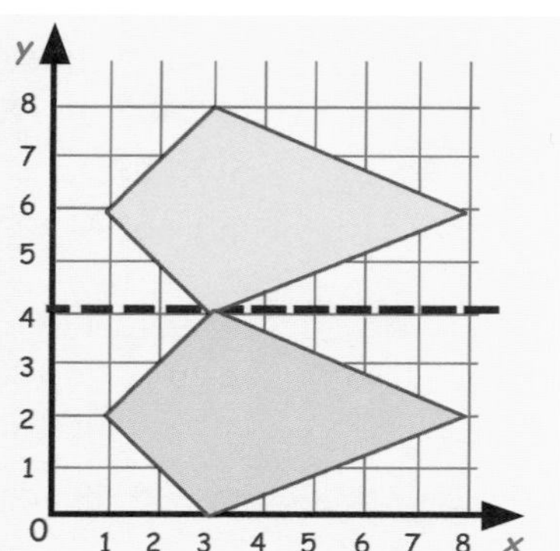

d A'(1, 2), B'(3, 4), C'(8, 2), D'(3, 0)

1. a $\frac{39}{100}$ b $\frac{4}{5}$ c $\frac{6}{25}$ d $\frac{1}{20}$

2. a 75% b 70% c 94% d 65%

3. a £24 b 35 cm c 40 g d $18

4. a £9 b £36

5. a 40 cm^3 b 16 cm^3

6. a 37 mm b 1·85 cm
c 3050 m d 65·8 km
e 23050 ml f 6·8 kg

7. a Dunhill b 0·477 secs

8. a 13 b 13 c 7
d 8 e 11 f 4

9. a ÷ b - c +
d x e - f ÷

0. a 8 b 13 c 10
d 14 e 7 f 12
g 7·5 h 45 i 6
j 25 k 100 l 4

1. a $\frac{1}{2}$ b $\frac{1}{5}$ c 1 d $\frac{1}{6}$
e $1\frac{1}{3}$ f $\frac{3}{8}$ g $\frac{3}{10}$ h $\frac{3}{8}$

2. a $3\frac{3}{5}$ b $4\frac{1}{4}$ c $5\frac{2}{3}$ d $9\frac{3}{4}$
e $4\frac{5}{8}$ f $2\frac{1}{6}$ g $2\frac{3}{5}$ h $6\frac{1}{3}$

3. a $1\frac{2}{3}$ b $3\frac{1}{3}$ c $7\frac{1}{8}$ d $14\frac{2}{5}$

4. a 0340 b 1755

5. a 7:45 pm b 8:05 am

6. a 2 min 25 sec b 5 min 1 sec

7. a 95 min b 195 mins

8. a 2 hrs 10 mins b 1507

9. a (i) 2 (ii) 10 (iii) 8 (iv) 6
b 14 floors

0. a (i) $\frac{1}{4}$ (ii) $\frac{1}{6}$ (iii) $\frac{1}{6}$ (iv) $\frac{5}{12}$
b (i) 60 (ii) 100 (iii) 80